Translated Texts for Byzantinists

The intention of the series is to broaden access to Byzantine texts from 800 AD, enabling students, non-specialists and scholars working in related disciplines to access material otherwise unavailable to them. The series will cover a wide range of texts, including historical, theological and literary works, all of which include an English translation of the Byzantine text with introduction and commentary.

Liverpool University Press gratefully acknowledges the generous continued support of Dr Costas Kaplanis, alumnus of King's College London, who was instrumental in setting up the series.

General Editors
Judith Ryder, Oxford
Elizabeth Jeffreys, Oxford
Judith Herrin, King's College London

Editorial Committee
Mary Cunningham, Nottingham
Charalambos Dendrinos, Royal Holloway
Niels Gaul, Edinburgh
Tim Greenwood, St Andrews
Anthony Hirst, London
Liz James, Sussex
Michael Jeffreys, Oxford
Costas Kaplanis, King's College London
Marc Lauxtermann, Oxford
Fr Andrew Louth, Durham
Brian McLaughlin, Independent Scholar
Rosemary Morris, York
Leonora Neville, University of Wisconsin-Madison
Charlotte Roueché, King's College London
Teresa Shawcross, Princeton
Mary Whitby, Oxford

Translated Texts for Byzantinists
Volume 12

The Disputatio
of the Latins and the
Greeks, 1234

Introduction, Translation, and Commentary by
Jeff Brubaker

Liverpool
University
Press

First published 2022
Liverpool University Press
4 Cambridge Street
Liverpool, L69 7ZU

Copyright © 2022 Jeff Brubaker

Jeff Brubaker has asserted the right to be identified as the author of this book in accordance with the Copyright, Designs and Patents Act 1988.

All rights reserved. No part of this book may be reproduced, stored in a retrieval system, or transmitted, in any form or by any means, electronic, mechanical, photocopying, recording, or otherwise, without the prior written permission of the publisher.

British Library Cataloguing-in-Publication Data
A British Library CIP Record is available.

ISBN 978-1-80085-678-3 cased

Typeset by Carnegie Book Production, Lancaster
Printed and bound by CPI Group (UK) Ltd, Croydon CR0 4YY

CONTENTS

Preface	vii
Abbreviations	xi
Map: Journey of the Friars from Constantinople to Nymphaion	xv
Introduction	1
1 Historiography	5
2 Terminology	9
3 Background	18
4 Pope and Patriarch	29
5 Sources	35
6 Who are the Friars?	47
7 Report of the Friars	58
8 Role of Emperor and Patriarch	83
9 Conclusions	91
Note on Translations	104
Texts	105
I Germanos to Gregory, 1232	107
II Germanos to Cardinals, 1232	115
III Gregory to Germanos, July 1232	121
IV Gregory to Germanos, May 1233	129
V Report of the Friars, 1234	133
Bibliography	199
Index	221

PREFACE

> Tragically, in later times we grew apart. Worldly concerns poisoned us, weeds of suspicion increased our distance and we ceased to nurture communion.
>
> Pope Francis I, December 2021

Toward the end of 2021, while I was completing work for the publication of this volume, Pope Francis I made a visit to Greece and Cyprus in an effort to bring the Roman Catholic and Greek Orthodox Churches closer together. The sentiment he expressed was conciliatory, lamenting the centuries of division within the Christian community. The most urgent headlines from the pope's trip to the eastern Mediterranean, however, were not about the olive branch of reconciliation; rather, they focused on a small group of hecklers who had assembled to protest the pope's visit. They accused Francis I of moving away from centuries of Christian orthodoxy, shouting 'Heretic!' at the pope.

These outbursts echo the result of a similar encounter between leaders from the Greek and Roman Churches that took place almost 800 years ago. Like the recent newspaper headlines describing the visit of the pope in 2021, the meeting of these clergymen in 1234 is frequently referenced by modern historians as a low point in the history of Christian relations. Rather than considering the origins of the meeting, or what the parties intended to accomplish, we rush to the ill-fated results and consider such encounters to always be inevitable failures.

The purpose of this text and translation is to shed greater light on the dialogue that took place so long ago. By examining the sources that have come to us from that meeting, and by making them accessible to a wider audience, we reach a fuller understanding of what the parties in the thirteenth century hoped to achieve. Approaching this material with an open mind, I hope the reader will conclude that no one in 1234 intended for their efforts to result in failure, and thus we might come to a fuller understanding of the events that followed. We cannot simply reject

viii   THE DISPUTATIO

attempts to end the schism of the churches as hopeless, but must consider how the disputants viewed the problem, and what might have been gained by seeking a peaceful resolution to the issues that divided them.

One hesitates to begin expressing gratitude to those who have contributed to this volume for fear of leaving someone out, or, worse yet, failing to put into words how important one's input was in bringing this project to fruition. Before beginning I must confess that all errors in the present translation remain entirely my own. This work owes much to Professor Michael Angold, who helped clarify the parameters of the present project from its inception over a cup of coffee while he waited to catch a train. He continued to support my efforts with advice and an early edition of his translation of the works of Nicholas Mesarites. The critiques and encouragement he has offered since that first conversation have been invaluable. Dr Philip Burton is largely responsible for any claim I might make today to being a competent translator. Indeed, he is nothing short of a wizard with Greek and Latin, and it was he who first helped me decipher the truly gruelling sections of the present text. I can only hope to replicate his patience and reassuring demeanour as a teacher. Much gratitude goes to Rev. Dr Joseph Munitiz, who gave freely of his time and expertise throughout this project. More than one source, buried in the libraries of Oxford, might have gone unexamined without his guidance. I am very grateful for his insights after reading through early drafts of this work. I must thank Professor Anthony Kaldellis, Dr Karl Bede Lackner, Professor Jonathan Shepard, Professor Leslie Brubaker, Professor Chris Wickham, Dr Alessandra Bucossi, and Professor Judith Herrin for their generosity and advice. I am especially grateful to Dr Tia Kolbaba and Professor Edward Siecienski for their suggestions, recommendations, and even their critiques through the translation and writing process. Special thanks go to Rev. Dr Judith Ryder, who patiently edited this work for Liverpool University Press. Her questions and comments have made this a better product.

Nothing I can say can accurately encapsulate the debt this project owes to my wife, Sarah. She was the one who offered constant encouragement, especially at times when this work seemed like it would never come to an end. Her patience and support are truly superhuman.

Finally, I must comment on the tremendous contributions of the late Dr Ruth Macrides, my great mentor and teacher. To say that she served as a model for my efforts does not do her justice. Fellow students of hers at the University of Birmingham will remember her encouraging words, her constant sense of humour, and her ability as an historian. While she never

PREFACE

managed to instill in me a correct pronunciation of Byzantine Greek (a lost cause long before I met her), she taught me that there was much more to reading a source. I will be forever grateful that she saw this project nearing its completion before leaving us so suddenly. I hope it makes her proud.

ABBREVIATIONS

Akropolites, *History* *The History*, ed. A. Heisenberg and P. Wirth, *Opera*, vol. 1 (Stuttgart: Teubner, 1978); transl. by R. Macrides, *George Akropolites, The History. Introduction, translation and commentary* (Oxford: Oxford University Press, 2007)

Auvray, *Reg.* L. Auvray, *Les Registres de Grégoire IX*, 4 vols (Paris: A. Fontemoing, 1896–1955)

Choniates, *Historia* *Nicetae Choniatae Historia*, ed. J.-L. van Dieten, 2 vols (Berlin/New York: De Gruyter, 1975); transl. by H. Magoulias, *O City of Byzantium: Annals of Niketas Choniates* (Detroit: Wayne State University Press, 1984)

Dölger, *Reg.* F. Dölger and P. Wirth, *Regesten der Kaiserurkunden des oströmischen Reiches, von 565–1453*, vol. III: *Regesten von 1204–1282* (revised edition) (Munich/Berlin: C.H. Beck, 1977)

Golubovich, 'Disputatio' G. Golubovich, 'Disputatio Latinorum et Graecorum seu Relatio apocrisiarorum Gregorii IX de gestis Nicaeae in Bithynia et Nymphaeae in Lydia (1234),' *Archivum Franciscanum Historicum* 12 (1919), 418–70

Grumel, *Reg.* V. Grumel, *Les Regestes des actes du Patriarcat de Constantinople*, I, fasc. 2 and 3: *les regestes de 715 à 1206*, revised edition (Paris: Institut français des études byzantines, 1989)

Hageneder, *Die Register Innocenz' III* O. Hageneder et al., *Die Register Innocenz' III*, 13 vols (Graz/Cologne, Rome, Vienna; Verlag der Österreichischen Akademie der Wissenschaften, 1964–2015)

THE DISPUTATIO

Huillard-Bréholles, *Historia diplomatica Friderici secundi*	J. Huillard-Bréholles, *Historia diplomatica Friderici secundi*, 6 vols (Paris: Excudebant Plon Fratres, 1852–1861)
Laurent, *Reg.*	V. Laurent, *Les regestes des actes du patriarcat de Constantinople*, I, fasc. 4: *Les regestes de 1208 à 1309* (Paris: Institut français des études byzantines, 1971)
Matthew Paris	Matthew Paris, *Chronica majora*, ed. H. Luard, vol. 3 (London: Longman, 1876); transl. by J. Giles, *Matthew Paris's English History from the year 1235 to 1273*, vol. 1 (London: Henry Bohn, 1889)
Mesarites I	A. Heisenberg, 'Neue Quellen zur Geschichte des lateinischen Kaisertums und der Kirchenunion: I. Der Epitaphios des Nikolaos Mesarites auf seinen Bruder Johannes,' *Sitzungsberichte der Bayerischen Akademie der Wissenschaften*, philos.-philol. und hist. Klasse, 1922, Abh. 5 (Munich, 1922), 3–75 [= A. Heisenberg, *Quellen und Studien zur spätbyzantinischen Geschichte* (London: Variorum Reprints, 1973), II, i]; transl. M. Angold, *Nicholas Mesarites: his life and works (in translation)* (Liverpool: Liverpool University Press, 2017), 141–92
Mesarites II	A. Heisenberg, 'Neue Quellen zur Geschichte des lateinischen Kaisertums und der Kirchenunion: II. Die Unionsverhandlungen vom 30. August 1206; Patriarchenwahl und Kaiserkrönung in Nikaia 1208: i. Die Disputation vom 30. August 1206; ii. Die Bitteschriften des griechische Klerus in Konstantinopel an den Kaiserhof von Nikaia und die kaiserliche Botschaft; iii. Reisebericht des Nikolaos Mesarites an die Mönche des Euergetisklosters in Konstantinopel,' *Sitzungsberichte der Bayerischen Akademie der Wissenschaften*, philos.-philol. und hist.

ABBREVIATIONS

xiii

Klasse, 1923, Abh. 2 (Munich, 1923), 3–46 [= A. Heisenberg, *Quellen und Studien zur spätbyzantinischen Geschichte* (London: Variorum Reprints, 1973), II, ii]; transl. M. Angold, *Nicholas Mesarites: his life and works (in translation)* (Liverpool: Liverpool University Press, 2017), 197–234

Mesarites III
A. Heisenberg, 'Neue Quellen zur Geschichte des lateinischen Kaisertums und der Kirchenunion: II. III – 'Der Bericht des Nikolaos Mesarites über die politischen und kirchlichen Ereignisse des Jahres 1214,' *Sitzungsberichte der Bayerischen Akademie der Wissenschaften*, philos.-philol. und hist. Klasse, 1923, Abh. 3 (Munich, 1923), 3–96 [= A. Heisenberg, *Quellen und Studien zur spätbyzantinischen Geschichte* (London: Variorum Reprints, 1973), II, iii]; transl. M. Angold, *Nicholas Mesarites: his life and works (in translation)* (Liverpool: Liverpool University Press, 2017), 251–96

Migne *PG*
J.P. Migne, *Patrologiae cursus completus: series Graeca*, 166 vols (Paris: Garnier Fratres, 1857–66)

Migne *PL*
J.P. Migne, *Patrologiae cursus completus: series Latina*, 217 vols (Paris: Garnier Fratres, 1841–1855)

ODB
Oxford dictionary of Byzantium, ed. A. Kazhdan and A. Talbot, 3 vols (Oxford: Oxford University Press, 1991)

Potthast, *Reg.*
A. Potthast, *Regesta Pontificum Romanorum inde ab anno post Christum natum MCXCVIII ad annum MCCCIV*, vol. 1 (Graz: Akademische Druck- U. Verlagsanstalt, 1957)

Richard of San Germano
Richard of San Germano, *Ryccardi de Sancto Germano notarii chronica*, ed. C. Garufi, *Rerum Italicarum Scriptores*, vol. 7, part 2 (Bologna, 1937).

xiv   THE DISPUTATIO

Tautu, *Acta*   A. Tautu, *Acta Honorii III (1216–1227) et Gregorii IX (1227–1241)* (Vatican: Typis Polyglottis Vaticanis, 1950)

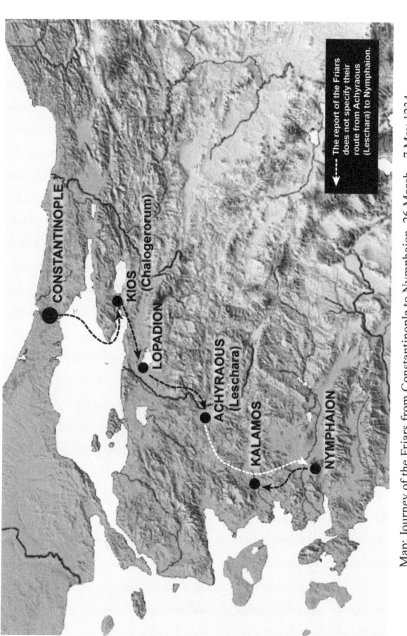

Map: Journey of the Friars from Constantinople to Nymphaion, 26 March – 7 May 1234

INTRODUCTION

The negotiations that took place in the early 1230s between Pope Gregory IX and Patriarch Germanos II are among the most important and well-documented attempts to bring about a union between the Western Roman and Eastern Greek Churches in the medieval period. This dialogue took place in the aftermath of the Fourth Crusade, which witnessed the sacking of Constantinople, the ancient capital of the Byzantine Empire, in 1204. In the decades that followed, often referred to as the period of 'exile' for the Byzantine regime in Nicaea, we find numerous examples of hostility and animosity between Greeks and Latins. Expelled from his native city and recalling the sacking of Constantinople in 1204, Niketas Choniates refers to the Latins as 'forerunners of Antichrist, chief agents and harbingers of his anticipated ungodly deeds.'[1] This adversarial relationship between east and west was not new in 1204. Byzantines and Latins frequently employed competing ecclesiastical and political claims to justify various instances of hostility in the centuries before the Fourth Crusade.[2] The Great Schism, the division between the Greek and Roman Churches, did not encourage good relations. The schism, often dated to 1054, more accurately reflects a growing rift between the two churches going back at least to the so-called Photian Schism of the ninth century, and possibly earlier.[3]

---

1 Choniates, *Historia*, 573 lines 7–9; transl. H. Magoulias, 315.

2 M. Angold, *Church and society in Byzantium under the Comneni, 1081–1261* (Cambridge: Cambridge University Press, 1995), 511–12.

3 For the growing rift, see T. Kolbaba, *The Byzantine lists: errors of the Latins* (Urbana: University of Illinois Press, 2000); T. Kolbaba, *Inventing Latin heretics: Byzantines and the filioque in the ninth century* (Kalamazoo, MI: Medieval Institute Publications, Western Michigan University, 2008); A. Louth, *Greek East and Latin West: the Church AD 681–1071* (Crestwood, NY: St Vladimir's Seminary Press, 2007); T. Kolbaba, 'The legacy of Humbert and Cerularius: traditions of the schism of 1054 in Byzantine texts and manuscripts of the twelfth and thirteenth centuries,' in *Porphyrogenita. Essays on the history and literature of Byzantium and the Latin East in honour of Julian Chrysostomides*, eds C. Dendrinos et al. (Aldershot: Ashgate, 2003), 47–62; H. Chadwick, *East and west: the making of a rift in the*

2   THE DISPUTATIO

Antagonists in this growing division pointed to some common problems as cause for the schism, namely the *filioque*, the use of leavened or unleavened bread in the Eucharist, and the extent of the primacy of the pope over his fellow bishops.[4] There is little evidence, however, that a clear understanding of these complicated problems was held by more than the educated elite. The complex and nuanced issues of practice and doctrine argued over in the schism of the churches probably held little sway over the average Byzantine or Latin layman. The account of Odo of Deuil, which chronicles the journey of the French king Louis VII on the Second Crusade in the mid-twelfth century, gives several examples of hostility between the Latin crusaders and their Byzantine hosts. Although the author, trained as a cleric of St Denis, devotes a good deal of his attention to what he perceives to be the religious errors of the Greeks, his record of the Second Crusade suggests that it was a lack of provisions at fair prices for the travelling crusaders, rather than religious differences, that was a primary cause for conflict.[5]

Church, from apostolic times until the Council of Florence (Oxford: Oxford University Press, 2005); S. Runciman, *The Eastern schism: a study of the papacy and the Eastern Churches during the XIth and XIIth centuries* (Oxford: Oxford University Press, 1955). For the Photian Schism, see F. Dvornik, *The Photian schism: history and legend* (Cambridge: Cambridge University Press, 1948; reprinted 1970). Tia Kolbaba has despondently noted that 1054 still appears as the definitive date of schism in textbooks, surveys, and Wikipedia: T. Kolbaba, 'Theological debates with the West, 1054–1300,' in *The Cambridge intellectual history of Byzantium*, ed. A. Kaldellis and N. Siniossoglou (Cambridge: Cambridge University Press, 2017), 480.

4 For the most thorough analysis of the *filioque* problem, see A. Siecienski, *The filioque: history of a doctrinal controversy* (Oxford: Oxford University Press, 2010). On the question of leavened versus unleavened bread, see M. Smith, *And taking bread...: Cerularius and the azyme controversy of 1054* (Paris: Beauchesne, 1978); J. Erickson, 'Leavened and unleavened: some theological implications of the schism of 1054,' *St Vladimir's Theological Quarterly* 14 (1970), 155–76. On the primacy of the pope, see A. Siecienski, *The papacy and the Orthodox: sources and history of a debate* (Oxford: Oxford University Press, 2017); A. Papadakis and J. Meyendorff, *The Christian East and the rise of the papacy: the church 1071–1453 A.D.* (Crestwood, NY: St Vladimir's Seminary Press, 1994).

5 For example, Odo of Deuil famously accuses the Greeks of washing altars after they were used by Latin priests, as if they had been defiled: Odo of Deuil, *De profetione Ludovici VII in orientem*, ed. and transl. V. Berry (New York: Columbia University Press, 1948), 54–55. He complains frequently about the lack of provisions for the crusaders provided by the Byzantines: Odo of Deuil, *De profectione*, 40–41, 66–67, 74–75. Niketas Choniates seems to justify Odo's complaints when he condemns his fellow Byzantines for taking advantage of their Latin customers by raising prices: Choniates, *Historia*, 66 lines 18–31, transl. H. Magoulias, 38–39. Angeliki Laiou provides an analysis of the impact of

INTRODUCTION   3

It was not until the sacking of Constantinople by the crusaders in 1204 that the idea of the Great Schism, previously confined to circles of scholars and theologians, became a new reality visible to larger segments of society.[6] Various authors writing in the years after the Fourth Crusade attest to the increasing interest in ecclesiastical matters and the tension surrounding those issues.[7] Nicholas Mesarites reports that arguments over religious doctrine and practice between Greeks and Latins held wide popular appeal in Constantinople shortly after 1204.[8] In one anecdote he describes a Latin of apparently unremarkable lineage who was incensed by the diversity of robes worn by Greek clergymen.[9] George Akropolites comments on the general anguish caused by ecclesiastical matters when

the crusades on local food production, explaining that Byzantine merchants, with their long and sustained tradition of sound coinage, would not have been willing to accept Frankish silver coins in trade as their purity and value could not be proven: A. Laiou, 'Byzantine trade with Christians and Muslims and the crusades,' in *The crusades from the perspective of Byzantium and the Muslim world*, ed. A. Laiou and R. Mottahedeh (Washington, D.C.: Dumbarton Oaks, 2001), 161–68.

6 It has been argued that it was the conquest of Constantinople that caused most Greeks to definitively reject papal primacy, see A. Papadakis, 'The Byzantines and the rise of the papacy: points for reflection, 1204–1453,' in *Greeks, Latins, and intellectual history, 1204–1500*, ed. M. Hinterberger and C. Schabel (Leuven: Peeters, 2011), 23; F. Dvornik, *Byzantium and the Roman Primacy* (New York: Fordham University Press, 1966), 56–57; D. J. Geanakoplos, *Byzantine east and Latin west: two worlds of Christendom in the Middle Ages and Renaissance; studies in ecclesiastical and cultural history* (Oxford: Basil Blackwell, 1966), 2; D. J. Geanakoplos, *Interaction of the 'sibling' Byzantine and western cultures in the Middle Ages and Italian Renaissance 330–1600* (New Haven, CT: Yale University Press, 1976), 10; A. Siecienski, *The papacy and the Orthodox*, 282; J. Gill, *Byzantium and the papacy, 1198–1400* (New Brunswick: Rutgers University Press, 1979), 12–13; N. Oikonomides, 'Byzantine diplomacy, A.D. 1204–1453: means and ends,' in *Byzantine diplomacy: papers from the twenty-fourth spring symposium of Byzantine Studies, Cambridge, March 1990*, ed. J. Shepard and S. Franklin (Aldershot: Ashgate, 1992), 75; M. Angold, 'After the Fourth Crusade: the Greek rump states and the recovery of Byzantium,' in *The Cambridge history of the Byzantine Empire, c. 500–1492*, ed. J. Shepard (Cambridge: Cambridge University Press, 2008), 735; D. Nicol, 'The crusades and the unity of Christendom,' Lecture to the friends of Dr. Williams's Library (London: Dr. Williams's Trust, 1986), 10.

7 Aristeides Papadakis and Alice Mary Talbot have argued that, after 1204, no writing by a Byzantine author was free of an anti-Latin attitude: A. Papadakis and A. M. Talbot, 'John X Camaterus confronts Innocent III: an unpublished correspondence,' *Byzantinoslavica* 33 (1972), 29.

8 Mesarites I, 48 line 22.

9 Mesarites III, 9 line 5–10 line 5.

4   THE DISPUTATIO

Cardinal Pelagius, the new papal legate to Constantinople in 1213, closed churches and threatened Greek clergy who refused submission to the authority of elder Rome.[10]

All of this indicates a heightened tension and anxiety surrounding the Great Schism, adding new urgency to attempts to bring about a union of the churches in the early thirteenth century. No longer was this a problem confined to circles of scholars and theologians. The matter was made more pressing by the chaotic political situation that developed as a result of the Fourth Crusade. Throughout the eastern Mediterranean there were Byzantines and Latins living as neighbours and enemies, subjects and rulers. The prospect of ending the schism would have real political implications, affecting how the two groups related to one another on a geo-political scale. Before 1204 the Byzantines had entertained the prospect of healing the schism as a method for engaging papal support against enemies, or potential enemies, far away. After 1204 ending the schism had become a necessary and important means for countering the incursions of Latin enemies at home. For the Latins, obtaining the recognition of western practices and doctrines from the Greek Church might very well justify the expense and bloodshed of the conquest of Constantinople, and perhaps the crusading movement itself. Innocent III expresses this belief shortly after the Fourth Crusade, suggesting that the conquest of Constantinople might soon be followed by the liberation of Jerusalem.[11] As the political stakes rose, so did the tensions in debates over the schism of the churches.[12]

It might seem remarkable, in this context often characterized by rivalry between Greeks and Latins, that we find attempts at ecclesiastical cooperation and unity such as the negotiations of the 1230s.[13] These episodes of repeated dialogue, culminating in the meetings of 1234, challenge the historical narrative of unremitting violence between

10 Akropolites, *History*, 29 line 20 – 30 line 2, transl. R. Macrides, 155.

11 Hageneder, *Die Register Innocenz' III*, vol. 7, no. 153, 263 lines 16–21. See also K. Setton, *The papacy and the Levant 1204–1571*, vol. 1, *The thirteenth and fourteenth centuries* (Philadelphia, PA: The American Philosophical Society, 1976), 1–26.

12 Francis Dvornik explained that, before 1204, theological dialogue had been 'rather polite and academic.' After the Fourth Crusade, these talks take on greater importance as a political and 'national' problem: F. Dvornik, *Byzantium and the Roman Primacy*, 14–15.

13 Another dialogue toward church union took place in the 1250s. On these negotiations, see J. Gill, *Byzantium and the papacy*, 88–96; A. Franchi, *La svolta politico-ecclesiastica tra Roma e Bizanzio (1249–1254): La legazione di Giovanni da Parma* (Rome: Pontificium Athenaeum Antonianum, 1981).

INTRODUCTION

the scattered Byzantine 'successor states' and the Latin invaders, most notably the Latin Empire of Constantinople, established by the crusaders in 1204. A greater focus on the sources describing the dialogue of 1234 creates a new paradigm in which the two sides emphasized diplomacy and theological debate, rather than violent force, as a means to solve the problems that divided them. That the negotiations of 1234 failed to bring about a union of the Greek and Roman Churches and resolve the animosity between Byzantines and Latins is less significant than the fact that both sides put forth honest efforts to reach a peaceful resolution. The potential benefits of a successful negotiation were highly sought after by both sides, and the eventual failure of these meetings held significant consequences for the ecclesiastical and diplomatic relationship between east and west.

1. Historiography

Modern scholars have tended to overlook the potential for success in the meetings of 1234, characterizing the encounter as a relatively insignificant negotiation that neither side took seriously. Such conclusions are common in the history of dialogues intended to bring about church union. Nearly a century ago Louis Bréhier described the history of attempts at church union as 'one of continued mortification, repeated checks, and perpetual failures.'[14] Such conclusions overlook the nuances of these meetings and the optimism for success exhibited by both sides before negotiations began. This is especially true of the meetings in 1234, which were the result of a long and serious correspondence between the heads of both churches. Even those scholars who have examined the events of 1234 specifically, however, have carried over Bréhier's bleak and dismal outlook.[15] Perhaps the most

---

14 L. Bréhier, 'Attempts at reunion of the Greek and Latin Churches,' in *Cambridge medieval history* 4, ed. J. Bury (Cambridge: Cambridge University Press, 1923), 594. This overall attitude is shared by Milton Anastos, who argued that all efforts toward church union were doomed due to the 'devotion to Byzantine orthodoxy and a proud nationalism' that limited the ability of the emperors to submit to compromise: M. Anastos, 'Constantinople and Rome: a survey of the relations between the Byzantine and the Roman Churches,' in *Aspects of the mind of Byzantium: political theory, theology, and ecclesiastical relations with the See of Rome*, ed. S. Vryonis and N. Goodhue (Aldershot: Ashgate, 2001), 60.

15 John Doran concluded that 'there was no prospect of a union of the Churches because each had a fundamentally different conception of the nature of ecclesiastical authority': J. Doran, 'Rites and wrongs: the Latin mission to Nicaea, 1234,' *Studies in Church History*

6 THE DISPUTATIO

succinct estimation of the dialogue of 1234 is that of Michael Angold, who said simply that union negotiations were 'doomed to fail.'[16] Each of these interpretations has tended to project the result of the meetings of 1234 onto the beginning, thus concluding that they never really had much chance of success and that the schism was destined to continue.[17]

The narrative of perpetual and unavoidable failure to end the schism maintained by modern scholarship may stem from a lack of emphasis on the sources that emerged from such proceedings – what we might refer to as the *'disputatio* genre.'[18] Alex Novikoff has noted that textual evidence of disputations, although avidly studied by theologians, have been largely neglected by historians.[19] Again, a comment by Louis Bréhier demonstrates this point perfectly. Bréhier said of the literature that emerged from the *disputatio* that 'nothing can surpass the monotony of these erudite treatises on the Procession of the Holy Ghost, of these dialogues and contradictory debates, which repeat over and over again the same arguments and appeal continually to the same authorities.'[20] It is true that such works tend to be

---

32 (1996), 131. John Langdon remarked that theological debate 'only served to exacerbate the seemingly irreconcilable difference between the Roman Catholic and Byzantine Greek Orthodox churches': J. Langdon, 'Byzantium in Anatolian exile: imperial vicegerency reaffirmed during Byzantino-Papal discussions at Nicaea and Nymphaion, 1234,' *Byzantinische Forschungen* 20 (1994), 199. Even the more balanced view of Tia Kolbaba has regarded the failure of church–union negotiations as an almost predetermined result. 'Each side usually failed to address the real and substantive arguments of the other, as polemic and point-scoring usually triumphed over any prolonged effort to understand': T. Kolbaba, 'Theological debates with the West,' 479.

16 M. Angold, *A Byzantine government in exile* (London: Oxford University Press, 1975), 15.

17 The opposing view, that healing the schism was indeed a real possibility, is found in the work of Aristeides Papadakis, who maintained that 'there is no evidence that either side deemed reconciliation impossible solely because of such factors, even after the forced latinization of the Byzantine Church and the partition of the empire in 1204': A. Papadakis, 'Byzantine perceptions of the Latin West,' *Greek Orthodox Theological Review* 36 (1991), 235. See also M. Stavrou, 'Heurs et malheurs du dialogue théologique gréco-latin au XIIIe siècle,' in *Réduire le schisme? Ecclésiologies et politiques de l'Union entre Orient et Occident (XIIIe–XVIIIe siècles),* ed. M. Blanchet and F. Gabriel (Paris: Peeters, 2013), 41–56.

18 The *disputatio* may be considered a sub-genre of polemic: O. Weijers, *In search of the truth: a history of disputation techniques from antiquity to early modern times* (Turnhout: Brepols, 2013), 175.

19 A. Novikoff, 'Towards a cultural history of scholastic disputation,' *American Historical Review* 117:2 (2012), 331–34. See also A. Cameron, *Arguing it out: discussion in twelfth-century Byzantium* (Budapest: Central European University Press, 2016), 10–12.

20 L. Bréhier, 'Attempts at reunion of the Churches,' 595.

INTRODUCTION

repetitive, and this may be why they are often overlooked. Other historians, such as Alexander Vasiliev, have mined documents that describe religious dialogue for information on political developments and completely disregarded any evidence that might shed light on Byzantine–Latin social or cross-cultural interactions.[21] The practice of making theological treatises and sources on doctrinal debate subservient to other, often more politically orientated material has become commonplace.

De-emphasizing the *disputatio* genre inherently distorts the historical narrative of Byzantine–Latin interaction. Several scholars have warned against the potential pitfalls of overlooking such material.[22] Tia Kolbaba has shown that the sources describing ecclesiastical dialogue tell us much about cross-cultural contacts. She wrote that it will 'sometimes be necessary to dip a toe into the deep waters of theological explanation.'[23] Averil Cameron's recent examination of dialogues under the Komnenoi emperors of the twelfth century demonstrated that the sources describing ecclesiastical debate between the Greek and Roman Churches can in fact tell us much about the development of Byzantine literature and cultural activity. The consequence of historians neglecting this material, she explained, is that much of our understanding of these sources is reduced to mere generalizations.[24] This is especially true for our understanding of the turbulent years following the Fourth Crusade. It will be impossible to build a complete paradigm of the interactions between Byzantines and Latins without including all pertinent material and avoiding the generalizations that have characterized that material. Unfortunately, sources describing theological debate have been largely overlooked as a method of Byzantine diplomacy with Latin powers. Alexander Kazhdan's nine

---

21 In his comments on the historical value of the works of Nicholas Mesarites, Alexander Vasiliev expressed his disregard for the numerous descriptions of church–union negotiations in the text, referring to them as 'mere rhetorical ejaculations on church troubles': A. Vasiliev, 'Mesarites as a source,' *Speculum* 13 (1938), 181.

22 A. Papadakis, 'Byzantine perceptions of the Latin West,' 234–35; J. Pelikan, *The Christian tradition: a history of the development of doctrine*, vol. 2, *The spirit of eastern Christendom* (Chicago, IL: University of Chicago Press, 1988), 170; M. Smith, *And taking bread*, 77–83; J. Erickson, 'Leavened and unleavened,' 156; T. Ware, *The Orthodox Church* (London: Penguin, 1997), 44; C. Schabel, 'The quarrel over unleavened bread in western theology, 1234–1439,' in *Greeks, Latins, and intellectual history, 1204–1500*, ed. M. Hinterberger and C. Schabel (Leuven: Peeters, 2011), 85–127.

23 T. Kolbaba, 'Theological debates with the West,' 483.

24 A. Cameron, *Arguing it out*, 10.

8   THE DISPUTATIO

techniques of Byzantine diplomacy, for example, include no mention of ecclesiastical dialogue.[25] Even scholars who promote a balanced approach, advocating for an inclusive analysis of political and theological concerns in Byzantine–Latin diplomacy, have failed to take into account the instances of church-union negotiations that took place during the period of exile from 1204 to 1261. Aristeides Papadakis suggested that theological debate returned to east–west relations only under Michael VIII Palaiologos, with the union proclaimed at Lyons in 1274.[26] This assertion completely disregarded the union negotiations of 1234 and other attempts under the Laskarid emperors in Nicaea, which formed the precedent for later talks.[27] In this way, Papadakis failed to properly address the theological encounters of the early thirteenth century and their significance in the relationship between Byzantines and Latins.

Few of these studies have given due attention to the correspondence between the pope and patriarch that forms the preliminaries to these negotiations and indicates the optimism held by both sides. By contrast, those historians who have examined the negotiations of 1234 have given the bulk of their focus to the report of the friars. This text, compiled by the very men who represented Gregory IX in 1234, gives an extraordinarily detailed account of the proceedings undertaken to bring union to the churches, but has also formed the basis for the 'doomed to fail' paradigm for this meeting. The friars' final words to the gathered Greek clergy, 'We found you heretics and excommunicates, and as heretics and excommunicates we leave you,' have become synonymous with the meeting itself.[28] It is the comment that many historians have most often used to characterize the negotiations as a whole, and thus readers neglect the nuances of the meeting. Some have even overlooked the possibility that the friars, whose report forms the main source for this encounter, may purposely have distorted the facts of the proceeding. The authors of this text almost certainly intended their words to explain to the pope why the meeting had failed. Depicting the patriarch

---

25 A. Kazhdan, 'The notion of Byzantine diplomacy,' in *Byzantine diplomacy: papers from the twenty-fourth spring symposium of Byzantine Studies, Cambridge, March 1990*, ed. J. Shepard and S. Franklin (Aldershot: Ashgate, 1992), 6.

26 A. Papadakis, *Crisis in Byzantium: the filioque controversy in the patriarchate of Gregory II of Cyprus (1283–1289)*, 2nd edn (Crestwood, NY: St Vladimir's Seminary Press, 1997), 1–2.

27 George Pachymeres, *Georges Pachymérès. Relations historiques*, ed. A. Failler, transl. V. Laurent vol. 2, III, IV (Paris: Peeters, 1999), 479.

28 Golubovich, 'Disputatio,' ch. 28, 463, lines 37–39.

INTRODUCTION 9

and his Greek clergy as bigoted and prejudiced against them serves that purpose. Indeed, the whole document appears to have been written after the anticipated union of the churches had collapsed. Thus, the authors of the report purposely portrayed the negotiations as 'doomed to fail,' because that is precisely what happened. It is understandable that historians would take the lead from what is contained in the sources, but we must be aware of the intentions of the authors of this material and their purpose in writing, and in this way challenge the overarching negative narrative surrounding the meeting of 1234, and the *disputatio* genre as a whole.

The best method for countering this negative narrative and correcting the oversight of evidence from the early thirteenth century is to make the sources more available to a wider audience. As our own world becomes increasing secular, and scholars call into question our understanding of the roles of church and state in Byzantium, it is more important than ever that we remember the crucial role of ecclesiastical dialogue in the relationship between east and west. A close examination of this material demonstrates that the meetings of 1234 were the result of a consistent and sincere correspondence between Gregory IX and Germanos II, and that both pope and patriarch approached church-union negotiation with high expectations.

2. Terminology

Classifying the encounter between ecclesiasts of the Greek and Roman Churches in 1234 as a *disputatio* requires some qualification. The Latin term denotes an 'argument' or 'discussion,' often in the form of debate or dialogue, but does not necessarily indicate hostility between the parties involved.[29] In its broadest form, the *disputatio* involved two disputants, or groups of disputants, one representing each side, offering arguments and counterarguments. This format of dialogue became popular with the rise of scholasticism in the Latin West and can be frequently observed in meetings between representatives of the Greek and Roman Churches.[30] In many ways,

---

29 P. Glare, ed., *Oxford Latin dictionary*, 2nd edn (Oxford: Oxford University Press, 2012), 609–10.

30 O. Weijers, *In search of the truth*; O. Weijers, *La 'disputatio' dans les facultés des arts au moyen âge* (Turnhout: Brepols, 2002); O. Weijers, 'The medieval *disputatio*,' in *Traditions of controversy*, ed. M. Dascal and H. Chang (Amsterdam and Philadelphia, PA: John Benjamins Publishing Company, 2007), 141–49; A. Novikoff, *The medieval culture of*

10 THE DISPUTATIO

identifying the first *disputatio* is as difficult a task as pinpointing the origin of the schism. Suffice it to say that, from the eleventh century, and especially under the Komnenoi emperors, who frequently entertained the prospect of church union as a means of advancing their foreign policy agenda with the papacy and other western powers, there are numerous examples of the *disputatio* between Byzantine and Latin scholars and theologians.[31] These encounters were not always official. The disputants who took part were not always sanctioned by the pope or patriarch, and it was not always the case that the emperor or some other ruler was present. Still, every example of the *disputatio* between Byzantines and Latins pertained to the diplomatic sphere just as much as it did to religious matters.

The friars who represented Gregory IX in 1234 use the noun *disputatio* to refer to their meetings with Germanos II and his clergy on 14 occasions.[32]

---

disputation: pedagogy, practice, and performance (Philadelphia: University of Pennsylvania Press, 2013).

31 The first took place under Alexios I Komnenos, when two papal envoys arrived in Constantinople in 1089 asking why the pope's name had been removed from the diptychs: J. Darrouzès, 'Les documents byzantins du XIIe siècle sur la primauté romaine,' *Revue des études byzantines* 23 (1965), 43–51; T. Kolbaba, 'The legacy of Humbert and Cerularius,' 59–60; H. Chadwick, *East and west*, 222–23; M. Kaplan, 'La place du schism de 1054 dans les relations entre Byzance, Rome et l'Italie,' *Byzantinoslavica* 54:1 (1993), 36; H. Cowdrey, 'The Gregorian Papacy, Byzantium, and the First Crusade,' in *Byzantium and the west, c. 850–c. 1200: proceedings of the XVIII spring symposium of Byzantine Studies, Oxford 30th March–1st April 1984*, ed. J. Howard-Johnston (Amsterdam: Verlag Adolf M. Hakkert, 1988), 162; S. Runciman, *The Eastern schism*, 61–62; J. Erickson, 'Leavened and unleavened,' 157. For the letter to Urban II from Patriarch Nicholas III that resulted from this meeting: W. Holtzmann, 'Unionsverhandlungen zwischen Kaiser Alexios I. und Papst Urban II. im Jahre 1089,' *Byzantinische Zeitschrift* 28 (1928), 62–64.

32 Golubovich, 'Disputatio,' 431 line 23; 434 line 4; 434 line 7; 435 line 38; 436 line 1; 437 line 19; 437 line 22; 444 line 22; 448 line 9; 448 line 15; 448 line 22; 450 lines 1–2; 452 lines 18–19; 461 line 30. Another often noted *disputatio* was held in Constantinople with Peter Grossolano, archbishop of Milan in 1112: Migne *PG* 127, cols 911–20; V. Grumel, 'Autour du voyage de Pierre Grossolanus archevêque de Milan, à Constantinple, en 1112. Notes d'histoire et de littérature,' *Échos d'Orient* 32 (1933), 22–33; A. Siecienski, *The filioque*, 111–13, 121; T. Kolbaba, 'Byzantine perceptions of Latin religious "errors": themes and changes from 850 to 1350,' in *The crusades from the perspective of Byzantium and the Muslim world*, ed. A. Laiou and R. Mottahedeh (Washington, D.C.: Dumbarton Oaks, 2001), 126–27, 138; J. Darrouzès, 'Les documents byzantins,' 51–59; H. Chadwick, *East and west*, 225. Perhaps the most recognized example of a *disputatio* under the Komnenoi is the meeting in 1136 between Anselm of Havelberg and Niketas of Nicomedia: Anselm of Havelberg, *Antikeimenon*, Migne *PL* 188, cols 1139–1248; transl. A. Criste and C. Neel, *Anselm of Havelberg, Anticimenon: on the unity of the faith and the controversies with the*

INTRODUCTION   11

Still, some caution is called for if scholars are to use the word as a more general form of categorization for discussions of ecclesiastical schism and church-union negotiations. After all, Byzantine authors of the early thirteenth century naturally did not use the Latin term *disputatio* to refer to these meetings, but employed a varied vocabulary of Greek terms. Nicholas Mesarites describes the discussions in late 1204 as διαλαλία, 'discourse,'[33] and διάλεξις, 'conversation.'[34] Mesarites, in discussing the meetings in 1206 and 1214, identifies them as ἆθλος, meaning 'contests' or 'spiritual struggles.'[35] Germanos II refers to the Latin arguments made in 1234 as ὁμολογία, 'confession.'[36] The most enigmatic identification is that of Nikephoros Blemmydes. He describes the 1234 meeting as a κοινὸν ἀθροισμόν, 'public assembly.'[37] In describing the *disputatio* with John of Parma in 1249/50, Blemmydes states that representatives of the Roman Church came to a σύλλογος, 'meeting,' in order to 'defend their definition of faith.'[38] There seems to have been little or no uniformity in how Byzantine authors characterized episodes of dialogue with representatives of the Roman Church.

Another potential problem of terminology is that referring to these meetings as *disputationes* might be seen to suggest a specialized format or formal conduct that was observed by both sides. Averil Cameron has correctly noted that the meetings between Byzantine and Latin theologians

---

Greeks (Collegeville, MN: Liturgical Press, 2010), 81–211; J. Darrouzès, 'Les documents byzantins,' 59–65; J. Lees, *Anselm of Havelberg: deeds into words in the twelfth century* (Leiden and New York: Brill, 1998), 40–47; S. Runciman, *The Eastern schism*, 115; J. Ryder, 'Changing perspectives on 1054,' *Byzantine and Modern Greek Studies* 35 (2011), 26; T. Kolbaba, 'On the closing of the churches and the rebaptism of Latins: Greek perfidy or Latin slander?' *Byzantine and Modern Greek Studies* 29 (2005), 43–45; A. Siecienski, *The filioque*, 121–23; H. Chadwick, *East and west*, 228–32.

33 Mesarites I, 48 line 22.

34 Mesarites I, 69 line 23. Nicholas of Otranto also uses the term διάλεξις to describe church-union negotiations in 1206: Nicholas of Otranto, *Nikolaia Hidruntskago tri ealici*, ed. Archimandrite Arsenij (Novgorod, 1896), 4.

35 Mesarites I, 51 line 12; Mesarites III, 19 line 15.

36 Germanos II, Ἀπάντησις, in *Chronikon Georgiou Phrantze tou protovestiariou eis tessara vivlia diairethen*, ed. F. Alter (Vienna, 1796), 139.

37 Nikephoros Blemmydes, *Nicephori Blemmydae Autobiographia sive curriculum vitae*, ed. J. A. Munitiz (Turnhout: Brepols, 1984), Book 2, ch. 25, 57 line 5; transl. J. A. Munitiz, *Nikephoros Blemmydes: a partial account* (Louvain: Spicilegium Sacrum Lovaniense, 1988), 107. It should be noted that J. Munitiz in this instance translated ἀθροισμόν as 'debate.'

38 ἐπὶ συστάσει τοῦ οἰκείου δόγματος, Nikephoros Blemmydes, *Autobiographia*, ed. J. Munitiz, Book 2, ch. 50, 67 lines 1–4; transl. J. A. Munitiz, *A partial account*, 119.

12   THE DISPUTATIO

'lacked the technical features of disputation as developed in western scholasticism.'[39] How then can we refer to church-union negotiation as a *disputatio*? Cameron's concern is a result of the fact that the exercise of disputation was becoming formalized in the Latin West over the thirteenth and fourteenth centuries. Although instances of dialogue and disputation had their roots in the ancient and late antique periods, it was not until the late twelfth and early thirteenth centuries that the practice became fully explored in western education. Anselm of Canterbury played a large role in reviving the practice in the Latin West.[40] By about 1200 the *disputatio* had become a central component of medieval university education.[41]

If we are to use the term *disputatio* to refer to a genre of literature or type of encounter between Byzantine and Latin ecclesiasts, it is necessary to separate the word from a sense of technical meaning. Thankfully, both Olga Weijers and Alex Novikoff have shown that the forms of such dialogue did not remain confined to the academic environment. Novikoff explained that the *disputatio* influenced various facets of medieval culture – namely poetry, polyphonic music, and Christian confrontations with Judaism.[42] The fact that current scholarship has not included Byzantine–Latin interactions and inter-Christian dialogue or negotiation between different Christian groups in its analysis of medieval disputation is most unfortunate.[43] Weijers concluded that, outside of the universities and academic circles of

---

39 A. Cameron, *Arguing it out*, 46.

40 A. Novikoff, *The medieval culture of disputation*, 34–61; A. Novikoff, 'Anselm, dialogue, and the rise of disputation,' *Speculum* 86 (2011), 387–418.

41 A. Novikoff, *The medieval culture of disputation*, 133–47; O. Weijers, 'The medieval disputatio,' 141–49.

42 A. Novikoff, 'Towards a cultural history of scholastic disputation,' 335–64.

43 The silence on the subject is particularly unusual when one considers the emphasis given to Anselm of Canterbury as a pioneer in reintroducing the method. His treatise on the procession of the Holy Spirit, a dialogue written to refute Greek doctrine at Bari in 1098 is viewed as a pivotal moment in western scholasticism. Still, modern scholars of the *disputatio*, while praising the work for its influence in western logic, have failed to trace its impact on the narrative of the schism of the churches: Anselm of Canterbury, *Opera omnia*, ed. F. Schmitt, vol. 2 (Rome, 1940), 175–219; transl. B. Davies and G. Evans, *Anselm of Canterbury: the major works* (Oxford: Oxford University Press, 1998), 390–434. Christopher Martin said only that Anselm's treatise had little impact on Greek theological thought, and then proceeded to trace a long history of Anselm's influence in western academic circles: C. Martin, 'Disputing about disputing: The medieval procedure of *positio* and its role in a dispute over the nature of logic and the foundations of metaphysics,' in *Traditions of controversy*, ed. M. Dascal and H. Chang (Amsterdam and Philadelphia: John Benjamins Publishing Company, 2007), 151–64.

INTRODUCTION

the Latin West, the word *disputatio* did not necessarily carry a technical meaning.[44] Furthermore, both scholars offered broad interpretations of the word *disputatio* that allow us to use it in the context of the meetings of 1234. Novikoff explained that the word might indicate a 'discussion,' 'conversation,' or the more intense 'dispute' or 'debate,' but in any case the word always refers to rational investigations and dialectical argumentation inherent in the term *disputatio*.[45] Weijers went further in explaining the wide range of possible interpretations of the word *disputatio*, indicating a 'treatment' or 'public discussion.'[46] Such conceptualizations, coupled with the dizzying variety by which Byzantine authors characterized these encounters, allow us to categorize the dialogue and negotiations of 1234 as a *disputatio*, but only in the broadest and most liberal sense.

Another possible pitfall in the area of terminology is how to refer to the diplomatic office of the friars who represented Pope Gregory IX in 1234. The status of these representatives can tell us much about what the pope expected from the meetings, and perhaps why they failed to bring about the desired union of the churches. Identifying the precise diplomatic status of these friars, however, presents a problem. It is impossible to speak of them as 'ambassadors' of the Roman Church. Donald Queller has explained that this term is particularly hazardous because of modern implications of the office that did not apply in the early thirteenth century.[47] Thus, we must refer to the friars who took part in the *disputatio* in contemporary terms, namely *nuncio* or *legatus*. Alternative terms do exist. *Apokrisiarios* is a term that turns up during the negotiations of 1234.[48] In their statement of faith regarding the procession of the Holy Spirit, the friars referred to themselves as '*apokrisiarii* of the lord pope Gregory, bishop of elder Rome.'[49] According to G. W. H. Lampe's *Patristic Greek Lexicon*, an *apokrisiarios* can indicate either a messenger or a legate.[50] Because of this

---

44 O. Weijers, *In search of the truth: a history of disputation techniques*, 100.

45 A. Novikoff, 'Towards a cultural history of scholastic disputation,' 339–40.

46 O. Weijers, *In search of the truth: a history of disputation techniques*, 100.

47 D. Queller, *The office of ambassador in the Middle Ages* (Princeton, NJ: Princeton University Press, 1967), ix; D. Queller, 'Thirteenth-century diplomatic envoys: *'Nuncii'* and *'Procuratores',' Speculum* 35 (1960), 196.

48 Golubovich, 'Disputatio,' ch. 7, 434 line 15; ch. 20, 450 line 18; ch. 23, 454 line 17; 455 line 4; ch. 27, 463 line 6.

49 J. Mansi, *Sacrorum conciliorum nova et amplissima collectio*, XXIII (Paris, 1903), col. 66.

50 G. Lampe, *A Patristic Greek lexicon* (Oxford: Clarendon Press, 1961), 198.

14 THE DISPUTATIO

inherent ambiguity, *apokrisiarios* should be understood as an all-inclusive diplomatic term and does not serve to delineate the power and authority of the friars as papal representatives. Another word to describe representatives, πρεσβεύς, is sometimes used by Byzantine authors, most frequently by Nicholas Mesarites. Henry George Liddell and Robert Scott's *Greek–English Lexicon*[51] and Lampe's *Patristic Greek Lexicon*[52] translate this word as 'ambassador,' but it can also have the meaning of 'advocate,' 'agent,' or 'intercessor.' Whereas other Byzantine authors employ πρεσβεύς to describe the representatives of secular powers,[53] Mesarites uses the term in both a secular and ecclesiastical context, for the representatives of the Roman Church who arrived in Nicaea in 1214,[54] and for himself as a representative of Theodore I Laskaris.[55] While the exact connotation of this word may be perplexing, this diplomatic term never surfaces in the context of the friars at the *disputatio* of 1234. *Nuncio* or *legatus*, therefore, offer us the clearest distinction of diplomatic authority for the friars as representatives of the papacy.

Richard Schmutz provided us with a thorough examination of the office of *nuncio* versus that of the legate, elucidating the differences between the two in medieval diplomacy.[56] He described the *nuncio* as a message-bearer, conveying the words and will of his principal without the authority to negotiate new agreements independent of prior instruction.[57] Donald Queller has gone even further, characterizing a *nuncio* as a 'speaking letter.'[58] There

---

51 The Greek πρέσβευτής has been identified as the equivalent of the Latin term *legatus*: H. G. Liddell and R. Scott, *Greek–English lexicon* (New York: Harper and Brothers, 1883), 1266.

52 G. Lampe, *A Patristic Greek lexicon*, 1129.

53 For example, both Nikephoros Gregoras and George Akropolites use the term πρέσβεις to describe a group of representatives from Bulgaria: Nikephoros Gregoras, *Byzantina Historia*, ed. L. Schopen, vol. 1 (Bonn: Weber, 1829), 29 line 16; Akropolites, *History*, 53 line 1, and 57 line 6. Another Byzantine author to employ the term, Theodore II Laskaris, in a letter to Nikephoros Blemmydes, refers to a 'spiritual embassy' – οἱ πνευματικοὶ πρέσβεις – sent to meet with Pope Innocent IV in 1250/1: N. Festa, *Theodori Ducae Lascaris Epistulae CCXVII* (Florence: Tipografia G. Carnesecchi e Figli, 1898), no. 18, 24 line 5.

54 πρέσβεις ἐκ Ῥώμης, Mesarites III, 19 line 9 – 34 line 8.

55 ἀπὸ τηλικούτου βασιλέως πρέσβυς, Mesarites III, 21 lines 32–33.

56 R. Schmutz, 'Medieval papal representatives, legates, nuncios, and judges-delegate,' *Studia Gratiana* 15 (1972), 456.

57 R. Schmutz, 'Medieval papal representatives,' 458.

58 D. Queller, 'Thirteenth-century diplomatic envoys,' 198; D. Queller, *The office of ambassador*, 225.

INTRODUCTION 15

are episodes of a *nuncio* stretching his authority into negotiation. A famous example of a *nuncio* overstepping his authority is reported in the account of Liudprand of Cremona. In 968 Liudprand was sent to Constantinople as an envoy of Otto I. There he met with the Byzantine emperor Nikephoros II Phokas, who pointed out that a previous *nuntius* from the west, Dominic the Venetian, had made promises on behalf of his principal that Otto I did not keep.[59] Examples such as this help to clarify the boundaries of the authority granted to a *nuncio*. They could not bind their principal to new agreements. Strictly speaking, therefore, the *nuncio* was a mere representative whose responsibility rarely extended beyond delivering written or spoken messages.

The legate appears to have had a more dynamic and nuanced authority. Schmutz defined the legate as 'a proctorial agent who exercised papal authority in the ordinary, ecclesiastical administration and, under special mandate, in diplomacy.'[60] He added that the key to identifying a legate versus a *nuncio* is best achieved via their mandate – usually included in a letter of recommendation given to the one who received the representative.[61] In the absence of a mandate, however, Schmutz suggested looking to the 'characteristic kinds of activity authorized by mandates' to indicate the presence of a legate.[62] Thus, if the envoy acted as though he had the authority to negotiate, we must consider whether or not such authority had been granted by his principal, perhaps in spoken rather than written instruction.

Although they have much to say about the issue, it is surprisingly difficult to decipher the diplomatic status of the friars as papal representatives based on the sources surrounding the *disputatio* of 1234. The letter from Gregory IX to Germanos II, dated 18 May 1233, introduces the friars to the patriarch, serving to prove their credentials. The pope explains that their purpose is to 'negotiate faithfully and discuss amicably' with the patriarch, but he does not identify them as either *nuncios* or *legatii*.[63] Both the terms appear prominently in the friars' report describing the *disputatio* of 1234 (Source V). In chapter 2 the patriarch asks the representatives from

---

59 Liudprand of Cremona, *Relatio de legatione Constantinopolitana*, ed. P. Chiesa, *Liudprandi Cremonensis opera omnia* (Turnhout: Brepols, 1998), 200 line 496 – 201 line 500; transl. P. Squatriti, *The complete works of Liudprand of Cremona* (Washington, D.C.: Catholic University of America Press, 2007), 257.

60 R. Schmutz, 'Medieval papal representatives,' 444.

61 R. Schmutz, 'Medieval papal representatives,' 445.

62 R. Schmutz, 'Medieval papal representatives,' 456.

63 Tautu, *Acta*, no. 193, 267 lines 4–5; see Source IV.

16   THE DISPUTATIO

Gregory IX 'whether we were legates of the lord Pope, and whether we wished to accept the honour due to legates.'[64] To this the friars answer that they were *simplices nuncios*, 'simple messengers,' and that they did not wish to claim the honours due to legates.[65] The patriarch determines that even the lowliest messenger of the pope deserved 'great reverence and honour.'[66] This episode has been enough to satisfy previous historians who investigated the *disputatio*, concluding that the friars held the position of a *nuncio*.[67] None of these scholars, however, have delved deeper into the report of the friars to clarify or corroborate their statement. Not long after their claim to be mere *nuncios*, the friars make a startling statement regarding the extent of their authority as papal representatives: 'The contents of the lord Pope's letters sufficiently explains our authority to you; and this we add, whatever we do well in this business the Roman Church will consider ratified and pleasing.'[68] This response may indicate some authority to negotiate on behalf of Gregory IX, perhaps suggesting that the friars were indeed legates, despite their protestations to the contrary. Other evidence contained within the friars' report suggests that their status as *nuncios* was not as straightforward as past scholars have argued.[69] All of this makes the terms we use to characterize the friars as papal represent-atives – be it as *nuncio* or *legatus* – very problematic.[70]

Finally, it may seem strange, especially to those in Byzantine Studies, to refer to the Western Church, the church presided over by the pope, as the 'Roman Church.' Western medievalists may see this as a given, seeing as the pope, who occupied the seat of St Peter, resided in Rome. Byzantinists,

---

64 Golubovich, 'Disputatio,' ch. 2, 428 lines 27–28.

65 Golubovich, 'Disputatio,' ch. 2, 428 lines 28–29.

66 Golubovich, 'Disputatio,' ch. 2, 429 lines 4–5.

67 J. Doran, 'Rites and wrongs in 1234,' 135; H. Chadwick, *East and west*, 238; R. Schmutz, 'Medieval papal representatives,' 444.

68 Golubovich, 'Disputatio,' ch. 3, 429 lines 16–19.

69 See ch. 11, in which the friars, translating a treatise by Nikephoros Blemmydes, refer to themselves as legates: Golubovich, 'Disputatio Latinorum et Graecorum,' ch. 11, 438 line 1; *Nicéphore Blemmydès: Œuvres théologiques: introduction, texte critique, traduction et notes*, ed. M. Stavrou, vol. 1 (Paris: Les Éditions du Cerf, 2007), 184 lines 1–2.

70 For a fuller discussion of the problem of the friars' diplomatic status and the implications for the ecclesiastical and diplomatic negotiations of 1234, see J. Brubaker, '*Nuncii* or *Legati*: what makes a papal representative in 1234,' in *Cross-cultural exchange in the Byzantine world, 300–1500 AD: selected papers from the XVII International Graduate Conference of the Oxford University Byzantine Society*, ed. K. Stewart and J. Wakeley (Oxford: Peter Lang International Academic Publishers, 2016), 115–28.

INTRODUCTION   17

however, would be quick to point out that the people we refer to as 'Byzantines' referred to themselves as 'Romans' throughout their history. Even during the period of so-called 'exile,' when a Latin regime occupied Constantinople from 1204 to 1261, the Byzantines continued to emphasize their Roman heritage.[71] The fact that certain alternatives, such as 'Hellene' or 'Greek,' might have taken on a new significance during the period does not negate the Byzantines' Roman identity.[72] In terms of ecclesiastical identity, however, and certainly in the context of the sources referring to the *disputatio* of 1234, 'Roman' refers explicitly to the Western Church of the Latins. The Byzantines refer to their own Church as the 'Greek Church.' This is by no means exclusive to the context of 1234. Paul Magdalino has

---

71 G. Page, *Being Byzantine: Greek identity before the Ottomans* (Cambridge: Cambridge University Press, 2008), 94–137; C. Roueché, 'Defining identities and allegiances in the Eastern Mediterranean after 1204,' in *Identities and allegiances in the Eastern Mediterranean after 1204*, ed. J. Herrin and G. Saint-Guillain (Aldershot: Ashgate, 2011), 1–5; C. Morrison, 'Thirteenth-century Byzantine "metallic" identities,' in *Liquid and multiple: individuals and identities in the thirteenth-century Aegean*, ed. G. Saint-Guillain and D. Stathakopoulos (Paris: Association des Amis du Centre d'Histoire et Civilisation de Byzance, 2012), 133–64; D. Smythe, 'Byzantine identity and labeling theory,' in *Byzantium, identity, image, influence: XIX International Congress of Byzantine Studies, University of Copenhagen, 18–24 August, 1996*, ed. K. Fledelius and P. Schreiner (Copenhagen: Eventus, 1996), 26–36; P. Magdalino, 'Hellenism and nationalism in Byzantium,' in P. Magdalino, *Tradition and transformation in medieval Byzantium* (Aldershot: Variorum, 1991), 1–29; A. Kaldellis, *Hellenism in Byzantium: the transformation of Greek identity and the reception of the classical tradition* (Cambridge: Cambridge University Press, 2007), 317–88; T. Shawcross, 'The lost generation (c. 1204–c. 1222): political allegiance and local interests under the impact of the Fourth Crusade,' in *Identities and allegiances in the Eastern Mediterranean after 1204*, ed. J. Herrin and G. Saint-Guillain (Aldershot: Ashgate, 2011), 9–37; A. Bryer, 'The late Byzantine identity,' in *Byzantium, identity, image, influence: XIX International Congress of Byzantine Studies, University of Copenhagen, 18–24 August, 1996*, ed. K. Fledelius and P. Schreiner (Copenhagen: Eventus, 1996), 49–50; E. Mitsiou, 'Networks of Nicaea: 13th-century socio-economic ties, structures and prosopography,' in *Liquid and multiple: individuals and identities in the thirteenth-century Aegean*, ed. G. Saint-Guillain and D. Stathakopoulos (Paris: Association des Amis du Centre d'Histoire et Civilisation de Byzance, 2012), 91–104.

72 R. Macrides, 'The thirteenth century in Byzantine historical writing,' in *Porphyrogenita: essays on the history and literature of Byzantium and the Latin east in honour of Julian Chrysostomides*, eds C. Dendrinos et al. (Aldershot: Ashgate, 2003), 63–76; M. Angold, *A Byzantine government in exile*, 30–31; P. Magdalino, 'Hellenism and nationalism in Byzantium,' 1–29; T. Papadopoulou, 'The terms Ῥωμαῖος, Ἕλλην, Γραικὸς the Byzantine texts of the first half of the 13th century,' *Byzantina Symmeikta* 24 (Athens, 2014), 157–76.

18   THE DISPUTATIO

pointed out that, 'in all their writings concerning the Roman church, the Byzantines habitually described themselves as Γραικοί in order to avoid confusion.'[73] The terms 'Roman Church' and 'Greek Church,' therefore, should be considered an issue of simplification, and not as any form of concession to the pope.

3. Background

The years following the capture of Constantinople by the Fourth Crusade were chaotic, violent, and uncertain. One historian has referred to the period from 1204 to 1261 as an 'orgy of violence.'[74] The almost constant state of warfare between Byzantines and Latins was punctuated by short periods of truce and diplomatic dialogue. With the Byzantine capital under crusader occupation, a number of Greek and Latin polities emerged to fill the vacuum of power.[75] The most successful of these were the so-called 'successor states,' of which the most important for the purpose of the current study is the Empire of Nicaea. The Anatolian city of Nicaea became a focal point of resistance against the Latins under Theodore Laskaris, who had already risen to prominence before the Fourth Crusade through his marriage to Anna, the daughter of Alexios III Angelos.[76] Both Greek and Latin sources describe how Laskaris consolidated his position in Nicaea and the surrounding area no later than 1206.[77] To the west the Byzantine aristocrat Michael Doukas founded a rival successor state in Epiros that reached the apogee of its power under his brother Theodore Doukas, who liberated the city of Thessalonike from Latin control in 1224.[78] Theodore

---

73 P. Magdalino, 'Hellenism and nationalism in Byzantium,' 11.

74 S. Reinert, 'Fragmentation (1204–1453),' in *The expansion of Orthodox Europe: Byzantium, the Balkans and Russia*, ed. J. Shepard (Aldershot: Ashgate, 2007), 308.

75 For an overview of the political fragmentation after 1204, see M. Angold, 'After the Fourth Crusade,' 731–58.

76 Akropolites, *History*, 9 lines 3–4; transl. R. Macrides, 118; Choniates, *Historia*, 508 lines 81–82; transl. H. Magoulias, 280.

77 Geoffrey of Villehardouin, *Histoire de la conquête de Constantinople par Geoffroi de Ville-Hardouin avec la continuation de Henri de Valenciennes*, ed. N. de Wailly (Paris: Hachette, 1909), ch. 313, 117; Choniates, *Historia*, 638; transl. H. Magoulias, 350; Akropolites, *History*, 10 lines 17–27; transl. R. Macrides, 118.

78 Medieval sources vary on the account of Michael Doukas and the foundation of the polity of Epiros, often referred to as a 'Despotate.' The most widely accepted story is that told by Geoffrey of Villehardouin, the chronicler of the Fourth Crusade, who states that

INTRODUCTION   19

Doukas had imperial ambitions that seriously threatened the claims of Theodore Laskaris and his successors in Nicaea.[79]

Although he had already proclaimed himself as emperor, Theodore Laskaris could not be crowned without the participation of a patriarch. The patriarch of Constantinople during the Fourth Crusade was John X Kamateros, who escaped the sacking of the city and fled to Thrace.[80] The

---

Michael Doukas attached himself to the crusader leader Boniface of Montferrat before striking out on his own: Geoffrey of Villehardouin, *Histoire de la conquête*, ed. N. de Wailly, ch. 301.113. See also Akropolites, *History*, 13 line 13 – 14 line 7; transl. R. Macrides, 124; *Vita* of St Theodora, Migne *PG* 127, col. 904 C; transl. A. M. Talbot, *Holy women of Byzantium: ten saints' lives in English translation* (Washington, D.C.: Dumbarton Oaks, 1996), 328. For secondary sources on the subject, see L. Stiernon, 'Les origines du Despotat d'Épire: A propos d'un livre recent,' *Revue des études byzantines* 17 (1959), 114–26; D. Nicol, *The Despotate of Epiros* (Oxford: Basil Blackwell, 1957), 14–15; A. Karpozilos, *The ecclesiastical controversy between the Kingdom of Nicaea and the Principality of Epiros (1217–1233)* (Thessalonike: Kentron Vyzantinōn Ereunōn, 1973), 33–34; G. Prinzing, 'Epiros, 1204–1261: historical outline – sources – prosopography,' in *Identities and allegiances in the Eastern Mediterranean after 1204*, ed. J. Herrin and G. Saint-Guillain (Aldershot: Ashgate, 2011), 81–82; R. Macrides, *George Akropolites, The History. Introduction, translation and commentary* (Oxford: Oxford University Press, 2007), 127 note 12. On the rise of his brother, Theodore Doukas, see Akropolites, *History*, 24 line 12 – 25 line 2; transl. R. Macrides, 145; R. Macrides, *George Akropolites, The History*, 146 note 6; D. Nicol, 'The fate of Peter of Courtenay, Latin Emperor of Constantinople, and a treaty that never was,' in *Καθηγήτρια: essays presented to Joan Hussey* (Camberley: Porphyrogenitus, 1988), 377–83. On the conquest of Thessalonike by Theodore Doukas, see Richard of San Germano, 119–20; Akropolites, *History*, 33 lines 14–19; transl. R. Macrides, 162; D. Nicol, *The Despotate of Epiros*, 63–64.

79 The imperial claims from Epiros created two Greek rivals for the exiled Byzantine throne: M. Angold, 'After the Fourth Crusade: the Greek rump states and the recovery of Byzantium,' 738; A. Karpozilos, *The ecclesiastical controversy*, 72–73.

80 Niketas Choniates comments on the flight of Kamateros from Constantinople after the Latin takeover, describing the patriarch as 'a perfect evangelical apostle, or rather, a true imitator of Christ': Choniates, *Historia*, 593 lines 8–9; transl. H. Magoulias, 326. Kamateros apparently refused to relocate to Nicaea. George Akropolites even reports that the patriarch offered his resignation rather than answer the summons of Theodore Laskaris: Akropolites, *History*, 11 lines 5–15; transl. R. Macrides, 119. Apostolos Karpozilos argued that the idea of Kamateros sending a written resignation of his office was based on a misunderstanding of the text, and that what the patriarch sent was only a refusal to Theodore's invitation to join him in Nicaea: A. Karpozilos, *The ecclesiastical controversy*, 19 note 18. For more, see Nikephoros Xanthopoulos, Migne *PG* 147, col. 464 D; Grumel, *Reg.*, no. 1202, 611–12; Dölger, *Reg.*, no. 1671, 2; M. Angold, 'Byzantium in exile,' in *The new Cambridge medieval history* V, ed. D. Abulafia (Cambridge: Cambridge University Press, 1999), 544; A. Gardner, *The Lascarids of Nicaea* (London: Messrs, Methuen and Co., 1912), 67.

20   THE DISPUTATIO

death of Kamateros in 1206 presented Laskaris with an opportunity.[81] George Akropolites explains that the notables of Nicaea assembled and appointed Michael IV Autoreianos the new patriarch of Constantinople on 20 March 1208. One of the first tasks for the new patriarch was the coronation of Theodore Laskaris as emperor on Easter Sunday, 6 April 1208.[82]

It is difficult to overemphasize the importance of the coronation of Theodore Laskaris as Byzantine emperor. The events of 1208 effectively restored the twin pillars of Byzantium – the patriarch and the emperor – in exile.[83] Of course, their claims ran counter to those of a Latin emperor and a Latin patriarch in Constantinople. The crusader conquest of the city in 1204 was followed quickly by the coronation of the first Latin emperor, the count of Flanders and Hainaut, as Baldwin I.[84] He was crowned by the new Latin

81 Choniates, *Historia*, 633 lines 57–59; transl. H. Magoulias, 347; Gill, *Byzantium and the papacy*, 34.

82 George Akropolites gives the impression that these events – the death of John X Kamateros, the proclamation of Theodore Laskaris as emperor, the appointment of Michael IV Autoreianos, and the coronation of Theodore as emperor – all happened in quick succession: Akropolites, *History*, 11 lines 15–18; transl. R. Macrides, 119. Theodore Laskaris was probably proclaimed emperor in 1205: B. Sinogowitz, 'Über das Byzantinische Kaisertum nach dem vierten Kreuzzuge (1204–1205),' *Byzantinische Zeitschrift* 45 (1952), 348–51. Other events almost certainly moved more slowly than Akropolites indicates. For more on the date of patriarchal appointment and coronation see A. Karpozilos, *The ecclesiastical controversy*, 22–23; M. Angold, 'After the Fourth Crusade,' 735; P. Guran, 'From empire to church, and back: in the aftermath of 1204,' *Revue des Études Sud-Est Européennes* 44 (2006), 62–63.

83 M. Angold, 'After the Fourth Crusade,' 734–35; M. Angold, 'Byzantine "nationalism" and the Nicaean Empire,' *Byzantine and Modern Greek Studies* 1 (1975), 50; S. Reinert, 'Fragmentation (1204–1453),' 309; R. Macrides, 'From the Komnenoi to Palaiologoi: imperial models in decline and exile,' in *New Constantines: the rhythm of imperial renewal in Byzantium, 4th–13th centuries*, ed. P. Magdalino (Aldershot: Ashgate, 1994), 280. For the opposing view, arguing that the coronation of Theodore I carried 'little constitutional significance,' as he had already possessed the symbols of power since his proclamation in 1205, see A. Karpozilos, *The ecclesiastical controversy*, 23.

84 The only contemporary description of the coronation of Baldwin I on 16 May 1204 is that of Robert of Clari. His account shows that the ceremony was at least partially modelled on the Byzantine example: Robert of Clari, *La conquête de Constantinople*, ed. and transl. P. Noble (Edinburgh: British Rencesvals Publications, 2005), XCVI.114–XCVII.17. See also F. Van Tricht, *The Latin* Renovatio *of Byzantium: the Empire of Constantinople (1204–1228)*, English translation by P. Longbottom (Leiden: Brill, 2011), 82–84; D. Jacoby, 'The Latin Empire of Constantinople and the Frankish states in Greece,' in *The new Cambridge medieval history* V, ed. D. Abulafia (Cambridge: Cambridge University Press, 1999), 530–31; K. Ciggaar, 'Flemish

INTRODUCTION

patriarch, the Venetian Thomas Morosini.[85] It seems that Pope Innocent III was initially unaware of the election of the Venetian to the patriarchate. He made no reference to the new patriarch in his first correspondence to the crusader army following their capture of Constantinople.[86] When he did learn about the appointment of Morosini Innocent III expressed displeasure at the manner of his election to the patriarchate.[87] Despite his concerns, however, the pope had little choice but to endorse the claims to ecclesiastical authority of Morosini.[88] Nicholas Mesarites records multiple attempts by the Latin patriarch and other representatives of the Roman Church to gain the submission of the Greek clergy who remained in Constantinople.[89] In each of these meetings, Mesarites describes the Latin position regarding the Greek Church as an ultimatum. The Greek clergy were told to accept

counts and emperors: friends and foreigners in Byzantium,' in *The Latin Empire: some contributions*, ed. V. van Aalst and K. N. Ciggaar (Hernen: A. A. Bredius Foundation, 1990), 43; J. Longnon, *L'Empire latin de Constantinople et la principauté de Morée* (Paris: Payot, 1949), 58–59; D. Queller and T. Madden, *The Fourth Crusade: the conquest of Constantinople*, 2nd edn (Philadelphia: University of Pennsylvania Press, 1997), 202.

85 Andrea Dandolo reports that the election of Morosini was unanimous: Andrea Dandolo, *Chronica per extensum descripta*, ed. E. Pastorello, *Rerum Italicarum Scriptores*, vol. 12, part 1 (Bologna, 1938), 280 lines 2–6.

86 Hageneder, *Die Register Innocenz' III*, vol. 7, no. 164, 290–91.

87 See the letter dated to 21 January 1205: Hageneder, *Die Register Innocenz' III*, vol. 7, no. 203, 354–59. See also *Gesta Innocentii III*, Migne *PL* 214, no. XCVI, cxlii D, no. C, cxliv C; transl. J. Powell, *The Deeds of Pope Innocent III by an anonymous author* (Washington D.C.: Catholic University of America Press, 2004), no. XCVI, 175, no. C, 184. For more on the election of Morosini as the first Latin patriarch of Constantinople see J. Gill, *Byzantium and the papacy*, 25, 27; A. Andrea, 'Innocent III and the Byzantine Rite,' in *Urbs Capta: the Fourth Crusade and its consequences*, ed. A. Laiou (Paris: Lethielleux, 2005), 118; J. Richard, 'The establishment of the Latin church in the empire of Constantinople (1204–1227),' in *Latins and Greeks in the Eastern Mediterranean after 1204*, ed. B. Arbel, B. Hamilton and D. Jacoby (London: Frank Cass, 1989), 50; G. Fedalto, 'Venice's responsibility in the break down of ecclesiastical unity between Rome and Constantinople,' in *The Fourth Crusade revisited. Atti della Conferenza Internazionale nell'ottavo centenario della IV Crociata 1204–2004. Andros (Grecia) 27–30 maggio 2004* (Vatican: Libreria Editrice Vaticana, 2008), 194–95; L. Santifaller, *Beiträge zur Geschichte des lateinischen Patriarchats von Konstantinopel (1204–1261)* (Weimar, 1938), 25–28.

88 A. Siecienski, *The papacy and the Orthodox*, 285–86.

89 The first of these encounters took place from November to December 1204: Mesarites I, 48–51; transl. M. Angold, 172–75. The second meeting took place on 30 August 1206: Mesarites II, 15–25; transl. M. Angold, 197–207. Another gathering was called by Cardinal Benedict of St Susanna, the papal legate, on 29 September and 2 October 1206; Mesarites I, 52–63; transl. M. Angold, 175–84.

22 THE DISPUTATIO

the authority of the pope and the Latin patriarch or face the consequences.[90] Rarely does Mesarites, or any other source, suggest that these meetings included an honest exploration of doctrinal issues dividing the Greek and Roman Churches, to say nothing of a possible compromise.

While the two parties fell short of a solution to the schism in the years immediately following the Fourth Crusade, attempts aimed at some form of ecclesiastical accommodation continued. The periodic cessation of hostilities provided new opportunities to attempt a union of the churches, as political and ecclesiastical matters went hand in hand. When Henry I, who took over as Latin emperor following the death of his brother Baldwin I in 1205, defeated the armies of Nicaea in 1211/2, it appears that negotiations toward a peace treaty overlapped with discussions of ecclesiastical matters.[91] Once again, the Greek Church was represented by Nicholas Mesarites, now metropolitan of Ephesos, who describes the encounter of 1214/15.[92] The authenticity of this dialogue in the account of Mesarites has been called into question. Numerous scholars have noted the similarities between the arguments Mesarites describes and those found in the *Sacred Arsenal*, a text written about a half century earlier by Andronikos Kamateros.[93] Although the account of the meetings in 1214/15 by Mesarites

90 Regarding Benedict of St Susanna, for example, Nicholas Mesarites identifies three occasions when the papal legate threatened the Greeks with punishment if they did not obey papal directives: Mesarites I, 52 lines 14–18, 62 lines 6–8, and 63 lines 9–11.

91 Henry I describes his victory over Theodore I Laskaris in a letter to the pope: G. Prinzing, 'Der Brief Kaiser Heinrichs von Konstantinopel vom 13. Januar 1212,' *Byzantion* 43 (1973), 415–17. See also Akropolites, *History*, 27 line 4 – 28 line 11; transl. R. Macrides, 148. The date for the resulting treaty has caused some debate, and is usually put somewhere between 1211 and 1214: Dölger, *Reg.*, no. 1684, 4; R. Wolff, 'The Latin Empire of Constantinople and the Franciscans,' *Traditio* 2 (1944), 209; T. Venning, *A chronology of the Byzantine Empire* (New York: Palgrave, 2006), 559; C. Foss, *Nicaea: A Byzantine capital and its praises* (Brookline, MA: Hellenic College Press, 1996), 61; M. Angold, *A Byzantine government in exile*, 111; F. Van Tricht, *The Latin Renovatio of Byzantium*, 353; J. Longnon, *L'Empire latin de Constantinople*, 145–46. It seems likely that the treaty was negotiated during this time, but not formalized until the end of 1214 or the beginning of 1215: B. Hendrickx, *Regestes des empereurs latins de Constantinople (1204–1261/1272)* (Thessalonike: Aristoteleian University of Thessaloniki, 1988), no. 129, 90; D. Nicol, 'The Fourth Crusade and the Greek and Latin empires,' in *Cambridge medieval history* IV/1, ed. J. Hussey (Cambridge: Cambridge University Press, 1966), 300; R. Macrides, *George Akropolites, The History*, 152 note 12.

92 Mesarites III, 19–46; transl. M. Angold, 262–89.

93 A. Bucossi, 'Introduction,' *Sacrum armamentarium. Pars prima* (Turnhout: Brepols, 2014), lvi–lvii; G. Spiteris, 'I dialogi di Nicolas Mesarites coi Latini: opera storica o finzione

INTRODUCTION   23

indicates possible plagiarism, Averil Cameron and others have suggested that the author's use of an earlier work may instead be characterized as 'intertextuality,' emphasizing continuity in how Byzantine intellectuals approached the problem of schism and perceived Latin religious errors.[94] Whatever the case, the meetings described by Mesarites again attest to the shared desire by both Byzantines and Latins to heal the schism.

The negotiations of 1214/15 were the last time a possible union of the Greek and Roman Churches was discussed during the reign of Theodore I Laskaris.[95] He was succeeded by his son-in-law, John III Vatatzes, on 15 December 1221.[96] The first decade of the new emperor's reign is remarkable for its near total lack of interaction with his Latin neighbours or the papacy. There was no repeat of the negotiations toward church union that had been favoured by his father-in-law, and almost no evidence of diplomatic exchanges with the Latin Empire of Constantinople. The sole exception surrounded Vatatzes' victory over a Latin army at Poimanenon in 1224. The Latin defeat and subsequent treaty reversed the earlier gains in Anatolia made by Henry I, confirming the Empire of Nicaea as the dominant force in the region.[97] After this episode, however, Vatatzes again

---

letteraria,' *Orientala Christiana Analecta* 204 (1977), 181–86. C. Palau, 'Nicholas Mésaritès: deux lettres inédites (Milan, *Ambrosianus* F 96 Sup., ff. 15v–16v),' in *Manuscripta Graeca et Orientalia, Mélanges monastiques et patristiques en l'honneur de Paul Géhin*, ed. A. Binggeli, A. Boud'hors and M. Cassin (Leuven: Peeters, 2016), 192; C. Palau, 'L'*Arsenale Sacro* di Andronico Camatero. Il proemio ed il dialogo dell'imperatore con i cardinali latini: originale, imitazioni, arrangiamenti,' *Revue Revue des études byzantines* 51 (1993), 20–36.

94 A. Cameron, *Arguing it out*, 31; I. Nilsson, '"The same story, but another": a reappraisal of literary imitation in Byzantium,' in *Imitatio – Aemulatio – Variatio*, ed. E. Shiffer and A. Rhoby (Vienna: Österreichischen Akademie der Wissenschaften, 2010), 195–208.

95 Theodore I did propose renewing overtures toward the papacy in 1220, but the initiative was blocked by the Greek clergy of Epiros: Laurent, *Reg.*, nos 1222–24, 29–31; V. Vasiljevski, 'Epirotica saeculi XIII,' *Vizantiiskii Vremennik* 3 (1896), nos 14–15, 264–67.

96 Akropolites, *History*, 32 lines 12–14; transl. R. Macrides, 159. For the date of his accession, see R. Macrides, *George Akropolites, The History*, 160 note 1.

97 George Akropolites provides a detailed account of the battle and its results: Akropolites, *History*, 35 lines 10–12; transl. R. Macrides, 166. Other accounts of the battle include Theodore Skoutariotes, ed. K. N. Sathas, Μεσαιωνικὴ Βιβλιοθήκη, vol. 7 (Paris, 1894), 469–70; George of Pelagonia, *Life of Vatatzes*, ed. A. Heisenberg, 'Kaiser Johannes Batatzes der Barmherzige. Ein mittelgriechische Legened,' *Byzantinische Zeitschrift* 14 (1905), 164, 221–24; Ephraem, *Historia Chronica*, ed. O. Lampsidis (Athens: Academia Atheniensis, 1990), vv. 7933–7973; Philippe Mouskes, *Chronique rimée de Philippe Mouskes*, ed. Le Baron de Reiffenberg, vol. 2 (Brussels, 1838), 409 vv. 23195–23206. See also B. Hendrickx, *Regestes des empereurs latins de Constantinople*, no. 158, 107–08; M. Angold, *A Byzantine*

24 THE DISPUTATIO

withdrew from interaction with the Latins.[98] The absence of diplomatic communication between Nicaea and the Latin West in this period is

government in exile, 111–12; D. Jacoby, 'The Latin Empire of Constantinople,' 529; F. Van Tricht, *The Latin* Renovatio *of Byzantium*, 368–71.

98 The evidence for any contact between the Empire of Nicaea and any Latin power is scant at best. George Akropolites records that the Greek residents of Adrianople in Thrace invited Vatatzes to liberate their city from the Latins following his victory at Poimanenon. The troops he sent were the first Nicaean force to cross into Europe. Vatatzes' army was made to withdraw soon after, however, not by the Latins, but by the armies of Theodore Doukas, ruler of Epiros: Akropolites, *History*, 38 line 6 – 40 line 20; transl. R. Macrides, 172.

Michael Angold has argued that the marriage of Vatatzes' sister-in-law, Eudokia Laskarina, to a Latin baron, Anselm of Cahieu, took place in 1228/9. It is possible, however, that this marriage was a formality stemming from the treaty negotiated after the Nicaean victory at Poimanenon and does not represent any new negotiation: M. Angold, 'The Latin Empire of Constantinople, marriage strategies,' in *Identities and allegiances in the Eastern Mediterranean after 1204*, ed. J. Herrin and G. Saint-Guillain (Aldershot: Ashgate, 2011), 54; see also J. Longnon, *L'Empire latin de Constantinople*, 169.

Ekaterini Mitsiou held that the diplomatic overtures between Vatatzes and Frederick II Hohenstaufen began as early as 1229, but the evidence for this early contact is highly suspect. Mitsiou has pointed to a letter from Frederick II to Vatatzes that is usually dated to the late 1240s: E. Mitsiou, 'Ideology and economy in the politics of John III Vatatzes (1221–1254),' in *Change in the Byzantine world in the twelfth and thirteenth centuries*, ed. A. Ödekan (Istanbul: Koç Üniversitesi Anadolu Medeniyetleri Araştırma Merkezi, 2010), 196; for the letter from Frederick II, see Huillard-Bréholles, *Historia diplomatica Friderici secundi*, VI.2, 921–22. See also Dölger, *Reg.*, no. 1721. Other evidence for early overtures between Vatatzes and Frederick II are found in the account of Richard of San Germano, who states that Matthew Orsini, count of Kephalonia, arrived at the court of Frederick II in November 1229 as a *nuntius de Romania ex parte Commiano*: Richard of San Germano, 164 lines 13–14. We can safely conclude that the *Commiano* mentioned here refers to an embassy not from Vatatzes but from Theodore Doukas, the ruler of Epiros who had close ties to the Komnenos family and who was the brother-in-law of Matthew Orsini: Aubry of Three Fountains, *Alberici monachi Triumfontium Chronica*, ed. P. Scheffer-Boichorst, Monumenta Germaniae Historica, Scriptores 23 (Hanover, 1874), 938, line 44; M. Angold, 'The Latin Empire of Constantinople,' 58.

Michel Balard and Ekaterini Mitsiou have also argued for diplomatic overtures between Vatatzes and Genoa around 1231, but the information here is vague and is not corroborated: M. Balard, 'The Genoese in the Aegean (1204–1566),' in *Latins and Greeks in the Eastern Mediterranean after 1204*, ed. B. Arbel, B. Hamilton and D. Jacoby (London: Frank Cass, 1989), 158–59; E. Mitsiou, 'Ideology and economy in the politics of John III Vatatzes,' 200. Mitsiou points to the comment about an embassy to Vatatzes in *Annali Genovesi di Caffaro e de' suoi continuatori dal MXCIX al MCCXCIII*, ed. L. Belgrano and C. Imperiale di Sant'Angelo, vol. 3 (Rome: Tipografia del Senato, 1923), 57 lines 13–18. Michael Angold has argued that, before the generous commercial privileges granted to Genoa by Michael VIII Palaiologos in 1261, the Italian maritime city had almost no contact with the Empire of Nicaea. He adds that Genoa does not seem to have done much business with the Latin Empire either, save for a single transaction in 1251: M. Angold, *A Byzantine government in exile*, 115.

INTRODUCTION 25

surprising and difficult to explain. John Langdon has argued that from 1225 to 1231 Vatatzes was engrossed in a large-scale conflict against the Seljuk Turks spanning the entire length of the eastern frontier of the Empire of Nicaea.[99] It is possible that this conflict monopolized the attention of the Byzantine emperor, making diplomacy with the Latins a lower priority.

The outburst of diplomatic activity between Vatatzes and various Latin powers in the early 1230s was the result of shifting foreign policy goals as well as an ecclesiastical crisis concerning the Greek subjects of the Latin kingdom on Cyprus. First, the war with the Seljuk Turks came to an end in late 1231 or early 1232, and the attention of the Turks was soon fixed on the Mongols invading from the east.[100] This allowed Vatatzes to focus on new opportunities for expansion across the Bosporos into Europe. The armies of Epiros had recently been defeated by the Bulgarians at Klokotnitza in 1230, creating a power vacuum in the Balkans and an opportunity for Vatatzes.[101]

---

99 John Langdon has suggested that these campaigns are ignored in the history of George Akropolites because he wrote under Palaiologan patronage and did not want to anger his patron by extolling the success and virtue of his popular predecessor: J. Langdon, *Byzantium's last imperial offensive in Asia Minor* (New Rochelle, NY: Caratzas, 1992), 1–4; J. Langdon, 'John III Ducas Vatatzes and the Venetians: the episode of his anti-Venetian Cretan campaigns, 1230 and 1234,' in *Novum millennium: studies in Byzantine history and culture dedicated to Paul Speck*, ed. C. Sode and S. Takács (Aldershot: Ashgate, 2001), 231.

Recently, John Langdon's interpretation has been called into question. Filip Van Tricht explained that the Seljuk Turks invaded the Empire of Nicaea in 1225 at the request of the Latin Empire, but he argued that this particular conflict lasted only one year: F. Van Tricht, *The Latin* Renovatio *of Byzantium*, 370–71. Dimitri Korobeinikov maintained that the Byzantines and Seljuk Turks enjoyed a 'special relationship' that continued from the twelfth to the thirteenth centuries, but, given the remarkable absence of information about Nicaean-Seljuk relations in the sources of the period, he could not contradict Langdon's thesis of intense warfare between the two parties: D. Korobeinikov, *Byzantium and the Turks in the thirteenth century* (Oxford: Oxford University Press, 2014), 156–59.

100 George Akropolites, *Opera*, ed. A. Heisenberg and P. Wirth, vol. 2 (Stuttgart: Teubner, 1978), 18 lines 14–25; A. Tartaglia, *Theodorus II Ducas Lascaris opuscula rhetorica* (Munich: Saur, 2000), 28 lines 97–106; D. Korobeinikov, *Byzantium and the Turks in the thirteenth century*, 159.

101 George Akropolites reports that the would-be emperor's army was crushed and he himself captured, along with several of his officials: Akropolites, *History*, 41 line 11 – 42 line 15; transl. R. Macrides, 25.178. For other accounts of the battle, see Richard of San Germano, 166; Aubry of Three Fountains, *Chronica*, ed. P. Scheffer-Boichorst, 927 lines 5–7. See also D. Nicol, *The Despotate of Epiros*, 109–11; M. Angold, 'After the Fourth Crusade,' 738; D. Angelov, 'Prosopography of the Byzantine world (1204–1261) in the light of Bulgarian sources,' in *Identities and allegiances in the Eastern Mediterranean after 1204*, ed. J. Herrin

26　THE DISPUTATIO

Second, the Greek subjects of the Latin regime on Cyprus began to appeal to Nicaea for protection from persecution. The island of Cyprus had been conquered by crusader armies in the late twelfth century, and by 1223 letters began to arrive in Nicaea from the island's Greek residents, complaining about the harsh treatment they had endured from their Latin rulers.[102] In 1231, 13 Greek monks of the Kantara monastery in Nicosia were executed by the Latin authorities on Cyprus after they refused to cease their condemnation of the practices of the Roman Church.[103] It appears that these monks had purposely sought conflict with the Latins, provoking the crisis in the hopes of martyrdom.[104] Archbishop Neophytos, in a letter to the emperor in Nicaea, suggested that the monks themselves were to blame for their fate.[105]

---

and G. Saint-Guillain (Aldershot: Ashgate, 2011), 104; F. Van Tricht, *The Latin Renovatio of Byzantium*, 386–87.

102 A. Beihammer, *Griechische Briefe und Urkunden aus dem Zypern der Kreuzfahrzeit. Die Formularsammlung eines königlichen Sekretars im Vaticanus Palatinus Graecus 367* (Nicosia: Zyprisches Forschungszentrum, 2007), no. 10, 158–59.

103 K. Sathas, *Μεσαιωνικὴ Βιβλιοθήκη*, vol. 2 (Paris, 1873), 20–39. Only 12 of the monks were executed. The 13th died in prison: C. Schabel, 'The quarrel over unleavened bread in western theology,' 85. An anonymous Greek chronicle describes various forms of torture inflicted on the monks during their three-year incarceration: L. Allatius, *De Ecclesiae Occidentalis atque Orientalis perpetua consensione libri tres* (Coloniae Agrippinae, 1648), 693–96. See also C. Schabel, 'Martyrs and heretics, intolerance of intolerance: the Greek–Latin azymo dispute and the execution of thirteen monks in Cyprus in 1231,' in *Greeks, Latins, and the Church in Early Frankish Cyprus*, ed. C. Schabel (Aldershot: Ashgate, 2010), 1–33; A. Beihammer and C. Schabel, 'Two small texts on the wider context of the martyrdom of the thirteen monks of Kantara in Cyprus, 1231,' in ΠΟΛΥΠΤΥΧΟΝ: *Αφιέρωμα στον Ιωάννη Χασιώτη*, ed. E. Motos Guirao and M. Morfakidis (Granada: Centro de Estudios Bizantinos, 2008), 69–81.

104 Gregory IX, responding to news about the monks in a letter to the Latin archbishop of Nicosia, dated 5 March 1231, ordered that the monks be regarded as heretics: N. Coureas and C. Schabel, eds, *The Cartulary of the Cathedral of Holy Wisdom of Nicosia* (Nicosia: Cyprus Research Centre, 1997), no. 69, 175–76. The letter is translated in C. Schabel, *The Synodicum Nicosiense and other documents of the Latin Church of Cyprus, 1196–1373* (Nicosia: Cyprus Research Centre, 2001), 296–97. Both Martin Hinterberger and Chris Schabel emphasized that the monks were martyred not because of their belief in the Greek rite but because of their continued condemnation of the Latin rite: M. Hinterberger, 'A neglected tool of Orthodox propaganda? The image of the Latins in Byzantine hagiography,' in *Greeks, Latins, and intellectual history, 1204–1500*, ed. M. Hinterberger and C. Schabel (Leuven: Peeters, 2011), 141; C. Schabel, 'The quarrel over unleavened bread in western theology,' 92.

105 A. Beihammer, *Griechische Briefe*, no. 26, 181 lines 37–45.

INTRODUCTION   27

The incident on Cyprus held dangerous implications for the relationship between Latin rulers and their Greek subjects throughout the eastern Mediterranean, threatening new waves of religious violence. It is interesting that in 1232, almost immediately following this crisis, five Franciscan friars appeared in Nicaea, impressing upon the Greek patriarch the need for reconciliation and union.[106] How these friars came to be in Nicaea is something of a mystery. They may have been in the East on a mission to preach and convert, but most historians have concluded that they were returning from a pilgrimage to the Holy Land. The disagreement arises from a lack of clarity in the sources.[107] Two documents attest to the arrival of the Franciscan friars in Nicaea in 1232. The first is a letter to the pope from Germanos II (Source I). The patriarch was clearly impressed by the friars' piety, remarking on their 'good companionship and unbreakable harmony ... as they proclaimed peace and good tidings between Greeks and Latins.'[108] Unfortunately, Germanos II gives little indication of the friars' business in the East, saying only that they had run into 'a particularly precarious situation' and that the emperor John III Vatatzes had intervened to help them.[109] Based on this evidence, it has been argued that the friars were harassed or even imprisoned by the Seljuk Turks while travelling through Anatolia, and were freed through the efforts of Vatatzes.[110]

---

106 Chris Schabel argued that the mission of the friars in Nicaea was a direct result of the execution of the Greek monks in Cyprus in 1231: C. Schabel, 'The quarrel over unleavened bread in western theology,' 86 note 3. See also A. Beihammer and C. Schabel, 'Two small texts,' 70.

107 Although none of the sources identify the five friars by name, some have speculated that among their number were Jacob of Russano or Adam of Oxford, who were known for their missionary activity in the East: S. Lagopates, *Γερμανὸς ὁ β΄, πατριαρχὴς Κωνσταντινουπόλεως-Νικαίας, 1222–1240: βίος, συγγράμματα καὶ διδασκαλία αὐτοῦ, ἀνέκδοτοι, ὁμιλίαι καὶ ἐπιστολαί* (Athens: Μορέας, 1913), 109; M. Roncaglia, *Les frères mineurs et l'église grecque orthodoxe au XIIIe siècle (1231–1274)* (Cairo: Le Caire Centre d'études orientales de la Custodie franciscaine de Terre-Sainte, 1954), 29–31. For the conclusion that the friars were returning from a pilgrimage see Golubovich, 'Disputatio,' 419; G. Golubovich, *Biblioteca Bio-bibliografica della Terra Sancta e dell' Oriente Francescana*, vol. 1 (Florence: Collegio di s. Bonaventura, 1906), 161–62; J. Hussey, *The Orthodox Church in the Byzantine Empire* (Oxford: Clarendon Press, 1986), 214; R. Wolff, 'The Latin Empire of Constantinople and the Franciscans,' 225; J. Gill, *Byzantium and the papacy*, 64; J. Langdon, *Byzantium's last imperial offensive in Asia Minor*, 69 note 113b; J. Doran, 'Rites and wrongs in 1234,' 133.

108 Tautu, *Acta*, no. 179a, 242 lines 7–24.

109 Tautu, *Acta*, no. 179a, 241 line 46 – 242 line 1.

110 G. Golubovich, *Biblioteca*, vol. 1, 161–62; vol. 2, 510–12.

28 THE DISPUTATIO

The second source mentioning the arrival of friars in Nicaea is an anonymous Greek chronicle. Until recently, this work was thought to survive only in a seventeenth-century edition by Leo Allatius.[111] Alexander Beihammer and Chris Schabel, however, have concluded that the work copied by Allatius is found in a sixteenth-century manuscript, Parisinus Graecus 1286.[112] The chronicle describes the friars in Nicaea immediately following an account of the execution of the Greek monks on Cyprus, suggesting a close relationship between the two. In this text, the Franciscans are depicted as papal 'spies' sent to the Empire of Nicaea, making their way with a pretense of going on a pilgrimage to Jerusalem, but really there to speak with Germanos II.[113] After speaking with the friars about the schism of the churches, the patriarch, 'full of all love and humility,' and with the approval of Vatatzes, initiated a correspondence with Gregory IX.[114]

This story presents very different implications for the mission of the five Franciscan friars in Anatolia. Whereas the letter from Germanos II indicates that their arrival and the subsequent reopening of union negotiations was a happy accident, the anonymous chronicle found in Allatius suggests otherwise. This work alleges that the friars' appearance in Nicaea was very much the covert plan of Gregory IX. In this way, the pope could commence negotiations with the Empire of Nicaea, which posed an ever greater threat to the Latin Empire of Constantinople, without being seen to make direct overtures. The patriarch would make the first gesture to the pope, not the other way around.[115] The problem with this version of events is that it is too much predicated on the outcome of these negotiations. The anonymous chronicle speaks frequently of the tyranny and deception of the Latins, and the pope in particular, suggesting that the author of the work was aware of the negative outcome of church-union negotiations in the

---

111 L. Allatius, *De Ecclesiae Occidentalis*, 693–96. The Greek text of the chronicle is reproduced in K. Sathas, *Μεσαιωνικὴ Βιβλιοθήκη*, vol. 2, πδ–πε. For a new edition of the text, see A. Beihammer and C. Schabel, 'Two small texts,' 77–81. It has been suggested that Allatius, who served as the custodian of the Vatican Library, may have had access to sources and materials that are no longer available: J. Langdon, *Byzantium's last imperial offensive in Asia Minor*, 68 note 113a.

112 A. Beihammer and C. Schabel, 'Two small texts,' 69–70.

113 ἀπέστειλάν τινας ἐγκαθέτους τῶν λεγομένων φραμηνουρίων: L. Allatius, *De Ecclesiae Occidentalis*, 694; A. Beihammer and C. Schabel, 'Two small texts,' 78 line 78.

114 ὁ πατριάρχης πεπληρωμένας πάσης ἀγάπης καὶ ταπεινοφροσύνης: L. Allatius, *De Ecclesiae Occidentalis*, 695; A. Beihammer and C. Schabel, 'Two small texts,' 79 lines 94–95.

115 J. Langdon, 'Byzantino-Papal discussions in 1234,' 200–01; Laurent, *Reg.*, no. 1256, 65.

INTRODUCTION   29

1230s and projected that understanding onto his description of events.[116] Whether or not we regard Gregory IX as a master of underhand diplomacy, the visit of the Franciscan friars to Nicaea prompted Germanos II to begin a correspondence with the pope regarding the union of the churches.[117]

4. Pope and Patriarch

The letters exchanged between Germanos II and Gregory IX between 1232 and 1234 are crucial for understanding how the two sides conceived of the Great Schism in the years after the Fourth Crusade. This correspondence conveys their ideas about how the schism came about, who was to blame, and how to fix the problem. In this way, the letters between pope and patriarch reflect their respective careers and priorities. The pontificate of Gregory IX was a mature expression of centuries of reform, making the papacy a force in political as well as ecclesiastical matters.[118] Gregory IX had spent nearly three decades as a cardinal before becoming pope following the death of Honorius III in 1227.[119] As the nephew of Innocent III, Gregory IX was especially influenced by his uncle's concept of the *plenitudo potestatis* (plentitude of power), by which Christ had given both sacred and secular authority to Peter and his successors.[120] This frequently put Gregory IX

---

116 A. Beihammer and C. Schabel concluded that the anonymous Greek chronicle was probably written in Nicaea between 1254 and 1261: 'Two small texts,' 69–70. John Langdon has noted that contemporaries tend to refer to John III Vatatzes as Ἰωάννης ὁ Δούκας, whereas the author of the anonymous chronicle identifies him as Ἰωάννης ὁ Βατάτζης: J. Langdon, *Byzantium's last imperial offensive in Asia Minor*, 68–69 note 113a. See also M. Roncaglia, *Les frères mineurs et l'église grecque orthodoxe*, 31.

117 R. Wolff, 'The Latin Empire of Constantinople and the Franciscans,' 225. Both the anonymous chronicle recorded by L. Allatius and the *Vita* of Gregory IX indicate that a letter from Vatatzes was sent along with that of the patriarch, but only the patriarch's letter has survived: L. Allatius, *De Ecclesiae Occidentalis*, 695; A. Beihammer and C. Schabel, 'Two small texts,' 79 lines 94–96; 'Vita Gregorii Papae IX,' ed. L. Muratori, *Rerum Italicarum Scriptores*, vol. 3 (Milan, 1723), 580; *Le Liber Censuum de l'Eglise Romaine*, ed. P. Fabre, vol. 2, fascimile 5 (Paris, 1905), 26.

118 C. Morris, *The papal monarchy: the western Church from 1050 to 1250* (Oxford: Clarendon Press, 1989), 79–133.

119 J. Watt, 'The papacy,' in *The new Cambridge medieval history*, vol. 5, *c. 1198–c. 1300*, ed. D. Abulafia (Cambridge: Cambridge University Press, 1999), 110.

120 A. Siecienski, *The papacy and the Orthodox*, 278; H. Schmidt, 'The papal and imperial concept of *plenitudo potestatis*: the influence of Pope Innocent III on Emperor Frederick II,' in *Pope Innocent III and his world*, ed. J. Moore (Aldershot: Ashgate, 1999), 305–14.

30 THE DISPUTATIO

at odds with secular rulers in the West.[121] Modern historians have characterized Gregory IX as more provocative than his uncle when it came to his relationship with kings and princes. Thomas Van Cleve described him as 'knowing little of conciliation or of patience,' and thus looking for conflict as soon as he became pope.[122]

Gregory IX is best known for his frequent conflicts with the western emperor Frederick II Hohenstaufen.[123] On 29 September 1227 the pope excommunicated Frederick II for the emperor's continued failure to take up his promised crusade.[124] While the emperor was away, Gregory IX attacked his territories in Italy.[125] Although the two reconciled in 1230, pope and emperor continued to be at odds.[126] Gregory IX continued to emphasize to Frederick that clerical authority superseded that of lay rulers, arguing that this had been established since the days of Constantine the Great.[127] Gregory IX excommunicated the western emperor again in 1239, citing similar reasons.[128] Confirming the place of the spiritual power over that of lay rulers, therefore, was a defining characteristic of his papacy.

121 W. Ullmann, *The growth of papal government in the Middle Ages: a study in the ideological relation of clerical to lay power*, 2nd edn (London: Messrs, Methuen and Co., 1962), 283.

122 T. Van Cleve, *The Emperor Frederick II of Hohenstaufen, Immutator Mundi* (Oxford: Oxford University Press, 1972), 190. See also C. Schabel, 'The quarrel over unleavened bread in western theology,' 102.

123 T. Van Cleve, *The Emperor Frederick II*, 194–207; D. Abulafia, *Frederick II: a medieval emperor* (New York: Oxford University Press, 1988), 164–201; J. Watt, 'The Papacy,' 134–35.

124 For the announcement of the excommunication of Frederick II: C. Rodenburg, ed., *Epistolae Saeculi XIII e regestis pontificum Romanorum*, vol. 1 (Berlin, 1883), no. 368, 281–85; Huillard-Bréholles, *Historia diplomatica Friderici secundi*, III, 23–30. Frederick II frequently took the crusading vow, but had postponed the promised expedition for various reasons: G. Loud, 'The papal "crusade" against Frederick II in 1228–1230,' in *The papacy and the crusades: proceedings of the VIIth conference of the Society for the Study of Crusades and the Latin East*, ed. M. Balard (Aldershot: Ashgate, 2011), 93–94; T. Van Cleve, *The Emperor Frederick II*, 96–97; D. Abulafia, *Frederick II*, 120–22.

125 Richard of San Germano, 147 line 14 – 148 line 3. See also G. Loud, 'The papal "crusade",' 91; N. Chrissis, *Crusading in Frankish Greece: a study of Byzantine–Western relations and attitudes, 1204–1282* (Turnhout: Brepols, 2012), 87; J. Watt, 'The Papacy,' 134; T. Van Cleve, *The Emperor Frederick II*, 196.

126 Richard of San Germano, 167–69. See also G. Loud, 'The papal "crusade",' 92, 103; T. Van Cleve, *The Emperor Frederick II*, 231–32.

127 C. Rodenburg, *Epistolae Saeculi XIII Regestis Pontificum Romanorum*, no. 703, 599–605, especially 604 lines 17–43.

128 Huillard-Bréholles, *Historia diplomatica Friderici secundi*, V.1, 286–89; T. Van Cleve, *The Emperor Frederick II*, 428–29; J. Watt, 'The Papacy,' 134–36; B. Arnold, 'Emperor

INTRODUCTION   31

Explaining the pope's attitude toward the Greek Church is somewhat more difficult. There is no question that the pope supported the Latin Empire of Constantinople against its Byzantine neighbours. Like Innocent III, Gregory IX believed that the stability and preservation of the Latin regime was vital for the success of a crusade to the Holy Land.[129] He therefore directed new crusades to support the regime in Constantinople, and even permitted those who had already taken the cross to redeem their vows in Constantinople rather than Jerusalem.[130] Gregory IX was less consistent regarding the ecclesiastical situation in the East. During the incident that resulted in the martyrdom of the Cypriot monks, Gregory IX wrote to Eustorge, the Latin archbishop of Nicosia, taking a firm position against those Greeks who publicly denounced Latin practices. The pope instructed that such individuals be treated as heretics.[131] This was a break with Gregory IX's predecessors, who had been content to refer to these individuals as 'schismatics.' It is important to realize, however, that the pope did not adopt such a harsh policy with the whole of the Greek Church. Indeed, when considered in a wider context, his instruction regarding Cyprus in 1231 appears to be something of an anomaly. In southern Italy, for example, when the archbishop of Bari wanted to impose rebaptism in the Latin rite on the local Greek population, the pope sought out a dialogue on the issue. In a letter to the bishop in February 1232, Gregory IX recommended surveillance rather than outright violence to impose uniformity in the matter.[132] We must conclude, therefore, that before 1234 Gregory IX was capable of some degree of tolerance with the Greek community, especially when their actions were relatively benign and did not challenge the doctrines, practices, and authority of the Roman Church.

Frederick II (1194–1250) and the political particularism of the German princes,' *Journal of Medieval History* 26:3 (2012), 242.

129 R. Spence, 'Gregory IX's attempted expeditions to the Latin Empire of Constantinople: the crusade for the union of the Latin and Greek churches,' *Journal of Medieval History* 5 (1979), 166.

130 Auvray, *Reg.*, II, no. 3363, 497–98; no. 4219, 957; no. 4631, 1178–79; no. 4632, 1179; no. 4633, 1179; no. 4608, 1173.

131 Potthast, *Reg.*, no. 8673, 745; N. Coureas and C. Schabel, *The Cartulary of the Cathedral of Holy Wisdom of Nicosia*, no. 69, 175–76. The letter is translated in C. Schabel, *The Synodicum Nicosiense*, 296–97.

132 Tautu, *Acta*, no. 173, 229. For more on this see J. Gill, *Byzantium and the papacy*, 74–75.

32   THE DISPUTATIO

The career of Germanos II displays a sharp contrast with that of Gregory IX. The future patriarch was born in Anaplous, on the European side of the Bosporos, in the second half of the twelfth century. Later in life he would defend his provincial origins as better than that of most Constantinopolitans.[133] Before the Fourth Crusade he served as a deacon in Hagia Sophia in Constantinople, and he fled the city some time after 1204. On 4 January 1223 he was elevated to the patriarchate of Constantinople in exile in Nicaea by John III Vatatzes.[134] As patriarch, Germanos II was influential in both domestic and foreign affairs as a staunch supporter of the emperor. Michael Angold has demonstrated that Germanos II was key in helping Vatatzes thwart an attempted coup by the brothers of his predecessor, thus consolidating the emperor's power early in his reign.[135] When Theodore Doukas had himself crowned emperor in Thessalonike in 1224, the patriarch was quick to press the imperial rights of Vatatzes over any challengers.[136] Nikephoros Blemmydes adds that a synod of bishops in Nicaea sent a letter to Theodore Doukas, warning him to put aside his imperial claims.[137] Thus, we must understand the patriarch as an advocate for the domestic interests of the emperor and a champion of the foreign policy of the Empire of Nicaea.[138] As opposed to

133 S. Lagopates, Γερμανὸς ὁ β´, πατριάρχης Κωνσταντινουπόλεως-Νικαίας, 282–83; H. Beck, *Kirche und theologische Literatur im byzantinischen Reich* (Munich: Beck, 1959), 667; P. Magdalino, 'Hellenism and nationalism in Byzantium,' 10. For more on the conceit after 1204 of those born in Constantinople, see P. Magdalino, 'Byzantine snobbery,' in *The Byzantine aristocracy, IX to XIII centuries*, ed. M. Angold (Oxford: British Archaeological Reports, International Series 221, 1984), 65.

134 For the encyclical letter of Germanos II to the people of Constantinople, see S. Lagopates, Γερμανὸς ὁ β´, πατριάρχης Κωνσταντινουπόλεως-Νικαίας, 350–53; Laurent, *Reg.*, no. 1233, 42–43.

135 M. Angold, 'After the Fourth Crusade,' 741. See also A. Karpozilos, *The ecclesiastical controversy*, 71.

136 In a letter to the clergy of Epiros, Germanos II condemns the actions of Demetrios Chomatenos, Archbishop of Ochrid, who performed the coronation of Theodore Doukas: Laurent, *Reg.*, no. 1243, 50–51; no. 1248. On the coronation of Theodore Doukas, see Akropolites, *History*, 33 line 14 – 34 line 5, transl. R. Macrides, 21.162. For the subsequent split between Germanos II and the clergy of Epiros, see A. Karpozilos, *The ecclesiastical controversy*, 70–99; J. Gill, 'An unpublished letter of Germanus, patriarch of Constantinople (1222–1240),' *Byzantion* 44 (1974), 138; M. Angold, 'After the Fourth Crusade,' 742; G. Prinzing, 'Epiros, 1204–1261: historical outline,' 83.

137 Nikephoros Blemmydes, *Autobiographia*, ed. J. Munitiz, Book 1, ch. 23, 14 lines 1–10; transl. J. A. Munitiz, *A partial account*, 56–57; Laurent, *Reg.*, no. 1239, 47.

138 M. Angold, *A Byzantine government in exile*, 47; M. Stavrou, 'Rassembler et rénover

INTRODUCTION
33

the antagonistic relationship that existed in the West between pope and emperor, Germanos II developed a cooperative and symbiotic relationship with the emperor in Nicaea.[139]

Several writings by Germanos II indicate his anti-Latin sentiments, but not to an extreme degree. The patriarch's attitude against the Latins and their church seems to have intensified later in life, especially after the *disputatio* of 1234. In 1223 he encouraged the Greeks of Cyprus to continue resisting pressure to recognize papal authority, but he also advised caution.[140] Germanos II warned against measures intended to provoke the Latins.[141] Some years later, in 1229, his attitude towards the situation in Cyprus changed, probably as a result of complaints from other Greek communities living under Latin rule and facing similar pressure.[142] Germanos II expressed anger that some Greeks on the island, including Archbishop Neophytos, had acknowledged the primacy of the pope.[143] Apparently, Germanos II had come to consider that the archbishop and several of the Greek clergy on Cyprus had become too compliant with the Latins on the island.[144] In one letter, Germanos II calls on the Orthodox of Cyprus to hold to the faith of their fathers and resist the Latins until death.[145] His instructions were apparently heeded by the 13 monks who sought martyrdom in 1231.

The anti-Latin attitude of Germanos II becomes more apparent later in his patriarchate. He expressed a growing distaste for the Latins and their practices and commented frequently on the distress caused him by

---

une Église en crise: la politique ecclésiale du patriarche Germain II (1223–1240),' in *Le patriarcat oecuménique de Constantinople et Byzance hors frontières (1204–1586)*, ed. M. Blanchet, M. Congourdeau and D. Muresan (Paris: Centre d'études byzantines, 2014), 23–36.

139 Petre Guran described the patriarchate in Nicaea, and that of Germanos II specifically, as a transitional period during which ecclesiastical authority began to transcend that of the political: P. Guran, 'From empire to church, and back,' 63–65.

140 K. Sathas, Μεσαιωνικὴ Βιβλιοθήκη, vol. 2, 5–14; Laurent, *Reg.*, no. 1234, 43–45.

141 K. Sathas, Μεσαιωνικὴ Βιβλιοθήκη, vol. 2, 9–10, 13.

142 M. Angold, *Church and society in Byzantium*, 520–21.

143 K. Sathas, Μεσαιωνικὴ Βιβλιοθήκη, vol. 2, 16.

144 Michael Angold explained this change of heart as a result of inroads made by the Latins, especially the mendicant orders, who called on the Greeks to adopt the customs and doctrines of the Roman Church: M. Angold, *Church and society in Byzantium*, 522–29.

145 A. Dondaine, '"Contra Graecos." Premiers ecrits polemiques des dominicains d'Orient,' *Archivum Fratrum Praedicatorum* 21 (1951), 428–30, at 430 lines 29–34.

34 THE DISPUTATIO

the efforts of Latin missionaries.[146] In an undated letter to the monks of St John the Baptist at Petra, the patriarch referred to the Latins as 'godless' and 'miserable.'[147] He went on to explain to the monks that 'the heresy of the Latins is almost the recapitulation of all the heresies that after the incarnate life on earth of Our Lord Jesus Christ have in the course of time been injected by the prince of evil into the holy and apostolic Church of God.'[148] Based on such evidence, we can surmise that Germanos II was, to say the least, cautious in his dealings with the Roman Church and concerned about papal attempts to assert its authority. At most, the patriarch was 'anti-Latin' in his demeanour, but less so before the *disputatio* of 1234.[149]

Thus, the experiences and priorities of Gregory IX and Germanos II before 1234 appear remarkably opposed to one another. It is safe to say that the pope advocated for the rights of the Church over imperial authority, whereas the patriarch enjoyed more of a partnership with imperial authority. Clearly, the two men had very different reasons for engaging in the affairs of secular rulers. Gregory IX spent much of his papacy countering the moves of the greatest secular ruler in Western Europe, Frederick II, while Germanos II used the authority of his patriarchate to endorse and advocate the power of his emperor. In addition, the experiences of the two men indicate that it would be very difficult for them to reach a compromise on the issue of union, although not entirely impossible. Nothing suggests that they would absolutely refuse the opportunity to approach the topic with an open mind, especially if the opportunity featured the prospect of advancing their goals in other areas.

---

146 Laurent, *Reg.*, no. 1287, 94–95; no. 1291, 98–99; no. 1303, 106. Again, Michael Angold has suggested that these comments are a reaction to the arrival of Dominican and Franciscan friars in the East: M. Angold, 'Michael VIII Palaiologos and the Aegean,' in *Liquid and multiple: individuals and identities in the thirteenth-century Aegean*, ed. G. Saint-Guillain and D. Stathakopoulos (Paris: Association des Amis du Centre d'Histoire et Civilisation de Byzance, 2012), 28.

147 J. Gill, 'An unpublished letter of Germanus,' 142 line 11 and 144 line 35.

148 J. Gill, 'An unpublished letter of Germanus,' 142 lines 26–30; transl. 143.

149 This conclusion runs counter to speculation that the patriarch's anti-Latin attitude stemmed from his experience in 1204, when he had been a deacon in Hagia Sophia at the time of the sacking of Constantinople by the crusaders: M. Roncaglia, *Les frères mineurs et l'église grecque orthodoxe*, 31–32.

INTRODUCTION   35

5. Sources

Understanding what the pope and patriarch hoped to gain is best achieved through the correspondence between them before the *disputatio* of 1234 took place. The tone of these letters is notably optimistic, with a clear expectation that real gains could be made toward bringing unity to the Churches. Germanos II begins the exchange by sending not one, but two letters to the leaders of the Roman Church, apparently carried west by the five Franciscans who visited Nicaea in 1232. One of these letters is addressed to the pope, preserved in the papal registers in both Greek and in Latin translation (Source I). The conciliatory tone of this letter stands in sharp contrast to the harsh advice he had given only a few years before to the Greeks of Cyprus resisting the persecutions of the Latins and their church. Germanos II refers to the Great Schism as 'great and of long duration,' adding that 'there is no one who shows compassion for the bride of Christ wearing a torn garment.'[150] He compares the division between the Greek and Roman Churches to Old Testament examples of schism, namely Cain and Abel, Esau and Jacob, Judaea and Israel, Jerusalem and Samaria.[151] Regarding the origins of the schism, the patriarch explains that 'contentious hands, indeed not those of soldiers, but ecclesiastic hands' brought about the separation.[152] Germanos II understood the sacking of Constantinople in 1204, therefore, as a symptom of the schism; a result rather than a cause. The real beginning of the division of the churches was brought about by ecclesiasts on both sides, thus it was up to ecclesiasts to heal the breach. The patriarch argues that this was possible by holding up disagreements over practice and doctrine to the 'mirror' of Scripture and the patristic writings.[153]

Such comments must have caused some excitement in Rome. They show that Germanos II was indeed open to the prospect of union. The patriarch's positive outlook, however, did not prevent him from taking Gregory IX to

---

150 Tautu, *Acta*, no. 179a, 243 lines 7–11.

151 Tautu, *Acta*, no. 179a, 243–44.

152 Tautu, *Acta*, no. 179a, 243 lines 1–7.

153 The analogy of the mirror appears frequently in the context of the *disputatio* of 1234 and the correspondence leading up to that meeting. Germanos II mentions it first here in his letter to the pope. Gregory IX uses it again in his reply, and later the friars refer to their treatise on the procession of the Holy Spirit as a 'mirror of the creed of the Roman Church': Tautu, *Acta*, no. 179a, 247–48; no. 179, 238; Golubovich, 'Disputatio,' ch. 29, 464 lines 29–30.

36 THE DISPUTATIO

task for what he considered to be the recent abuses of the Roman Church. Germanos II emphasizes the Latin persecution in Cyprus, which had produced 'new martyrs.'[154] The patriarch explains that bishops should be good shepherds, leading their flocks by example.[155] The implication being, of course, that the pope and his Latin bishops in the East were failing to provide that good example.

The second letter sent by Germanos II in 1232 is addressed to the Cardinals of the Roman Church (Source II).[156] Again, the patriarch expresses his optimism that a gathering of learned churchmen could solve the problems presented by the schism:

> For often God concealed from one what he revealed to another, and thus through counsel he introduced what he has revealed to the public and gain is distributed to all the subject multitude. If there are many counsellors, and they are prudent and wise, how much profit, how much advantage to all governed [and] subject people![157]

Germanos II continues by calling on the cardinals to give good advice to the pope, encouraging Gregory IX to compromise. 'God alone is in want of nothing, nor needs help from anyone,' he says, adding that 'all men need the cooperation of one another even if they are exceedingly gifted with pride and wisdom.'[158] As in his letter to the pope, Germanos II expresses his displeasure at the current division of the churches. He notes that, in the past, when Rome had been threatened by barbarian peoples, it was 'liberated' by the Greeks.[159] In his own day, however, Byzantines and Latins are 'divided as enemies by bitter separation. We injure and are injured by one another and avoid communion with one another as if it were harmful to the soul.'[160]

---

154 Tautu, *Acta*, no. 179a, 246 lines 14–17.

155 Tautu, *Acta*, no. 179a, 246. For a bad example of a Latin bishop, see C. Schabel, 'Antelm the Nasty, first Latin archbishop of Patras (1205-ca. 1241),' in *Diplomatics in the eastern Mediterranean 1000–1500*, ed. M. Parani and C. Schabel (Leiden: Brill, 2008), 93–137.

156 Aloysius Tautu stated that the only version of this letter to survive was the Latin translation, probably produced within the Curia: Tautu, *Acta*, no. 179b, 252. Christos Armpatzis, however, has identified and published a Greek original: C. Armpatzis, 'Ανέκδοτη επιστολή του πατριάρχη Κωνσταντινουπόλεως Γερμανού Β΄ προς τους καρδιναλίους της Ρώμης (1232),' *Αθήνα: Εταιρία Βυζαντινών Σπουδών* (2006), 363–78.

157 Tautu, *Acta*, no. 179b, 250 lines 1–5.

158 Tautu, *Acta*, no. 179b, 251 lines 23–25.

159 Tautu, *Acta*, no. 179b, 251 line 8; R. Spence, 'Gregory IX's attempted expeditions,' 168.

160 Tautu, *Acta*, no. 179b, 251 lines 11–13.

INTRODUCTION   37

These comments indicate once more that Germanos II was sincere in his hopes for a successful negotiation that would bring about church union.

Although these letters convey a particularly optimistic hope for ending the schism, in neither does Germanos II come across as particularly naïve. He is fully aware of the challenge posed and the difficulty in reaching a compromise. In the first letter to Gregory IX the patriarch acknowledges that both sides believed in the validity of their position: 'We know that this is said by the church of the Greeks, and by that of the Latins; for no one is able to see genuine disgrace in his own face, if one does not look into a mirror.'[161] In the letter to the Cardinals Germanos II goes so far as to suggest that the schism of the churches, deplorable as it was, may have been God's will. He compares the division between the Greek and Roman Churches to the disagreements between the apostles Paul and Peter described in the New Testament.[162] The patriarch adds that their conflict was 'not some sort of fight or ill-timed rivalry,' but was intended to bring about a more profound accommodation appropriate to the time.[163] The argument, therefore, is that disagreement between Peter and Paul was ordained by God in order to clarify the positions of the church. As the conflict between Peter and Paul was the will of God, so was the schism between the Greek and Roman Churches. However, this was only a temporary situation. While God might ordain that there be a schism at one time, he would surely ordain that the schism be healed in another. Such a statement, it seems, is the patriarch's way of rationalizing the state of separation of the two churches. What had happened to divide them was 'supposed' to happen, and now the wise men from both sides were 'supposed' to come together to resolve the issue.

The letter to the cardinals is also significant for its insights into the patriarch's view of papal primacy. Germanos II refers to Peter as the 'leader of the group of disciples of Christ, the rock of the faith,' and asks that he be corrected if he did indeed fail to revere the pope's apostolic tradition.[164] However, the patriarch notes that even Peter was capable of error, referring to the gospel story of the rooster's crow shaking the foundation of Peter's faith.[165] The story served to show, according to the interpretation of Germanos II, that the pope was not infallible. Just as

---

161 Tautu, *Acta*, no. 179a, 248 lines 5–11.
162 Tautu, *Acta*, no. 179b, 251; Galatians 2:11.
163 Tautu, *Acta*, no. 179b, 251 lines 20–22.
164 Tautu, *Acta*, no. 179b, 251 lines 26–27.
165 Tautu, *Acta*, no. 179b, 251; Matthew 26:69–75.

38   THE DISPUTATIO

Peter needed the rooster's crow to rouse his tested faith, the pope required the advice of sound and educated men, such as the cardinals, to avoid the wrongs that had brought about schism. Furthermore, the patriarch refrains from addressing Rome as the 'mother church.' The analogy of the Roman Church as a 'mother' and the Greek Church as a 'daughter' appears frequently in the writings of western theologians. In a letter to Michael VII in 1073 Pope Gregory VII described the relationship between Rome and the *ecclesia Constantinopolitana* 'as daughter to mother.'[166] In 1199 Pope Innocent III called on the Greek 'daughter' church to return to her 'mother' in his letter to Patriarch John X Kamateros.[167] This interpretation implies the primacy of Rome over all other churches, and ran counter to the eastern understanding of the hierarchical rule of the five senior patriarchs, or Pentarchy.[168] Germanos II rejects this analogy and deference to the popes, instead referring to elder Rome as the 'elder sister' of the Greek Church.[169]

The patriarch ends his message with a reference to the vast number of Christians who look to him for guidance. He refers to the Ethiopians, Syrians, Georgians, Lazi, Alans, Goths, Khazars, the 'innumerable Russian peoples,' and the 'conquering kingdom of the Bulgarians.'[170] The comment is probably intended as a hint to the cardinals about what could be gained through an agreed union, but it may also be a veiled reference to political realities. After defeating Theodore Doukas and the armies of Epiros at Klokotnitza only two years before Germanos II wrote this letter, the Bulgarian regime had proved itself a particularly powerful force in the Balkans, one that could threaten the continued survival of Latin Constantinople.[171]

---

166 *Gregorii VII Registrum*, ed. E. Caspar, Monumenta Germaniae Historica, Epistolae selectae, vol. 1 (Berlin, 1920), 29 lines 30–33; transl. H. Cowdrey, *The register of Pope Gregory VII, 1073–1085* (Oxford: Oxford University Press, 2002), 20.

167 Hageneder, *Die Register Innocenz' III*, vol. 2, no. 200(209), 383–89, especially 387 line 27 – 388 line 21. For more on the papacy's concept of its relationship with the prelates of Constantinople, see W. Duba, 'The status of the patriarch of Constantinople after the Fourth Crusade,' in *Diplomatics in the eastern Mediterranean 1000–1500*, ed. M. Parani and C. Schabel (Leiden: Brill, 2008), 65–71.

168 H. Chadwick, *East and west*, 226: A. Siecienski, *The papacy and the Orthodox*, 186–88; J. Pelikan, *The Christian tradition*, vol. 2, 164; A. Andrea, 'Latin evidence for the accession date of John X Camateros, Patriarch of Constantinople,' *Byzantinische Zeitschrift* 66 (1973), 357; G. Fedalto, 'Venice's responsibility,' 185–201.

169 Tautu, *Acta*, no. 179b, 252.

170 Tautu, *Acta*, no. 179b, 251 lines 43–46.

171 As we will see, an alliance between Nicaea and Bulgaria, directed against Latin Constantinople, was one of the consequences of the failure of the negotiations of 1234:

INTRODUCTION   39

By referring to the Bulgarians and their victories, therefore, Germanos II may well be making an implied threat, warning the cardinals that the prospects for the Roman Church in the East were about to decline dramatically and that they had better make the best of the current opportunity.

An unusual problem when considering these letters from Germanos II is posed by the work of Matthew Paris, an English chronicler of the thirteenth century. In his *Chronica majora* Paris includes a Latin translation of the patriarch's letters to Gregory IX, but the text found in his work does not exactly match the text of the letters found in the papal register.[172] Aloysius Tautu offered some possible solutions to these anomalies, suggesting that Paris may have made his translation from a lost Greek original, or that the edition in the papal register omitted certain parts that Paris did not leave out when he made his Latin translation.[173]

This interpretation, that Matthew Paris had access to a now lost original version of the letters, is almost certainly incorrect. There is ample cause to doubt the authenticity of Paris's version of these letters. Multiple scholars have called into question the reliability of Matthew Paris as a source. Richard Vaughan's estimation of Paris was as a 'careless, inaccurate, and frequently unreliable writer.'[174] Björn Weiler has noted that Paris had a tendency to rewrite the letters that he copied into his chronicle, and Suzanne Lewis explained that Paris frequently altered texts to reflect his own opinions, feelings, and prejudices.[175] The discrepancies that appear in the correspondence between pope and patriarch as preserved by the papal

---

Akropolites, *History*, 48 line 22 – 49 line 5, transl. R. Macrides, 31.191; Nikephoros Gregoras, *Historia*, ed. L. Schopen, 29 lines 15–18; Andrea Dandolo, *Chronica*, ed. E. Pastorello, 295 lines 1–2.

172 For the version of the patriarch's letter to Gregory IX preserved by Matthew Paris, see Matthew Paris, 448–55; transl. J. Giles, 98–104. For Germanos II's letter to the cardinals, see Matthew Paris, 455–60; transl. J. Giles, 104–08. For Gregory IX's reply to Germanos II, dated 1232, see Matthew Paris, 460–66; transl. J. Giles 108–14. For the final letter of the correspondence, from the pope to the patriarch dated 1233, see Matthew Paris, 466–69; transl. J. Giles, 114–16.

173 Tautu, *Acta*, no. 179a, 249; no. 179b, 252. For an earlier debate over the discrepancies in the Latin edition of this letter, see M. Roncaglia, *Les frères mineurs et l'église grecque orthodoxe*, 35–36.

174 R. Vaughan, *Matthew Paris* (Cambridge: Cambridge University Press, 1958), 131.

175 B. Weiler, 'Matthew Paris on the writing of history,' *Journal of Medieval History* 35 (2009), 256; S. Lewis, *The art of Matthew Paris in the Chronica Majora* (Berkeley: University of California Press, 1987), 56.

40 THE DISPUTATIO

register versus those of Matthew Paris must be understood as interpolations by the English chronicler.[176]

Gregory IX's response to the overtures from Germanos II reveal him to be open to discussions about a possible union of the churches (Source III). The letter, dated to 26 July 1232, responds to both the patriarch's letter to the pope and to the cardinals.[177] There is no indication that the cardinals sent a reply of their own. The pope addresses the issues raised by the patriarch in a point for point approach. He discusses the 'mirror' analogy mentioned by Germanos II – namely the gospels and the patristic writings – and remarks that the Roman Church found nothing contrary in this mirror when properly interpreted.[178] The pope stoutly defends his interpretation of papal primacy, agreeing with Germanos II that Christ will always be the head of the church, but adding that 'the foundations of the church in the holy mountains and the citizens of heavenly Jerusalem are read to have been built upon the foundation of the apostles and prophets. Among these the first and principal is the most blessed Peter.'[179] The pope does not argue with Germanos II about the mother analogy of the Roman Church, but instead employs the analogy of the body to describe papal primacy. 'Just as the multitudes of senses remain in the head,' so the 'orders of the faithful' – priests, monks, and laity – rely on the papacy.[180] Gregory IX answers the patriarch's charge about the fallibility of Peter. 'In your letter, as if under a form of criticism, [was mentioned] that Peter was moved three times from the gates, being roused by the crowing of the rooster.'[181] The pope argues that the episode served to teach Peter to endure and to have pity, allowing him more easily to show the spirit of leniency to those returning to the unity of the church.[182] In the same way, he proposes to welcome the Greek Church back into his flock. 'If you, out of a sense of compassion, return to the primacy and judgment of the Apostolic See ... we will have compassion for your suffering and,

---

176 Suzanne Lewis referred to his additions to the letters of Germanos II as 'the most substantial interpolation Matthew Paris is known to have made in his documentary texts': S. Lewis, *The art of Matthew Paris*, 131.

177 M. Roncaglia, *Les frères mineurs et l'église grecque orthodoxe*, 42.

178 Tautu, *Acta*, no. 179, 238 lines 39–42.

179 Tautu, *Acta*, no. 179, 236 lines 5–8.

180 Tautu, *Acta*, no. 179, 236 line 10. Here, the pope personifies the 'orders of the faithful' with Noah, Daniel, and Job.

181 Tautu, *Acta*, no. 179, 238 lines 13–15.

182 Tautu, *Acta*, no. 179, 238.

INTRODUCTION

41

with the Apostle, will commiserate in your pain.'[183] Gregory IX, in effect, argues that the failings of Peter and the papacy are not failings, but the hallmarks of mercy and forgiveness that he will use in pursuing union with Germanos II.

The papal response addresses the comments made in Germanos II's letter about the conflict between Peter and Paul. Gregory IX indicates that what we perceive to be a conflict between the apostles has little in common with the current schism between the Greek and Roman Churches. Rather, theirs was a result of their differing missions. He points out that, while Peter preached to the Jews, Paul preached to the Gentiles, and thus was less bound by Judaic law.[184] Any conflict between the two, therefore, must be understood as a result of their evangelical missions. Even if they did preach to different peoples, the two preached one church, and Gregory IX is adamant that Peter was at the head of that church.[185] He argues that Peter's authority 'was clearly confirmed by the words of the Lord,' and that he alone received the keys to the kingdom of heaven.[186] Moreover, the pope comments that 'a body with more than one head is monstrous and the one without a head is without a leader.'[187] In other words, a union of the churches would be impossible without some acknowledgement of the primacy of Rome.

On this point, Gregory IX gives some indication of his view of the cause of the schism between the churches. He states that 'the Lord foresaw that the Church of God would be crushed by tyrants, mangled by heretics and divided by schismatics,' and thus gave authority to Peter.[188] The implication is that the Greek Church had been beset by troubles, largely of an internal nature. 'Heretics and schismatics' is almost certainly a reference to Byzantium's long history of struggles with divergent groups and ideologies, while being 'crushed by tyrants' is probably an allusion to the role of the emperor in the ecclesiastical affairs of the Greek Church.[189] The pope expands on this line of thought, discussing the comment by Germanos II about who was to blame for the schism:

---

183 Tautu, *Acta*, no. 179, 238 lines 23–26.
184 Tautu, *Acta*, no. 179, 236 line 38 – 237 line 1.
185 Tautu, *Acta*, no. 179, 237.
186 Tautu, *Acta*, no. 179, 237 lines 16–17.
187 Tautu, *Acta*, no. 179, 237 lines 22–23.
188 Tautu, *Acta*, no. 179, 237 lines 27–29.
189 According to Petre Guran, before 1208 the priorities of the emperor often overruled those of the ecclesiastical establishment: P. Guran, 'From empire to church, and back,' 63.

42 THE DISPUTATIO

When the Church of the Greeks withdrew from the unity of the Roman See, that which had been free at once lost the privilege of ecclesiastical liberty. It became the slave of secular power, so that, by the righteous judgment of God, she who refused to recognize the sacred primacy in Peter, reluctantly endured an earthly lord.[190]

Gregory IX is clearly under the impression that the patriarch, or his predecessors, would have happily acknowledged the primacy of Rome, thus ending the schism, had it not been for what he considered to be the 'caesaropapist' interference of the Byzantine emperor.[191] This idea appears to be contrary to historical precedent, as it was usually the emperor, not the patriarch, who sought ecclesiastical dialogue and improved relations with the Roman Church. Anthony Kaldellis has demonstrated that Patriarch Michael Kerularios was careful not to contradict the foreign policy goals of Constantine IX Monomachos in his conflict with Cardinal Humbert in 1054.[192] It was probably the emperor Alexios I Komnenos, rather than the

---

190 Tautu, *Acta*, no. 179, 237 lines 35–39.

191 The use of the term 'caesaropapism' is problematic in the church of Byzantium, where the principle was never formally accepted: J. Meyendorff, *Byzantine theology: historical trends and doctrinal themes* (New York: Fordham University Press, 1979), 5–6. Steven Runciman has explained that popes never fully understood the relationship of church and state in the East. They believed that Byzantine emperors exercised a complete form of caesaropapism over the church, when this was not the case: S. Runciman, *The Eastern schism*, 102. Aristeides Papadakis has shown that western misconceptions of the role of the emperor in the Greek Church continued well into the late Byzantine period: A. Papadakis, 'The Byzantines and the rise of the papacy,' 32. Gilbert Dagron has noted that charges of caesaropapism were frequently used to insult Byzantines: Dagron, G., *Emperor and priest: the imperial office in Byzantium*, transl. J. Birrell (Cambridge: Cambridge University Press, 2003), 283. For the competing view, that caesaropapism was indeed as one of the impediments to church union, see D. J. Geanakoplos, *Byzantine east and Latin west*, 86. The role of the Byzantine emperor in the schism of the churches continued to be a concern of western thinkers, even during the Council of Ferrara-Florence some 200 years after the *disputatio* of 1234: R. Price, 'Precedence and papal primacy,' in *Sylvester Syropoulos on politics and culture in the fifteenth-century Mediterranean: themes and problems in the memoirs*, ed. F. Kondyli et al. (Aldershot: Ashgate, 2014), 39. For more on the problem of caesaropapism in Byzantium, see D. J. Geanakoplos, 'Church and state in the Byzantine Empire: a reconsideration of the problem of caesaropapism,' *Church History* 34 (1965), 381–403; J. Skedros, '"You cannot have a church without an empire": political orthodoxy in Byzantium,' in *Christianity, democracy, and the shadow of Constantine*, ed. G. Demacopoulos and A. Papanikolaou (New York: Fordham University Press, 2016), 219–31.

192 A. Kaldellis, *Streams of gold, rivers of blood: the rise and fall of Byzantium 955 A.D. to the First Crusade* (Oxford: Oxford University Press, 2017), 204–05. For more on the role

INTRODUCTION   43

patriarch, who took the initiative to invite Peter Grossolano, archbishop of Milan, to discuss theological problems in Constantinople in 1112.[193] Even after the Fourth Crusade, Theodore I Laskaris was eager to meet with envoys sent by Cardinal Pelagius in Herakleia Pontike in 1214, despite the objections of Patriarch Theodore II Eirenikos.[194]

With so many examples of the Byzantine emperor supporting negotiations toward church union, how do we account for Gregory IX's harsh distrust of secular authority and concerns about caesaropapism in the East? The answer, almost certainly, can be derived from the pope's own policies, specifically with respect to the emperor in the west, Frederick II. Since coming to the papal throne, Gregory IX had been at odds with the western emperor, pressing him to fulfill his crusader vow. When he finally excommunicated Frederick II in 1227, the pope initiated a series of schemes to undermine the emperor's authority. He urged the clergy of the Kingdom of Sicily to stop paying taxes to the emperor, hired mercenaries and marshalled an army to attack his holdings in Italy, and attempted to threaten Frederick II's position in Germany with the election of a rival king.[195] The struggle confirmed Gregory IX in his determination that the power of kings and emperors was a threat to the church.[196] This undoubtedly skewed his view of the Byzantine emperor and his role in the Greek Church, as well as his approach to negotiating an end to the schism. The pope's letter to Germanos II in 1232 ends, as one might expect, with a

---

of Kerularios in 1054, see R. Mayne, 'East and west in 1054,' *The Cambridge Historical Journal* 11:2 (1954), 133–48; F. Dvornik, *Byzantium and the Roman Primacy*, 132–33; E. Chrysos, '1054: Schism?' *Cristianità d'Occidente e cristianità d'Oriente* 1 (Spoleto, 2004), 549; S. Runciman, *The Eastern schism*, 49.

193 Grossolano's speech on the procession of the Holy Spirit is addressed to Alexios I Komnenos, not to the patriarch: Migne *PG* 127, cols 911–20; S. Runciman, *The Eastern schism*, 108; T. Kolbaba, 'Byzantine perceptions of Latin errors,' 138.

194 Eirenikos did not attend the meetings in Herakleia Pontike, never met with the representatives of the Roman Church, and later chided Nicholas Mesarites for his conduct during his encounter with Cardinal Pelagius in Constantinople: Mesarites III, 34, 47.

195 T. Van Cleve, *The Emperor Frederick II*, 203–05. D. Abulafia, *Frederick II*, 194–201; G. Loud, 'The papal "crusade",' 91–103.

196 Paul Magdalino, pointing to twelfth-century examples, has argued that caesaropapism was becoming increasingly prevalent in the West, and was perhaps influenced by Byzantine precedents: P. Magdalino, 'The phenomenon of Manuel I Komnenos,' in *Byzantium and the west, c. 850–c. 1200: proceedings of the XVIII spring symposium of Byzantine Studies, Oxford 30th March–1st April 1984*, ed. J. Howard-Johnston (Amsterdam: Verlag Adolf M. Hakkert, 1988), 185.

44 THE DISPUTATIO

reference to the story of the prodigal son,[197] calling on the Greek Church to give up its errant ways and return to unity with Rome.[198]

The final correspondence between pope and patriarch, dated 18 May 1233, was delivered by the friars who arrived for the *disputatio* in Nicaea in January 1234 (Source IV). Gregory IX expounds on two important concepts in this letter to the patriarch. The first reaffirms his belief that secular interference perpetuated the schism, while the second puts particular emphasis on the problem of leavened or unleavened bread in the Eucharist. In regards to secular interference, the pope, as Germanos II had already done, refers to Old Testament examples to demonstrate his point. The pope states that the schism of the Greeks was anticipated by that brought about under Jerobo'am, who 'made Israel to sin' as a result of political circumstances.[199] From the New Testament, Gregory IX points to the story of the two swords, which he interprets to be the material and the spiritual sword.[200] 'When Jesus spoke to the disciples about the acquisition of the spiritual sword, they offered two in that place, which the Lord said are sufficient, clearly for the governance of the spiritual and the temporal crime.'[201] The pope argues that both swords were bequeathed to the church, but, while one was to be employed by the church, the other was to be used for the church – 'One [is to be wielded] by the priest, the other at the command of the priest by the soldier.'[202] This letter conveys to Germanos II the pope's view that the secular ruler acts for the benefit of the church, and under its direction, the implication being that such an arrangement had been violated by the Byzantine emperors, and their actions required correction in order for union to be achieved.[203]

The other issue addressed by Gregory IX in this letter is the use of leavened versus unleavened bread, or azymes, in the Eucharist. The pope gives a very generous interpretation of the divergent views, which seems

---

197 Luke 15:11–32.

198 Tautu, *Acta*, no. 179, 239.

199 Tautu, *Acta*, no. 193, 266; 1 Kings 12:25–33.

200 Luke 22:38.

201 Tautu, *Acta*, no. 193, 266 lines 17–20.

202 Tautu, *Acta*, no. 193, 266 lines 28–29.

203 Gilbert Dagron has argued that such a distinction between sacred and secular authority, although never denied by the Greek Church, was never officially adopted in Byzantium: G. Dagron, *Emperor and priest*, 293. For a more recent examination of the role of the Byzantine emperor in the Greek Church, see R. Macrides, 'Emperor and church in the last centuries of Byzantium,' *Studies in Church History* 54 (2018), 123–43.

INTRODUCTION

to offer an outline to a possible solution and indicates his willingness to compromise with Germanos II. He argues that differences in the Greek and Latin rite did not denote a different or alien sacrament, merely a different interpretation. Gregory IX employs as an analogy a story from the Gospel of John, in which the 'younger disciple,' presumably John, ran ahead of Peter to the tomb of Christ. Although he arrived first, John did not enter the tomb, whereas Peter entered and saw the funerary clothes set aside.[204] Gregory IX identifies John as the Greek Church, 'running ahead to the tomb' – in other words, running ahead to the faith.[205] The pope praises the Greeks, commenting that they rightly boasted a tradition of being among the first to adopt Christianity.[206] The Latins, however, Gregory IX associates with Peter, 'entering the tomb,' and thus gaining a greater understanding of the faith.

> But the Latin, following scripture, with the elder Peter, had earlier entered the tomb, from which proceeds spiritual meaning, and saw laying there the linens, which had covered the most holy Body, designating the Church, and he observed the separate napkin which had been over the head. Thus he chose to celebrate the more marvelous sacrament of the glorified body in the azymes of purity.[207]

Such an interpretation perpetuates the concept of the pope as the father figure, giving guidance to those under his authority. The Greeks in this comparison are not described strictly as being in error – both the Greeks and the Latins are associated with disciples, as shown in the gospels. Rather Gregory IX explains the divergence in practice as a problem of clarification. What the Greeks do is not wrong, but it can be more right.

Indeed, Gregory IX goes on to comment that it did not matter if the bread used for the Eucharist was leavened or unleavened. He explains to Germanos II that 'bread, simple before the sacrifice, is bread, but in truth when transubstantiation is brought about by the [pronouncement of] the words of the lord, it is not bread, and therefore it may be called neither leavened nor unleavened.'[208] This statement gives us a glimpse

---

204 John 20:1–10.
205 Innocent III had previously compared the Greek Church to John and the Roman Church with Peter: Hageneder, *Die Register Innocenz' III*, vol. 7, no. 154, 265; W. Duba, 'Status of the patriarch of Constantinople,' 74.
206 Tautu, *Acta*, no. 193, 267.
207 Tautu, *Acta*, no. 193, 267 lines 31–36.
208 Tautu, *Acta*, no. 193, 267 lines 36–38.

46   THE DISPUTATIO

of what Gregory IX may have considered as a possible compromise. He is essentially offering to recognize the Greek use of leavened bread as an orthodox practice. The pope may have expected a similar gesture in return – that Germanos II and the Greek Church would announce that the use of unleavened bread in the Eucharist was permissible. There is a clear connection between this offer and the circumstances surrounding the Cypriot monks who were executed in 1231. Latin authorities on Cyprus punished the monks not because of their own practice but because the monks themselves refused to cease their condemnation of the use of azymes in the Roman Church. Gregory IX could well have hoped that an agreement of mutual respect for the two different practices in the Eucharist would prevent similar incidents in the future, and allow for more positive relations between Greeks and Latins.

What conclusions can we draw from the correspondence between Gregory IX and Germanos II? Both emphasize the issue of papal primacy in their letters, and the patriarch had shown considerable generosity in his respect for the place of the papacy in church hierarchy. At the other church-union negotiations following the Fourth Crusade, the primacy of Rome had been a central topic. All indications suggest that the same would be true in the coming meeting in 1234. As we shall see, however, this was not to be the case. Another issue we might expect to be raised is that of secular authority over the Greek Church. The pope shows tremendous concern over the role of the emperor in church matters, thus we might expect the papal representatives to request that the ruler in Nicaea be excluded from the proceedings. Instead, John III Vatatzes plays an active role in the *disputatio* in Nicaea and Nymphaion, conversing often with Gregory IX's envoys. Both Gregory IX and Germanos II allude to the situation in Cyprus and the Greek monks who were executed there in 1231 in their letters, but no source indicates that Cyprus itself was ever discussed at the meeting in 1234.

In many ways, the *disputatio* of 1234 appears disconnected from the exchange between pope and patriarch. In one crucial aspect, however, the talks that emerge from the correspondence very accurately reflect the will and intention of the two ecclesiastical leaders. Both the pope and patriarch mention the 'mirror of scripture and patristic writings' as a basis for correcting errant doctrines and practices. Each believed that an honest and faithful reading of the gospels and other texts would correct theological error and prove their own position to be orthodox. In other words, theological matters would be paramount in the coming *disputatio*.

INTRODUCTION   47

The papacy had learned from the failure of the meetings in 1204 and 1206 that they could not force union upon the Greek Church. They were going to have to address the problem of the schism in theological terms. This is not to say that political matters do not appear in the talks at Nicaea and Nymphaion. In fact, political matters arise often in the report on the *disputatio*, but the discussions between the patriarch and the papal envoys concentrate on theological differences between the two churches, and in that way strive to bring union.

6. Who are the Friars?

Gregory IX's final letter to Germanos II introduces four friars as his representatives to the Greek Patriarch. They include two Dominicans, identified as Hugo and Peter, and two Franciscans, Haymo and Rodulphus. The pope describes them as 'men of virtue, famous for their devotion, renowned for their moral reputation and gifted with the knowledge of the Sacred Scriptures.'[209] Because much was at stake in these negotiations, we can conclude that the pope had a great deal of faith in these friars to execute his policies and represent the theological as well as political interests of the Roman Church. Unfortunately, our information about these men is incomplete. It is possible, however, to build profiles of these men, especially based on their status as friars. We know that the mendicant orders had been active in the East, making contacts and developing skills that would be of benefit in papal diplomatic dealings with Nicaea.[210] Gregory IX had sent friars as missionaries to numerous peoples in the East, including the Cumans,[211] Ruthenians,[212] Nestorians,[213] and Jacobites.[214] As we have already seen, the successful proselytizing

---

209 Tautu, *Acta*, no. 193, 267 lines 1–3.

210 R. Spence, 'Gregory IX's attempted expeditions,' 167, 173; J. Moorman, *A history of the Franciscan Order: from its origins to the year 1517* (Oxford: Clarendon Press, 1968), 298.

211 Auvray, *Reg.*, I, no. 139, 77; no. 187, 108; no. 556, 359.

212 Potthast, *Reg.*, no. 9458, 807.

213 Auvray, *Reg.*, II, no. 3791, 720.

214 Auvray, *Reg.*, II, no. 3789, 719. Gregory IX's predecessors, Innocent III and Honorius III, had also sent similar missions to the East, see, for example, the appointment of a papal legate to bring the Ruthenians into unity with the Roman Church, 7 October 1207: Hageneder, *Die Register Innocenz' III*, vol. 10, no. 138, 231–33.

48 THE DISPUTATIO

missions of the mendicant friars in the Byzantine East had caused Germanos II some concern.[215] Western monastic orders were present in the region almost immediately after 1204.[216] Franciscan friars were active in the Latin Empire almost as soon as their order was recognized as the Order of the Friars Minor by Pope Innocent III in 1210.[217] The images depicting St Francis of Assisi found in the Kalenderhane Camii in modern Istanbul represent the earliest known frescoes of the saint.[218] By 1220, the Franciscans had a house at Pera, and admiration for their ascetic way of life was spreading among the Greeks.[219] The Dominicans appeared in Latin Constantinople later.[220] Like the Franciscans, they were active

215 David Jacoby has argued that the aggressive propaganda of the Dominican and Franciscan friars in Latin territories greatly antagonized the Greeks: D. Jacoby, 'From Byzantium to Latin Romania: continuity and change,' in *Latins and Greeks in the Eastern Mediterranean after 1204*, ed. B. Arbel, B. Hamilton and D. Jacoby (London: Frank Cass, 1989), 24.

216 Malcolm Barber identified nearly a dozen Cistercian houses in the Latin territories of Greece in the years after 1204: M. Barber, 'Western attitudes to Frankish Greece in the thirteenth century,' *Mediterranean Historical Review* 4 (1989), 113, 118. Nickiphoros Tsougarakis counted over 100 Latin monastic houses in Greece founded between 1204 and 1500, including 40 such establishments founded by about the middle of the thirteenth century: N. Tsougarakis, *The Latin religious orders of medieval Greece, 1204–1500* (Turnhout: Brepols, 2012), xx. See also E. Fisher, 'Monks, monasteries and the Latin language in Constantinople,' in *Change in the Byzantine world in the twelfth and thirteenth centuries* (Istanbul: Koç Üniversitesi Anadolu Medeniyetleri Araştırma Merkezi, 2010), 391.

217 Elizabeth Fisher maintained that the Franciscans were active in proselytizing in Constantinople, as portions of the rule of their order have been found translated into Greek: E. Fisher, 'Monks, monasteries and the Latin language in Constantinople,' 391. See S. Salaville, 'Fragment inédit de traduction grecque de la Règle de saint François,' *Échos d'Orient* 28 (1929), 167–72.

218 The frescoes are now on display at the Istanbul Archeological Museum: C. Striker and D. Kuban, *Kalenderhane in Istanbul: the buildings, their history, architecture, and decoration* (Mainz: Zabern, 1997), 128–42, 155–70. Michael Angold argued that the Franciscans remained in the monastery after 1261: M. Angold, 'Michael VIII Palaiologos and the Aegean,' 28.

219 J. Hussey, *The Orthodox Church in the Byzantine Empire*, 214; R. Wolff, 'The Latin Empire of Constantinople and the Franciscans,' 214.

220 Although the Dominican province of Greece was established at the General Chapter of 1228, it is unclear when the first friars of that order arrived in the region. The first Dominican house in Constantinople appeared in 1233. By 1248, there were still only a handful of Dominican establishments in Greece. For more on this problem, see N. Tsougarakis, *The Latin religious orders of medieval Greece*, 169–74; M. Angold, 'After the Fourth Crusade,' 743; E. Fisher, 'Monks, monasteries and the Latin language in Constantinople,' 391; R. Loenertz, 'Les établissements dominicains de Péra-Constantinople,' *Échos d'Orient* 34

INTRODUCTION 49

in preaching to the Greek communities living under Latin rule. The anonymous *Contra graecos*, composed in 1252, is probably the work of a Dominican friar residing in the city for the purpose of encouraging the Greeks to accept the supremacy of the pope.[221]

Their commitment to scholarship meant that the mendicant orders were quite capable of debating doctrinal matters with the theologians of the Greek Church.[222] The thirteenth-century Franciscan chronicler Thomas of Eccleston states that it was only after succeeding in theological learning that members of his order went on to conduct the affairs of preaching.[223] As Michael Angold explained, the mendicant orders 'introduced a spirit of reasoned dialogue' that the Greeks could appreciate.[224] Several Dominican and Franciscan friars rose to prominent positions in the universities of Western Europe, especially at Oxford and Paris. Chris Schabel has conducted a thorough study of the internal debate around azymes and the Greek use of leavened bread in western universities.[225] A central academic focus of the orders was foreign languages.[226] The prominent English Franciscan Roger Bacon was a strong advocate for linguistic study. He rated the study of languages as one of the principal aspects of the curriculum at Oxford[227] and argued that learning the Greek language was necessary

---

(1935), 332–49; R. Wolff, 'The Latin Empire of Constantinople and the Franciscans,' 213 note 2.

221 A. Dondaine, 'Contra Graecos,' 320–30. This work became the basis for all future anti-Greek polemics produced by the Dominicans: A. Kaldellis, *Hellenism in Byzantium*, 359.

222 Due to their training in the schools and universities of the Latin West, Edward Siecienski refers to the *disputatio* of 1234 as the 'first encounter between the Greeks and Latin scholasticism': A. Siecienski, *The filioque*, 125–26.

223 Thomas of Eccleston, *Tractatus De Adventu Fratrum Minorum in Angliam*, ed. A. Little (Manchester: Manchester University Press, 1951), 27; transl. A. Little, *The coming of the Friars Minor to England and Germany* (London: J. M. Dent and Sons, 1926), 38.

224 M. Angold, 'After the Fourth Crusade,' 743.

225 Chris Schabel concluded that, while both groups tended to refrain from absolutely condemning the practice of the Greek Church, the comments of the Dominicans were more hostile than those of the Franciscans: C. Schabel, 'The quarrel over unleavened bread in western theology,' 85–127. See also A. Little, *Franciscan papers, lists, and documents* (Manchester: Manchester University Press, 1943), 56.

226 E. Fisher, 'Monks, monasteries and the Latin language in Constantinople,' 392; A. Little, *Studies in English Franciscan history, being the Ford Lectures, delivered in the University of Oxford in 1916* (Manchester: Manchester University Press, 1917), 195–208.

227 Roger Bacon, *Opera quaedam hactenus inedita*, ed. J. Brewer (London: Longman, 1859), 91.

50 THE DISPUTATIO

for correcting theological errors and preaching to the Greek people.[228] The bilingual ability of the friars – especially of the Franciscans – made them prime candidates for diplomatic service.[229]

The diplomatic resumé of the Franciscans is particularly impressive.[230] Gregory IX is known to have employed the friars in his dealings with the western emperor.[231] Matthew Paris writes that the friars of the Dominican and Franciscan orders had become the 'selected agents and messengers' of the pope, and that they were found in the service of kings.[232] Using the friars as representatives to the Byzantine emperor was thus a natural extension of diplomatic activities already undertaken in the West. Franciscans played a significant and continuous role in communications between Nicaea and Latin Constantinople, as well as with the West, serving as representatives for both Latins and Byzantines.[233] Salimbene de Adam tells us that he once encountered a Franciscan friar, also named Salimbene, who had been born in Constantinople and was half-Italian and half-Greek. The Salimbene in question was in the West serving as a 'messenger' from Vatatzes.[234] Franciscans and Dominicans served as envoys and advisors to the Latin emperors John of Brienne and Baldwin II.[235] John of Brienne is considered to have been particularly attached to the Franciscans, and possibly joined the order before he died.[236] Both orders would continue to exert influence

228 G. Golubovich, *Biblioteca*, vol. 2, 404–11.

229 J. Hussey, *The Orthodox Church in the Byzantine Empire*, 215.

230 John Moorman noted that Franciscans were employed frequently as emissaries of the pope throughout the thirteenth century – in 1234, 1248, and 1262: J. Moorman, *A history of the Franciscan Order*, 298–99. See also A. Little, *Franciscan papers, lists, and documents*, 55–57; A. Little, *Studies in English Franciscan history*, 195–213.

231 T. Van Cleve, *The Emperor Frederick II*, 192–93.

232 Matthew Paris, 627 lines 12–13; transl. J. Giles, 244. It was probably friars who served to carry to Germany the message of the second excommunication of Frederick II in 1239: Matthew Paris, 621; transl. J. Giles, 239–40.

233 M. Angold, 'Byzantium in exile,' 555.

234 Salimbene says of the messenger that he was 'not a learned man,' but did note that he spoke good Latin and Greek, as well as Italian: Salimbene de Adam, *Cronica*, ed. G. Scalia, vol. 1 (Turnhout: Brepols, 1998), 489 lines 18–24; transl. J. Baird, *The Chronicle of Salimbene de Adam* (Binghamton, NY: Center for Medieval and Early Renaissance Studies, 1986), 321.

235 M. Barber, 'Western attitudes to Frankish Greece in the thirteenth century,' 113.

236 Salimbene de Adam, *Cronica*, ed. G. Scalia, 63 lines 16–17; transl. J. Baird, *The Chronicle of Salimbene de Adam*, 18. Robert Wolff concluded that John of Brienne entered the Franciscan order shortly before his death. He even speculated that John of Brienne knew St Francis of Assisi personally, having met him in Damietta, during the crusade to

INTRODUCTION   51

and serve in a diplomatic capacity in the years following 1261.[237] John Parastron, a Franciscan, served as an envoy from Michael VIII Palaiologos to Louis IX of France in 1270 and was the interpreter on the Byzantine delegation to Lyons in 1274.[238] Another example of a bilingual friar is Simon of Constantinople, a Dominican who fled the city in 1261 for Negroponte and returned to the capital in 1299. He kept up a correspondence with numerous Byzantines, encouraging his Greek-speaking friends to learn Latin.[239]

All of this suggests that the friars who represented Gregory IX in 1234 had a great deal of training and were perhaps capable in the Greek language. Unfortunately, neither the letters of Gregory IX nor the report written by the friars themselves confirm such a background for any particular individual. We are forced, therefore, to deduce the identity and background of each individual friar. We know least about the two Dominicans, Hugo and Peter of Sézanne. Both appear to have been of French origin. Hugo is a true mystery. The friars' report gives no direct clues to his identity. However, a notable Dominican with the same name, Hugo of St Cher, is known to have been active in academic circles in the early thirteenth century. He was born in 1200 and studied at the university in Paris. After joining the Dominican order in 1225, he taught in Paris from 1230 to 1235.[240] Salimbene de Adam reports that 'venerable Hugo'

Egypt, in 1219/20: R. Wolff, 'The Latin Empire of Constantinople and the Franciscans,' 214–21, 231–34.

237 Michael Angold argued that Michael VIII Palaiologos made use of the Franciscans order to help advance his union policy, as well as reconcile the Latins of Constantinople to Byzantine rule after 1261: M. Angold, 'Michael VIII Palaiologos and the Aegean,' 28–29.

238 Elizabeth Fisher speculated that John Parastron was of Venetian origins: E. Fisher, 'Monks, monasteries and the Latin language in Constantinople,' 392–93. See also M. Angold, 'Michael VIII Palaiologos and the Aegean,' 28–29. According to George Pachymeres, John Parastron had such a devoted following in Constantinople that the people attempted to have him canonized: George Pachymeres, ed. Failler, vol. 2, 475–77.

239 E. Fisher, 'Monks, monasteries and the Latin language in Constantinople,' 393–94; M. Congourdeau, 'Note sur les Dominicains de Constantinople au debut du 14e siècle,' *Revue des études byzantines* 45 (1987), 175–81; M. Congourdeau, 'Frère Simon le Constantinopolitan, OP (1235?–1325?),' *Revue des études byzantines* 45 (1987), 165–74.

240 Hugo of St Cher set the precedent for the methodology of future scholars in the West, such as Thomas Aquinas: J. Fisher, 'Hugh of St. Cher and the development of mediaeval theology,' *Speculum* 31 (1956), 57–69. For more on his thought and career, see C. Jerman, 'Hugh of St. Cher,' *Dominicana* 44 (1959), 338–47; F. Gigot, 'Hugh of St-Cher,' *The Catholic encyclopaedia* (1910), 521; W. Principe, *The theology of the hypostatic union in the early*

THE DISPUTATIO

was elevated to the post of cardinal bishop of St Sabine by Pope Innocent IV in the 1240s, after he had gained a reputation for his commentary on the Bible.[241] While we cannot say with any certainty that this is the same Hugo who took part in the *disputatio* of 1234, he is just the sort of individual Gregory IX would have appointed to the embassy if his goal was to win over the Greeks, and the circumstantial evidence certainly fits.[242]

The other Dominican, Peter of Sézanne, was a prior and lector who is depicted as a notable missionary.[243] Gerard de Frachet preserves a description of Peter's activities while on this mission, given in the first person, and apparently set in Constantinople in 1233 before the friars had reached Nicaea.[244] Peter states that he had travelled east 'with other brothers from the lord pope, to settle, if possible, the controversy of the modern Greeks.'[245] In Constantinople, Peter encountered a Muslim man, described as 'a religious man with political powers who dressed modestly.'[246] After the man was imprisoned for blasphemy, Peter encouraged him to convert to the Christian faith. The individual in question was eventually baptized

---

thirteenth century, vol. 2, *Hugh of Saint-Cher's theology of the hypostatic union* (Toronto: Pontifical Institute of Medieval Studies, 1970).

241 Salimbene de Adam, *Cronica*, ed. G. Scalia, 266 lines 23–30; transl. J. Baird, *The Chronicle of Salimbene de Adam*, 166.

242 Francis Gigot, writing over a century ago, was the first scholar to assert that Hugo of St Cher acted as an envoy to Constantinople on behalf of Gregory IX in 1233, but he said nothing of his role in negotiations in Nicaea: F. Gigot, *Catholic encyclopaedia*, 521. An entry in the more recent *New Catholic encyclopedia* made no mention of a mission on behalf of the pope to the East: A. Smith, 'Hugh of Saint-Cher,' in *New Catholic encyclopedia*, 2nd edn, vol. 7 (Washington, D.C.: Catholic University of America Press, 2002), 193–94. Colman Jerman noted Hugo of St Cher's experience as a papal envoy to Germany, but did not indicate a diplomatic assignment to the East in the 1230s: C. Jerman, 'Hugh of St. Cher,' 342–43. For more on the likelihood that the Dominican friar mentioned representing the pope in 1234 can be identified as Hugh of St Cher, see J. Brubaker, '"You are the heretics!" Dialogue and disputation between the Greek East and the Latin West after 1204,' in *Interfaith dialogue and disputation in the medieval Mediterranean*, ed. B. Catlos and A. Novikoff, *Medieval encounters* 24, no. 5/6 (Leiden: Brill, 2018), 623–24.

243 Golubovich, 'Disputatio,' 419; R. Wolff, 'The Latin Empire of Constantinople and the Franciscans,' 225 note 48.

244 Gerard de Frachet, *Vitae Fratrum Ordinis Praedicatorum necnon Cronica Ordinis*, ed. B. Reichert (Leuven: Charpentier and Schoonjans, 1896), 218–20; transl. P. Conway, *Lives of the Brethren of the Order of Preachers* (London: Aquin Press, 1955), 198–201. The text of this story is also found in G. Golubovich, *Biblioteca*, vol. 2, 302–03.

245 G. Golubovich, *Biblioteca*, vol. 2, 302.

246 G. Golubovich, *Biblioteca*, vol. 2, 302.

INTRODUCTION   53

with the name Paul.[247] Even if we address this story of conversion with the appropriate caution, it still tells us much about the activities of the mendicant orders and about Peter of Sézanne himself. We can say with some assurance that he was an avid missionary.

Although we know more about the Franciscan friars who took part in the papal embassy to Nicaea in 1234, our knowledge is still quite limited. Rodulphus of Remis is thought to have been born in France, hence the name 'Remensis,' but he may have been raised in England.[248] Thomas of Eccleston identifies Rodulphus as an Englishman who 'came to England after many years of toil, and after giving himself to the contemplative life at Salisbury for a long space, made a happy end.'[249] No additional information is given.

The individual we know best of all the friars is Haymo of Faversham. Born in southern England, Haymo is the only one of the friars we know who did not have French origins.[250] Thomas of Eccleston regards Haymo as a man 'of authority and renown.'[251] He writes that Haymo practised such severe penitence that he was left feeble and weak.[252] In addition to his devotion and piety, Haymo was known for his skills as a preacher. Within the account of Thomas of Eccleston is a famous story in which Haymo, immediately after having entered the Franciscan Order, volunteered to preach to a large crowd that had gathered at St Denis on Easter Sunday, 14 April 1224.[253] His words were so moving, Thomas of Eccleston tells us, that Haymo spent the next three days hearing the confessions of the entire congregation.[254]

---

247 The story itself is very telling about the actions of the mendicant orders in Constantinople under the Latin regime. The man is said to have gone to the Franciscans upon his release, who then delivered him to Peter and the Dominicans, who instructed him in Christian doctrine: G. Golubovich, *Biblioteca*, vol. 2, 302–03.

248 Golubovich, 'Disputatio,' 419; M. Roncaglia, *Les frères mineurs et l'église grecque orthodoxe*, 45.

249 Thomas of Eccleston, *Tractatus*, ed. A. Little, 73 lines 6–8; transl. A. Little, *The coming of the Friars Minor*, 88.

250 Golubovich, 'Disputatio,' 419.

251 Thomas of Eccleston, *Tractatus*, ed. A. Little, 27 lines 12–13; transl. A. Little, *The coming of the Friars Minor*, 38.

252 Thomas of Eccleston, *Tractatus*, ed. A. Little, 27; transl. A. Little, *The coming of the Friars Minor*, 39.

253 Haymo entered the Franciscan Order at St Denis on Good Friday, 12 April 1224: Little, *Franciscan papers, lists, and documents*, 57.

254 Thomas of Eccleston, *Tractatus*, ed. A. Little, 28; transl. A. Little, *The coming of the Friars Minor*, 40.

54 THE DISPUTATIO

After returning to England as one of the first Franciscans in the country, possibly as early as September 1224,[255] Haymo spent some time teaching at Oxford before going on to similar positions at Paris, Tours, Bologna, and Padua.[256] Haymo was made the provincial minister to England in 1239,[257] and only about a year later was elevated to the post of minister general of the Franciscan order, following the death of Albert of Pisa.[258] After a tenure as minister general in which he is thought to have done much to promote the study of theology as well as preaching,[259] Haymo died in 1244.[260]

Even with the sparse evidence we have for the careers of these men, it is clear that the papal representatives who championed the position of the Roman Church in the *disputatio* of 1234 had strong ties to both the academic and missionary activities of the mendicant orders. Still, we are left with certain questions regarding the conduct of the friars during the *disputatio*. For example, which of them spoke Greek? Nowhere in their report of the proceedings do the friars indicate that an interpreter was provided for them. It is difficult to imagine that the Greeks at Nicaea

---

255 Little, *Franciscan papers, lists, and documents*, 56–57; Moorman, *A History of the Franciscan Order*, 100.

256 Thomas of Eccleston, *Tractatus*, ed. A. Little, 28; transl. A. Little, *The coming of the Friars Minor*, 40–41. As *magister theologiae* in Paris, Haymo was a colleague of Hugo of St Cher in educational circles in Paris: M. Roncaglia, *Les frères mineurs et l'église grecque orthodoxe*, 44.

257 Thomas of Eccleston, *Tractatus*, ed. A. Little, 69; transl. A. Little, *The coming of the Friars Minor*, 82–83.

258 Thomas of Eccleston, *Tractatus*, ed. A. Little, 85–86; transl. A. Little, *The coming of the Friars Minor*, 103–04; J. Doran, 'Rites and wrongs in 1234,' 131 note 2. Haymo of Faversham is the only Englishman to have occupied the post: A. Little, *Franciscan papers, lists, and documents*, 57. John Moorman remarked that Haymo was the first Minister General to be trained in the universities, and thus the first who could be referred to as an 'academic': J. Moorman, *A history of the Franciscan Order*, 107. A remark by Salimbene de Adam suggests that the choice of Haymo for the post was in some way related to the conflict between the papacy and the western emperor. 'In the year 1240, Albert of Pisa, Minister General of the Order of the Friars Minor, died, and Brother Haymo of England was appointed in his place, since Brother Elias had bolted the Order and joined the Emperor Frederick': Salimbene de Adam, *Cronica*, ed. G. Scalia, 254 lines 17–20; transl. J. Baird, *The Chronicle of Salimbene de Adam*, 157.

259 J. Moorman, *A history of the Franciscan Order*, 107–08.

260 Salimbene de Adam, *Cronica*, ed. G. Scalia, 267 lines 19–20; transl. J. Baird, *The Chronicle of Salimbene de Adam*, 166. A commentary on the works of Aristotle may well be a surviving work of Haymo, but it may also be ascribed to Simon of Faversham: A. Little, *Franciscan papers, lists, and documents*, 58 note 1.

INTRODUCTION 55

were unprepared for the Latin disputants, thus they almost certainly would have had capable interpreters on hand for the coming discussions. Such was the case for previous church-union negotiations. During the *disputatio* between Anselm of Havelberg and Niketas of Nicomedia in 1136, a Latin in the imperial service, Moses of Bergamo, was employed to translate for both sides.[261] The Latins provided their own interpreter in the person of Nicholas of Otranto on two occasions – the *disputatio* between Cardinal Benedict and the Greek clergy in Constantinople in 1206, and the proceedings in Constantinople and Herakleia Pontike in 1214–1215.[262] Yet the report of the friars does not indicate that they employed an interpreter, nor does it suggest that their hosts offered such a service, despite the fact that Latins were present and probably in the service of the Nicaean regime, and almost certainly bilingual. Thus, one or more of the friars must have had a strong knowledge of the Greek language, at least good enough to translate for the rest to understand.[263] Their report on the *disputatio* never records a complaint about a lack of understanding, nor does it state that the friars asked for an interpreter or for the discussions to be slowed down due to lack of comprehension. Instead, the friars' report describes the linguistic competence of one or more of their number, referring to 'one of our brothers, upon whom the Lord had bestowed favour in the literature of the Greeks.'[264] Not only does this suggest that the friars came to Nicaea with their own interpreter, but we must consider that the phrase 'one of our brothers' does not preclude the possibility that more than one of the friars had a working knowledge of the Greek language.[265]

One episode in the report of the friars indicates that their skill and experience in the study of Greek texts was put to use even before they had reached Nicaea. The friars record that the Greek disputants were most perturbed when their Latin adversaries employed Greek patristic sources

---

261 Anselm of Havelberg, *Antikeimenon*, Migne *PL* 188, col. 1163 B; transl. A. Criste and C. Neel, *Anticimenon*, 86.

262 J. Hoeck and R. Loenertz, *Nikolaos-Nektarios von Otranto, Abt von Casole: Beiträge zur Geschichte der ost-westlichen Beziehungen unter Innozenz III. und Friedrich II.* (Ettal: Buch-Kunstverlag, 1965), 41–44.

263 Golubovich, 'Disputatio,' 426.

264 Golubovich, 'Disputatio,' ch. 12, 443 lines 3–4.

265 Henry Chadwick was not as impressed with the bilingual ability of the friars. He maintained that, as soon as the language became the least technical, neither side at the *disputatio* could have comprehended the other: H. Chadwick, *East and west*, 243.

56 THE DISPUTATIO

to endorse the positions of the western church.[266] While many, if not all of these writings were almost certainly available in the West, the friars themselves state that they obtained these and other Greek works in the libraries of Constantinople before their arrival in Nicaea. Indeed, the friars refer to a 'plentiful multitude of Greek books' they found in Constantinople and brought with them for the *disputatio*.[267] The fact that Greek texts would have been available in Latin-occupied Constantinople should come as no surprise. It would have been a simple matter for the friars to have gained access to Greek patristic texts in the libraries of the churches and monasteries of Constantinople, preserved there long before 1204. The language of their report – stating that they found these works in Constantinople – would even suggest that the friars made a conscious choice to stop there before the *disputatio* began, identifying texts that would be useful and how they might be employed to refute the arguments of the Greeks.

The most profound example of the proficiency of the friars in the Greek language is their translation of documents composed during the talks in Nicaea and Nymphaion. The friars display an ability to translate texts both from Greek to Latin and from Latin to Greek. This is clearly visible in an early episode of the *disputatio* in Nicaea, after the friars have presented a set of reasons which support the Latin view on the procession of the Holy Spirit.[268] When the Greek disputants ask that a list of the reasons be put in writing, the friars obliged them. Their report specifically states that the writing was first presented in Latin, and that the Greeks requested that 'it be translated into Greek for them.'[269] Much is implied by this statement. Not only are the friars clearly capable of translating, but the fact that the Greeks ask them to provide a Greek translation suggests that they trust the

---

266 Golubovich, 'Disputatio,' ch. 7, 434–35. Tia Kolbaba has noted that the Byzantines, apparently unaware of the new logical and dialectical tools being used in the Latin West, had rejected the role of philosophy in theology, preferring instead to base their positions on the writings of the fathers. The fact that the friars appeared in Nicaea prepared to use both patristic and analytic resources, therefore, demonstrates their preparedness for the *disputatio* and willingness to debate the issues on the terms of the Greek Church: T. Kolbaba, 'Theological debates with the West,' 486. See also P. Magdalino, 'Enlightenment and repression in twelfth-century Byzantium: the evidence of the canonists,' in *Byzantium in the 12th century: canon law, state and society*, ed. N. Oikonomides (Athens: Etareia Byzantinon kai Metabyzantinon Meleton, 1991), 357–73.

267 Golubovich, 'Disputatio,' ch. 7, 434 lines 8–9.

268 Golubovich, 'Disputatio,' ch. 8, 435–36.

269 Golubovich, 'Disputatio,' ch. 8, 436 lines 26–27.

INTRODUCTION   57

linguistic ability of the friars.[270] When the Greeks respond to this document with a treatise of their own, the friars set about translating that work from Greek into Latin.[271]

While all of this testifies to the competence of one or more of the friars with the Greek language, the evidence available does not allow us to definitively identify which of the friars performed the translation. One individual we can safely rule out is Peter of Sézanne. In the story of his conversion of a Muslim in Constantinople, Peter himself remarks that he spoke to the man in question through 'a companion who knew Greek and Latin.'[272] The implication, therefore, is that Peter himself was not bilingual. As for the other three, any or all could have had some ability to interpret. No evidence exists to allow us to rule out Rodulphus of Remis. If the Hugo who served as the papal representative in 1234 is the same Dominican whom Salimbene de Adam praised for his commentary on the Bible and who was promoted by the pope to Cardinal of St Sabine, it stands to reason that he would have had some familiarity with the Greek language. The long career of Haymo of Faversham in the universities of Western Europe – especially at Oxford, where Roger Bacon rated linguistic studies so important – is a strong indication that he would have been well versed in the Greek language. Unfortunately, the sources we have show only that languages were a major part of the curriculum only after Haymo's tenure at Oxford. He may have been instrumental in bringing the study of languages to the English university. We simply cannot say with any certainty. Haymo's time at the universities of France and Italy is another hint at his bilingual ability, but again we cannot say this definitively. All we can say with any certainty is that someone in the papal delegation in 1234 had an impressive understanding of the Greek language.

Another question surrounding the friars and their actions as papal representatives in 1234 concerns who wrote their report on the proceedings. It is entirely possible that the document was written by committee, as the report seems to reflect the common efforts of each of the

---

270 As mentioned above, 63–64, it is unusual that the Greeks did not employ their own translators.

271 Golubovich, 'Disputatio,' ch. 10, 437. For the original Greek of this treatise, see M. Stavrou, *Œuvres théologiques*, vol. 1, 184–205; P. Canart, 'Nicéphore Blemmyde et le mémoire adressé aux envoyés de Grégoire IX (Nicée, 1234),' *Orientalia Christiana Periodica* 25 (1959), 319–25. For the Latin translation of the friars, see Golubovich, 'Disputatio,' ch. 11, 438–42.

272 G. Golubovich, *Biblioteca*, vol. 2, 302.

58   THE DISPUTATIO

four friars. Girolamo Golubovich, however, has insisted that it is necessary to identify a chief secretary or reporter among them.[273] While others have noted a strong possibility that one of the Franciscans was the definitive author,[274] Golubovich argued strongly that the report was composed by Rodulphus of Remis.[275] The most convincing evidence to suggest that Rodulphus performed this function is derived from a statement on the issue of the procession of the Holy Spirit put forward by the friars during the *disputatio*.[276] At the end of the statement, in order to show that all agreed with the content and the argument, each one of the friars signed their name. Each friar identified himself as an *apokrisiarios* of Gregory IX, and three of the friars added that they 'believed and felt' in agreement with the contents of the document.[277] The only friar to state otherwise was Rodulphus, who stated 'thus I write, and thus I believe.'[278] The word *subscribo* seems to demonstrate that it was Rodulphus who authored the statement of faith on the procession issue, and implies that it was he who was responsible for composing all other documents produced by the papal representatives, including the report given to Gregory IX describing the *disputatio*.[279]

7. Report of the Friars

The *disputatio* between the friars and Germanos II took place in two phases: first at Nicaea in January 1234, and then at Nymphaion from March to May 1234. The only other source for these meetings is found in the writings of Nikephoros Blemmydes, the famous monk, scholar, and teacher who, unfortunately, was present for only the first phase of the *disputatio* at Nicaea. Some have suggested that Blemmydes was harshly anti-Latin, and that he was restrained by those elements in Nicaea that wanted to

---

273   Golubovich, 'Disputatio,' 425.

274   M. Roncaglia, *Les frères mineurs et l'église grecque orthodoxe*, 47–48.

275   Girolamo Golubovich attempted to argue, on purely circumstantial evidence, that the individual revealed nationalist tendencies in the report: Golubovich, 'Disputatio,' 425–26.

276   Golubovich, 'Disputatio,' ch. 24, 455–58. A Greek and Latin edition of this document is preserved in J. Mansi, *Sacrorum conciliorum*, XXIII, cols 61–66.

277   J. Mansi, *Sacrorum conciliorum*, XXIII, col. 66.

278   J. Mansi, *Sacrorum conciliorum*, XXIII, col. 66.

279   R. Wolff, 'The Latin Empire of Constantinople and the Franciscans,' 226; Golubovich, 'Disputatio,' 425–26.

INTRODUCTION   59

explore the opportunity for compromise with the papal representatives.[280] In addition, his account of the meeting focuses primarily on his own role in the *disputatio*, and is not as detailed as that left by the friars.[281] The report of the friars gives day to day information about their activities and negotiations. It demonstrates that the negotiations were not solely of an ecclesiastical nature but also concerned a great deal of foreign policy between western powers and the Empire of Nicaea. The political nature of this meeting cannot be understood apart from the theological discussions. The course, tenor, and objectives of those discussions determined what progress might be made in the area of foreign policy, and thus cannot be ignored. This dual nature of the *disputatio* is apparent at the outset of the friars' report, when they relate that they were met upon their approach to Nicaea on 15 January 1234 by messengers from both the emperor and the patriarch.[282] This would not be the last time that Germanos II and Vatatzes communicated with the friars independently of one another during the *disputatio*. Through the whole of the report, the friars indicate that they received messengers or met privately with either the patriarch or emperor on several separate occasions. The frequency of this isolated communication forces us to consider whether Germanos II and Vatatzes were pursuing separate agendas toward the negotiations with Rome.

The friars do not describe meeting personally with Germanos II until the day after their arrival in Nicaea. After a cordial greeting and

---

280 John Langdon described Blemmydes as 'a Byzantine ecclesiastic extremist who had to be purged from the proceedings if any semblance of the dialogue was to be maintained': J. Langdon, 'Byzantino-Papal discussions in 1234,' 212 note 58. John Doran suggested that the anti-Latin position of Blemmydes caused Vatatzes to refuse his appointment to the patriarchate following the death of Germanos II: J. Doran, 'Rites and wrongs in 1234,' 143. For the opposite view, that Blemmydes was open to compromise, especially on the procession issue, see H. Chadwick, *East and west*, 240; A. Siecienski, *The filioque*, 125–26; A. Papadakis, 'The Byzantines and the rise of the papacy,' 36.

281 Nikephoros Blemmydes, *Autobiographia*, ed. J. Munitiz, Book 2, ch. 25, 57 – ch. 41, 64; transl. J. A. Munitiz, *A partial account*, 106–14. Joseph Munitiz noted that Blemmydes, writing his autobiography some years after the fact, presents the issues somewhat differently than he did in the treatise itself. However, Munitiz concluded that 'there is no explicit contradiction' between the treatise and the recollection of Blemmydes some years later: J. A. Munitiz, *A partial account*, 8–10. Munitiz suggested the possibility that Blemmydes had a copy of his treatise from 1234 on hand when he wrote the account of his life, and simply omitted and adapted certain passages: J. Munitiz, 'A reappraisal of Blemmydes' first discussion with the Latins,' *Byzantinoslavica* 51 (1990), 25.

282 Golubovich, 'Disputatio,' ch. 1, 428 lines 6–9.

60   THE DISPUTATIO

delivering the letter from Gregory IX (Source IV), the patriarch inquires of the friars' diplomatic status, to which they insist that they are mere *nuncios*.[283] There is a degree of unease discernible in the friars' response to this question, which they immediately interpret as an attempt by the Greeks to scheme and take advantage.[284] The emphasis the friars place on their status as *nuncios* is clearly meant to avoid any attempt by the Greek Church to regard the following meeting as a council. The friars apparently saw the gathering of Greek prelates and quickly determined that Germanos II would attempt to force their compliance to an agreement the Roman Church might later regret. Although the friars refer to this as a 'trick,' we might consider this as another indication of the patriarch's sincere expectation of ending the schism of the churches. What the papal representatives dismiss so quickly as a ploy may well have been the genuine hopes of the patriarch, which were probably quickly dispelled by the friars' negative response.

The friars describe a peculiar incident that took place during their time in Nicaea that reveals much about the degree to which Latins and Byzantines coexisted within the Empire of Nicaea, a phenomenon not often illuminated in the sources.[285] Shortly after arriving in Nicaea, the friars seek from the patriarch a church in which to hold mass and pray for guidance on the subject of azymes.[286] The mass, held on 18 January, was apparently a special occasion. The friars report that all the Latins in Nicaea were in attendance: 'The Latins, French, English and diverse nations assembled that they might hear the divine rites.'[287] Many of these westerners may have

---

283 Golubovich, 'Disputatio,' ch. 2, 428 line 27 – 429 line 1.

284 Golubovich, 'Disputatio,' ch. 2, 429 lines 1–4.

285 Several studies have focused on the fate of Greeks living under Latin regimes after 1204, but rarely do we gain a glimpse of the opposite phenomenon. See D. Jacoby, 'From Byzantium to Latin Romania: continuity and change,' 1–44; P. Lock, *The Franks in the Aegean 1204–1500* (London: Longman, 1995), 266–309; P. Lock, 'The Latin emperors as heirs to Byzantium,' in *New Constantines: the rhythm of imperial renewal in Byzantium, 4th–13th centuries*, ed. P. Magdalino (Aldershot: Ashgate, 1994), 295–304; A. Kaldellis, *Hellenism in Byzantium*, 338–52; F. Van Tricht, *The Latin* Renovatio *of Byzantium*, 24–39; M. Kordoses, *Southern Greece under the Franks (1204–1261): A study of the Greek population and the Orthodox Church under the Frankish dominion* (Ioannina: University of Ioannina Press, 1987); T. Shawcross, 'Lost generation,' 9–37.

286 Golubovich, 'Disputatio,' ch. 3, 430 lines 7–9.

287 The reading of this section, *convenerunt Latini, Francigene, Anglici et diverse nationes ut divina audirent misteria*, is open to interpretation: Golubovich, 'Disputatio,' ch. 4, 430 lines 11–12. Girolamo Golubovich suggested that the author of the report was

INTRODUCTION 61

been mercenaries in the service of Vatatzes.[288] The participation of Latins residing in Nicaea provoked a controversy. The friars explain that, after the services, 'a certain lamenting and weeping Latin came to us, saying that his own priest had condemned him, because he had attended our mass.'[289] It seems that the Latin in question had been attending services with a Greek priest who then punished him for attending the Latin service. The friars immediately bring the matter to the attention of Germanos II, whom they depict as attempting 'to conceal rather than correct this dreadful deed.'[290] When the patriarch realizes the extent of the transgression, he brings forth the offending priest, strips him of his robes and parades him through the streets. According to the friars, it was only after they intervened on behalf of the priest that the punishment was stopped.[291]

The depiction of this incident serves an interesting purpose for the friars and their report. First, it shows their reader a degree of anti-Latin feeling that was already prevalent in the Empire of Nicaea. If they could demonstrate that a general animosity towards the Latins, their practices, and their church was already present among the Byzantines of Nicaea the friars might elicit a greater sympathy from their audience and foreshadow a possible cause for the eventual failure of their negotiations. Certainly, the portrayal of the patriarch's hesitation at addressing the matter – and then his overreaction – serves to represent the friars in a more enlightened and merciful light. They might even appear more noble by daring to continue their efforts among a stubborn and indignant people.

This exchange also represents the first of many instances in which the friars accuse their Byzantine hosts of scheming or deception. Their report of meetings in Nicaea alleges some type of ploy, evasion, or fraud perpetrated by the patriarch or his spokesmen on a total of six separate occasions.[292] Some of the accusations are vague, but others indicate a

---

emphasizing the French in Nicaea. The crux of the matter is whether the friars are discerning 'French' and 'English' as distinct from the 'Latins,' thus identifying three groups, or if they are attempting to delineate the French and the English within the larger group of 'Latins.' It is the difference between saying the *Latins, French and English assembled,* and the *Latins – French and English – assembled*: Golubovich, 'Disputatio,' 425.

288 C. Foss, *Nicaea: A Byzantine capital and its praises,* 66; M. Angold, *A Byzantine government in exile,* 188–201.

289 Golubovich, 'Disputatio,' ch. 4, 430 lines 13–14.

290 Golubovich, 'Disputatio,' ch. 4, 430 lines 17–18.

291 Golubovich, 'Disputatio,' ch. 4, 430 lines 18–25.

292 Golubovich, 'Disputatio,' chs. 2, 4, 7, 8, 9, 13.

62   THE DISPUTATIO

growing concern among the friars over the honesty of their hosts.[293] Twice during the meetings in Nicaea Germanos II claimed that he was unwell, in circumstances that appear rather dubious.[294] It is possible that he feigned illness as a way to gain time for his side to prepare.[295] At one point, the emperor reprimands the friars for making syllogistic arguments in theology, and asks that they limit their evidence and refrain from the philosophical approach. 'Your task is to show simply, without philosophy, the truth of the question. Nor are you to proceed syllogistically, since from such debates arise controversies and quarrels. It is better that you proceed simply.'[296] The friars quickly call the emperor's motives into question, pointing out that the Greeks have employed 'complex and elaborate answers' against them, suggesting a dense, philosophical argument.[297] Later, the patriarch and his clergy do indeed put forward a syllogistic argument. The friars make a point of describing the argument as 'wicked,' noting their expectation that both sides would forego such methods.[298] On other occasions, the friars accuse the Greeks of delaying the proceedings in order to prepare their response or hide their confusion. According to the report of the friars, their opponents 'laboured to disguise their own confusion and contrived excuses for their sin.'[299] When they wanted to change the subject, the friars state that the Greeks delayed the talks with 'trifles and nonsense.'[300]

Accusing the Greek disputants of misconduct is an effective way for the friars to again elicit sympathy from their readers, but it is interesting that the friars too appear capable of dissembling, although they never describe

---

293 Henry Chadwick concluded that the accusations by the friars of 'disingenuous behaviour' on the part of the Greeks are not justified even by their own account of the events: H. Chadwick, *East and west*, 243.

294 Golubovich, 'Disputatio,' ch. 5, 431 lines 18–21; ch. 10, 437 lines 17–19.

295 This is supposition. The report of the friars makes no claim of their 'suspicions' about the patriarch's wellbeing. Henry Chadwick read a great deal into the statements of the friars about the patriarch's illness. He claimed that they believed it to be 'a diplomatic illness,' but no such suspicion is voiced by the friars themselves, or from any other source: H. Chadwick, *East and west*, 240.

296 Golubovich, 'Disputatio,' ch. 8, 436 lines 2–5; Once again, Henry Chadwick offered an interpretation that is plausible, but is not explicitly indicated by the text. He suspected, in this case, that syllogistic arguments to prove articles of faith made the emperor nervous: H. Chadwick, *East and west*, 239.

297 Golubovich, 'Disputatio,' ch. 8, 436 lines 9–10.

298 Golubovich, 'Disputatio,' ch. 9, 436 lines 35–36.

299 Golubovich, 'Disputatio,' ch. 13, 443 lines 38–39.

300 Golubovich, 'Disputatio,' ch. 13, 444 line 18.

INTRODUCTION   63

their own actions as such. During one session of the *disputatio* the friars clearly frustrated the Greek clergy by refusing to answer the question, 'who added to the creed?,' by which the patriarch and his companions sought to understand how the *filioque* came to be accepted by the Roman Church.[301] Rather than offer a direct response, the friars evade the question, and even answer with a question of their own. The friars go so far as to describe the exchange as a part of their opponent's overall scheming, as the Greeks 'devised how they might be able to confuse us with little questions or deceive us with words.'[302] The accusation is particularly ironic as the friars later use a series of complex questions to trick one Greek spokesman into professing a heretical position.[303]

Clearly, both sides were hoping to employ the complexity of the topics to confound their opponents and claim victory in the *disputatio*. Such accusations also suggest that the Greeks and Latins had different expectations of how the proceedings would take shape. The friars seem to have been looking forward to a relatively rapid series of sessions in which they would proceed quickly from one topic to the next, whereas the Greeks were happy to take their time and muse about the enormity of the theological issues being discussed.[304]

The friars' report indicates that, during their time in Nicaea, the two parties engaged in debate over theological issues for a period of eight days. Neither side was keen to commence the proceedings, preferring the other to present the first matter for debate.[305] Considering his correspondence with the pope, it would seem that Germanos II had expected the papal representatives to approach with an offer to begin negotiations toward union. The friars clarify that this was not their purpose:

> We have not been sent to debate with you about some article of faith about which we or the Roman Church are in doubt, but rather that with you we may have a friendly debate about your doubts. Therefore it will be yours to reveal [those doubts] and ours, by the grace of God, to enlighten.[306]

---

301 Golubovich, 'Disputatio,' ch. 7, 434–35.

302 Golubovich, 'Disputatio,' ch. 7, 434 lines 9–11.

303 Golubovich, 'Disputatio,' ch. 7, 435.

304 Nikephoros Blemmydes states that long speeches were made by both sides during the discussions, adding that such was to be expected: Nikephoros Blemmydes, *Autobiographia*, ed. J. Munitiz, Book 2, ch. 26, 57 lines 11–12; transl. J. A. Munitiz, *A partial account*, 107.

305 Golubovich, 'Disputatio,' ch. 3, 429 lines 19–21.

306 Golubovich, 'Disputatio,' ch. 3, 429 lines 21–25.

64 THE DISPUTATIO

The friars came to Nicaea prepared to listen to the Greeks' criticisms of Latin doctrine and practice, and to defend the positions of the Roman Church. They apparently expected the patriarch and his assembled clergy to initiate the discussions.

Analysis of the correspondence between Gregory IX and Germanos II shows that the pope was concerned with matters related to papal primacy and caesaropapism, suggesting that these matters would dominate discussion at the *disputatio*. The pope even considered whether it was secular interference in the Greek Church that had caused the schism.[307] Although this matter was of paramount importance in his letters, it was not mentioned by Gregory IX's representatives in Nicaea in 1234. The friars never protest over the presence or participation of the emperor during the *disputatio*, and even appeal to him when the proceedings become hostile. The other matter so often appearing in the correspondence between pope and patriarch, but which does not explicitly arise during the *disputatio*, is papal primacy. Indeed, the words 'papal primacy' are never actually recorded in the report of the friars. It is unusual that such a central topic in earlier church-union discussions is absent from the *disputatio* of 1234.[308] The closest the disputants come to addressing the topic is when the friars pose the following question: 'It is true and agreed by all that the Greek Church was subordinate, just like the other Christian nations that are spread far and wide throughout the whole world. What then was the reason or cause whereby she withdrew from obedience to the Church of Rome?'[309] Since the Greeks decline to answer this question, we must conclude that they steered the talks away from this particular topic.

---

307 Similar concerns were expressed at the Council of Ferrara-Florence some 200 years later: R. Price, 'Precedence and papal primacy,' 39.

308 The absence of the papal primacy issue from 1234 is often overlooked by historians. Tia Kolbaba has described the *disputatio* of 1234 as an anomaly in church-union negotiations, thus explaining the lack of discussion over papal primacy. She insisted that, even if it was not discussed directly, papal primacy was still the primary issue between the two churches: T. Kolbaba, 'Byzantine perceptions of Latin errors,' 128 note 49, 130. John Doran argued that papal primacy was always the underlying problem throughout the *disputatio* of 1234, even if the issue was never directly addressed: J. Doran, 'Rites and wrongs in 1234,' 136–38. Chris Schabel explained that the Greeks never viewed papal primacy as a theological issue; thus, they avoided the topic in 1234. Even he, however, argued that the *disputatio* of 1234 dealt indirectly with the primacy of the Roman See: C. Schabel, 'The quarrel over unleavened bread in western theology,' 86, 94.

309 Golubovich, 'Disputatio,' ch. 3, 429 lines 29–32.

INTRODUCTION   65

It was only after some prodding from the friars that the Greeks put forward the two theological matters that would occupy the discussions of 1234 – disagreement over the procession of the Holy Spirit, and the Sacrament of the Eucharist.[310] That the Greeks would consider the *filioque* a paramount issue causing division is no surprise. The *disputatio* was being conducted very near the site where that creed was first established, and the Greeks made a special point of showing that site to the friars upon their arrival.[311] Indeed, their hosts probably pointed out that monument with future discussions about the *filioque* in mind. The other matter – leavened versus unleavened bread in the Eucharist – cannot have surprised the friars.[312] Not only was this a central focus in such discussions since 1054, but Gregory IX had addressed the problem at great length in his most recent letter to Germanos II.[313] Thus, the friars were certainly prepared to debate both issues.

The friars, prepared to begin discussion about the azymes, express surprise when Germanos II suddenly changes the topic of debate to the *filioque*.[314] The discussion on this matter focused on 20 separate pieces of textual evidence, namely patristic writings, the canons of the ecumenical councils, and Scripture.[315] Analysis of these quotations shows that

---

310 Golubovich, 'Disputatio,' ch. 3, 429 lines 38–39. Nearly a century earlier, Odo of Deuil had pinpointed these two issues as the most alarming cause of division between Greeks and Latins: Odo of Deuil, *De profectione Ludovici VII in orientem*, ed. and transl. V. Berry, 56–57.

311 Golubovich, 'Disputatio,' ch. 1, 428.

312 Joseph Gill maintained that the azymes question was placed among the central issues of the *disputatio* because of the incident of the 'lamenting and weeping Latin' who had attended the services held by the friars: J. Gill, *Byzantium and the papacy*, 271 note 67. This is impossible since the parameters of the *disputatio* were established before that incident occurred.

313 Tautu, *Acta*, no. 193, 267. Henry Chadwick suspected that the Dominican friars were especially eager to discuss the Eucharist, as they had recently had some success debating the topic with the Greek abbot of St Mamas: H. Chadwick, *East and west*, 239; Laurent, *Reg.*, no. 1287, 94–95.

314 The friars give no explanation for the Greek demand that discussion of azymes be tabled, referring only to their hosts' 'stubborn insistence': Golubovich, 'Disputatio,' ch. 5, 430 line 29.

315 The breakdown of these references is as follows: 13 quotes from the church fathers – Cyril of Alexandria, Basil of Caesarea and Athanasios, one reading of the creed as proclaimed by the First Council, 325, one reading of the creed as proclaimed by the Second Council, 381, and five quotes from the New Testament, three of which appear in the treatise by Nikephoros Blemmydes: see Source V, ch. 11. The only biblical reference by the friars at

66 THE DISPUTATIO

both sides saw Cyril of Alexandria as speaking for their interpretation in regards to the procession problem. Only two other church fathers – Athanasios and Basil of Caesarea – are quoted during the *disputatio*, and then only sparingly.[316] The works of Cyril are put forward five times each by the Greeks and the friars, but a breakdown of those instances is even more revealing. During the dialogue itself, the spokesmen of the patriarch make independent references to only one work of Cyril, his letter to John, Patriarch of Antioch,[317] and then only at the outset of talks on Friday, 29 January.[318] The other quotes from Cyril put forward by the Greeks appear in the treatise by Nikephoros Blemmydes.[319] The friars, on the other hand, quote Cyril five times from four different works.[320] Moreover,

Nicaea is John 16:13, which they quote twice: Golubovich, 'Disputatio,' ch. 7, 435 lines 1–2 and lines 12–13.

316 The friars reference Athanasios's exposition on the faith in their efforts to prove the procession of the Holy Spirit from the Son: Athanasios, *Expositio Fidei*, Migne *PG* 25, col. 208 A; ed. P. Schaff and H. Wace, *Athanasius: select works and letters. Nicene and Post-Nicene Fathers*, vol. 4, Second Series (Peabody, MA: Hendrickson Publishers, 1995), 366; Golubovich, 'Disputatio,' ch. 6, 433 line 37 – 434 line 1. The works of Basil of Caesarea are referenced twice by the Greeks, but only in the treatise by Nikephoros Blemmydes. For the first reference: Basil of Caesarea, *Liber de Spiritu Sancto*, caput XVIII, Migne *PG* 32, col. 152 B; ed. P. Schaff, *Basil: letters and selected works. Nicene and Post-Nicene Fathers*, vol. 8, Second Series (Grand Rapids, MI: Christian Classics Ethereal Library), 201; Golubovich, 'Disputatio,' ch. 11, 439 lines 16–17. For the second: Basil of Caesarea, *Epistle* 38, Migne *PG* 32, col. 331 C; ed. P. Schaff, *Basil: letters and selected works*, 429; Golubovich, 'Disputatio,' ch. 11, 439 lines 27–29.

317 Cyril of Alexandria, *Epistle* 39, Migne *PG* 77, cols 173–82; transl. J. McGuckin, *St Cyril of Alexandria: the Christological controversy. Its history, theology and texts* (Leiden: Brill, 1994), 343–48.

318 The Greeks make two references to this letter: Golubovich, 'Disputatio,' ch. 6, 431 lines 28–34; ch. 6, 432 lines 4–12. A third reference to the work of Cyril is presented by the Greeks, but only as an extension of what the friars had already referenced: Golubovich, 'Disputatio,' ch. 12, 443 lines 22–30.

319 Once again, these reference only one work by Cyril, his exposition on the Gospel of John: Cyril of Alexandria, *In Ioannis Evangelium*, Book X, Migne *PG* 74, cols 283–446; transl. N. Russell, *Cyril of Alexandria* (London: Routledge, 2000), 96–129. For these references see Golubovich, 'Disputatio,' ch. 11, 439 lines 17–21, and lines 21–22.

320 The first is from Cyril of Alexandria, *De Adoratione et cultu in spiritu et veritate*, Liber I, Migne *PG* 68, col. 148 A; Golubovich, 'Disputatio,' ch. 6, 433 lines 23–25. The second is from Cyril's letter to Nestorius: Cyril of Alexandria, *Epistle* 17, Migne *PG* 77, col. 118 C; transl. L. Wickham, *Cyril of Alexandria: select letters* (Oxford: Clarendon Press, 1983), 26–27; Golubovich, 'Disputatio,' ch. 6, 433 lines 26–30. The third is derived from his exposition on the Nicaean Creed: Cyril of Alexandria, *Epistle* 55, Migne *PG* 77, col. 316 D; transl. J. McEnerney, *St. Cyril of Alexandria: letters 51–110* (Washington, D.C.: Catholic

INTRODUCTION   67

the friars' efforts to find Greek patristic works supporting the *filioque* become apparent during the discussions. When the Greeks ask that the friars prove the truth of procession from the Son, the friars respond 'let your saints prove it,' and begin immediately with quotations from Cyril.[321] The conclusion must be that they came to Nicaea well prepared to use the works of Greek patristic fathers to prove their interpretation of the procession question.[322]

For some time, the *disputatio* revolved around the question 'why is the Holy Spirit called the Spirit of Truth?'[323] The friars propose a three-part answer, the so-called 'trilemma,' which was intended to prove procession from the Son. It suggests three possibilities – the Holy Spirit is called the Spirit of Truth because the Son and Spirit are of the same substance, or because the Spirit goes out to creation through the Son, or because the Spirit proceeds from the Son. The friars explain that the first two options are impossible, leaving only procession from the Son.[324] It was in answer to this trilemma that Nikephoros Blemmydes wrote his extensive treatise on the procession of the Holy Spirit.[325] Blemmydes emphasizes the difficulty in producing the document. According to his account, he was given only short notice to compose the treatise, and he strained to present his argument in simple language so that it

University of America Press, 1987), 34; Golubovich, 'Disputatio,' ch. 6, 433 lines 33–36. The fourth and fifth references are both from Cyril's Ninth Anathema: Cyril of Alexandria, *Explicatio duodecimo capitum*, Anathema IX, Migne *PG* 76, col. 308 C–D; Golubovich, 'Disputatio,' ch. 12, 443 lines 6–10, and Migne *PG* 76, cols 308 D – 309 A: Golubovich, 'Disputatio,' ch. 12, 443 lines 11–14. For a translation of Cyril's Ninth Anathema, see N. Russell, *Cyril of Alexandria*, 186.

321 Golubovich, 'Disputatio,' ch. 6, 433 line 21.

322 The friars point out that several western church fathers do support the *filioque* and, while they give the names of these saints – Augustine, Gregory, Jerome, Ambrose, and Hilary – their works are never cited during the *disputatio*: Golubovich, 'Disputatio,' ch. 7, 435 lines 6–7.

323 Golubovich, 'Disputatio,' ch. 7, 435 line 12 – ch. 8, 436 line 28.

324 Golubovich, 'Disputatio,' ch. 8, 436 lines 13–28. The presentation of the trilemma is also conveyed in the account of Nikephoros Blemmydes. However, the order is altered: Nikephoros Blemmydes, *Autobiographia*, ed. J. Munitiz, Book 2, ch. 27, 57 line 1 – 58 line 11; transl. Munitiz, 107–08.

325 Source V, ch. 11. The nearly complete Greek edition of this translation can be found in M. Stavrou, *Œuvres théologiques*, vol. 1, 184–205. See also P. Canart, 'Nicéphore Blemmyde et le mémoire,' 319–25. Patriarch Philotheos Kokkinos, writing against Nikephoros Gregoras in the fourteenth century, incorrectly attributes this document to Germanos II: Philotheos Kokkinos, *Antirretike* VI, *PG* 151, cols 910–15.

68 THE DISPUTATIO

could be understood by all.[326] While 'simple' and 'difficult' are relative terms, the treatise compiled by Blemmydes presents some of the most complex language of the *disputatio*.[327] Still, the friars show great skill in translating the work, which they include in their report.[328] The treatise employs patristic evidence as well as rational argument to conclude that procession is a hypostatic property particular to the Spirit.[329] Thus, 'if procession belongs to one, it is clear that emission also will belong to one,' namely the Father.[330] If emission were a property belonging to both Father and Son, Blemmydes argues, then there would be two Spirits.[331]

Nikephoros Blemmydes could not help but indicate his pride in the argument of the treatise. His account of the *disputatio* relates that it was accepted by all his fellow Greeks, and adds that the papal representatives found it 'irrefutable.'[332] The friars' report does not suggest such a

---

326 Nikephoros Blemmydes, *Autobiographia*, ed. J. Munitiz, Book 2, ch. 29, 58 lines 3–5; transl. J. A. Munitiz, *A partial account*, 108–09. John Langdon viewed these comments as emblematic of the tendency of Blemmydes towards false modesty: J. Langdon, 'Byzantino-Papal discussions in 1234,' 211.

327 Clive Foss referred to the contribution of Blemmydes as the 'most dramatic act' of the *disputatio*: C. Foss, *Nicaea: A Byzantine capital and its praises*, 69.

328 Golubovich, 'Disputatio,' ch. 11, 438–42. The characterization of this episode offered by Henry Chadwick, while plausible, is once again given to exaggeration. He argued that the friars 'felt unsure of the correctness of their hasty translation.' No such uncertainty is apparent in the report of the friars: H. Chadwick, *East and west*, 240. Paul Canart noted that the Latin translation remains very close to the original Greek: P. Canart, 'Nicéphore Blemmyde et le mémoire,' 314–15. Too literal a translation may have been an impediment to the final product. Joseph Munitiz has commented that anyone having only the Latin translation of the treatise would be very confused: J. Munitiz, 'A reappraisal of Blemmydes' first discussion with the Latins,' 21.

329 Golubovich, 'Disputatio,' ch. 11, 441 line 30 – 442 line 36.

330 Golubovich, 'Disputatio,' ch. 11, 442 lines 7–8. Cf. M. Stavrou, *Œuvres théologiques*, vol. 1, 202 lines 21–23.

331 Golubovich, 'Disputatio,' ch. 11, 442 lines 11–16. The problem may also be in the Latin concept of shared origination of the procession of the Spirit. Such a concept violates the individuality of the hypostases of the Trinity. 'In the divine Triad, the Monad is not prior to the threeness: that is, not first Monad then a Dyad, and finally a Triad. The Latins make the first principle a Dyad': H. Chadwick, *East and west*, 240. For more on the response of Blemmydes to the trilemma of the friars, as well as changes in the recollection of his argument some years later in his autobiography, see J. Munitiz, 'A reappraisal of Blemmydes' first discussion with the Latins,' 22–23.

332 ἀπρόσβλητα. He adds that the patriarch was greatly emboldened by the argument of the treatise: Nikephoros Blemmydes, *Autobiographia*, ed. J. Munitiz, Book 2, ch. 41, 64 lines 3–4; transl. J. A. Munitiz, *A partial account*, 114. Joseph Munitiz suggested that the report

INTRODUCTION

69

glowing reception of the document. Their report introduces the document with four sharp criticisms, describing the work as one of falsehoods and heresies.[333] The friars state that the emperor 'wished to cover up the disgrace [of the Greeks]' when he realized that the assembled learned men could not defend the treatise.[334] He therefore suggests the work be put aside, 'because it produces only controversy,' and that the disputants return to evidence found in patristic texts.[335] The friars read from Cyril's Ninth Anathema, which anathematized any who argued that the Spirit was alien from the Son.[336] This reading was almost certainly a response to the treatise put forth by Blemmydes. At this point the emperor himself contributes to the debates, stating that in the Ninth Anathema Cyril was speaking against heresy, and thus 'he spoke more than was proper.'[337] The friars answer that even if Cyril was speaking against heretics, his words were still true, and that his argument supported procession from the Son.[338]

---

of the friars and the treatise by Blemmydes shows that the Greeks and Latins had a similar approach to argumentation: J. Munitiz, 'A reappraisal of Blemmydes' first discussion with the Latins,' 23.

333 The friars allege that the document maintains two falsehoods, a heresy that Christ was not from eternity, and an errant accusation of false syllogism: Golubovich, 'Disputatio' ch. 10, 437 lines 28–37. Joseph Munitiz has gone into great detail in examining these criticisms. He found that the accusation of heresy is only true when a statement from the treatise is taken out of context. According to Munitiz, the criticisms 'inspire little conviction, and appear shallow.' He concluded that the friars did not judge the treatise of Blemmydes fairly: J. Munitiz, 'A reappraisal of Blemmydes' first discussion with the Latins,' 23–24.

334 Golubovich, 'Disputatio,' ch. 12, 442 lines 37–38.

335 Golubovich, 'Disputatio,' ch. 12, 442 line 38 – 443 line 1. It is noteworthy that Nikephoros Blemmydes, despite his claim that the treatise was so positively received, promptly left Nicaea and went to Ephesos: Nikephoros Blemmydes, *Autobiographia*, ed. J. Munitiz, Book 2, ch. 41, 64 lines 5–6; transl. J. A. Munitiz, *A partial account*, 114. John Langdon pointed out that Blemmydes does not return for the second round of talks in Nymphaion, and concluded that it was Vatatzes who was particularly displeased by the argument of the treatise. Langdon argued that the emperor viewed Blemmydes as one of those clerics who opposed compromise with the Latins, and therefore excluded him from continued participation in the *disputatio*: J. Langdon, 'Byzantino-Papal discussions in 1234,' 212. See also H. Chadwick, *East and west*, 240.

336 Golubovich, 'Disputatio,' ch. 12, 443 lines 6–10 and lines 11–14: Cyril of Alexandria, *Explicatio duodecimo capitum*, Anathema IX, Migne *PG* 76, col. 308 C – 309 A; transl. N. Russell, *Cyril of Alexandria*, 186.

337 Golubovich, 'Disputatio,' ch. 12, 443 lines 32–33.

338 Golubovich, 'Disputatio,' ch. 12, 443 lines 33–36.

70   THE DISPUTATIO

On the final day of theological debate during their time in Nicaea the friars explain that they no longer wish to discuss the procession issue. The language in their report indicates that they were becoming increasingly frustrated by the Greeks, whom the friars describe as stubborn and unwilling to consider the Latin argument. 'If you flagrantly do not wish to assent to the truth, what more will we be able to show to you?'[339] Instead, the friars want to move on to the issue of azymes, and the patriarch consents. The friars follow with a presentation of their position. Unfortunately, the friars are unusually brief in their description of this discussion. We can imagine that it was similar in content to the comments on leavened versus unleavened bread we find in the letter from Gregory IX to Germanos II,[340] but if this was the case the friars do not say. Instead, the report of the friars relates that the patriarch asked to be allowed to consult with his fellow patriarchs, due to the complexity of the issue.[341] The friars grant the patriarch's request, but insist that they cannot remain in Nicaea for a continuation of the talks, repeating their mandate from the pope that prohibited them from attending a council.[342] With this, the theological discussions during the first phase of the *disputatio* of 1234 were complete, and the friars return to Constantinople soon after.

There was a considerable delay between the first phase of negotiations in Nicaea and the second in Nymphaion. The report of the friars includes no mention of their activities during the month of February, while they were presumably waiting in Constantinople. In March, the friars receive letters from both the emperor and patriarch in Nicaea, calling on them to return and participate in the proposed council.[343] These letters have not survived, but the friars describe the patriarch's messages as 'filled with sadness.'[344] The patriarch apparently suggested that the friars' mission would be viewed with suspicion by the Greek Church if they did not join the council.[345] Germanos II also wrote to others in Constantinople, asking that they urge the friars to return to the *disputatio*, and 'promising that if we [the friars] went to the council, we would return to the curia

---

339 Golubovich, 'Disputatio,' ch. 13, 444 lines 3–5.
340 Tautu, *Acta*, no. 193, 266–68.
341 Golubovich, 'Disputatio,' ch. 13, 444 lines 23–27.
342 Golubovich, 'Disputatio,' ch. 13, 444 lines 28–40.
343 Golubovich, 'Disputatio,' ch. 16, 445–46.
344 Golubovich, 'Disputatio,' ch. 16, 445 lines 29–30.
345 Golubovich, 'Disputatio,' ch. 16, 445 lines 33–34.

INTRODUCTION 71

with great joy.'[346] According to the friars, the letter from Vatatzes offered to send the friars back to Rome aboard a ship he was then preparing for the journey. They would be accompanied by his own envoys to the pope, indicating that the emperor expected a positive resolution to the *disputatio*.[347] All of this blatantly disregards the earlier protestations by the friars that their mandate had forbidden them from attending a council,[348] but also shows that elements within the Greek Church, or at least the emperor, still held out hope for an agreement. They may even have been encouraged by some of the discussions in Nicaea.

The friars do not take lightly their decision to return to the *disputatio*. They clearly understood that doing so would violate their mandate as papal representatives. To explain their decision, they devote considerable space to explaining their actions. The friars relate that they consulted the clergy of Constantinople, and even the Latin emperor, John of Brienne, all of whom recommended returning to the *disputatio*.[349] Their report even goes to the length of describing the desperate situation facing the Latin Empire, which was surrounded by enemies and abandoned by allies.[350] Their remarks are an important eyewitness account describing the sorry state of Constantinople under the Latins only 30 years after the Fourth Crusade.[351] They suggest that the Latin elite in Constantinople were particularly concerned about the possible threat posed by the Empire of Nicaea, and were eager for any opportunity for diplomatic contact that might pacify the ambitions of Vatatzes. It is also possible, given that the friars had consulted with the Latin emperor, that their mission now included negotiating a truce between Nicaea and Constantinople. All of this again demonstrates the mingling of religious and political priorities in decision making.

---

346 Golubovich, 'Disputatio,' ch. 16, 446 lines 2–3.

347 Golubovich, 'Disputatio,' ch. 16. 446 lines 3–7.

348 R. Wolff, 'The Latin Empire of Constantinople and the Franciscans,' 226.

349 Golubovich, 'Disputatio,' ch. 16, 446 lines 18–19. That the Latin emperor would support continued negotiations toward church union is particularly remarkable. Guy Perry explained that the entire prospect of ending the schism was a 'lurking threat' to the Latins in Constantinople, whose position was certainly a possible part of the bargain. There was always the possibility that the pope, the main patron of the Latin Empire, might sacrifice Constantinople 'on the altar of ecclesiastical reunion': G. Perry, *John of Brienne: King of Jerusalem, Emperor of Constantinople, c. 1175–1237* (Cambridge: Cambridge University Press, 2013), 170.

350 Golubovich, 'Disputatio,' ch. 16, 446 lines 7–17.

351 R. Wolff, 'The Latin Empire of Constantinople and the Franciscans,' 227.

THE DISPUTATIO

Having explained their reasoning for returning to the *disputatio*, the friars proceed to give a detailed account of their journey into Anatolia. This account is particularly important because it is the only instance in which the friars describe their journey. They give no information about how they first arrived at Nicaea in January of 1234, nor how they returned to Constantinople.[352] The journey to rejoin Germanos II and Vatatzes from the end of April to the beginning of May 1234 is the only travel the friars describe in detail.[353] Unfortunately, even this journey leaves historians with questions. The letters from the emperor and patriarch had asked the friars to meet them at 'a certain Leschara,' but the friars give no indication about whether this indicates a town or a simple structure for lodging or fortification. Their spelling of the word varies throughout the report, giving *Leschara, Leschera, Alescheran, Lescherea* and *Lescaram*. An eighteenth-century edition of the friars' report refers to this place with the Greek word $Λέσχερα$.[354] Girolamo Golubovich suspected that this came from the Greek word $λέσχη$, indicating a place for 'study, meetings, entertainment and lodging.' Taking this to be correct, Golubovich maintained that Leschara was a palace or lodging built, or possibly inherited, by Vatatzes. However, Golubovich left open the possibility that Leschara denotes a village, in which case he put its location just south of Lopadion on the road to Nymphaion, about one day's journey.[355] His estimation that Leschara was one day from Lopadion is not clarified by any statement by the friars, and it is possible that the location was some distance further from Lopadion. All the friars say for certain is that Leschara was a four-day journey from Nymphaion.[356] One possible location indicated by Leschara is Achyraous, a fortress originally built by John II Komnenos overlooking the tributary to the Makestos (Simav) River. Achyraous controlled the road from the Propontis and the Mysian plain to the regions of Lydia and Ionia, and rests conveniently between

---

352 Henry Chadwick stated that the friars departed from Rome and travelled through Constantinople to reach Nicaea in January 1234. While both assertions are highly probable, neither is explicitly stated by the friars in their report: H. Chadwick, *East and west*, 238.

353 See the map of this journey on p. xv.

354 J. Quetif and J. Echard, *Scriptores ordinis praedicatorum recensiti, notisque historicis et criticis illustrati*, vol. 1 (Paris, 1719), 919.

355 Golubovich, 'Disputatio,' 447 note 4. Joan Hussey agreed, describing Leschara as a village not far from Nymphaion: J. Hussey, *The Orthodox Church in the Byzantine Empire*, 216 note 74. See also Dölger, *Reg.*, no. 1737a, 12.

356 Golubovich, 'Disputatio,' ch. 18, 447 lines 18–19.

INTRODUCTION

73

Lopadion in the north and Nymphaion to the south.[357] The fortress came under Latin occupation following Henry I's victory over Theodore I Laskaris in 1211/2, and Frederick Hasluck has pointed out that Achyraous was referred to as *Esseron* or *Sycheron* by the Latins.[358] Hélène Ahrweiler gave the possible identification of *Laquera* for Achyraous.[359] Any of these terms could easily be corrupted into *Leschara*. This is by no means a definitive identification, but the location of Achyraous, between Lopadion and the friars' eventual destination of Nymphaion, neatly fits the facts.

The friars' journey began on 26 March 1234. They report that they sailed from Constantinople to *Chalogerorum*, identified as Kios, the modern port of Gemlik.[360] From there they travel to Lopadion, modern Ulubad,[361] and continue on to Leschara, arriving some time before 6 April 1234.[362] They do not find Vatatzes waiting to greet them. Instead, the friars receive word from the emperor asking them to continue on and join him at Nymphaion.[363] The report again carefully delineates between

---

357 Choniates, *Historia*, 33 lines 65–67; transl. H. Magoulias, 19.

358 F. Hasluck, *Cyzicus: being some account of the history and antiquities of that city, and of the district adjacent to it, with the town of Apollonia ad Rhyndacum, Miletupolis, Hadrianutherae, Priapus, Zeleia, etc.* (Cambridge: Cambridge University Press, 1910), 93–94, 133. For the Latin occupation of Achyraous: Akropolites, *History*, 27–28; transl. R. Macrides, 15.149. Germanos II, who spent time in Achyraous at the monastery of St George Paneumorphos before being elevated to the patriarchate, makes reference to the Latin occupation: Xanthopoulos, Migne *PG* 147, col. 465 C; S. Lagopates, Γερμανὸς ὁ β΄, πατριαρχὴς Κωνσταντινουπόλεως-Νικαίας, 216 lines 10–19. For more on Achyraous, see W. Ramsay, *Historical geography of Asia Minor* (London: John Murray, 1890), 156; C. Foss and D. Winfield, *Byzantine fortifications: an introduction* (Pretoria: University of South Africa, 1986), 146; C. Foss, 'The defenses of Asia Minor against the Turks,' *Greek Orthodox Theological Review* 27:2 (1982), 161–66; R. Macrides, *George Akropolites, The History*, 152 note 14.

359 H. Ahrweiler, 'L'histoire et la géographie de la région de Smyrne entre les deux occupations turque (1081–1317), particulièrement au XIIIe siècle,' *Travaux et Mémoires* 1 (1965), 69.

360 Not to be confused with Chios, the island in the Aegean Sea: W. Ramsay, *Historical geography of Asia Minor*, 180. For the identification of Chalogerorum as Kios, see Golubovich, 'Disputatio,' 446 note 7.

361 F. Hasluck, *Cyzicus*, 78–83; Golubovich, 'Disputatio,' 447 note 2; W. Ramsay, *Historical geography of Asia Minor*, 160; C. Foss, 'The defenses of Asia Minor,' 159–61; C. Foss and D. Winfield, *Byzantine fortifications*, 145.

362 The friars do not specify their date of arrival at Leschara. However, their report tells us that they received correspondence from Vatatzes on 6 April, apparently after they had arrived: Golubovich, 'Disputatio,' ch. 17, 447 lines 4–10.

363 Golubovich, 'Disputatio,' ch. 17, 447 lines 8–11.

74 THE DISPUTATIO

communications between the friars and the emperor and the friars and the patriarch. The friars respond to Vatatzes that they have come to Leschara to meet with Germanos II, and cannot leave until they hear from him. A letter from the patriarch arrives soon after, informing the friars that he was on his way to Nymphaion, and asking them to meet him there.[364] Thus, the friars depart for Nymphaion, and arrive there on 12 April 1234. The patriarch arrives the following day.[365]

The journey of the friars provokes several questions regarding the nature of the negotiations in 1234, as well as the approach taken to the meetings by Vatatzes and Germanos II. Their actions, as reported by the friars, suggest that emperor and patriarch held different goals and expectations, at least going into the second phase of the *disputatio*. We have already seen that Vatatzes and Germanos II maintained separate communications and interactions with the friars. The journey and correspondence surrounding the resumption of the *disputatio* in Nymphaion opens certain new possibilities regarding their intentions. The friars give no indication of where Germanos II was travelling from, thus we are left to wonder at his whereabouts before arriving at Nymphaion. The quick succession of events following the friars' refusal of the invitation from Vatatzes to the message from Germanos II indicates that the emperor and patriarch were together, but the report states that the Vatatzes was already in Nymphaion, while the patriarch was not. It is most unfortunate that the letters from Vatatzes and Germanos II to the friars during this sequence do not survive. The comments by the friars, our only source for this episode, cause us to surmise that Vatatzes placed such a high emphasis on the arrival of the friars in Nymphaion that he very rapidly called on the patriarch, wherever he was, to send word to the friars to meet him there. The possible implication is that the emperor and patriarch were not on the same page, and that Vatatzes was pressuring Germanos II in his dealings with the friars.

The beginning of the second phase of the *disputatio* at Nymphaion is marked by the friars' anxious desire to complete the talks and return as quickly as possible to the West. According to their report, this desire is frequently met with disappointment. First, Germanos II delays the proceedings, citing the need to await the arrival of other Greek clergy. The emperor asks for further delays, noting the upcoming Easter holiday.[366]

---

364 Golubovich, 'Disputatio,' ch. 17, 447 lines 11–17.
365 Golubovich, 'Disputatio,' ch. 17, 447 lines 18–21.
366 Golubovich, 'Disputatio,' ch. 18, 447 line 22 – 448 line 18.

INTRODUCTION 75

Even when theological debate does recommence in Nymphaion, the friars are frustrated by yet further delays and pauses in the meetings. Of the nearly two weeks the friars remain in Nymphaion, they describe meeting with Germanos II and his clergy to continue the *disputatio* on only five days.[367] The constant obstruction that is caused, according to the friars, by the Byzantines, like the complexities of their journey to Nymphaion, serves to add to the purpose of the friars' report. Their testimony emphasizes the difficulty of the task before them. The emperor and patriarch claim a desire to negotiate, doing everything in their power to urge the friars to rejoin the discussions, but when the friars finally consent to further negotiations the Byzantines prolong the *disputatio* and avoid any resolution. When the friars conclude that the negotiations will not have the desired result they begin to plan their departure. The friars seek permission from Vatatzes to leave Nymphaion for Constantinople on three occasions.[368] The first came almost immediately after the *disputatio* in Nymphaion began, on Wednesday, 26 April, after only two sessions of talks with the patriarch and his clergy.[369] Each time the emperor convinces them to remain. It was only after the friars decide to abstain from food until they gained permission from Vatatzes that they finally departed from Nymphaion.[370] The persistent emphasis on leaving Nymphaion found in the report serves to convince the reader that the *disputatio* is not going well, suggesting that the Byzantines were determined to sabotage the proceedings. This perspective is reiterated frequently during the second phase of the *disputatio* conducted at Nymphaion, but should not be exaggerated. We must consider this was another method for the friars to elicit sympathy from their reader, as they project the end of the proceedings at Nymphaion onto the rest of their report.

The constant reference to the attempts by Germanos II and his clergy to delay or sabotage the talks carries over the theme of the 'scheming Greeks' already seen during the first phase at Nicaea. On at least six occasions, during this portion of the report, the friars make comments that allude to the tricks and ploys of their hosts, either to delay talks or to

367 Monday, 24 April; Wednesday, 26 April; Friday, 28 April; Saturday, 29 April; Thursday, 4.
368 Wednesday, 26 April, Golubovich, 'Disputatio,' ch. 21, 452 lines 13–16; Tuesday, 2 May, ch. 26, 461 lines 30–31; Thursday, 4–6 May, ch. 28–29, 464 lines 1–8.
369 Golubovich, 'Disputatio,' ch. 21, 452 lines 13–16.
370 Golubovich, 'Disputatio,' ch. 28, 464 lines 1–3.

THE DISPUTATIO

change the topic. If we expand our analysis to the period during which the friars were waiting for the second phase of the *disputatio* in Nymphaion to begin on 24 April, we find the total number of accusations of deception reaches seven. The first day of talks at Nymphaion is particularly charged with examples of mistrust from the friars. On that occasion, the patriarch opens the proceedings with a request that the friars give a summary of what was discussed at Nicaea for the benefit of those who were not present for those talks. While such a request may appear reasonable to the outside observer, the friars immediately react to it with suspicion. They had looked forward to discussing the problem of azymes, but conclude from the patriarch's request that 'he was dissembling in answering our question, wishing to bring us back to the issue of the Holy Spirit.'[371] The discussions then devolve into an argument over the topic of the second phase of talks.

Another instance of alleged 'scheming' by the patriarch comes when he proposes a compromise on the topic, suggesting that the Byzantine position on azymes should be put into writing. Again, the friars suspect that he does not want to answer the question, and instead wishes to 'pass over it by dissembling, and to disguise it with their writing.'[372] The friars respond that a written response is inappropriate: 'Writing is done namely for those who are absent and not for those present. Therefore, seeing as we are present, answer us as though we were present.'[373] Eventually, the friars relent, and the patriarch asks to pause the proceedings to allow time to compile the Greek response on the azymes question. Again, the friars interpret the request for a delay as an example of deception.[374] They even go so far as to repeat their question to Germanos II and his clergy, so that there can be no confusion over the topic of their next meeting.[375]

---

371 Golubovich, 'Disputatio,' ch. 19, 448 lines 24–26. Henry Chadwick characterized the reaction of the friars to the request to give a summary of the arguments made at Nicaea as 'alarm.' He also remarked that the friars were aware that the Greeks felt themselves better able to argue over the *filioque* than azymes: H. Chadwick, *East and west*, 241. The friars never express such confidence in their knowledge of the feelings of their opponents.

372 Golubovich, 'Disputatio,' ch. 19, 449 lines 35–36.

373 Golubovich, 'Disputatio,' ch. 19, 449 lines 38–39.

374 John Doran has argued that their unwillingness to debate leavened versus unleavened bread 'is the clearest sign in the whole mission that the Greeks were in fact intolerant of diversity': J. Doran, 'Rites and wrongs in 1234,' 141. See also H. Chadwick, *East and west*, 241.

375 Golubovich, 'Disputatio,' ch. 19, 450 lines 8–14.

INTRODUCTION 77

The increasing tension generated by the 'scheming Greeks' provokes one of the most dramatic encounters of the *disputatio* on 26 April. Apparently frustrated by their hosts, the friars make a number of accusations against the Greek clergy, including the washing of altars after their use by Latin clergy,[376] forcing Latins who take part in Greek services to renounce azymes, and expelling the pope from their diptychs.[377] The response to these charges is equally harsh. For the first time in the *disputatio*, the Byzantines use the events of 1204 to highlight Latin wrongdoings and the evils of the Roman Church:

> When your Latins seized Constantinople, they shattered churches, demolished altars, stealing gold and silver, throwing relics of the saints into the sea, they trampled holy icons and they made churches into stables for mules, so that the prophecy appeared fulfilled: *God, the nations came into your inheritance, they defiled your holy temple, they laid low Jerusalem.*[378]

The friars respond by insisting that the Roman Church was not responsible for alleged Latin atrocities in the Fourth Crusade. 'If these things were done, the people who did them were laity, sinners, and excommunicates, presuming to commit such actions on their own authority. The whole Church should not be charged, for these things were done presumptuously by certain wicked persons.'[379] Michael Angold interpreted this admission of guilt as a particular diplomatic blunder on the part of the friars.[380] It was the first time papal representatives had distanced themselves from those events, and their decision to condemn the actions of the crusaders in 1204

---

376 The accusation is identical to that made by Odo of Deuil during the Second Crusade: Odo of Deuil, *De profectione Ludovici VII in orientem*, ed. and transl. V. Berry, 54–55. It is noteworthy that the friars never make this accusation in relation to the services they performed in a church in Nicaea on Wednesday, 18 January: Golubovich, 'Disputatio,' ch. 4, 430 lines 10–25.

377 Golubovich, 'Disputatio,' ch. 20, 451 lines 16–26. The last charge sparked a debate about whether it was the pope or the patriarch who first expelled the other from their diptychs. The exchange is remarkably similar to that which took place in 1089 between representatives of Pope Urban II and Alexios I Komnenos: T. Kolbaba, 'The legacy of Humbert and Cerularius,' 51, 59–60.

378 Golubovich, 'Disputatio,' ch. 20, 451 lines 29–35; Psalm 79:1.

379 Golubovich, 'Disputatio,' ch. 20, 452 lines 3–6. John Doran maintained that the accusation of Latin atrocities in 1204 left the friars 'somewhat flustered': J. Doran, 'Rites and wrongs in 1234,' 140. While this might well have been the case, the friars themselves give no such indication of this reaction in their report.

380 M. Angold, 'After the Fourth Crusade,' 744.

THE DISPUTATIO

as those of 'sinners and excommunicates' is in stark contrast to the view of Pope Innocent III, who concluded that the sacking of Constantinople had been 'God's will.'[381]

The friars express a clear intention to focus their discussions at Nymphaion on the issue of leavened versus unleavened bread in the Eucharist. They put the issue to Germanos II and his clergy with the following question: 'Are we able to accomplish the body of Christ in azymes, or not?'[382] After some upheaval, the Greek clergy respond that it is impossible to perform the Eucharist in unleavened bread.[383] From there the discussion revolves around the story of the Last Supper, debating whether the bread used by Jesus and his disciples was leavened or unleavened.[384] Unconvinced, the friars announce before the patriarch and the council that the Greek argument concerning azymes amounts to heresy and those who defend it are heretics.[385] They insist that the Greeks could only hold such a position out of either ignorance or malice, and call on them to defend their answer with Scripture and patristic authorities.[386] The Byzantines make reference to the letters of Paul, describing the Last Supper.[387] They respond that the bread in that instance – which they describe simply as *artos*, the Greek word for bread – implies 'leavened bread.' They explain that *artos* denotes 'completed bread, the risen bread, the leavened bread.'[388] The

---

381 Innocent III explains the events of 1204 to Theodore I Laskaris as 'divine punishment': Hageneder, *Die Register Innocenz' III*, vol. 11, no. 44(47), 63 lines 1–3.

382 Golubovich, 'Disputatio,' ch. 19, 449 lines 1–2.

383 Golubovich, 'Disputatio,' ch. 22, 453 lines 26–28. Tia Kolbaba has demonstrated that the emphasis on the discussion of the Eucharist for Gregory IX, and thus the emphasis placed on the issue in the report of the friars, is a result of the developing doctrine of transubstantiation taking place in the Latin West in the twelfth and thirteenth centuries. The primary concern for the friars, therefore, would not be whether the bread of the Eucharist was either leavened or unleavened; rather, they sought from the Greek clergy an acceptance of the new doctrine: T. Kolbaba, 'Theological debates with the west,' 490–92. Whatever the priority for the friars, the response by the patriarch and his clergy, that it was 'impossible to perform the Eucharist in unleavened bread,' makes clear that the issue for them was not some new doctrine but the validity of the Latin Eucharist itself.

384 Golubovich, 'Disputatio,' ch. 22, 453 line 30 – 454 line 11.

385 Golubovich, 'Disputatio,' ch. 25, 458 lines 19–21.

386 The friars explain that they were astonished to find that none of the Greek clergy gathered for the council had a copy of either the Old or New Testament on hand: Golubovich, 'Disputatio,' ch. 25, 458 line 21 – 459 line 4.

387 1 Corinthians 11:23.

388 Golubovich, 'Disputatio,' ch. 25, 459 lines 8–9. For a full discussion of the word *artos*, its origins and its implications, see J. Erickson, 'Leavened and unleavened,' 159.

INTRODUCTION 79

friars begin to question this assumption, concluding that *artos* can denote either leavened or unleavened bread, and cannot itself definitively indicate either form.[389] This position, open to either form during the Eucharist, is reminiscent of Gregory IX's last letter on the issue of azymes.[390] The friars conclude that the Last Supper was a Passover meal. Thus Jesus, who always observed Jewish custom, would have celebrated it with azymes.[391]

In arguing for the use of unleavened bread, the friars put forward a vast number of patristic quotations. During the second phase of the *disputatio*, neither side employed syllogistic argument, but instead rested their position on references to Scripture and patristic writings. Together, the two parties made a total of 29 such references during the meetings in Nymphaion.[392] The most prolific references were to Cyril of Alexandria, John Chrysostom and Epiphanios of Cyrus. As was the case in Nicaea, Cyril of Alexandria was the most popular source during the *disputatio*. He is cited a total of six times from five different works, but always by the friars, never by the Greek clergy.[393] One work of John Chrysostom, his

---

389 Golubovich, 'Disputatio,' ch. 25, 459 lines 9–30.

390 Tautu, *Acta*, no. 193, 267 lines 36–38 (Source IV).

391 Golubovich, 'Disputatio,' ch. 25, 459 line 30 – 461 line 20. The disagreement over whether the Last Supper was a Passover meal is a result of discrepancies in the gospels. The three Synoptic Gospels, Mark, Matthew, and Luke, describe it as a Passover meal, while John suggests that it took place before Passover. For more on this issue see J. Doran, 'Rites and wrongs in 1234,' 142; J. Pelikan *The Christian Tradition*, vol. 2, 177–78; A. Gilmore, 'The date and significance of the Last Supper,' *Scottish Journal of Theology* 14:3 (1961), 256–69; C. Humphreys, *The mystery of the Last Supper: Reconstructing the final days of Jesus* (Cambridge: Cambridge University Press, 2011).

392 These references are as follows: 21 quotes from the church fathers – Athanasios, Gregory Thaumaturgus, Gregory of Nyssa, Cyril of Alexandria, John Chrysostom, Epiphanios of Cyprus, Pope Damasus I and Basil of Caesarea; three from the Old Testament; four from the New Testament; one from the canons of the Council of Ephesos, 431. One reference, Psalm 79:1, is made by the chartophylax when describing Latin atrocities in 1204: Golubovich, 'Disputatio,' ch. 20, 451 lines 33–35. Thus, it is possible to consider the quote as being outside of theological discussion. In their report the friars state that most references to John Chrysostom and Epiphanios of Cyprus were not spoken aloud during the *disputatio*, but were included in their recollection of events because they bolstered the Latin position on azymes: Golubovich, 'Disputatio,' ch. 25, 460 line 19 – 461 line 20.

393 Cyril of Alexandria, *Liber de recta in Dominum nostrum Iesum Christum fide*, Migne *PG* 76, cols 1133–200; Cyril of Alexandria, *Scholia de Incarnatione Unigeniti*, Migne *PG* 75, cols 1369–412; transl. J. McGuckin, *St Cyril of Alexandria: the Christological controversy*, 294–335; Cyril of Alexandria, *Explicatio duodecimo capitum*, Anathema IX, Migne *PG* 76, col. 308 C–D and cols 308 C – 309 A; transl. N. Russell, *Cyril of Alexandria*, 186–87; Cyril

80 THE DISPUTATIO

Homily on the Gospel of Matthew, was cited four times,[394] as was a single work of Epiphanios of Cyprus, the *Panaria.*[395]

The friars make an impressive use of Greek patristic authors – Athanasios, Gregory Thaumaturgus, Gregory of Nyssa, Cyril of Alexandria, John Chrysostom, and Epiphanios of Cyprus – to enhance their arguments, citing their works on 18 occasions.[396] The patriarch and his clergy, in contrast, make only three such references – once to John Chrysostom[397] and once to Basil of Caesarea.[398] The third patristic reference by the Byzantines is from the work of Damasus I, who was the only pope to be quoted in the whole course of the *disputatio* at either Nicaea or Nymphaion.[399] Once again, the numerous Scriptural and patristic references during the *disputatio* indicate the extent to which both sides were prepared for theological debate. We should be cautious when considering the comparatively slim number of references made by the Byzantine disputants, as our knowledge of their arguments is dependent on the report of their Latin opponents. What we should take away from this analysis is that the friars, at least, had prepared for the discussions in a different and more comprehensive way than Latin disputants had done in previous church-union negotiations since the Fourth Crusade. We can safely conclude that the friars were thoroughly versed in the issues that had caused the schism and had approached the negotiations toward union with a serious and genuine desire for success. Their attitude and approach to the *disputatio* stands in stark contrast to the Latins who

of Alexandria, *Epistle* 40, Migne *PG* 77, col. 184 D; transl. L. Wickham, *Cyril of Alexandria, select letters,* 39; Cyril of Alexandria, *Epistle* 48, Migne *PG* 77, col. 249 C–D.

394 John Chrysostom, *In Matthaeum. Homilia* LXXXI (al. LXXXII), Migne *PG* 58, cols 729–30, 738; ed. P. Schaff, *St. Chrysostom: Homilies on the Gospel of Saint Matthew: Nicene and Post-Nicene Fathers,* vol. 10 (Grand Rapids, MI: Christian Classics Ethereal Library), 842, 852.

395 Epiphanios of Cyprus, *Adversus Haereses,* 'Against the Ebionites,' Lib. I, tom. 2, Migne *PG* 41, col. 441 B–C; 'Against the Marcionites,' Lib. I, tom. 3, Migne *PG* 41, col. 761 B – 764 B; transl. F. Williams, *The Panarion of Epiphanius of Salamis, Book I (Sects 1–46),* 2nd edn (Leiden: Brill, 2009), 149, 334.

396 Eleven of the references to Greek patristic sources by the friars are made in their treatise on the procession of the Holy Spirit: Golubovich, 'Disputatio,' ch. 24, 455–58. In this treatise, the friars are clearly making a point to use Greek patristic authors. They even point out that they could refer to various Latin church fathers – Ambrose, Augustine, and Jerome – but refrain from doing so: Golubovich, 'Disputatio,' ch. 25, 456 lines 24–26.

397 Golubovich, 'Disputatio,' ch. 25, 459 line 36 – 460 line 1.

398 Golubovich, 'Disputatio,' ch. 27, 463 lines 20–26.

399 Golubovich, 'Disputatio,' ch. 27, 463 lines 13–17.

INTRODUCTION

81

took part in the meetings described by Nicholas Mesarites in 1204 and 1206, or any other union negotiation since the Fourth Crusade.

According to an agreement made between the two parties, in exchange for debate over the issue of azymes, the friars provided the patriarch and his clergy with a treatise on the issue of procession.[400] This text stands in sharp contrast to the Greek document on the issue of azymes, which was much shorter in length and featured far fewer sources.[401] It seems that on the day the friars handed this document to their opponents, 29 April, it was set aside to be examined and discussed later. Germanos II and his spokesmen make no response to the treatise on the procession of the Holy Spirit until the final day of the *disputatio* in Nymphaion, 4 May. The report of the friars explains that a large multitude of lay people had been invited to hear the discussions that day.[402] The patriarch opens the proceedings by expressing his desire to proclaim the Latin position on procession throughout the eastern world, 'so that all will hear and understand the faith of the Roman Church.'[403] The text gives the impression that Germanos II thought this measure would help other Byzantines to dispute Latin theology; thus he was probably disappointed when the friars announce their delight in the idea, as they too wished 'everyone in the eastern Church to know and learn and faithfully keep the creed of the Roman Church.'[404]

Following this exchange, a Greek spokesman produced and read aloud another document, referencing the friars' treatise on the *filioque*.[405] After the friars clarify a matter of translation, the Greek clergy launch into a melee of textual evidence, arguing in favour of procession from the Father alone. At this point the report of the friars becomes rather vague, summarizing the points and references made by Germanos II and his clergy. They cease to give precise references for the evidence put forward by their opponents. When the arguments apparently cause a good deal of commotion in the assembled crowd, the patriarch calls for silence in what the friars perceive to be a threatening manner.[406] The friars portray the

---

400 Golubovich, 'Disputatio,' ch. 24, 455–58.

401 Golubovich, 'Disputatio,' ch. 23, 454–55.

402 Golubovich, 'Disputatio,' ch. 27, 462 lines 30–32. Although they do not ascribe any reaction to the audience, we may consider that the sight of such a crowd made the friars nervous.

403 Golubovich, 'Disputatio,' ch. 27, 462 lines 36–39.

404 Golubovich, 'Disputatio,' ch. 27, 463 line 40 – 464 line 2.

405 Golubovich, 'Disputatio,' ch. 24, 455–58.

406 Golubovich, 'Disputatio,' ch. 28, 463 lines 27–28.

82 THE DISPUTATIO

patriarch's actions not as a call for calm but as an attempt to 'stir up the people' against them.[407] They give no proof for this accusation, and instead interject before Germanos II can make a statement, asking him directly whether he believes the Holy Spirit to proceed from the Son. When he answers that he does not, the friars deliver their final verdict.

> Blessed Cyril, who presided over the third council, anathematizes all those who do not believe this. Therefore, you are anathematized. Likewise, you believe and say that the body of Christ cannot be made in azymes. But this is heretical, therefore, you are heretics. Thus we found you heretics and excommunicates, and as heretics and excommunicates we leave you.[408]

The friars relate that they fled the meeting as the Byzantines shouted back 'you are the heretics!'[409] In this manner the theological debates at Nymphaion came to a close. It was clearly the intention of the friars to elicit shock from their readers by the drama of the final events of the *disputatio*, but we should not allow this to overwhelm our analysis of the proceedings. We must consider the theological topics discussed, and ask why the friars continued to participate in the proceedings, especially after their own report on the *disputatio* gives the impression that the meeting had deteriorated into hostilities long before their departure from Nymphaion.

As we have seen, the friars frequently asked Vatatzes for permission to leave the second phase of the *disputatio*, yet they allow themselves to be convinced to remain, especially because they hoped to discuss the issue of the Eucharist. The controversy over the proper form of bread to use in the Sacrament was put forward at every meeting of the *disputatio* in Nymphaion, and the friars frequently express their frustration at what they perceive to be attempts by the patriarch and his clergy to change the subject to the *filioque*. It is safe to conclude, therefore, that an agreement on the problem of azymes was a foremost priority for the friars, and that they genuinely believed a compromise on the matter was possible. Gregory IX had put forward a proposal for a compromise in his last letter to Germanos II, the very letter introducing the friars as his representatives. The proposed compromise, in which both sides would mutually respect the practice of the other, was almost certainly the basis for each proposal made by the friars, even until the last day of the *disputatio* in Nymphaion. The friars, probably acting on

407 Golubovich, 'Disputatio,' ch. 28, 463 lines 28–29.
408 Golubovich, 'Disputatio,' ch. 28, 463 line 34 – 464 line 1.
409 Golubovich, 'Disputatio,' ch. 28, 464 line 1.

INTRODUCTION 83

instruction from the pope, may have sought an agreement on the issue of the Eucharist that might form the basis for a larger negotiation on the topic of church union. Why this failed to come to pass is not some inevitable result, but a consequence of the shifting desires, priorities, and intentions of those involved, not the least of which were those of the emperor and the patriarch.

8. Role of Emperor and Patriarch

The report of the friars makes clear that both Vatatzes and Germanos II exercised enormous influence during the *disputatio*, but several episodes indicate that the two men were following separate policies regarding the papal representatives. Some historians have concluded that Vatatzes favoured negotiations with Rome as a means of advancing his agenda against Constantinople, whereas Germanos II was opposed to such discussions.[410] Robert Wolff has argued that the emperor pressured the patriarch to begin a correspondence with Gregory IX because he was concerned about the potential threat posed by the new Latin emperor, John of Brienne.[411] That the patriarch would accede to the emperor's wishes to entertain talks toward union is in keeping with traditional views of Byzantine custom and what we know about Germanos II and his attitude toward the emperor.[412] To draw the conclusion, however, that Germanos II resented having to undergo these negotiations from the beginning is perhaps going too far. In any event, it is worth examining what the report of the friars tells us about the emperor and the patriarch, and their respective motivations and intentions regarding the *disputatio*.

Their depiction of the emperor throughout the *disputatio* demonstrates his optimism during the talks. Vatatzes appears as a friend of the friars,

---

410 J. Doran, 'Rites and wrongs in 1234,' 132–33; N. Chrissis, *Crusading in Frankish Greece*, 94; L. Bréhier, 'Attempts at reunion of the Churches,' 607–08; J. Langdon, 'Byzantino-Papal discussions in 1234,' 213–22.

411 R. Wolff, 'The Latin Empire of Constantinople and the Franciscans,' 225. John of Brienne did invade Anatolia in 1233, but his campaign is generally considered a failure: Akropolites, *History*, 47 line 4 – 48 line 14; transl. R. Macrides, 190. Guy Perry has noted that the arrival of John of Brienne tended to provoke fear among his enemies, even if that fear was not always warranted: G. Perry, *John of Brienne*, 172–73.

412 Michael Angold noted that patriarchs of Constantinople tended to leave the initiative for church-union negotiations up to the emperor: M. Angold, *Church and society in Byzantium*, 506.

84   THE DISPUTATIO

and eager for compromise. He even takes part in some of the theological debates. The friars' positive depiction of the emperor may reflect a genuine demeanour. The prospect of regaining Constantinople from the Latins was a consistent focus of foreign policy in the Empire of Nicaea after 1204. A possible compromise on church union presented the possibility of regaining the city through peaceful means, which must have been very appealing to Vatatzes.[413] The progress of the discussions determined the foreign policy pursued by Vatatzes, and his negotiating position from day to day. Germanos II, on the other hand, is described by the friars as duplicitous, scheming, and dishonest, using ploys and delay tactics to change the subject of the *disputatio* and perhaps sabotaging the proceedings altogether. It is unclear if this was the original intention of Germanos II, or if his outlook on the *disputatio* changed over time.[414] Whatever the case, the friars' report makes it very clear that the they believed the emperor and patriarch to have very different motivations and priorities.

One issue that seems to indicate that emperor and patriarch were pursuing different goals during the *disputatio* is the fact that the two often employed different messengers and messages when communicating with the friars. From the outset of the *disputatio*, even before the friars first arrived at Nicaea, the report indicates that Vatatzes and Germanos II pursued separate and independent communications with the papal representatives.[415] We have seen that during their journey to Leschara and then to Nymphaion, the friars communicated independently with the emperor and then the patriarch. The friars' comments suggest that they continued to receive separate communications from the emperor and from the patriarch throughout the meetings. For example, when the patriarch

---

413 The liberation of Constantinople from Latin control was the primary focus of most of the Byzantine successor states, especially that of the Empire of Nicaea, from 1204 to 1261: P. Magdalino, 'Hellenism and nationalism in Byzantium,' 18; A. Kaldellis, *Hellenism in Byzantium*, 367; J. Langdon, *Byzantium's last imperial offensive in Asia Minor*, 5. John Doran has explained that the emperor's ambitions around Constantinople required him to make overtures to the papacy. Even if he did take the city by force, Vatatzes would still need the good will of the pope to maintain his borders and protect Constantinople in the long term: J. Doran, 'Rites and wrongs in 1234,' 133.

414 John Langdon has argued that Germanos II decided that the dialogue with the friars was fruitless during the early stages of the discussions at Nicaea: J. Langdon, 'Byzantino-Papal discussions in 1234,' 213.

415 The friars report that they were met by imperial messengers, 'sent by the Emperor himself, and notifying us of the joy in his heart at our arrival,' and only later were greeted by messengers from the patriarch: Golubovich, 'Disputatio,' ch. 1, 428 lines 6–11.

INTRODUCTION

was ill and unable to meet on 25 January, it was he who first informed the friars of his condition. Not long after, additional messengers arrived from Vatatzes, again informing the friars of the patriarch's condition. When Germanos II recovered and was able to return to the *disputatio*, it was not his messengers but those of the emperor who requested the friars return to the debates.[416]

Most of these examples suggest that maintaining separate messengers and communication was a formality. Vatatzes and Germanos II no doubt kept each other aware of developments and plans. The inclination to employ their own messengers was probably an issue of etiquette, and not an indication that the two were pursuing separate agendas. One example from the friars' report, however, indicates that there may have been more to the separate communications. After the collapse of the talks on 4 May the friars depart from Nymphaion for their return journey to Constantinople. Near the town of Kalamos they are approached by two messengers, one representing the emperor, the other the patriarch and the council at Nymphaion. The emperor's messenger 'benevolently reproaches' the friars for leaving without gaining the blessing of Germanos II and the council.[417] The messenger from the council – who we later learn was the chartophylax, Aulenos – repeats this sentiment, but also puts forward an unusual demand.[418] He has with him the document the friars presented to the council concerning the *filioque*, and insists that the friars exchange it for the document they have been given describing the Greek position on azymes.[419] After they refuse to give up the document, which the friars consider to be a scandal for the Greek Church, Aulenos informs them that they will not be able to leave the borders of the Empire of Nicaea until they have surrendered the Greek document on azymes.[420]

The friars resolve to disregard the warning, and prepare to depart anyway, apparently in secret. Before leaving, however, they inquire of the

---

416 Golubovich, 'Disputatio,' ch. 10, 437 lines 18–22.

417 Golubovich, 'Disputatio,' ch. 29, 464 lines 11–15. The friars had gained permission to depart from Vatatzes before leaving Nymphaion: Golubovich, 'Disputatio,' ch. 29, 464 line 6.

418 Golubovich, 'Disputatio,' ch. 29, 464 lines 21–22; ch. 30, 465 line 15.

419 Golubovich, 'Disputatio,' ch. 29, 464 lines 22–24. For the document by the friars describing the Latin position on the procession of the Holy Spirit: Golubovich, 'Disputatio,' ch. 24, 455 line 24 – 458 line 17. For the document outlining the Greek position on azymes: Golubovich, 'Disputatio,' ch. 23, 454 line 17 – 455 line 10.

420 Golubovich, 'Disputatio,' ch. 29, 464 lines 33–37; 465 lines 1–3.

86   THE DISPUTATIO

'soldier who came on behalf of the Emperor' whether he has been sent to apprehend the friars.[421] He answers: 'On the contrary, I have come to speed you on your way.'[422] The status of this soldier is something of a question. His presence among the friars is not mentioned before this incident, meaning he may have been sent by Vatatzes to meet the friars at Kalamos.[423] It is also possible that he was assigned by the emperor to accompany the friars during their journey from Nymphaion to Latin territory. Such an interpretation is supported by his response that he has been sent 'to speed them on their way' back to Constantinople. When the chartophylax realizes that the friars intend to leave despite his injunction he approaches the Byzantines accompanying them and threatens to excommunicate anyone who continues to help the Latins.[424] We would be right to question the authority of the chartophylax to carry out a sentence of excommunication. The statement may have been an invention of the friars, again intended to elicit the sympathy of their reader, or it may have been a depiction of a genuine threat put forward by the chartophylax at that time. In any event, the companions of the friars abandon them and they continue alone and on foot.[425] They proceed for some time until the aforementioned soldier sent by the emperor overtakes them. According to the friars, the soldier begs them to return to the safety of their lodging, adding that he would thwart the threats of the chartophylax.[426] The friars' report depicts this plea as a genuine act of concern for their safety and gives no evidence of duplicity on the part of the soldier. However, by convincing the friars to pause their journey the soldier has placed them at the mercy of the chartophylax, who soon arrives and forcibly takes from them the document he had demanded.[427]

This incident is the only occasion on which the representatives of the emperor and patriarch pursue blatantly separate agendas. The friars depict the representative of the emperor, in the form of the soldier-guide, as solely concerned with their safe conduct back to Constantinople, while portraying the ecclesiastical messenger, the chartophylax, as a villain who harassed

---

421 Golubovich, 'Disputatio,' ch. 30, 465 lines 9–11.
422 Golubovich, 'Disputatio,' ch. 30, 465 line 12.
423 H. Chadwick, *East and west*, 243.
424 Golubovich, 'Disputatio,' ch. 30, 465 lines 15–18.
425 Golubovich, 'Disputatio,' ch. 30, 465 lines 19–21.
426 Golubovich, 'Disputatio,' ch. 30, 465 lines 30–33.
427 Golubovich, 'Disputatio,' ch. 30, 465 lines 35–38.

INTRODUCTION 87

and robbed them in a brutal manner. Once again, the episode is certainly intended to emphasize to the pope the trials the friars endured, but in so doing it has the effect of shaping our view of events. Just as the friars take every opportunity in their report to portray the patriarch and his clergy as conniving and scheming – a trait that is never applied to the emperor – likewise those traits are applied to the ecclesiastical representative, the chartophylax. The drama of the incident provokes our suspicion, and the lack of detail at this point in the report of the friars leaves us in the dark, which may have been their purpose. Perhaps it happened just as the friars related. Perhaps they exaggerated the evils of the chartophylax. It may have been that the soldier was operating with the same goal as the messenger from the council and this fact was unknown or unreported by the friars in order to confine the condemnation of the reader to Germanos II. In any event, enough questions exist for us to view the incident itself with some hesitation. The fact that they employed representatives and messengers independent of each other cannot be considered to indicate that Vatatzes and Germanos II pursued separate goals throughout the *disputatio*.

One incident in the friars' report is particularly revealing about the emperor's goal in the negotiations. On their final day in Nicaea, the friars met personally with Vatatzes, whom they depict as eager to make an agreement before the papal representatives depart for Constantinople. According to the friars, the emperor enquired how 'the Patriarch and the Church of the Greeks might be able to be reconciled with the Church of the Romans.'[428] When the friars answer that the Greek Church must obey the Roman Church, Vatatzes presses further, asking the friars: 'If the lord Patriarch wished to submit to the Church of the Romans, would the lord Pope restore to him his right?'[429] The word *ius* here is open to interpretation. While it certainly refers to the Greek patriarch's authority in Constantinople, it may also imply restoring the city to the Byzantine emperor. If this interpretation is correct, the offer from Vatatzes should be understood as offering the submission of his church in exchange for control of Constantinople.[430]

---

428 Golubovich, 'Disputatio,' ch. 14, 445 lines 1–3.

429 Golubovich, 'Disputatio,' ch. 14, 445 lines 7–8.

430 R. Wolff, 'The Latin Empire of Constantinople and the Franciscans,' 226; M. Angold, *Church and society in Byzantium*, 523; A. Siecienski, *The papacy and the Orthodox*, 294; J. Doran, 'Rites and wrongs in 1234,' 139. For an alternative interpretation of *ius*, see J. Langdon, 'Byzantino-Papal discussions in 1234,' 213.

88 THE DISPUTATIO

This episode once more illustrates that the *disputatio* of 1234 was a unique confluence of ecclesiastical and political interests. The implications of the exchange are tremendous. The emperor appears willing to consent to all papal demands in exchange for restored Byzantine control over Constantinople. The response of the friars to such dramatic proposals is also telling. They are careful not to commit the pope to any one course of action, but they do leave open the door to a possible compromise that would suit all parties.[431] Their response, and the exchange itself, shows the full extent of the relationship between ecclesiastical and political matters, and the impossibility of untangling one from the other. This episode, however, also provides evidence for a possible rift between the emperor and Germanos II. According to the friars, the patriarch was present during the encounter, but said nothing.[432] He appears in the friars' report simply to have been a passive observer. His silence suggests that Vatatzes had pressured him to be present, and that Germanos II was less than enthusiastic about a possible agreement.[433]

It is notable that this is the last time the friars describe a meeting with both Vatatzes and Germanos II outside the context of theological debate. In Nicaea the friars never meet with Vatatzes without the patriarch present, but at Nymphaion the friars record four instances when the friars converse with the emperor alone.[434] The frequency and tenor of these private meetings, as well as the general absence of Vatatzes from the theological debate in the second phase of the *disputatio*, suggest that the role of the emperor was much changed between Nicaea and Nymphaion. During the first phase at Nicaea Vatatzes personally presided over the theological discussions on six of eight occasions, including each of the first five. More than half of those discussions were held in the imperial residence, and Vatatzes even added his own voice to the ecclesiastical discussions on five occasions.[435] In contrast, during the second phase of

---

431 Golubovich, 'Disputatio,' ch. 14, 445 lines 9–11.

432 Golubovich, 'Disputatio,' ch. 14, 444–45.

433 J. Langdon, 'Byzantino-Papal discussions in 1234,' 212–14.

434 Golubovich, 'Disputatio,' ch. 18, 448 lines 9–18; ch. 21, 452 line 13 – 453 line 10; ch. 26, 461 line 36 – 462 line 26; and ch. 28, 464 lines 1–5.

435 The emperor clarifies the question about additions to the creed on 19 January: Golubovich, 'Disputatio,' ch. 5, 431 lines 13–17. On 21 January, he entered debate about the Spirit of Truth: Golubovich, 'Disputatio,' ch. 7, 435 lines 9–14. Vatatzes warns the friars against the use of syllogism on 23 January: Golubovich, 'Disputatio,' ch. 8, 435 line 37 – 436 line 5. He recommends that the treatise on the procession issue, composed by Nikephoros

INTRODUCTION 89

the *disputatio*, three of the five meetings were held at the home of the patriarch in Nymphaion, and the emperor was present to hear the debate on only two occasions. The friars record him speaking in the presence of the council only once.[436] Again, the friars repeatedly characterize Vatatzes as courteous and patient, eager for debate and compromise. This is juxtaposed with their depiction of Germanos II, who is described as rude and boastful.

The shifting roles of emperor and patriarch in the friars' report is evident in their meetings in Nymphaion on 15 April, before the theological discussions had resumed. The friars ask the patriarch when they will return to the *disputatio*, to which he arrogantly responds: 'We are amazed by the Brothers, when we have 30 headings against you, and you wish to be dealt with in a moment.'[437] When the friars go to Vatatzes and relate what the patriarch has said, the emperor makes excuses for further delaying the *disputatio*, allowing other Greek prelates to join the proceedings.[438] He does not repeat the rudeness displayed by Germanos II, and it is even possible that Vatatzes wanted more Greek clergy present in order to increase the number of voices speaking in favour of union with Rome. The friars' depiction of Vatatzes as generous and benevolent in meetings apart from Germanos II appears again following the exchange of accusations between the friars and the patriarch's clergy on 26 April. After the chartophylax confronts the friars with stories of Latin atrocities in Constantinople in 1204,[439] the papal representatives go to the emperor, who was not present for that exchange, and relate to him what was said.[440] The emperor responds by reassuring the friars that such negative dialogue would not have taken place had he been present, adding that he wishes to hear the arguments of both sides.[441] He even announces his intention to send the friars to Italy onboard his own ships, accompanied by an embassy

---

Blemmydes, be put aside on 25 January: Golubovich, 'Disputatio,' ch. 12, 442 line 37 – 443 line 3. Finally, on that same day, the emperor engages the friars in debate over Cyril of Alexandria's ninth anathema: Golubovich, 'Disputatio,' ch. 12, 443 lines 31–37.

436 On 28 April, the friars record that Vatatzes began the day's proceedings by defending the wish of many Greek prelates to hear an account of what had been discussed at Nicaea: Golubovich, 'Disputatio,' ch. 22, 453 lines 17–21.

437 Golubovich, 'Disputatio,' ch. 18, 448 lines 6–8.

438 Golubovich, 'Disputatio,' ch. 18, 448 lines 8–9.

439 Golubovich, 'Disputatio,' ch. 20, 451 lines 26–34.

440 Golubovich, 'Disputatio,' ch. 21, 452 lines 13–15.

441 Golubovich, 'Disputatio,' ch. 21, 452 lines 18–21.

90 THE DISPUTATIO

from Nicaea carrying gifts for the pope.[442] The friars respond that they could not, in good conscience, escort an embassy to Rome without hope of an agreement, to which Vatatzes seems to react with some confusion.[443] Nevertheless, the emperor appears to retain some hope for continued negotiations. The meeting ends with Vatatzes promising to speak to the clergy of his church, urging them to return to the *disputatio*.[444]

All of this suggests that Vatatzes continued to hold out hope for a successful conclusion of the *disputatio* during the talks in Nymphaion. That the first phase of the *disputatio* at Nicaea came to an end without an agreement to heal the schism does not appear to have eliminated the Byzantine emperor's hopeful outlook for reaching a compromise. The friars depict him as a driving force behind theological dialogue, while Germanos II appears as scheming and deceitful. That the friars would portray such a sympathetic image of the emperor is surprising, especially given Gregory IX's expressed concerns about the interference of lay authorities in perpetuating the schism. In his letter to Germanos II in 1232, the pope had argued strongly that the role of the emperor in Byzantium was largely to blame for the division of the churches (Source III).[445] This issue is one area in which the friars' report does not reflect the attitudes found in the correspondence between pope and patriarch.

The final meeting between Vatatzes and the friars, again without the patriarch present, came on 3 May, at which the emperor made an extremely provocative offer to the papal representatives. In what appears to be a last ditch hope to salvage some sort of an agreement on church union, Vatatzes tells the friars that he would be willing to support the use of unleavened bread in the Greek Church if the Roman Church were willing to surrender their insistence on the *filioque*.[446] The emperor states that such a compromise would be in keeping with his experience in the political realm, in which parties reached peace through the exchange of lands or castles. It is significant that the emperor would compare the schism of the churches to a territorial dispute. It suggests that he approached the problem from a very practical point of view, commensurate with his experience. This exchange is also remarkable in that it was the last time Vatatzes

---

442 Golubovich, 'Disputatio,' ch. 21, 452 lines 21–26.
443 Golubovich, 'Disputatio,' ch. 21, 452 line 26 – 453 line 7.
444 Golubovich, 'Disputatio,' ch. 21, 453 lines 9–10.
445 Tautu, *Acta*, no. 179, 237 lines 35–39.
446 Golubovich, 'Disputatio,' ch. 26, 461 line 37 – 462 line 10.

INTRODUCTION 91

strove for compromise. The friars refuse the proposal, insisting that they would not surrender one iota of their faith, at which time they describe a sudden change in the emperor's outlook.[447] They say he became upset, responding to the friars' rejection by saying 'I do not now hear the term[s] of peace.'[448] It is probably at this point that the emperor's optimism finally wore out. Throughout the proceedings he had offered possible agreements and spoke amicably with the friars. Even when the friars had insisted that they could not present an embassy from Vatatzes to the pope he persisted in his hopeful outlook.[449] Now, however, the friars depict the mood of the emperor changing for the worse, and his own statement attests to a realization that an agreement might not be possible.

Some historians have argued that Vatatzes became increasingly cynical about the possibility of a positive outcome to the meetings, and that this is why he became less personally engaged in theological discussions at Nymphaion.[450] Unfortunately, because our understanding is confined to the perspective of the friars, we cannot address this with any real confidence. The emperor's absence from encounters between the friars and the Greek clergy at Nymphaion can be attributed to any number of matters requiring his attention. It is only in this final meeting between Vatatzes and the friars, just before the *disputatio* comes to a close and near the end of the friars' report, that can we say with any sense of certainly that all parties have finally given up on a possible church union in 1234.

9. Conclusions

The collapse of the *disputatio* in 1234 led directly to renewed hostilities between the Empire of Nicaea and the Latin Empire of Constantinople. John III Vatatzes initiated a series of military campaigns into the Balkan peninsula, creating advantageous alliances and making the Empire of Nicaea a foremost power in the Eastern Mediterranean. The experience of 1234 had confirmed the position of Patriarch Germanos II as definitively

---

447 Golubovich, 'Disputatio,' ch. 26, 462 lines 10–22. John Doran wrongly stated that the friars insisted the Greek Church should agree to all the demands of the Roman Church: J. Doran, 'Rites and wrongs in 1234,' 142.
448 Golubovich, 'Disputatio,' ch. 26, 462 line 23.
449 Golubovich, 'Disputatio,' ch. 21, 452 lines 36–39.
450 H. Chadwick, *East and west*, 242; J. Doran, 'Rites and wrongs in 1234,' 142–43.

92   THE DISPUTATIO

anti-Latin. Shortly after the friars departed Nymphaion, he and his clergy issued a response, the Ἀπάντησις, to the Latin theological position.[451] Germanos II questions the selection of sources and authorities used to validate the Latin belief in the *filioque*, asking why, if the argument of the friars represented truth, had so many authorities – prophets, gospels, church fathers – misled their followers? 'If someone is the teacher, and knows that the Spirit proceeds from the Father and the Son, and does not teach this, but says that the Father is always the cause of the Spirit, and the son is never the cause, is he worthy of blessing, or of eternal condemnation?'[452] The patriarch proceeded to advocate a more aggressive position against the Latins' political as well as ecclesiastical affairs after 1234. In a homily against the Bogomils he praises Vatatzes for his wars against the Franks, to whom he referred as 'dogs.' '[And surrounded in] their city they are weakened and bark in vain. John, our God-guarded autokrator, baptizes them in their blood.'[453] The patriarch's commitment to the anti-Latin position is confirmed by the fact that the issue of church union is never again broached in his lifetime.

The failure of the negotiations in 1234 prompted two specific responses from the pope. First, Gregory IX abandoned his attempts to heal the schism through diplomacy and called for a new crusade against the Byzantines in Nicaea.[454] Nikolaos Chrissis has shown that the pope's plans for crusading to protect Latin Constantinople were more ambitious than anything

---

451 This work survives in a fourteenth-century Greek text in the Austrian National Library, published over 200 years ago: Germanos II, Ἀπάντησις, ed. Alter, 140–49. See also A. Nikolov, 'The medieval Slavonic "dossier" of the Great Schism: historical narrations and lists of Latin errors among the Balkan Slavs,' in *Contra Latinos and Adversus Graecos: the separation between Rome and Constantinople from the ninth to the fifteenth century*, ed. A. Bucossi and A. Calia (Leuven: Peeters, 2020), 297–310.

452 ἐάν ᾖ τὶς διδάσκαλος, καὶ γινώσκῃ ὅτι τὸ πνεῦμα ἐκ τοῦ πατρὸς καὶ τοῦ υἱοῦ ἐκπορεύεται· καὶ οὐ διδάσκει οὕτως· ἀλλὰ πάντοτε τὸν πατέρα αἴτιον λέγει τοῦ πνεύματος, τὸν υἱὸν δὲ οὐδέποτε, μακαρισμοῦ ἐστιν ἄξιος, ἢ κατακρίσεως αἰωνίου· Germanos II, Ἀπάντησις, ed. Alter, 141.

453 Καὶ κυκλώσωσι τὴν ἰδίαν πόλιν λιμαγχονούμενοι καὶ βαΰζοντες μάταια. Ἰωαννης ὁ βαπτίσας αὐτοὺς τοῖς αἵμασιν ἑαυτῶν, ὁ θεοφρούρητος ἡμῶν αὐτοκράτωρ, Migne *PG* 140, col. 641 B. No modern scholar dates this homily by Germanos II, but the reference to the Latins 'surrounded in Constantinople' would seem to suggest a date after the siege of 1234/5.

454 Auvray, *Reg.* III, no. 3395, 512–13. Nikolaos Chrissis has emphasized that Gregory IX's calls for a crusade in support of Latin Constantinople were in keeping with the precedent set down by Innocent III: N. Chrissis, 'The city and the cross: the image of Constantinople and the Latin Empire,' *Byzantine and Modern Greek Studies* 36 (2012), 21, 23.

INTRODUCTION 93

previously attempted, and that Gregory IX was increasingly willing to divert resources from other expeditions to support the Latin Empire.[455] Writing to Béla IV, king of Hungary, on 10 December 1234, Gregory IX announces that those who went to the aid of Latin Constantinople would attain 'the same remission of sins which they would have received if they assisted the aforementioned Holy Land in person.'[456] Only a month later the same message was sent to those preaching the crusade in France.[457] Gregory IX even attempted to enlist the aid of Frederick II Hohenstaufen for a crusade in the Balkans, telling the western emperor that the Greek people spread heresy, that they were abominations detested by God, and that they represented a severe threat to the God-fearing Latins.[458]

The second response from the pope to the contentious end of the *disputatio* was to excommunicate Vatatzes. Excommunicating the Byzantine emperor as a result of the failure of the *disputatio* in 1234 might seem unusual considering that the report of the friars portrays, perhaps inadvertently, that Vatatzes was a driving force toward union during the negotiations. Yet blaming the emperor for interference in ecclesiastical issues is consistent with the pope's outlook. The circumstances of Gregory IX's excommunication of the Byzantine emperor has not been addressed by modern scholars, perhaps because the sources describing this action are meagre and scattered. No bull of excommunication for Vatatzes has survived, therefore we cannot be certain when he was excommunicated. However, every source that attests to his excommunication is dated after 1234. It is possible, therefore, to regard the excommunication as part of the pope's reaction to the failure of the *disputatio* in Nicaea and Nymphaion.

---

455 Gregory IX began by planning parallel expeditions to Constantinople and the Holy Land. As it became increasingly difficult to raise support for the Latin Empire, however, Gregory IX was more likely to grant indulgences to crusaders who travelled to Constantinople, just as if they had gone to Jerusalem: N. Chrissis, *Crusading in Frankish Greece*, 115.

456 *concedimus veniam peccatorum, quam habituri forent, si predicte terre sancte personaliter subvenirent*, A. Theiner, *Vetera monumenta historica Hungariam sacram illustrantia*, vol. 1 (Rome: Typis Vaticanis, 1863), no. 249, 141 lines 20–21; Auvray, *Reg.* II, no. 2872, 217–18. Gregory IX exerts considerable effort to enlist Hungary in his crusade against the Empire of Nicaea. He frequently writes to the king and clergy of Hungary to encourage them to join the expedition: R. Spence, 'Gregory IX's attempted expeditions,' 163–76; N. Chrissis, *Crusading in Frankish Greece*, 83–120.

457 Auvray, *Reg.* II, nos 2909–11, 232–33.

458 C. Rodenburg, *Epistolae Saeculi XIII Regestis Pontificum Romanorum*, no. 724, 622–23.

94 THE DISPUTATIO

The earliest mention of the excommunication is in a letter of 1236 from Gregory IX to the archbishops of Hungary, in which the pope refers to *Vatacii excommunicati*, 'the excommunicated Vatatzes,' implying that the excommunication had already taken place.[459] Only two years later, in a letter to Frederick II dated 17 March 1238, Gregory IX again refers to the excommunication of Vatatzes, presenting it in relation to the *disputatio* of 1234.[460] The pope describes his attempts to negotiate with the Greek Church.

> We sent Dominican and Franciscan Friars to Vatatzes ... to the said Patriarch of Nicaea and the prelates and bishops under him ... urging them with paternal warnings and supplications ... to return to Catholic union. But they, as we learnt from the trustworthy report of the Friars, put forward a variety of errors against orthodox faith and, stopping their ears like the asps, could by no warning be induced to come back to the way of ecclesiastical unity. At this We were very much saddened, and ... against the said schismatical Vatatzes and his supporters, We publicly renew their excommunication once every year.[461]

This statement makes clear that Gregory IX envisioned the excommunication as punishment for the stubbornness of the Greeks, who would not listen to his 'paternal warning.'

The final evidence for the excommunication of Vatatzes comes much later, and is included as part of the canons of the Council of Lyons in 1245. The meeting did not produce an official bull of excommunication for Vatatzes, but his excommunication is mentioned in the papal bull deposing Frederick II. At that meeting, Pope Innocent IV condemns Vatatzes as 'an enemy of God and the church who, together with his counsellors

---

459 A. Theiner, *Vetera monumenta historica Hungariam*, no. 255, 144 line 6.

460 Tautu, *Acta*, no. 236, 314–15; Potthast, *Reg.*, no. 10542, 893; Auvray, *Reg.* II, no. 4110, 902–03; C. Rodenburg, *Epistolae Saeculi XIII Regestis Pontificum Romanorum*, no. 725, 623–24; Huillard-Bréholles, *Historia diplomatica Friderici secundi*, V, 181–83.

461 *Propter quod exemplo summi pastoris ovem perditam ad ovile dominicum propriis cupientes humeris reportare, ad Vatacium, dictum patriarchum Nicaenum, praelatos et clerum sibi subditos, Fratres Praedicatores et Minores, in lege divina plene paritos, transmisimus, paternis apud ipsos monitis et precibus insistentes, ut a sumno mortis exurgerent et fugientes a ventura ira, illucescente illis supernae claritatis lumine, se unioni catholicae reformarent. At ipsi sicut ex ipsorum Fratrum veridical relatione percepimus, diversos contra fidem orthodoxam proponentes errores et obturantes more aspidis aures suas, nullis potuerunt induci monitis, ut in viam redirent ecclesiasticae unitatis. Super quo vehementi dolore turbati, ne frustra sit nobis evellendi et plantandi coelitus collate potestas, contra dictum Vatacium schismaticum et eius fautores, qui excommunicati a nobis semel in annis singulis nuntiantur:* Tautu, *Acta*, no. 236, 314 lines 15–29; translated in J. Gill, *Byzantium and the papacy*, 272 note 91.

INTRODUCTION   95

and supporters, was solemnly separated by excommunication from the communion of the faithful.'[462]

None of these sources give us a definitive date for the excommunication of Vatatzes. The letters of Gregory IX, however, make clear that the measure was in response to the events of 1234. No text exists indicating that the predecessor of Vatatzes, Theodore I Laskaris, was himself excommunicated. Indeed, in their report the friars state that Vatatzes himself spoke of Theodore I's relationship with the papacy as altogether positive.[463] Thus, we must conclude that Vatatzes was the first of the Byzantine emperors in Nicaea to be excommunicated by the pope, and that this act was a reaction to the failure of church-union negotiations in 1234.

All of Gregory IX's frustrations at the failure of the *disputatio* are on display in a letter he wrote to Vatatzes, dated to 21 May 1237, warning that the Byzantine emperor would be punished by crusading armies if he continued to harass Latin Constantinople.[464] In a document which remains the only writing attributed to Vatatzes that has come down to us, the emperor scoffs at the pope's warnings.[465] The reply from Vatatzes is filled with irony and sarcasm. He even expresses an anxious optimism at the prospect of the new crusade promised by Gregory IX:

> Hearing this news, we were filled with much gladness and became full of happy expectations, reckoning according to reason that these avengers of the holy places will begin their revenge from our fatherland, and they will subject to a just punishment those holding it captive, as they defile the holy dwellings, insult the sacred vessels, and show every wickedness against Christians.[466]

---

462 *Dei et ecclesiae inimico a communione fidelium per excommunicationis sententiam cum adiutoribus, consiliatoribus et fautoribus suis solemniter separato*: ed. and transl. N. Tanner, *Decrees of the ecumenical councils*, vol. 1, *Nicaea I to Lateran V* (London: Georgetown University Press, 1990), 282 lines 36–39. This excommunication is also mentioned in the work of Matthew Paris, in his description of the Council of Lyons in 1245: Matthew Paris, *Chronica majora*, ed. H. Luard, vol. 4 (London: Longman, 1877), 453 lines 27–30; transl. J. Giles, *Matthew Paris's English History from the year 1235 to 1273*, vol. 2 (London: Henry Bohn, 1853), 84.

463 Golubovich, 'Disputatio,' ch. 21, 453 lines 1–2.

464 V. Grumel, 'L'Authenticité de la lettre de Jean Vatatzès, empereur de Nicée, au Pape Grégoire IX,' *Échos d'Orient* 29 (1930), 455–56; Auvray, *Reg*. II, no. 3693, 659–60.

465 V. Grumel, 'L'Authenticité de la lettre de Jean Vatatzès,' 450–58. There is some question regarding whether Gregory IX ever received the letter from Vatatzes: E. Mitsiou, 'Ideology and economy in the politics of John III Vatatzes,' 204 note 123.

466 *Τούτων ἀκούσαντες ἡμεῖς πολλῆς ἐπλήσθημεν τῆς θυμηδίας καὶ χρηστῶν ἐλπίδων μεστοὶ γεγόναμεν λογισάμενοι κατὰ τὸ εἰκός, ὅτι οἱ τῶν ἁγίων τόπων οὗτοι ἐκδικηταὶ ἀπὸ*

96   THE DISPUTATIO

The statement overflows with sardonic contradiction. Vatatzes implies that a true crusade should seek to punish those who have committed atrocities against Christians, such as those done in Constantinople in 1204.[467] Thus, he recommends that the crusaders should join him in restoring Constantinople to Byzantine rule! We can only imagine how the pope might have reacted to the suggestion that his crusade ought to attack, rather than defend, the Latin Empire.

The humour expressed by Vatatzes was not simply an idle threat, but was instead part of the emperor's explicit response to the failure of the parties to achieve a union of the churches. Following the departure of the friars in 1234, the emperor in Nicaea formalized an alliance with the Bulgarian ruler John II Asen. Since his victory at Klokotnitza in 1230, Asen had emerged as the most powerful ruler in the region, and the most potent threat to Constantinople.[468] A positive relationship had already developed between Vatatzes and Asen by 1233, as evidenced by the mission of Christopher of Ankyra, the exarch of Germanos II in the Balkans.[469] A letter from Christopher indicates that Asen was reconsidering his relationship with the Latins, and would look favourably toward dialogue

---

τῆς ἡμετέρας ἄρχονται πατρίδος τῆς τοιαύτης ἐκδικίας καὶ τοὺς αἰχμαλωτιστὰς αὐτῆς ἐκδίκῳ καθυποβαλοῦσι τιμωρίᾳ ὡς βεβηλώσαντας ἁγίους οἴκους, ὡς τοῖς θείοις σκεύεσιν ἐνυβρίσαντας, ὡς πᾶσαν ἀνοσιουργίαν ἐπιδειξαμένους κατὰ Χριστιανῶν: L. Pieralli, *La corrispondenza diplomatica dell'imperatore byzantino con le potenze estere nel tredicesimo secolo (1204–1282). Studio storicodiplomatistico ed edizione critica* (Vatican: Archivio segreto vaticano, 2006), no. 2, 125 lines 72–78.

467 Many of the comments made by Vatatzes in this response are similar to those made by Pope Innocent III when he condemned crusader actions in 1204: Hageneder, *Die Register Innocenz' III*, vol. 8, no. 232, 244–48. See also N. Chrissis, *Crusading in Frankish Greece*, 110–11; A. Papayianni, 'The papacy and the Fourth Crusade in the correspondence of the Nicaean emperors with the popes,' in *The papacy and the crusades: proceedings of the VIIth conference of the Society for the Study of the Crusades and the Latin East*, ed. M. Balard (Aldershot: Ashgate, 2011), 162.

468 For Bulgarian gains following the battle of Klokotnitza, see Akropolites, *History*, 42 line 15 – 43 line 3; transl. R. Macrides, 25.179.

469 For more on the mission of Christopher of Ankyra, see A. Karpozilos, *The ecclesiastical controversy*, 91; J. Langdon, 'The forgotten Byzantino-Bulgarian assault and siege of Constantinople, 1235–1236, and the breakup of the *entente cordiale* between John III Ducas Vatatzes and John Asen II in 1236 as background to the genesis of the Hohenstaufen-Vatatzes alliance of 1242,' in *Byzantina kai metabyzantina*, vol. 4, *Byzantine studies in honor of Milton V. Anastos*, ed. S. Vryonis (Malibu: Undena Publications, 1985), 123–24 note 5.

INTRODUCTION 97

with Nicaea.[470] Christopher's efforts gave Vatatzes an obvious avenue to pursue following the collapse of talks with the pope in 1234.[471]

George Akropolites records that the two rulers formalized their alliance at Kallipolis, which Vatatzes had recently seized from Venetian control.[472] While we do not know the exact date of their meeting – either late 1234 or early 1235 – we can rest assured that Vatatzes approached the prospect of alliance with Bulgaria as a result of the failed *disputatio* with the friars in 1234.[473] No source relating to those talks indicates whether Nicaea and Bulgaria had already reached an agreement and planned for an attack on Constantinople. In the report of the friars Vatatzes never makes mention of his relationship with the Bulgarian ruler, nor does he attempt to use that relationship to threaten the friars as papal representatives or as representatives of Latin Constantinople. While it is impossible to make an argument *ex silentio*, one might expect Vatatzes to have used the alliance to exert pressure on the friars to be more amenable to a compromise. We must, therefore, consider that no alliance yet existed during negotiations with the friars. The alliance was sealed by the marriage of Helen, daughter of Asen, to Theodore, the son of Vatatzes and future Byzantine emperor.[474]

---

470 See Christopher's letter to John II Asen in E. Kurtz, 'Christophoros von Ankyra als Exarch des Patriarchen Germanos II,' *Byzantinische Zeitschrift* 16 (1907), 141–42.

471 Sources disagree about who first sought the alliance. George Akropolites states that it was Vatatzes who first sent an embassy to propose an alliance: Akropolites, *History*, 48 line 22 – 49 line 5; transl. R. Macrides, 31.191. Nikephoros Gregoras, on the other hand, reports that an embassy from Bulgaria was sent to meet Vatatzes: Nikephoros Gregoras, *Historia*, ed. L. Schopen, 29 lines 15–18. Comments on the origin of this alliance by Andrea Dandolo are vague, but give the initiative to Asen: Andrea Dandolo, *Chronica*, ed. E. Pastorello, 295 lines 1–2.

472 Akropolites, *History*, 50 lines 9–19; transl. R. Macrides, 33.194.

473 Some have put the Nicaean–Bulgarian alliance at the end of 1234: J. Langdon, 'The forgotten Byzantino-Bulgarian assault,' 105; Dölger, *Reg.*, vol. 3, no. 1745, 14. Guy Perry has commented that Vatatzes sought the alliance with Bulgaria immediately following the *disputatio* of 1234: G. Perry, *John of Brienne*, 173. Robert Wolff put the alliance in 1235: R. Wolff, 'The Latin Empire of Constantinople, 1204–1261,' in *A history of the crusades*, ed. K. Setton, vol. 2 (Madison, WI: University of Wisconsin Press, 1969), 219. In a letter to the king of Hungary under the year 1235, Gregory IX mentions the seizure of Kallipolis by Vatatzes: A. Theiner, *Vetera monumenta historica Hungariam*, no. 249, 140–41. Presuming that the pope was well and promptly informed, we can safely conclude that the alliance between Vatatzes and John II Asen was confirmed in early 1235 at the latest.

474 George Akropolites records that Vatatzes, along with Helen and her mother, crossed to the Asian side of the Hellespont, where they met with the empress Eirene and Theodore, and the 'union of the children was concluded': Akropolites, *History*, 50 lines 19–25; transl.

98   THE DISPUTATIO

Several sources testify that Gregory IX was alarmed by the union between Nicaea and Bulgaria,[475] and the new allies demonstrated the threat they posed by promptly occupying Latin territory in Thrace and besieging Constantinople in 1235. Byzantine sources give few details for this joint action.[476] Latin sources, on the other hand, dwell so much on this siege that Guy Perry has referred to it as the 'defining event' of the reign of John of Brienne as Latin emperor.[477] The Latin Empire was saved only by the timely arrival of naval reinforcements from Italy and Frankish Greece.[478]

R. Macrides, 33.194. It does appear that Asen had second thoughts about the alliance and the marriage of Helen to Theodore in particular. George Akropolites explains that Asen forcibly retrieved Helen from her husband before their marriage was consummated. A series of sudden deaths, however, convinced the Bulgarian ruler that he was being divinely punished for breaking his oath to Vatatzes, and Asen promptly returned his daughter to her husband: George Akropolites, *History*, 52–53, 54–57; transl. R. Macrides 34.197–98, 36.200–01.

475 In a letter from 1236 Gregory IX instructs the clergy of neigbouring Hungary to announce the excommunication of John II Asen if he refused to break his alliance with Vatatzes: A. Theiner, *Vetera monumenta historica Hungariam*, no. 255, 144; Tautu, *Acta*, no. 214, 290; Auvray, *Reg.* II, no. 3156, 391. Nikolaos Chrissis mistakenly interpreted the letter as announcing the excommunication of John II Asen: N. Chrissis, *Crusading in Frankish Greece*, 102 note 71. However, Gregory IX clearly states that the excommunication is pending a final warning given to the Bulgarian Tsar. 'When we diligently warned the noble man Asen in our letters, we commanded that he end his association with the excommu-nicate Vatatzes, removing himself entirely from the molestation of the Latins, since if the aforesaid noble does not desire in this part to acquiesce to our warnings, you will arrange to excommunicate him and all his supporters and protectors, publicly announcing their excommunication' – *Cum nobilem virum Assanum litteris nostris monuerimus diligenter, ut a societate Vatacii excommunicati omnino recedens ab infestatione desisteret Latinorum, mandamus, quatenus si dictus nobilis monitis nostris acquiescere non curaverit in hac parte, ipsum et omnes in hoc adiutores ac fautores ipsius excommunicare curetis, ac eos excommunicatos publice nuntiantes*: A. Theiner, *Vetera monumenta historica Hungariam*, no. 255, 144 lines 5–9.

476 George Akropolites gives only vague statements about overrunning Latin positions, taking much booty, and turning the land into a 'Scythian desert': Akropolites, *History*, 51 lines 7–13; transl. R. Macrides, 33.195. Nikephoros Gregoras states that Vatatzes inspected the walls of Constantinople during the summer of 1235 before returning home: Nikephoros Gregoras, *Historia*, ed. L. Schopen, 30 lines 6–12. The only Byzantine source to describe the engagements of 1235 is the much later account of George of Pelagonia: George of Pelagonia, *Life of Vatatzes*, ed. A. Heisenberg, 222. See also J. Langdon, 'The forgotten Byzantino-Bulgarian assault,' 106, 109.

477 G. Perry, *John of Brienne*, 157. For a full discussion of the Latin sources discussing the siege of Constantinople by Vatatzes in 1235, see J. Langdon, 'The forgotten Byzantino-Bulgarian assault,' 105–35, especially 122 note 2.

478 Venice dispatched 25 galleys to Constantinople in 1235: Martin de Canale, *La*

INTRODUCTION   99

The particulars of the siege of 1235/36 need not delay us here. It is sufficient to note that the alliance between Vatatzes and Asen nearly brought Constantinople back into Byzantine control almost three decades before Michael VIII Palaiologos entered the city in 1261.[479] What is most significant for our purpose is that Vatatzes, rebuffed in his overtures to the pope, responded to the events of 1234 with a diplomatic triumph that nearly ended the story of Latin Constantinople.

The alliance with Bulgaria and the siege of 1235 represents a serious shift in the foreign policy of the Empire of Nicaea in Europe. Whereas circumstances had required Theodore I Laskaris to explore diplomatic initiatives regarding the Latins, Vatatzes after 1234 committed to near constant warfare against his enemies in Europe and an antagonistic posture regarding the papacy.[480] The campaigns Vatatzes directed in the Balkans in the 1230s and 1240s transformed the balance of power in the region. Before the negotiations with the papacy in 1234, the Empire of Nicaea had no stronghold in Europe; less than a decade later Nicaea had emerged as the foremost power in the region and an urgent threat to Latin Constantinople.

This achievement was secured by yet another alliance, this time between Vatatzes and Frederick II Hohenstaufen, the western emperor and frequent opponent of papal ventures. He had a keen interest in the Eastern Mediterranean. As king of Sicily and Jerusalem, Frederick II had a key

---

chronique des Veniciens de maistre Martin da Canal, ed. F. Galvani, *Archivio storico italiano*, series 1, VIII (Florence, 1845), 365; Andrea Dandolo, *Chronica*, ed. E. Pastorello, 295 lines 8–13; Lorenzo de Monacis, *Historiae Venetae*, ed. F. Cornelius, *Rerum Italicarum Scriptores*, vol. 8 (Venice, 1758), 147; Marino Sanudo the Younger, *Vite de' duchi di Venezia*, ed. L. Muratori, *Rerum Italicarum Scriptores*, vol. 22 (Milan, 1733), col. 552. Philippe Mouskes describes reinforcements coming to Constantinople from Pisa, Genoa, Venice, and from Geoffrey II Villehardouin: Philippe Mouskes, *Chronique*, ed. Reiffenberg, vol. 2, 620, vv. 29238–245. Aubry of Three Fountains discusses the reinforcements from Frankish Greece in some detail: Aubry of Three Fountains, *Chronica*, ed. P. Scheffer-Boichorst, 938 line 45 – 939 line 9.

479   John Langdon has said that Vatatzes came within 'an ace' of gaining Constantinople: J. Langdon, 'The forgotten Byzantino-Bulgarian assault,' 105.

480   The renewed militarism in the Empire of Nicaea under Vatatzes is best expressed by the *Imperial Statue*, a 'mirror of princes' by Nikephoros Blemmydes, written c. 1250, that praises the Byzantine emperor for his military feats: Nikephoros Blemmydes, *Imperial statue*, ed. and transl. H. Hunger and I. Ševčenko, *Des Nikephoros Blemmydes Βασιλικὸς Ἀνδριάς und dessen Metaphrase von Georgios Galesiotes und Georgios Oinaiotes. Ein weiterer Beitrag zum Verständnis der byzantinischen Schrift-Koine* (Vienna: Verlag der Österreichischen Akademie der Wissenschaften, 1986), 136–39.

100 THE DISPUTATIO

role in the affairs of the region. Some have suggested that he inherited and enhanced the vision of a Mediterranean empire held by his father, Henry VI.[481] He had often intervened in the Balkan region. Benvenuto di San Giorgio records that the western emperor gave large sums to William VI, marquis of Montferrat, who led an expedition to defend Thessalonike from Theodore Doukas in 1224.[482] Frederick II later seems to have shifted positions, possibly as a result of his excommunication by Gregory IX, supporting the cause of Theodore Doukas in the region.[483] Theodore's defeat at Klokotnitza meant that he was no longer a suitable ally for advancing Hohenstaufen policies, forcing Frederick II to find new partners in the East. He found in Vatatzes a ruler with similar problems. As mentioned above, Frederick II was often at odds with the papacy and was more than once the target of excommunication. He had that in common with Vatatzes. Thomas Van Cleve has explained that the western emperor increasingly viewed the pope not as a spiritual leader but as a temporal rival, and adds that Frederick II considered an end to papal interference in secular matters a

481 T. Van Cleve, *The Emperor Frederick II*, 9; D. Nicol, 'The Fourth Crusade and the Greek and Latin empires,' 275; M. Angold, 'Byzantium in exile,' 558; S. Borsari, 'Federico II e l'Oriente bizantino,' *Rivista Storica Italiana* 63 (1951), 279. Thomas Madden, however, has questioned whether the Hohenstaufen held grand designs for a Mediterranean empire: T. Madden, 'Vows and contracts in the Fourth Crusade: the Treaty of Zara and the attack on Constantinople in 1204,' *International History Review* 15 (1993), 443 note 3.

482 Benvenuto di San Giorgio, *Historia Montis-Ferrati ab origine marchionum illius tractus usque ad annum MCCCCXC*, ed. L. Muratori, *Rerum Italicarum Scriptores*, vol. 23 (Milan, 1733), col. 376 C–E; Huillard-Bréholles, *Historia diplomatica Friderici secundi*, II, 425–27. Nikolaos Chrissis has argued that Frederick II's support for William VI had more to do with the fact that the marquis was a vassal of the emperor, and that Frederick II had not joined the Latin cause in the Balkans: N. Chrissis, *Crusading in Frankish Greece*, 88. Filip Van Tricht has rejected this interpretation, insisting that Frederick II's loan to William VI was part of a larger ploy by the Hohenstaufen emperor to increase his influence over Latin Constantinople: F. Tricht, *The Latin Renovatio of Byzantium*, 384–85 note 127. See also S. Borsari, 'Federico II e l'Oriente bizantino,' 280.

483 George Akropolites records that Theodore Doukas commanded an army of 'Romans and Italians' at Klokotnitza, possibly referring to a force of auxiliaries sent by Frederick II: Akropolites, *History*, 41 lines 18–24, transl. R. Macrides, 25.178. Gregory IX excommunicated all Latins who fought with Theodore Doukas: Auvray, *Reg.* I, no. 332, 204–05. See also D. Nicol, *The Despotate of Epiros*, 109, 112 note 12; A. Kiesewetter, 'Die Heirat zwischen Konstanze-Anna von Hohenstaufen und Kaiser Johannes III. Batatzes von Nikaia (Ende 1240 oder Anfang 1241) und der Angriff des Johannes Batatzes auf Konstantinopel im Mai oder Juni 1241,' *Römische Historische Mitteilungen* 41 (1999), 246–48 note 19; Langdon, 'The forgotten Byzantino-Bulgarian assault,' 133 note 55.

INTRODUCTION   101

necessary step to maintaining imperial authority.[484] As enemies of the pope, Vatatzes and the western emperor were natural allies. The most important expression of their cooperation came in the marriage between Vatatzes and Constanza-Anna, the illegitimate daughter of Frederick II, in 1241.[485]

The correspondence between Frederick II and Vatatzes makes clear that opposing the papacy and its goals were the paramount focus of the allies. It is unfortunate that none of the replies from Vatatzes have come down to us, but the letters addressed to the Byzantine emperor from Frederick II assure the reader that it was animosity toward Rome that brought the two together. In a letter dated to 1248 the western emperor apprises Vatatzes on the progress of his conflict with the pope. He described 'hateful prelates' who plotted against him in secret, urging his subjects to rebellion.[486] The letter is based in the belief that it is the responsibility of princes to resist the evil ambitions of the church. Frederick II even expresses his envy for Vatatzes, who was free from the intrigues and plots of the pope.[487] Another letter, dated to 1250,[488] described 'manifest deceit and snares, which those

---

484 T. Van Cleve, *The Emperor Frederick II*, 187, 412. See also D. Nicol, *The Despotate of Epiros*, 144.

485 Anthony Kaldellis has described this union as the best way possible for Vatatzes to annoy the pope: A. Kaldellis, *Hellenism in Byzantium*, 372. The dating for this union has presented something of a problem for historians, who have placed it anywhere between 1241 and 1245. Andreas Kiesewetter has conclusively shown the marriage to date between May and June 1241, noting that a donation to the monastery of Lembos dated to March 1242 was made during the reign of Vatatzes and his new wife: Kiesewetter, 'Die Heirat zwischen Konstanze-Anna von Hohenstaufen und Kaiser Johannes III,' 239–50; see F. Miklosich and J. Müller, *Acta et diplomata graeca medii aevi sacra et profana*, vol. 4, *Acta et diplomata monasteriorum et ecclesiarum orientis tomus primus* (Vienna: Carolus Gerold, 1871), no. 20, 66 lines 4–5. In addition, two contemporary authors place the marriage in the thirteenth year of the reign of Doge Jacopo Tiepolo of Venice, i.e. 1242: Lorenzo de Monacis, *Historiae Venetae*, ed. F. Cornelius, 147 lines 36–68; Andrea Dandolo, *Chronica*, ed. E. Pastorello, 298 line 10: Both authors describe the union using the pluperfect, 'having already taken place': R. Macrides, *George Akropolites, The History*, 275 note 19. For more on this marriage see D. Nicol, 'Mixed marriages in Byzantium in the thirteenth century,' *Studies in Church History* 1 (1964), 164; J. Munitiz, 'A "wicked woman" in the 13th century,' *Jahrbuch der österreichischen Byzantinistik* 32:2 (1982), 529–37.

486 Huillard-Bréholles, *Historia diplomatica Friderici secundi*, VI.2, 685 line 21 – 686 line 2.

487 Huillard-Bréholles, *Historia diplomatica Friderici secundi*, VI.2, 686 lines 5–7. See also J. Martin, 'O felix Asia! Frédéric II, l'Empire de Nicée et le 'césaropapisme',' *Travaux et Mémoires* 14, *Melanges Gilbert Dagron* (2002), 473–83.

488 One edition of this letter is dated to October: F. Miklosich and J. Müller, *Acta et Diplomata Graeca Medii aevi*, vol. 3, no. 19, 75. Another is dated to July: E. Merendino,

102 THE DISPUTATIO

who pretend to be at the head of the church have woven against us, and perjuries, which they make every day, being committed to our death and taking the assurance of our stability and good health, they incited everyone to make difficulty for us.[489] These letters indicate that the western emperor expected a sympathetic response from Vatatzes as a fellow prince who had himself suffered from the schemes of the papacy.

All of this allows us to consider the accord between Vatatzes and Frederick II as an agreement between likeminded rulers. The western emperor had a history of disagreement with the papacy, and the emperor in Nicaea had recently failed to reach an agreement with papal representatives. In this regard, we must consider the alliance between Vatatzes and Frederick II, much like the alliance with John II Asen, as the direct result of the failure of the *disputatio* of 1234. That meeting's failure to end the schism and return Constantinople to Byzantine control had prompted Vatatzes to seek out others who opposed papal influence.[490] In Frederick II he found a powerful western ruler who had already developed an ideology opposing papal authority over secular affairs.[491] That the two would join their efforts against their common enemies is hardly surprising.

Each of these developments – the alliances between Vatatzes and John II Asen, the alliance between Vatatzes and Frederick II, the rise of Nicaean power in the Balkans, and the increased threat to Latin Constantinople

---

'Quattro lettere greche di Federico II,' in *Atti della Accademia di Scienze Lettere e Arti di Palermo*, vol. 34, series 4, part 2 (Palermo, 1974–1975), no. 3, 333.

489 Γνωρίζομεν τοίνυν αὐτῇ ὅτι οἱ τῆς Μάρκας καὶ Ῥωμανιόλας πιστο ἡμῶν, τοῦ κρείττονος καὶ ἐπιτερπεστέρου μέρους τῆς Ἰταλίας ὄντες, μαθόντες τὴν φανερὰν ἀπάτην καὶ τὰς δολοπλοκίας, ἃς οἱ δοκοῦντες προεστάναι τῶν ἐκκλησιῶν ἔρραπτον καθ' ἡμῶν, καὶ τὰς ἐπιορκίας ἃς ἐποίουν καθ' ἑκάστην τὸν ἡμέτερον βεβαιούμενοι θάνατον, καὶ τῆς ἡμετέρας εὐσταθείας καὶ εὐεξίας λαβόντες πληροφορίαν, ἅπαντες πρὸς τὴν ἡμετέραν ηὐτομόλησαν δεσποτείαν· E. Merendino, 'Quattro lettere greche di Federico II,' no. 3, 332 lines 10–17. See also F. Miklosich and J. Müller, *Acta et Diplomata Graeca Medii aevi*, vol. 3, no. 19, 75; N. Festa, 'Le lettere greche di Federigo II,' *Archivo storico Italiano* 13 (1894), no. 4, 29.

490 This does not negate the possibility that Vatatzes and Frederick II had already laid the foundation for cooperation and been in contact before 1234, but such a relationship seems less probable: E. Mitsiou, 'Ideology and economy in the politics of John III Vatatzes,' 196; J. Langdon, 'The forgotten Byzantino-Bulgarian assault,' 113.

491 Frederick II needed allies to oppose the designs of the papacy: S. Borsari, 'Federico II e l'Oriente bizantino,' 285. Even before his first excommunication, Frederick II had formulated and issued a strong statement listing the papal abuses done upon him in 1226. His letter does not survive, but its contents can be gleaned from the reply of Pope Honorius III: C. Rodenburg, *Epistolae Saeculi XIII Regestis Pontificum Romanorum*, no. 296, pp. 216–22; Huillard-Bréholles, *Historia diplomatica Friderici secundi*, II.1, 588–99.

INTRODUCTION   103

– were direct results of the failure of church-union negotiations in 1234. The result of that *disputatio* had immediate political ramifications in the Eastern Mediterranean and beyond. Alexander Maiorov has shown that the collapse of dialogue between Rome and Nicaea had far-reaching consequences, even causing a rift between the papacy and the Rus princes.[492] Negotiations toward ending the schism of the churches would not begin again until 1250.[493] These, and the precedent of dialogue at Nicaea and Nymphaion in 1234, were instrumental in bringing about the Union of Lyons in 1274.[494]

With so much depending on the *disputatio* of 1234, it is evident that more attention must be paid to the details of the negotiation. It is not sufficient to disregard church-union dialogues as inevitable failures or to summarize that perpetual schism was the result of political demands overriding those of the church. Examination of the sources surrounding 1234 shows that, if anything, political concerns prompted the parties to explore ways to end the schism, and that the Byzantine emperor in particular considered church union an effective and plausible reality that would allow him to further other, more pragmatic goals. Examination of the correspondence between Gregory IX and Germanos II reveals these pressures to compromise, and the report of the friars demonstrates how political and theological matters intermingled and would continue to influence one another for centuries to come.

---

492 A. Maiorov, 'Church-union negotiations between Rome, Nicaea and Rus, 1231–1237,' *Orientalia Christiana Periodica* 84 (2018), 385–405.

493 A. Franchi, *La svolta politico-ecclesiastica tra Roma e Bizanzio*; K. Setton, *The papacy and the Levant*, 70–71; J. Gill, *Byzantium and the papacy*, 88–96; A. Siecienski, *The filioque*, 126; A. Siecienski, *The papacy and the Orthodox*, 293–303; M. Angold, 'Byzantium in exile,' 555–56; W. Norden, *Das Papsttum und Byzanz. Die Trennung der beiden Mächte und das Problem ihrer Wiedervereinigung bis zum Untergange des byzantinischen Reichs (1453)* (Berlin: Behr, 1903), 362–66; L. Bréhier, 'Attempts and reunion of the Churches,' 608; J. Hussey, *The Orthodox Church in the Byzantine Empire*, 217–18; M. Angold, *Church and society in Byzantium*, 525–27.

494 George Pachymeres refers to the church-union negotiations under John III Vatatzes as a precedent for the Union of Lyons: George Pachymeres, ed. Failler, vol. 2, 479. See also A. Siecienski, *The papacy and the Orthodox*, 303–09; J. Gill, *Byzantium and the papacy*, 120–41; D. Angelov, *Imperial ideology and political thought in Byzantium*, 72: T. Kolbaba, 'Repercussions of the Second Council of Lyon (1274): theological polemic and the boundaries of orthodoxy,' in *Greeks, Latins, and intellectual history, 1204–1500*, ed. M. Hinterberger and C. Schabel (Leuven: Peeters, 2011), 43–68.

NOTE ON TRANSLATIONS

The goal of these translations is to follow the original text as faithfully as possible while rendering it into comprehensible English. Details will be provided when compromises are made. While there are multiple editions of the letters available, the following translations have focused on the text edited by Aloysius Tautu, as those are the most recent. The lone exception is the letter from Germanos II to the Roman Cardinals (Document II), for which the Greek text has been published by Christos Armpatzis.

TEXTS

I

PATRIARCH GERMANOS II
TO POPE GREGORY IX, 1232

Editions and translations

A. Tautu, *Acta Honorii III (1216–1227) et Gregorii IX (1227–1241)* (Vatican: Typis Polyglottis Vaticanis, 1950), no. 179a, 240–49

K. N. Sathas, *Μεσαιωνικὴ Βιβλιοθήκη*, vol. 2 (Venice, 1873), 39–46

J. Mansi, *Sacrorum conciliorum nova et amplissima collectio,* XXIII (Venice, 1779), 48–56

Matthew Paris, *Chronica majora*, ed. H. Luard, vol. 3 (London: Longman, 1876), 448–455; transl. J. Giles, *Matthew Paris's English History from the year 1235 to 1273*, vol. 1 (London: Henry Bohn, 1889), 98–104

Letter of the most holy lord Germanos, archbishop of Constantinople, new Rome and ecumenical patriarch, sent to Pope Gregory.

Oh Lord, save; oh Lord, grant success.[1] For you are the precious cornerstone, the chosen, the honoured, according to the words by which the prophet addresses you,[2] and I establish you as the foundation of this negotiation that will benefit the whole world.[3] For I have learned this from you, that anyone who believes in you will not be dishonoured,[4] nor will he be shaken from the foundation of his hopes. And this is the truth, and no one would dare oppose it, unless he had been plainly instructed by the father of

---

1 Psalm 118:25. It is worth noting that Germanos II here is reading the Septuagint, or Greek Old Testament, which at times will appear unusual to those accustomed to reading most modern English translations based on the Hebrew version. In the case of the Psalms, the numbering followed here follows the New Revised Standard Version.

2 Isaiah 28:16.

3 Rather than addressing the pope immediately, Germanos II here addresses Christ, appealing to him to arbitrate the dispute.

4 Isaiah 28:16.

108 THE DISPUTATIO

lies. It is your work as cornerstone to reconcile in the union of faith those matters divided in opinion. And Paul, in a voice even greater than that of Isaiah, bears witness that you proclaim peace to those near and far,[5] and by opening wide your arms upon the cross you summon together the furthest reaches of the *oikoumene*[6] to piety and draw them into fatherly embrace. Thus, I seek from you the unwavering path that leads to salvation. Prosper my discourse,[7] you who are the living word of the father, the all-powerful and *enhypostatic*[8] wisdom of God. Construct in me the framework[9] of this business. Be the foundation and the roof of it, you who, according to the theological voice of John,[10] are called the alpha and the omega, the infinite beginning and end of everything. This is our prayer.

And having first lifted our eyes to the heavenly heights, whence we prayed our help would come,[11] we now turn this discourse to you, most holy pope, who have obtained the primacy of the highest seat, that you will deign to come down a little from the summit of your glory. If indeed you are the imitator of God who dwells in the heights and looks down on things below,[12] give consideration to my words, though I am but humble and of weak voice. I shall commence; bend your ear graciously and admit my words. The manifold wisdom of God, which brings forth everything out of nothing, and continues to sustain them providentially in being, often starts from small matters, [and from them] later builds up great deeds which give benefit and salvation to all. For Joseph, as we know, was made a slave sold for silver, and was thrown into a prison pit and separated from the prisoners.[13] But what does Scripture say? The king sent and freed him and

---

5 Ephesians 2:17. The Latin translation does not include the name and description of Paul, although the unattributed quotation is kept, introduced simply by *tu enim*: Tautu, *Acta*, no. 179a, 240.

6 i.e. 'the inhabited world.' See *ODB* III, sub Oikoumene.

7 i.e. λόγος.

8 i.e. 'personified,' from ἐνυπόστας, referring to Christ: G. Lampe, *A Patristic Greek lexicon*, 485–86. See also 'Enhypostasia' in F. Cross and E. Livingstone, *Oxford dictionary of the Christian Church*, 3rd edn (Oxford: Oxford University Press, 2005), 549–50. The Latin text of this letter in the papal register translates the word ἐνυπόστας into *consubstantialis*: Tautu, *Acta*, no. 179a, 240 lines 33–34, suggesting a rift or misconception in their Trinitarian theology.

9 From οἶκον, thus keeping the metaphor of the cornerstone.

10 Revelation 21:6.

11 Cf. Psalm 121:1.

12 Psalm 113:5–6.

13 Genesis 37:28.

PATRIARCH GERMANOS II TO POPE GREGORY IX   109

even made him ruler of the people. How glorious, how marvellous, how God was glorified through these happenings, has not escaped your notice.

To what purpose is this example? What does it suggest? These present holy brothers will explain to your holiness how, finding themselves in a particularly precarious situation, and in fear of being condemned,[14] they approached the most holy and mighty emperor, my autokrator,[15] who deemed them worthy of consideration, and presented them to our most humble person. The good companionship and unbreakable harmony of these brothers, whose number was equal to the wise virgins,[16] was such that the lamp of their deeds and the light which emanates from it shines before men toward the glory of the heavenly father, and the oil of the wise they continually add to their good works, lest the light go out, and they revert to the sleep of apathy and be barred entry to the kingdom.[17] All of them were without staff, wearing only a single garment, and unshod.[18] Now I surmise that their feet were, as the Apostle says, made beautiful,[19] as they proclaimed[20] peace and good tidings between Greeks and Latins. In short, they were wholly nimble and the swiftest runners, hastening to come to Christ, the summit of all good things, which attaining, they will stay the course and attain their desire. These men, therefore, who are *humble brothers* before God,[21] being thus united in thought and purpose, and fulfilling a group in the number of five, seemed to us a good sign, and led us to have high hopes that, with the help of God, the Christ-loving unity and harmony of the five patriarchates would come about. They entered our house, according to divine providence, which I believe

---

14 οἱ περιστατικῷ τινι συναντήματι καὶ φόβῳ τῶν κατακρίτων: Tautu, *Acta*, no. 179a, 241 line 46 – 242 line 1. The Latin wording, *periculosus occursus iniutus carcer*, more explicitly suggests that the friars were imprisoned, perhaps carrying over the reference to Joseph by way of comparison: Tautu, *Acta*, no. 179a, 241 line 41 – 242 line 1.

15 i.e. John III Vatatzes. The Latin text makes no mention of the emperor's role in coming to the aid of the friars.

16 i.e. five. See Matthew 25:2.

17 Matthew 25:1–13.

18 Cf. Matthew 10:10.

19 Romans 10:15; Isaiah 52:7.

20 The Greek verb used here is εὐαγγελιζουμένων, literally to 'evangelise' or to 'preach the good news': Tautu, *Acta*, no. 179a, 242 line 22.

21 οἱ κατὰ Θεὸν εὐτελεῖς ἀδελφοί: Tautu, *Acta*, no. 179a, 242 line 30, *Minores Fratres* in the Latin: i.e. Franciscans. The lack of precision in how Germanos II refers to the friars may be due to the fact that the order was still a relatively recent phenomenon, see Introduction Section 6.

110   THE DISPUTATIO

governs everything to advantage. After many words had been exchanged between us, more than other things we discussed the long-lasting schism of the seamless garment of piety, woven from on high, and bestowed upon the catholic church of the Christians by the hands of the apostles.[22] The distinguished gatherings of the holy fathers and teachers encircled it with a belt, but contentious hands, indeed not those of soldiers, but ecclesiastic hands have visibly divided and torn [the garment]. The schism is great and of long duration, and there is no one who shows compassion for the bride of Christ wearing a torn garment, or laments her disgrace.

David also, I believe, laments this in the psalms, saying: *they were separated, yet they were not heavy of heart.*[23] For if we had been heavy of heart, we would have been distraught, we would have suffered and been in distress. And if we had experienced such affliction and distress, we would have called on the name of the Lord.[24] He would have been among us, as earlier he was among his disciples, making peace, and addressing uncertainty. Indeed, are his very entrails not being mauled?[25] Does he not grieve at the disagreement? Yes, exceedingly. For he is the Father, more loving than all fathers,[26] and he cannot endure to see those he loves[27] separated from each other by hatred, consuming one another in the manner of fish, as the greater demonstrate arrogance towards the lesser, and the strong trample on the weak. Did Peter, the fisher of men, teach you to do thus – Peter who, contrary to his former conduct, led those who were caught from death to life? Oh! Who will give water to my head and my eyes, font of my tears, that I may lament throughout the days and nights over the destruction of new Zion,[28] the church gathered from the nations? How have the chosen people of God been divided into Judah and Israel, and our cities into Jerusalem and Samaria? For the same occurred in the

22 Cf. John 19:23–24.

23 Cf. Psalm 35:15–16.

24 Psalm 50:15; 116:17.

25 A visceral image of the Church being torn apart.

26 The Greek word here, φιλοστοργότερος, refers to the 'tender affection' of a parent to a child: Tautu, *Acta*, no. 179a, 243 line 26; while the Latin, *piisimus*, speaks of tender affection: Tautu, *Acta*, no. 179a, 243 line 30.

27 The Greek word φίλτατα refers to those 'dearest' or 'most beloved': Tautu, *Acta*, no. 179a, 243 line 27, while the Latin translation of this word, *pignera*, refers to those one is 'bound' or 'pledged to,' almost in a legal sense, suggesting the language of ownership and transactions over that of fatherly affection: Tautu, *Acta*, no. 179a, 243 line 31.

28 Cf Jeremiah 9:1.

PATRIARCH GERMANOS II TO POPE GREGORY IX   111

case of Cain and Abel, and Esau and Jacob, who were brothers by nature but enemies and contrary in thought. I hesitate to put forth this example, lest I dishonour the role of brotherhood and seem to steal the birthright of the first-born. Besides, our father has not grown old, nor has his sight diminished, and to those unjustly oppressed he shows his blessing.[29] Now these things are indeed bitter, and to your perceptive heart they gnaw insatiably at the bones.[30]

Now, what remains to be said is more grievous and fearful than all dangers, and both sharper and more piercing than any cutting dagger or two-edged sword, against whichever men it is brought down, either Latins or Greeks. What is this? Let us hear what Paul said: *If we, or an angel from heaven, preaches to you something different to what you have received, let him be anathema.*[31] And he does not strike with this sword only once, but a second time, that he might cause greater pain by the second blow, so that those who fear the death of the soul[32] will seek the care of a physician.

Now what do I say? Let us shake off every other care, every thought, every confusion from our heart, as dirt from our feet, and with all zeal examine whom this trouble and two-edged sword cuts, and what limbs have been cut away from the ecclesiastical whole, of which the head is Christ. For [if it cut] us Greeks, show us the blow, dress the wound, since we brothers are at risk of destruction. Be persuaded by Solomon, the wise man who says in the proverb: *brothers are made useful in adversity.*[33] Better yet, listen to God himself, who gave wisdom to Solomon, when he said through the prophet: *if you bring forth what is worthy from what is unworthy, you will be as my mouth.*[34] Wherefore we Greeks are free

---

29 The Latin here reads somewhat differently: 'Besides, our father is neither old nor do his eyes grow dim, *but residing in heaven, he sees all things clearly* and bestows his blessing upon all those who are unjustly oppressed.' – *Verumtamen nec pater noster senuit nec oculi eius caligaverunt, sed in coelis existens, liquide omnia videt et hiis qui iniuste oppressi sunt benedictionem largitur:* Tautu, *Acta,* no. 179a, 244 lines 9–14.

30 Again, the Latin reads somewhat differently from the Greek: 'Now these things are indeed bitter, and to *the* perceptive heart *they are like maggots in the bones, if they are frequently remembered.*' – *Sunt quippe sunt haec amara et intelligenti cordi tinea ossium, si frequenter ad memoriam deducantur:* Tautu, *Acta,* no. 179a, 244 lines 14–17.

31 Galatians 1:8.

32 ψυχικὸν: Tautu, *Acta,* no. 179a, 244 line 30.

33 Proverbs 17:17.

34 Jeremiah 15:19.

112   THE DISPUTATIO

from cuts and wounds from the accursed sword.[35] The deepest cuts are made against the Italians and Latins. The blade presses down to slay and destroy some, but we believe you will not allow yourselves to be harmed by ignorance and harmful passions, to be separated from the inheritance of Christ, for whom each of us would endure countless deaths, if it were possible. That discord and disagreement over dogma, and the dissolution of canonical rules, and the alteration of the customs handed down from the fathers: these are the walls that separate what had once been united in the bond of peace and concord.[36] When the *oikoumene* becomes one whole it will proclaim [this] aloud.[37]

Hence it is that enemies come against one another without making peace, destroying one another,[38] sealing the ecclesiastical gates against all kinds of holy acts, so that God could not be praised by Greek voices.[39] Only one thing was lacking, and it too has now happened, that the opportunity might arise for martyrdom, and the tyrannical tribunal be set up, and the throne of martyrdom be opened, that we may descend into the arena of martyrdom, to take up the good fight, and be crowned by the right hand of the all-mighty. The famous island of Cyprus knows what I say. It saw clearly the new martyrs and soldiers of Christ, who first crossed the sea of the tears of contrition, and for a long time were purified by the sweat that comes from the terrible suffering of the body. In the end they passed

---

35 τῆς μαχαίρας τοῦ ἀναθέματος: Tautu, *Acta*, no. 179a, 245 lines 11–12, i.e. 'the blade that causes anathema.' The Latin translation of this phrase is much less clear as to whether the Greeks have avoided such wounds, saying instead *Si autem nos quidem Graeci sine plaga sumus*, or '*If* we Greeks are free from cuts … ': Tautu, *Acta*, no. 179a, 245 lines 12–13.

36 Put simply, Germanos II charges that it is the Latins who have erred, not the Greeks.

37 This following is found in the Latin text and preserved by Matthew Paris, but is not found in the original Greek – Bearing witness to the Lord, invoking heaven and earth in testimony, which we, being united in your hands, and you with us, we urgently ask that we make a careful search to the depths of truth, with the invocation of the Holy Spirit, so that we will no longer be disfigured by the schismatic and unjust scandal, or be slandered by Latins, nor you corrupted by Greeks. And that we may arrive at the kernel of truth, many powerful and noble men would obey you if they did not fear the unjust seizures and reckless enforcement of power and excessive servitude that you extort from them: Tautu, *Acta*, no. 179a, 245–46; Matthew Paris, 452. For a slightly different translation, see transl. J. Giles, 101–02.

38 A possible reference to the events of 1204.

39 A possible reference to the actions of Cardinal Pelagius, who, according to George Akropolites, attempted to oppress the Greek population when he was papal legate to Constantinople in 1213: Akropolites, *History*, 29 line 20 – 30 line 2, transl. R. Macrides, 155.

PATRIARCH GERMANOS II TO POPE GREGORY IX 113

through fire and water, and God, the judge of the contest, led them to heavenly relief.[40]

Are these things good, most holy successor of the apostle Peter? Does the disciple of Christ – Christ who is gentle and humble of heart – command this? Does he instruct the elders thus in his letter when he says: *I call on the elders among you, myself a fellow-elder and witness to the sufferings of Christ, and fellow partaker of the glory that is to be revealed, tend the flock of God among you, not by force but willingly, not for shameful gain but eagerly, not to gain dominion over those allotted to you, but being as examples to your flock. And when the chief shepherd is made known, you will receive the unfading crown of glory.*[41] This is the teaching of Peter, and those who do not obey it will see. That part of the letter, which affords us some consolation, [is where he] commands those still suffering under various trials to rejoice, so that the proof of our faith might be found to be worth much more than the gold that perishes. It has been tested through fire, that it might bring praise, glory and honour at the appearance of Jesus Christ.[42]

But give heed [to us], holy lord, most sympathetic and gentle of all the previous arch-priests of elder Rome, and bear with these words, which contain bitterness, for they are the product of a suffering heart, and allowance is given to men of discretion who speak sharply out of grief. Gird up your loins like a man and light your lamp of wise judgement.[43] Seek the lost coin of union in faith,[44] and we will share in the labours with your holiness. We will not spare our feeble body, nor make excuses regarding old age, nor the long journey. For when the task is particularly strenuous, so much greater are the wreaths of victory. For each will receive according to his own labour,[45] as said Paul, for whom, as a runner, the whole inhabited world was a stadium, and who won the glorious wreath.

We are not in ignorance, oh most holy lord, that just as we Greeks assert that we uphold the correct belief and live piously in all things, and that in nothing are we in error with respect to apostolic and patristic doctrines, the

---

40 Germanos II here refers to the recent execution of several Greek monks on the Latin-controlled island of Cyprus in 1231.

41 1 Peter 5:1–5.

42 1 Peter 4:12–13.

43 Again, referring to the parable of the wise virgins, Matthew 25:1–13.

44 Luke 15:8–10.

45 1 Corinthians 3:8.

THE DISPUTATIO

church of Elder Rome also maintains the same about itself, and because it does not think it has been in error in any way, it does not ask for cure or correction. We know that this is said by the church of the Greeks, and by that of the Latins; for no one is able to see genuine disgrace in his own face, if one does not look into a mirror, or is told by another, or understands the appearance in some other way, whether ugly or not.[46] We also have mirrors that are both plentiful and most clear, namely the luminous gospel of Christ, the letters of the apostles, the books of the theological fathers. Let us examine these. They will teach us what kind of spirit each man holds, either corrupted, or genuine. The one who is summoned to the trial of the mirror must confess, when he departs, however unwillingly, to having seen the deformed face.

May God make haste to crush Satan under our feet,[47] may the peace-maker crush the war-maker, may he who is the cause of every good crush the one who hates good, may the God of love crush the stumbling block.[48] And may he send to us, shepherds of rational sheep, his angel announcing great joy, as long ago, upon his birth in the flesh, he sent to the shepherds of sheep and beasts without reason, and deem us worthy to sing that marvellous hymn: *Glory to God in the highest, and on earth peace, goodwill to men.*[49] And may we greet each other with a holy kiss: *the grace of our lord Jesus Christ, the love of God the Father, and the fellowship of the Holy Spirit, be with us all. Amen.*[50]

46 James 1:23.
47 Romans 16:20.
48 i.e. the devil.
49 Luke 2:14.
50 2 Corinthians 13:12–14.

II

PATRIARCH GERMANOS II
TO THE ROMAN CARDINALS, 1232

Editions and Translations

A. Tautu, *Acta Honorii III (1216–1227) et Gregorii IX (1227–1241)* (Vatican: Typis Polyglottis Vaticanis, 1950), no. 179b, 249–52

Christos Armpatzis, Ἀνέκδοτη ἐπιστολή τοῦ πατριάρχη Κωνσταντινουπόλεως Γερμανοῦ Β΄ πρὸς τοὺς καρδιναλίους τῆς Ρώμης (1232),' *Ἀθήνα: Εταιρία Βυζαντινών Σπουδών* (2006), 373–78

Matthew Paris, *Chronica majora*, ed. H. Luard, vol. 3 (London: Longman, 1876), 455–60; transl. J. Giles, *Matthew Paris's English History from the year 1235 to 1273*, vol. 1 (London: Henry Bohn, 1889), 104–08

Letter to all the Cardinals of Rome.

Most holy and admired and wise cardinals of the most holy pope and elder Rome and the apostolic throne.

Good counsel, together with help and support in things which must be done, are certainly a good thing in this life, and necessary for all. For often God concealed from one what he revealed to another, and thus through counsel he introduced what he has revealed to the public and gain is distributed to all the subject multitude. If there are many counsellors, and they are prudent and wise, how much profit, how much advantage to all governed [and] subject people. For if the man without counsel is an enemy to himself, as Solomon and truth say,[1] then clearly he who has much and good counsel will bring many friends to his favor and will attract his friends.[2] The prophet Isaiah bears witness that [consultation] is both

---

1 Proverbs 11:14; Luke 14:31.

2 τοὺς αὐτοῦ φίλους ἐφελκύσεται: Armpatzis, Ἀνέκδοτη ἐπιστολή τοῦ πατριάρχη Κωνσταντινουπόλεως Γερμανοῦ Β΄ πρὸς τοὺς καρδιναλίους τῆς Ρώμης (1232),' 373 lines

116   THE DISPUTATIO

divine and heavenly when he calls the *enhypostatic*[3] word of the father and the angel of great counsel 'the wonderful counsellor.'[4] Clearly, taking counsel from the father is thought of in a way befitting the divinity for the removal of disagreements between persons, for according to the nature of the divinity there is both one design and one will of the Father, the Son, and the Spirit. Great, therefore, is the esteem for good counsellors, who are of like mind with the Ruler and Lord, if the counsellors are acceptable to him [and they work] for the salvation of humanity.

Since, therefore, by the goodwill of heavenly providence, which arranges everything to consensus, great and reputable Rome enriched you worthy counsellors with her greatest majesty and honor, distinguishing yourselves above all previous cardinals in terms of judgement and reverence, as the most pious friars expressed to our humility,[5] I beseech your holiness,[6] rise above the spiritual contest, don the armor of the spirit, and bring down the dividing wall of ancient enmity that is within the Frankish church.[7] For your weapons are capable of overcoming such obstacles, and tearing down this division you will make peace between those who are separated. You will unite with the bonds of love and common faith the things which have been broken apart for a long time.[8] You will become wonderful counsellors

13–14. The Latin here reads 'he also attracts enemies,' *et ipsos etiam attrahit inimicos*: Tautu, *Acta*, no. 179a, 250 line 8.

3 Again, Germanos II uses the term ἐνυπόστας, or *enhypostatic*, which the Latin translation in the papal register made into *consubstantialis*: Tautu, *Acta*, no. 179b, 250 line 9. The same issue appears in the Latin translation of his first letter: See Source I; Tautu, *Acta*, no. 179a, 240 lines 33–34.

4 Isaiah 9:6. On the 'angel of great counsel,' i.e. Christ, see J. Trigg, 'The angel of great counsel: Christ and the angelic hierarchy in Origen's theology,' *Journal of Theological Studies* 42 (1991), 35.

5 A reference to an apparent conversation between Germanos II and the five Franciscans who met with him in 1232.

6 Literally, 'the holiness among you,' τῆς ὑμῶν ἱερότητος: Armpatzis, Ἀνέκδοτη ἐπιστολή του πατριάρχη Κωνσταντινουπόλεως Γερμανού Β´ πρὸς τοὺς καρδιναλίους τῆς Ρώμης (1232),' 374 line 28.

7 Ephesians 2:14. The use of 'Frankish' here to describe the western church is unusual. Germanos II may be making a play on words, i.e. the 'division,' φραγμοῦ, and the Franks, φραγκικῆς: Armpatzis, Ἀνέκδοτη ἐπιστολή του πατριάρχη Κωνσταντινουπόλεως Γερμανού Β´ πρὸς τοὺς καρδιναλίους τῆς Ρώμης (1232),' 374 line 30. Thus, the implication being that, whatever problems exist, they are due to the Latins. The Latin here misses the play on words, reading 'the Church of the Latins and the Greeks': Tautu, *Acta*, no. 179a, 250 line 23.

8 The Latin adds 'of peace and love and common faith': Tautu, *Acta*, no. 179a, 250 lines 25–26.

PATRIARCH GERMANOS II TO THE CARDINALS   117

pleasing to God for the most holy and exalted pope, recognizing that this man is desiring of the spirit, a peace-maker, most gentle, and as is suggested by his name[9] is always watchful and praying, awaiting the time when his Ruler will come[10] and deem him worthy of the sweetest blessings, he who, in the candour of his heart, tends to the people of Christ and in the wisdom of his own hands guides them to the pastures of paradise. For hands in scripture indicate action.

Now, being confident in the honest promise of the all-powerful Christ who accomplishes his power in our weakness,[11] we have advanced a proposal of union and offered a peaceful letter to the most holy pope.[12] I pray to the king of the heavens, who bore the form of a servant for us, his unworthy servants, who was exalted upon the cross and lifted up to himself those who had fallen into the pit of vice, that he would banish from our hearts all arrogance which is excited against our brotherly union, and illuminate our purpose with the light of knowledge. In order that we all say the same of him and not have schism within us, let us be reconciled in the same mind and in the same judgement,[13] and let it not be said between us, just as it was among the Corinthians, that *I belong to Kephas, or I belong to Paul, or I belong to Apollo, or I belong to Christ*,[14] but everyone be called 'of Christ,' which is why we are called Christians, and greet one another in the peace of Christ and carry within that evangelical voice, saying, that which is ordained to be first, shall be last;[15] and the apostolic teaching says this, *One Lord, one faith, one baptism*.[16] Once, all Italians and Greeks assembled under this

---

9 The name of the pope, Gregory, and the Greek word γρηγορος, meaning 'watchful': G. Lampe, *A Patristic Greek lexicon*, 324.

10 Matthew 24:45–47.

11 Cf 2 Corinthians 12:9.

12 See Source I.

13 1 Corinthians 1:10.

14 1 Corinthians 1:12. Interestingly enough, the order of names differs from what is found in the Latin, where it reads 'I belong to Paul, or I belong to Apollo, or I belong to Cephas,' *ego quidem sum Pauli, ego autem Apollo, ego autem Cephae*: Tautu, *Acta*, no. 179b, 250 lines 44–45.

15 Cf Mark 9:35. The preceding does not appear in the Latin version of this letter: Tautu, *Acta*, no. 179b, 251; Armpatzis, 'Ἀνέκδοτη επιστολή του πατριάρχη Κωνσταντινουπόλεως Γερμανού Β´ προς τους καρδιναλίους της Ρώμης (1232),' 375 line 57.

16 Ephesians 4:5. Added in the Latin version by Matthew Paris – Let us be allowed to confess truth, and you take on the form of friends, and it be possible to confess the truth without punishment. Because it is also written: *the words of a wise man who speaks truth*

118   THE DISPUTATIO

same faith, under the same canons, living peaceably with one another, defending one another, crushing the enemies of the church. [Those] who were persecuted from the east,[17] where the tyranny of heretics reigns, ran with great haste to great Rome, as to the unshaken tower of strength. And Rome, often made subject under the nations,[18] was liberated from [this] tyranny by the empire of the Greeks.[19] Agapetus and later Vigilius sought refuge in Constantinople from uprisings in Rome.[20]

and corrects are as nails fixed in deep (Ecclesiastes 12:11). And although much truth creates enemies, which I do fear, still I will confess. The division of our unity proceeded from the tyranny of your oppression and the demands of the Roman Church, which is made a step-mother instead of mother, who has driven away her own children long ago, like a rapacious bird expelling her young. How much more humble and prone to her, so much more she despises them and holds them all the more worthless, not recalling the gospel saying: *whoever exalts himself will be humbled* (Matthew 23:12). Therefore, may modesty govern you, and may Roman greed, although it is natural to her, be calmed for a while and let us begin the search for truth; and having undertaken the search for truth, both sides will be returned to the solidarity of union: Tautu, *Acta*, no. 179b, 252 note 4; Matthew Paris, 457 lines 16–32.

17 A possible reference to the Arab invasions of the seventh century, which claimed several eastern provinces from Byzantine control.

18 The Greek term here, ἐθνῶν, is open to interpretation: Armpatzis, Ἀνέκδοτη ἐπιστολή τοῦ πατριάρχη Κωνσταντινουπόλεως Γερμανοῦ Β΄ πρὸς τοὺς καρδιναλίους τῆς Ρώμης (1232),' 376 line 64. The phrase may imply that the same 'tyranny of heresy' that reigns in the East once threatened Rome itself.

19 Rome had been attacked by Arab raiders as recently as 846: T. Lankila, 'The saracen raid of Rome in 846: an example of maritime *Ghazw*,' in *Travelling through time: essays in honour of Kaj Öhrnberg*, ed. S. Akar, J. Hämeen-Anttila and I. Nokso-Koivisto, *Studia Orientalia* 114 (Helsinki: Finnish Oriental Society, 2013), 93–120. However, by this reference, Germanos II may also be recalling the long Byzantine wars fought in Italy against the Goths and Lombards: M. Whittow, *The making of Orthodox Byzantium, 600–1025* (Basingstoke: Macmillan, 1996), 298–303.

20 The Latin text adds that the two popes were 'received with honor,' *honorifice fuere recepti*: Tautu, *Acta*, no. 179b, 251 line 10.

Agapetus, pope from 535 to 536, travelled to Constantinople as an envoy of the Ostrogothic king Theodahad, and there became involved in arguments within the Eastern Church: *Liber Pontificalis: texte, introduction et commentaire*, ed. L. Duchesne, vol. 1 (Paris: Thorin, 1886), 287–89; transl. R. Davis, *The Book of Pontiffs (Liber Pontificalis): the ancient biographies of the first ninety Roman bishops to AD 715* (Liverpool: Liverpool University Press, 1989), 59.52–53; *ODB* I, sub Agapetus I; E. Ferguson, ed., *Encyclopedia of early Christianity*, 2nd edn (London: Garland Publishing, 1998), 25–26. Vigilius was pope from 537 to 555. He had spent time in Constantinople as a representative of the pope before his own papacy. He was heavily involved in the Three Chapters controversy: *Liber Pontificalis*, ed. L. Duchesne, vol. 1, 296–302; transl. R. Davis, *The Book of Pontiffs*, 61.56–59; *ODB* III,

PATRIARCH GERMANOS II TO THE CARDINALS   119

Now, alas, we have been divided as enemies by bitter separation. We injure and are injured by one another and avoid communion with one another as if it were harmful to the soul. What, therefore, can we say? If it is us who are laid low, raise us up. Do not seek our physical downfall, but look to the spiritual resurrection and we will give thanks to you as the patrons of our salvation. If, however, the error and origin of the scandal came from elder Rome and the successors of the apostolic throne of Peter, acknowledge his apostolic words, which Paul writes to the Galatians, saying thus: *When Peter came to Antioch, I opposed him to his face, because he was to be blamed,*[21] and other things. Paul says such thereafter, reproaching Peter. In addition, this opposition was intended to arouse not some sort of fight or ill-timed rivalry but a stronger economy[22] which aroused a timely agreement.[23] Do you see what a good thing it is for brother to be helped by brother? Indeed, God alone is in want of nothing, nor needs help from anyone. All men need the cooperation of one another even if they are exceedingly gifted with pride and wisdom. If I have not revered the great apostle Peter, leader of the group of disciples of Christ, the rock of the faith, I would remind you of how the rock of that foundation was shaken and moved by a miserable woman, as Christ, who knew his

---

sub Vigilius; E. Ferguson, *Encyclopedia of early Christianity*, 1161. For more on both of these figures see A. Siecienski, *The papacy and the Orthodox*, 188–89.

Added in the version by Matthew Paris – They were guarded and protected, although, as may have been a welcome exchange, you never offered us sanctuary or aid in difficult circumstances. But it is right that we be generous even toward the ungrateful. Even for pirates are the seas subdued and God causes the sun to rise over the just as well as the unjust (Matthew 5:45). Alas: Tautu, *Acta*, no. 179b, 252 note 5; Matthew Paris, 458 lines 12–16.

21 Galatians 2:11.

22 οἰκονομίας: Armpatzis, 'Ἀνέκδοτη ἐπιστολή τοῦ πατριάρχη Κωνσταντινουπόλεως Γερμανοῦ Β´ πρὸς τοὺς καρδιναλίους τῆς Ρώμης (1232),' 376 line 79, i.e. how God orders the world: *ODB* III, sub *Oikonomia*; E. Ferguson, *Encyclopedia of early Christianity*, 825–27. Thus, while God might ordain that there be schism at one time, he might well ordain that the schism be healed in another.

23 Added in the version by Matthew Paris – Indeed, they were tightly joined by Christ in the bond of affection, agreeing in faith and doctrine, and separated by no ambition or greed. Would that you were more like them in these matters! However, it produces a modicum of offense in our minds that, being greedy only for possessions, you can scratch everywhere for gold and silver from the flock, yet you call yourselves disciples of him who said: *I have no gold and silver* (Acts 3:6). You subject kingdoms to tribute, having accumulated money in business. Unlearn in actions what you preach with your words. May temperance moderate you, that you may be an example to us and an example to the whole world: Tautu, *Acta*, no. 179b, 252 note 7; Matthew Paris, 458 line 33 – 459 line 10.

120   THE DISPUTATIO

decisions, and *whose judgements are a great deep,*[24] allowed to happen, using the aforementioned rooster to remind [Peter]. [Christ] reminded Peter of the prophecy and the sound of the rooster roused him from the sleep of despair.[25] Being roused, [Peter] washed his face in tears and confessed to God and to all the world, becoming the model of repentance, lifting up the keys of the kingdom and running quickly to all men and saying: *Does he who falls not rise again?*[26] Rise, [you] who have fallen, look upon me and hasten to follow me to paradise, whose gates I have received the authority to open.

I write these things to your holiness only for recollection, for I know that you are filled with all wisdom and knowledge. But being persuaded by the wisdom of Solomon I have written these words, for he said: *give opportunity to the wise and wisdom will be added to him; teach the just and he will hasten to receive.*[27] This alone will I add, [and then] I will end my piece: that there are many and great nations of like mind and in fellowship with us Greeks in all things. First, in the first part of the East, dwell the Ethiopians, then all the Syrians, to the north the most manly Iberians,[28] the Abasgs,[29] the Lazi, the Alans, the Goths, the Khazars, the innumerable Russian peoples, and the conquering kingdom of the Bulgarians.[30] All of these hold to our church as a mother, remaining unshaken in the ancient orthodoxy. May holy God, who was made flesh for us and has been placed as head of the church of the nations, assemble all into a unity of faith and deem the church of the Greeks with its first, elder sister, I mean Rome, worthy to glorify the prince of peace, Christ, for the sake of union of faith and agreement for the restoration of orthodoxy from antiquity.[31] May all you cardinals be guided by the all-powerful hand of God so that, as great merchants you might find anchor in the calm harbour of the kingdom of the heavens. The grace of God be with all of you. Amen.

24 Psalm 36:6.
25 Matthew 26:69–75.
26 Jeremiah 8:4; Micah 7:8.
27 Proverbs 9:9.
28 i.e. Georgians and Armenians: *ODB* II, sub Iberians.
29 i.e. Georgians: *ODB* I, sub Abchasia; *ODB* II, sub Georgia. This group does not appear in the Latin text: Tautu, *Acta*, no. 179b, 251.
30 Certainly a reference to the Bulgarian victory at Klokotnitsa in 1230.
31 Added in the version by Matthew Paris – May he give brotherly affection to you: Tautu, *Acta*, no. 179b, 252 note 12; Matthew Paris, 460 lines 15–16.

III

POPE GREGORY IX TO PATRIARCH GERMANOS II, 26 JULY 1232[1]

Editions and translations

A. Tautu, *Acta Honorii III (1216–1227) et Gregorii IX (1227–1241)* (Vatican: Typis Polyglottis Vaticanis, 1950), no. 179, 235–39

J. Mansi, *Sacrorum conciliorum nova et amplissima collectio*, XXIII (Venice, 1779), 55–59

Matthew Paris, *Chronica majora*, ed. H. Luard, vol. 3 (London: Longman, 1876), 460–66; transl. J. Giles, *Matthew Paris's English History from the year 1235 to 1273*, vol. 1 (London: Henry Bohn, 1889), 108–14

The verdict of blessed Peter on the church. Every question of faith is to be referred to his seat. The Roman Church is the head and mistress of all churches; the defender of ecclesiastical liberty.

… to the archbishop of the Greeks.

When your fraternal letters were presented to us and our brothers by your messenger, and received with the appropriate courtesy, and their tenor more fully understood, we resolved to send to your presence religious men of praiseworthy life and proven knowledge, to bear the words of life and to explain more fully our will and that of our brothers.

But, since *from the eater came forth food and from the strong came sweetness,*[2] lest the honeycomb from the mouth of the dead lion should appear despised by the father,[3] in order to avoid embarrassment on the

---

1 Auvray, *Reg.*, II, no. 849, 523; Potthast, *Reg.*, no. 8981, 770.

2 Judges 14:14.

3 In the story, Samson offers the honey to his mother and father, but does not tell them from where he obtained it: Judges 14:5–9.

THE DISPUTATIO

part of the writer, we gave thought to a reply, that your letters might not seem to be despised if no response were given, *because a wise man will become wiser through listening, and understanding he will hold his course.*[4] – Although Christ, as you relate in your letter, is the first and principal foundation of the faith that we confess, and it is not possible to place another before him,[5] nevertheless we read that next are the apostles and prophets, secondary foundations, because the foundations of the church in the holy mountains[6] and the citizens of heavenly Jerusalem are read to have been built upon the foundation of the apostles and prophets.[7] Among these the first and principal is the most blessed Peter, who, not without cause, but by particular prerogative deserved to hear from the Lord: *You will be called Cephas,*[8] which is interpreted *head:*[9] So, just as the multitude of senses remain in the head, from which by hidden courses they flow out to individual limbs, as other parts of a river flow from its source, thus there are three orders of the faithful in the Church: Noah, Daniel and Job – namely prelates, those who practice continence and those who are married – were seen by Ezekiel in his vision of those who are to be saved.[10] The Lord built his Church for the faithful, who are every kind of fish caught in his net,[11] not as a house made from the forest of Lebanon,[12] nor a hall of pillars,[13] nor a home for the daughter of Pharaoh,[14] but upon a rock in the form of Peter. It was he [who received] primacy from the principal, who drank rivers from the font of the mind of the lord. It is from him that the means of salvation should be sought, with all patience and learning, not in emphatic or arrogant resistance, so that the jagged stones of doubt might be removed from the darkness of the mind.

4 Proverbs 1:2.

5 1 Corinthians 3:11.

6 Cf. Psalm 87:1.

7 Ephesians 2:20.

8 John 1:42.

9 Gregory IX's text here diverges somewhat from what is found in the Gospel of John. The Vulgate at the end of John 1:42 reads *quod interpretatur Petrus*, while Gregory IX has written *quod interpretatur caput*: Tautu, *Acta*, no. 179, 236 line 9. In his copy of the letter, Matthew Paris has kept with the text found in Scripture: Matthew Paris, 461 line 11.

10 Ezekiel 14:14.

11 Cf. Luke 5:1–11; John 21:1–14.

12 1 Kings 7:2.

13 1 Kings 7:6.

14 1 Kings 7:8.

POPE GREGORY IX TO PATRIARCH GERMANOS II 123

If you make a distinction for time and place, you will find that your assertion, that Paul resisted Peter to his face,[15] does not negate this, because [the episode] is read as a matter of divine dispensation by the orthodox Fathers.[16] While Peter strove to gain the Jews by professing the law of Moses, Paul, avoiding circumcision, strove with all his strength to gain the gentiles by this pretense. On this point you will also censure Paul, because when he travelled in Syria and Cilicia and had arrived at Derbe and Lystra, he circumcised Timothy, the son born from a gentile father and a believing mother.[17] Secondly and thirdly, you will blame either yourself or Paul, when he sailed to Syria and Priscilla and Aquila were with him, and for fear of the Jews they shaved his head at Kenchreai, as the Nazarites[18] who had accordingly made a vow were accustomed to do, in accordance with the commandment of Moses, there he cut his hair in accordance with the law.[19] If, dearest brother, you distinguish the mystery of grace and office of authority[20] in full understanding and examine the zeal of Peter and Paul, who thirsted only for souls, you will find disagreement in doctrine between them neither in death, where shared faith and suffering truly made them brothers,[21] nor in their teaching while they were alive. Peter, before the stubborn heads of the Jews, and Paul, before the gentile people, laboured in different languages and rites, supplying milk to infants and solid food to the initiated.[22] And yet, when they had reached the fullness of time, each preached one Lord, one faith, one baptism, and other articles of faith according to the grace given to him by the Lord in one same spirit. For Paul, with Peter, exercised the mystery of grace, according to the word of the Lord spoken generally to Peter and the other Apostles, who said: *if you*

---

15 Galatians 2:11.

16 In other words, Divine Will ordained that Peter and Paul were to be in conflict then, but not ever after.

17 Acts 16:3; Numbers 6:18; Judges 16:17.

18 A subgroup of Israelites who took vows of purity concerning the consumption of the produce of the vine and observing restrictions on cutting one's hair: F. Cross and E. Livingstone, *Oxford Dictionary of the Christian Church*, 1134.

19 Acts 18:18; also cf. Acts 21:22–26. Gregory IX seems to have conflated different episodes of the New Testament.

20 *dignitatis mysterium et auctoritatis officium*: Tautu, *Acta*, no. 179, 236 lines 34–35. Gregory IX is indicating that Peter and Paul shared in the 'mystery of grace,' but only Peter held the 'office of authority.'

21 Gregory IX is making the point here that both Peter and Paul achieved martyrdom in Rome, thus enhancing papal authority.

22 Cf. 1 Corinthians 3:2.

124 THE DISPUTATIO

forgive the sins of any, they are forgiven, and if you retain those of any, they are retained.[23] And yet, [Paul] recognized the office of authority bestowed separately to Peter, just as to the principle and font of the gospel of the Lord, from the same authority: *whatever you bind on earth will be bound in heaven and whatever you loosen over earth will be loosened in heaven also.*[24] For that reason [Paul] came to Jerusalem, and with him and others he preached the gospel, in accordance with revelation, lest he had run, or continued to run, in vain.[25] Again this is confirmed by the word of the Lord, when it was commanded to Peter alone, that if his brother sinned, he should forgive him *not seven, but even seventy times seven times.*[26] To Peter alone were his sheep entrusted. He exerted such particular power of miracles that through the streets the infirm were placed in beds and pallets that they might be healed by his shadow.[27] His authority is clearly confirmed by the words of the Lord, said only to him: *Put out into the deep water* and turning to the others: *let down your nets for the catch.*[28] Therefore, Peter alone received the keys of the kingdom of heaven on earth because of the excellence of his faith, with which truth he recognized the two natures in one Christ when he said: *You are Christ, son of the living God.*[29] As there is one Lord, one faith, one baptism, there is one leader and one body of the Church militant, and a body with more than one head is monstrous and the one without a head is without a leader. Thus remains the governance of the general Church, which he [Peter], with Paul and the others from the gentiles, assembled from Greeks, Latins, [and] barbarians, obviously through what has been said, the Lord appointed as head of his own and his successor. However, the Lord foresaw that the Church of God would be crushed by tyrants, mangled by heretics, and divided by schismatics, and he said: *I prayed for you, Peter, that your faith will not fail and that you, when you have turned back, will strengthen your brothers.*[30] From this is clearly inferred that every question of faith should be brought to the seat of Peter.

But grieving we return to the issue at hand, using the words of your letter [when you said] the full-length and seamless tunic of the true Joseph

23 John 20:23.
24 Matthew 16:19.
25 Galatians 2:1–2.
26 Matthew 18:22.
27 Acts 5:15.
28 Luke 5:4; i.e. it is for Peter to steer the ship, but it is for all the apostles to cast their nets.
29 Matthew 16:16.
30 Luke 22:32.

POPE GREGORY IX TO PATRIARCH GERMANOS II   125

was certainly presumptuously torn, not by the hands of soldiers but by the opinions of ecclesiastical persons. But let us consider who tore it. When the Church of the Greeks withdrew from the unity of the Roman See, that which had been free at once lost the privilege of ecclesiastical liberty. It became the slave of secular power, so that, by the righteous judgment of God, she who refused to recognize the sacred primacy in Peter, reluctantly endured an earthly lord. Under which, despising not a little, fading by degrees, professing a deformed faith and becoming lukewarm in brotherly love, unchecked, she wandered free through the field of licentiousness, so that, without rebuke from anyone, she concealed what was forbidden under what was permitted, and withdrew from the Temple of Peter, retreating from the Lord as if ejected by the Lord into the court outside, which John did not measure with his staff, having been restrained by the Lord, because it is given to the nations. Already you see clearly that this has happened.[31] Although Elias and Elisha shone as great lamps in that gloomy place, Samaria withdrew from the temple of the Lord and from Judah and from the confession of the true faith, prefiguring the idolatry that was to come, worn out in the permanent carnage of war and heavy burden of sins.[32] [Samaria] was given to [other] nations, banished outside as punishment for fornication and idolatry, by which they were separated from the Lord.[33] If the church of the Greeks proposes to have Paul for itself, she should recognize him with Peter, or by a successor to Peter and the Vicar of Christ, when shown in the basilica of the Apostles, which was built by Constantine.[34] Likewise is observed the mystery of the office, although it was mentioned in your letter, as if under a form of criticism, that Peter was moved three times from the gates, roused by the crowing

---

31 Cf. Revelation 11:1–2.

32 Thus, the fate of Samaria foreshadows the state of the Greek Church.

33 A. Crown, ed., *The Samaritans* (Tübingen: Mohr, 1989). On the Samaritans under crusader rule, see C. MacEvitt, *The crusades and the Christian world of the east: rough tolerance* (Philadelphia: University of Pennsylvania Press, 2008), 11–13.

34 The Church of the Holy Apostles in Constantinople is described by Nicholas Mesarites: Nicholas Mesarites, *Description of the Church of the Holy Apostles, Constantinople,* ed. A. Heisenberg, *Grabeskirche und Apostelkirche. Zwei Basiliken Konstantins: Untersuchungen zur Kunst und Literatur des ausgehenden Altertums* (Leipzig: Hinrichs, 1908), II, 10–96; ed. G. Downey, 'Nikolaos Mesarites: description of the Church of the Holy Apostles at Constantinople,' *Transactions of the American Philosophical Society* 47 (1957), 855–924: transl. M. Angold, *Nicholas Mesarites: his life and works (in translation)* (Liverpool: Liverpool University Press, 2017), 75–133. See also *ODB* II, sub Holy Apostles in Constantinople.

126 THE DISPUTATIO

of the rooster,[35] and yet he was made the gatekeeper of paradise, as one who leads clearly ought to know suffering and compassion. And three times it was said particularly to him, concerning the office of his authority: *thou feed* and not: *Ye feed my sheep,*[36] not [the sheep] of others, so that he might transmit to his successors the model of the true shepherd. Thus, in a spirit of leniency he might restore the departed, those who wandered from the Church, who had freely professed the worship of the Christian name, to the unity of the Church, and expel the prideful, according to the word of the Apostle, and deliver them to Satan for the destruction of the flesh,[37] restoring the unwilling to the flock. But if you, out of a sense of compassion, return to the primacy and judgment of the Apostolic See, like a true Israelite grieving with contrition over the tearing of Joseph's sown tunic,[38] we will have compassion for your suffering and, with the Apostle, will commiserate in your pain. And we will give thanks to him who opened the eyes of the man born blind,[39] humbly praying that just as he brightened the eyes of Tobias with the bile of a fish,[40] he may illuminate the hearts of the church of the Greeks, and yours, so that in our time and yours he will, by divine providence, restore us to one flock and one shepherd.

Therefore, dearest brother, take the scroll which John discusses in the Apocalypse, *and eat, although it will be bitter to your stomach,*[41] because the thorns of contrition will prick in the beginning, yet in your mouth will be sweet as honey, according to the word of the groom saying in the Psalms: *Your song will sing in my ears, your voice is sweet.*[42] Examine your understanding of wisdom without any irrational anger and you will find that the Roman Church, the head and instructress of all churches, [when she looks into] the mirror that you have proposed – namely the gospel and letters and dogma of the other doctors – finds nothing in interpretation or dispensation that is contrary to what is laid down by the statutes of the Holy Fathers in the unity of faith and spirit with which it does not agree. You will

35 Matthew 26:69–75.

36 John 21:15–19. This difference here is between *Pascite*, a second plural imperative, and *Pasce*, second singular imperative. Thus, Christ is understood as saying *You, Peter, feed my sheep*, and not *You, disciples, feed my sheep*.

37 1 Corinthians 5:5.

38 Genesis 37:23.

39 John 9:1–39.

40 Tobit 6:3–9.

41 Revelation 10:9.

42 Song of Solomon 2:14.

POPE GREGORY IX TO PATRIARCH GERMANOS II   127

find, in the opening of this book, that the Roman Pontiff is made everything in everything, not for shameful profit or whim, but being driven by his brothers through divine inspiration, so that all men may find salvation. At once he becomes the servant of the servants of God. For his brothers and fellow bishops he makes himself a wall against heretics, and with them he opposes schismatics and tyrants for the preservation of ecclesiastical liberty. And although there may be some exceptions, nevertheless the Roman Church breathes free from all attacks in modern times. But if the church of the Greeks would patiently endure, to use your words, the words that sting, rather than the dangers to their souls which hitherto came and continue to come from their division, distress should have given them sufficient understanding, for in their hands the ecclesiastical order is divided between the hostile eastern peoples, ecclesiastical liberty is repressed and ecclesiastical dignity is trampled under foot, for there is no one among all the dear ones to console her,[43] since the leaderless refused to return to the leader of the Church. *Therefore return Shu'lammite, return; return, so that we may look upon you,*[44] for then a brother will properly be able to be helped by a brother. If the son, who squandered everything in loose living, is inspired by the Lord to rise and say: *Father, I have sinned against heaven and before you, now I am not worthy to be called your son, make me as one from your servants,*[45] then the father, running to meet him not as a servant, but returning as a son, first will offer a robe and then kill the fatted calf,[46] making a public banquet. He will proclaim [the son] with joy to all the faithful of Christ, because the brother and son who had died has been restored to life, and the money which had been wasted has been found.[47] Thus, when you have been received with dignity into the bosom of the mother Church, you will plainly see truth in the mirror of truth, which the Latin Church preserves in unity of faith, which accepts neither stain nor wrinkle.[48]

Given at the Lateran, 7 days before the kalends of August, in the sixth year [of our pontificate].

---

43 Lamentations 1:2.
44 Song of Solomon 6:13.
45 Luke 15:21.
46 Luke 15:22–23.
47 Luke 15:8–10.
48 Ephesians 5:27.

IV

POPE GREGORY IX
TO PATRIARCH GERMANOS II,
18 MAY 1233[1]

Editions

A. Tautu, *Acta Honorii III (1216–1227) et Gregorii IX (1227–1241)* (Vatican: Typis Polyglottis Vaticanis, 1950), no. 193, 266–68

J. Mansi, *Sacrorum conciliorum nova et amplissima collectio*, XXIII (Venice, 1779), 59–62

Matthew Paris, *Chronica majora*, ed. H. Luard, vol. 3 (London: Longman, 1876), 466–69; transl. J. Giles, *Matthew Paris's English History from the year 1235 to 1273*, vol. 1 (London: Henry Bohn, 1889), 114–16

Whether the sword of the church that has been given reveals a difference of ritual of the two churches.

… To the archbishop of the Greeks.

Since, when it comes to witnessing to the truth, ignorance of Scriptures may be the cause of errors, it is expedient for all to read and to listen to them; because divine inspiration was stored [in these writings] for the teaching of those who follow, with a desire to warn modern peoples. Truly, the division of the tribes under Jerobo'am, who made Israel to sin, as it is read,[2] clearly foreshadows the schism of the Greeks; and the multitude of abominations in Samaria [foreshadows] the heresies of the multitude who have separated from the worship of the true Temple of the Lord, namely reverence for the Roman Church. Just as Chrysostom, Nazianzus, Basil the Great and Cyril shone forth in the meeting of dissenters, it was according

---

1 Auvray, *Reg.*, I, no. 1316, 738; Potthast, *Reg.*, no. 9198, 787.
2 1 Kings 12 and 13.

130   THE DISPUTATIO

to the [will of the] same summit of heavenly counsel, which desired Elijah, Elisha, and the sons of the prophets, to remain among the idolaters.

Now then, as in other letters, which we sent to you previously,[3] we explained more widely this and other matters, authority and reason, which are ordained for the primacy of the Roman Church, to which we add the following, that from reading the gospel, we consider both swords to pertain to the Roman Pontiff. Because when Jesus spoke to the disciples about the acquisition of the spiritual sword,[4] they offered two in that place, which the Lord said are sufficient, clearly for the governance[5] of the spiritual and the temporal crime. If you allow that the material sword relates to temporal force, listen carefully to what the Lord says to Peter in the gospel of Matthew: *Put your sword back in its place.*[6] By saying *your [sword]*, he indicated the material sword, with which he had struck the servant of the chief of priests. Concerning the spiritual [sword], no one is in any doubt, since [the Lord] united in him – that is, in Peter – the supreme power of binding and loosing, in a way that pertained peculiarly to him. Thus, both swords are bequeathed to the Church, but one must be wielded by the Church; the other for the Church, to be unsheathed by the hand of the secular prince. One [is to be wielded] by the priest, the other at the command of the priest by the soldier.

In order that this and other things, after a careful investigation of the truth, should bring you to feel the love that should be present, we decided to send to you the present advocates – Hugo and Peter of the Preachers,[7] Haymo and Rodulphus, Brothers of the Order Minor,[8] men of virtue, famous for their devotion, renowned for their moral reputation and gifted with the knowledge of the Sacred Scriptures, which we have described to you in the aforementioned letters – so that, should you decide to negotiate faithfully and discuss amicably with them about all the matters in question, you will be able to hear the voice of thunder in the wheel which was below the wheel of Ezekiel;[9] and see in the glassy sea that one Adam, appointed to the work and care for paradise, was assigned one wife, prefiguring the

---

3 Source III; Tautu, *Acta*, no. 179, 235–39.

4 Luke 22:38.

5 From *cohibitionem*, which can also mean 'restriction' or 'coercion': Tautu, *Acta*, no. 193, 266 line 19.

6 Matthew 26:52.

7 Order of the Preachers, i.e. the Dominicans.

8 i.e. Franciscans.

9 Ezekiel 1 and 10.

POPE GREGORY IX TO PATRIARCH GERMANOS II   131

one Lord Jesus Christ, begotten in justice and the sanctity of truth, and his one bride, the Church.[10] Also, Lamech, whose [name] means humiliation because he divided his one wife into two, was made bloody and killed a man to his own detriment.[11] Likewise, there were other [wives], besides [Noah's], who are not named but were present in the ark when the flood had utterly devastated [the land], and who were under the captaincy of the one sailing patriarch who saved a few souls under the number of perfection.[12] Also, the Lord gave the law [to Moses] a second [time], not different but the same.[13] Also the two Cherubim, who stand over the propitiation,[14] do not face in two different directions, but their gaze is fixed on one spot.[15] And finally Joseph had but one ankle-length tunic,[16] just like the one seamless robe of our Saviour.[17]

Still, if your rite, different from ours, causes a sense of doubt about the most sacred Sacrament of the Eucharist, then hear that the mystery of our salvation, celebrated alike by Greeks and Latins, is not other or a different mystery, belonging as it does to the one Lord Jesus Christ, who, previously capable of suffering when he took on flesh for our sake, is now entirely free from suffering, even as he is from death. The Greek – running ahead to the faith with the younger of the disciples and not ungrateful for such grace,[18] choosing to be reminded daily of the honour by which God, out of compassion for human misery, chose to become a human capable of suffering,[19] has determined that the host offered should be leavened. So, following what the apostle says, that is that the [whole] lump is corrupted by the leaven,[20] the corruption, to which the body of the lord, before the resurrection, was subject, is made manifest in the leaven [of the host]. But

10 Gregory IX here is arguing that Old Testament examples prefigure the current situation. Adam is equated with Christ, while Eve is the Church.

11 Genesis 4:19–23.

12 The flood story states that Noah brought onto the ark with him seven other individuals – his wife, his three sons, and their three wives: i.e., seven others were preserved. Only Noah and his three sons are identified. Nowhere are the wives given names: Genesis 6–8. For more on the 'number of perfection' see 1 Peter 3:20; 2 Peter 2:5.

13 Exodus 34:1.

14 i.e. the 'Mercy Seat,' atop the Ark of the Covenant.

15 Exodus 25:18–20.

16 Genesis 37:3.

17 John 19:23.

18 John 20:1–10.

19 From *passibilis*: Tautu, *Acta*, no. 193, 267 line 28.

20 1 Corinthians 5:6–8; Galatians 5:9. Both references say *totam massam*.

132 THE DISPUTATIO

the Latin, following scripture,[21] with the elder Peter, had earlier entered the tomb, from which proceeds spiritual meaning, and saw laying there the linens, which had covered the most holy Body, designating the Church, and he observed the separate napkin which had been over the head.[22] Thus he chose to celebrate the more marvellous sacrament of the glorified body in the azymes of purity.[23] Certainly[24] the bread, simple before the sacrifice, is bread, but in truth when transubstantiation is brought about by the [pronouncement of] the words of the lord, it is not bread,[25] and therefore it may be called neither leavened nor unleavened, but rather it is believed to be the true bread, which descended from heaven and bestowed life to the world.[26]

The anointing Spirit and sound understanding have taught these and other things to the See of Peter. If you would only go in. Follow the younger disciple, who at last saw and believed, so that with all understanding you would sing truly with us that psalm of David: *behold how good and pleasant it is when brothers dwell in unity.*[27]

Given at the Lateran, on the fifteenth kalends of June, in the seventh year of our pontificate.

---

21 'Following scripture' here comes from *secutus litterae*: Tautu, *Acta*, no. 193, 267 line 32. A different reading is found in the text preserved by Matthew Paris, which reads 'following freely,' from *libere*: Matthew Paris, 469 line 5.

22 John 20:7.

23 1 Corinthians 5:8.

24 The papal register reads *utique*, 'certainly': Tautu, *Acta*, no. 193, 267 line 36. The text preserved by Matthew Paris, however, reads *uterque*, 'both/either': Matthew Paris, 469 lines 10–11.

25 The reference to transubstantiation is not found in the version of the letter preserved by Matthew Paris: Tautu, *Acta*, no. 193, 267 lines 37–38; Matthew Paris, 469.

26 John 6:51.

27 Psalm 133:1.

V

THE DISPUTATIO
BETWEEN THE LATINS AND GREEKS

Edition

G. Golubovich, 'Disputatio Latinorum et Graecorum seu Relatio apocrisiarorum Gregorii IX de gestis Nicaeae in Bithynia et Nymphaeae in Lydia (1234),' *Archivum Franciscanum Historicum* 12 (1919), 428–65

Part I. *Held at Nicaea in Bithynia*

1. In the year of the Lord 1233,[1] in the month of January, we from the Order of Dominicans, Brother Hugo and Brother Peter; and from the Order of Franciscans, fr. Aymo and fr. Rodulphus, messengers of the lord Pope, were sent to the archbishop of the Greeks. We reached Nicaea on the first Sunday after the Octave of Epiphany,[2] at about the evening hour. But before we reached the city, many imperial messengers sent by the Emperor himself came often to meet us, greeting us on behalf of the Emperor and notifying us of the joy in his heart at our arrival. In addition, messengers from the Patriarch himself came honourably and often to meet us. And finally the canons of the greater church themselves, coming a distance from the city, cordially received us with joy and they all together led us to the city with honour and reverence.[3] And when we begged to be led to the great church in order to pray they led us to another church, where the first council was celebrated,[4] revealing to

---

1 1234.

2 15 January 1234.

3 References to *nuntii Imperatoris, nuntii ipsius Patriarche* and *ipsi canonici ecclesie* sent to greet the friars denotes the importance placed on these meetings by the Byzantines, but also suggests that Germanos II and Vatatzes were pursuing distinct goals in the *disptuatio* independent of one another.

4 The friars do not make explicitly clear which church in Nicaea they consider to be 'the greater church,' (*maiorem ecclesiam*): Golubovich, 'Disputatio,' 428 line 12. It may have

134   THE DISPUTATIO

us the holy Fathers, the ones present at the same council, depicted on the walls. Then after a tour of the city we were led to the hospice[5] which the lord

been the Church of St Sophia in Nicaea, the setting for the Seventh Ecumenical Council in 787, the Church of Hyakinthos, or some other structure: C. Mango, 'The meeting-place of the first ecumenical council and the church of the Holy Fathers at Nicaea,' *Deltion tes Christianikes Archeologikes Etaireias* 26 (2005), 32: C. Foss, *Nicaea: A Byzantine capital and its praises*, 101–03, 111.

The first council referred to here is the first ecumenical council in Nicaea in 325: *ODB* II, sub Nicaea I; E. Ferguson, *Encyclopedia of early Christianity*, 810–12; M. Edwards, 'The First Council of Nicaea,' in *The Cambridge history of Christianity*, vol. 1, *Origins to Constantine*, ed. M. Mitchell and F. Young (Cambridge: Cambridge University Press, 2006), 552–67. Clearly, the church to which the friars were taken is where the Byzantines believed the council had taken place over nine centuries earlier. Eusebios of Caesarea identifies this as a wing of the imperial palace: *Vie de Constantin: texte critique*, ed. F. Winkelmann (Paris: Les Éditions du Cerf, 2013), 3.10.362–64; transl. A. Cameron and S. Hall, *Eusebius: life of Constantine* (Oxford: Clarendon Press, 1999), 264. The structure was later adapted as a shrine and decorated with images of individuals said to have been present at the First Council of Nicaea. From these images the church took its name, the Church of the Fathers. This structure suffered a great deal of damage in its many centuries. Prokopios indicates that Justinian rebuilt or restored the structure along with other buildings in the city: Prokopios, *De aedificiis*, ed. G. Dindorf, vol. 3 (Bonn: Weber, 1838), V.3.313 line 19 – 314 line 14; transl. A. Stewart, *Of the buildings of Justinian by Procopius (circ. 560 AD)* (London: Palestine Pilgrims Text Society, 1888), 130–31. Theophanes tells us that the church was damaged along with large parts of the city after an Arab siege in 727. He also remarks on the miraculous powers of the images of the council Fathers on the walls of the church: Theophanes, *Chronographia*, ed. C. de Boor (Leipzig: Teubner, 1883), 405 line 18 – 406 line 31; transl. C. Mango and R. Scott, *The chronicle of Theophanes Confessor* (Oxford: Clarendon Press, 1997), 560–61. Finally, Michael Attaleiates reports that both the Church of the Fathers and St Sophia were brought down in an earthquake in 1065: Michael Attaleiates, *Historia*, ed. I. Pérez Martín, *Miguel Attaliates: introduccion, edicion, traduccion y comentario* (Madrid: Consejo Superior de Investigaciones Científicas, 2002), 68 lines 12–24; transl. A. Kaldellis and D. Krallis, *The History, Michael Attaleiates* (Cambridge, MA: Harvard University Press, 2012), 15.5, 166–67. Cyril Mango concluded that what remained of the Church of the Fathers in the thirteenth century was a domed *oaton*, or egg-shaped building, which had been attached to the original imperial palace of the fourth century: C. Mango, 'The meeting-place of the first ecumenical council,' 33. Germanos II himself delivered a homily in the church: S. Lagopates, Γερμανὸς ὁ β΄, πατριαρχὴς Κωνσταντινουπόλεως-Νικαίας, 214–17.

Promptly rushing the friars to the Church of the Fathers served a particular purpose. Germanos II almost certainly sought to impress the papal envoys, reminding them that the city of Nicaea held a central place in the formation of Christian doctrine and had a long history of correcting theological error. In this way, the tour given to the friars may be understood as a form of diplomatic intimidation, as well as an attempt to give the encounter the character of a new council of the church.

5 It is notable that the friars were lodged in what they refer to as a *hospitium*: Golubovich, 'Disputatio,' 428 line 17. Many embassies to the Byzantine capital of Constantinople before

THE REPORT OF THE FRIARS 135

Emperor had honourably made ready for us, accompanied by the clergy and a multitude of people. In this hospice, as men overcome by travel, we found comforts for the necessities of the body prepared in abundance.

2. On the following Monday,[6] the lord Patriarch summoned us. We presented ourselves before him and his assembled clergy, greeting the Patriarch himself first on behalf of the lord Pope, and then for our own part. Having first explained our purpose after our fashion, and after giving thanks for the honours and kindness bestowed on us by him, we offered the letter from the lord Pope to the same [Patriarch].[7] He accepted the letter, kissed the bull, and looking back at his own clergy he added: *'Peter, Paul.'*[8] Afterwards, he posed us a question along these lines: whether we were legates of the lord Pope, and whether we wished to accept the honour due to legates. To this we answered, testifying that we were simple messengers, and that we did not wish to receive the honour of legates. Also, taking into consideration such a multitude of clergy, and because we wished to avoid their usual tricks and stratagems, again with protestations we said that we were sent not to a council, but to the Patriarch himself.[9] When we refused the honour offered to us, [the Patriarch] still asserted that great reverence and honour be shown even to the lowliest messenger of the lord Pope.[10] After many words were professed by both sides in public, finally we took

---

1204 were housed in large residences or palaces. Liudprand of Cremona, serving as an envoy from Otto I to Nikephoros II Phokas in 968, complains that he was housed in an 'ugly, waterless, wide-open' residence that, nonetheless, was built of marble (*domum marmoream*), indicating that it was indeed a palace – *domum marmoream, invisam, inaquosam, patulam*: Liudprand of Cremona, *Relatio*, ed. P. Chiesa, 187 line 33; transl. P. Squatriti, *The complete works of Liudprand*, 23.

    6 16 January 1234.

    7 This is the letter from Gregory IX to Germanos II dated 18 May 1233: Source IV; Tautu, *Acta*, no. 193, 266–68.

    8 The reference to 'Peter, Paul' is probably a metaphor by Germanos II referring to the Greek and Roman Churches. Peter's association with Rome is evident, and Paul's association with the East comes from his missionary work in the Aegean Sea and elsewhere. Germanos II made this allusion to Peter and Paul, and their disagreements, often in his correspondence with Gregory IX and again when writing to the Cardinals of the Roman Church: Tautu, *Acta*, no. 179a, 240; no. 179b, 251.

    9 This clarification seems to indicate the friars' conception of the pope's mandate for their mission. They insist that they were sent specifically to have dealings with the patriarch, and not his assembled clergy.

    10 That the friars would find it necessary to include in their report to Rome the patriarch's insistence on giving *magnam reverentiam et honorem etiam minimo nuncio domini Pape*

136   THE DISPUTATIO

our leave and were honourably restored to our aforementioned hospice by his own clergy.

3. On Tuesday,[11] at a proper and fitting hour, we received imperial messengers who summoned us to appear before the Emperor.[12] Thereupon, having been properly presented, we greeted him, and after we had thanked him for the kindness and honours presented to us, we were amicably received. There we found the Patriarch with his clergy, and we related the reason for our arrival and business, adding that the Patriarch had received a letter containing all these things.[13] Then a question about our authority was raised to which we responded thus: 'The contents of the lord Pope's letters sufficiently explains our authority to you; and this we add, whatever we do well in this business the Roman Church will consider ratified and pleasing.'[14] They said: 'Then let us proceed in this business.' And when many lines of reasoning had been put forward from one side to the other as to whether we or they should begin the question, we said: 'We have not been sent to debate with you about some article of faith about which we or the Roman Church are in doubt, but rather that we may have a friendly debate with you about your doubts. Therefore it will be yours to reveal [those doubts] and ours, by the grace of God, to enlighten.' To which they

indicates the extent to which Germanos II (and probably the emperor John III Vatatzes) wish the proceedings to go well.

11   17 January 1234.

12   John III Vatatzes.

13   It seems that no letter was sent from the pope to the emperor. Because of the threat Vatatzes posed to the Latin Empire of Constantinople, it is surprising that Gregory IX did not take advantage of this opportunity to correspond directly with the emperor in Nicaea in the hopes of alleviating that danger: M. Angold, 'After the Fourth Crusade,' 738–39; J. Langdon, 'Vatatzes and the Venetians,' 231; F. Van Tricht, *The Latin* Renovatio *of Byzantium*, 368, 386. The absence of correspondence between Gregory IX and Vatatzes on this occasion is even more significant when one considers previous attempts by popes to elicit Nicaean support for the Latin Empire. In 1208/9, for example, Pope Innocent III wrote to Theodore I Laskaris, calling on him to recognize the imperial claims of Henry I: Hageneder, *Die Register Innocenz' III*, vol. 11, no. 44(47), 61–64.

14   This statement contradicts what the friars had previously said about their diplomatic powers. In ch. 2 they had insisted to Germanos II that they were *simplices nuncios,* 'simple messengers,' and that they did not hold the status of legates. If they had been mere *nuncios* they would not have had the power to ratify anything on behalf of their principal, the pope. See R. Schmutz, 'Medieval papal representatives,' 458. We must therefore be cautious in accepting too quickly the friars' own statements regarding their authority. For more on this issue, see J. Brubaker, *'Nuncii* or *Legati,'* 115–28.

THE REPORT OF THE FRIARS

137

answered thus: 'Say yourselves what they are.' Thus considering that they were attempting to gain time, we answered: 'Although it is not for us to put forward your questions, lest we waste this time fruitlessly, this is what the Roman Church especially wonders: It is true and agreed by all that the Greek Church was subordinate, just like the other Christian nations that are spread far and wide throughout the whole world. What then was the reason or cause whereby she withdrew from obedience to the Church of Rome?' They did not wish to respond to this either, but they asked that we explain our case.[15] Therefore we considered their sophistry, and since the Greeks applaud analogies, we put forward the following example to the public: 'There is a lender and the creditor. Who took the debt from the creditor? Which of them should give an account to the other, why the debt has not been paid?' Confounded by this analogy, a discussion was held and they gave the following response: 'We say that there are two reasons: one is the *procession of the Holy Spirit*,[16] the other is *the Sacrament of the altar*.'[17] To this we responded thus: 'If these are the reasons and not others, why have you removed yourselves from obedience to the Church of Rome? Let us see if these are or ought to be sufficient causes for such disobedience.' And we added: 'Since this is a difficult subject, and our meagre station will not be able to reach [an answer], where His Majesty is inclined, tomorrow we will commit ourselves to prayer and the celebration of mass invoking the Holy Spirit, so that by grace the Spirit itself might pour into our minds and the truth of its procession will be made clear. But because we do not have a place or oratory or church, we ask that the lord Patriarch assign an oratory to us.' And he assigned to us a church[18] suitably close to our residence.

4. That morning,[19] when we celebrated the divine [rites] in the aforementioned church, the Latins, French, English and diverse nations assembled

---

15 Edward Siecienski noted that the Byzantines were constantly 'reacting' to western developments, putting the Eastern Church 'at a distinct tactical disadvantage, since their Latin counterparts almost always came to the table better prepared and with the benefit of doctrinal unanimity': A. Siecienski, *The filioque*, 9–10.

16 i.e. the *filioque*.

17 i.e. azymes, or leavened versus unleavened bread in the Eucharist.

18 Without a specific place reference it may never be possible to identify what church was offered to the friars or where they stayed while in Nicaea. Clive Foss identified numerous Byzantine churches mentioned in textual sources but which cannot be located today: C. Foss, *Nicaea: A Byzantine capital and its praises*, 110.

19 Wednesday, 18 January 1234.

138 THE DISPUTATIO

that they might hear the divine mysteries. But having finished the mass, and after the divine [mysteries] had been duly performed, a certain lamenting and weeping Latin came to us, saying that his own priest had condemned him, because he had attended our mass.[20] Listening to this we grieved, and taking counsel we sent two of our brothers to the Patriarch, telling him that this dreadful action had been done as an insult to God and the whole church. When he heard this, the Patriarch wished to conceal rather than correct this dreadful deed. However, seeing that we thought this action to be a great insult, he sent that priest to us with other priests, who deprived the aforementioned priest of his priestly robes, and thus stripped, they paraded him through the town all the way back to the home of the Patriarch. And because some said that he did it out of naivety and not out of malice, lest we appear unmerciful from the beginning, we asked the Patriarch himself that, being content with these punishments, he would spare the naivety of the aforementioned priest.

5. Because of this, on Thursday,[21] when we had assembled in the imperial palace[22] for the debate, we wished first to discuss the Sacrament of the altar, so that we might understand what they thought about our Sacrament. Refusing, they stubbornly insisted that first we discuss the procession of the Spirit. And thus the debate began with them asking whether we wished to propose or to answer. We said: 'It will be for you to state your doubts about this article, and it will be for us to respond to these doubts.' To this the Patriarch said: 'And you will listen.' Therefore, in their midst rose the Chartophylax, who is called the treasurer of the patriarchal church,[23]

20 Henry Chadwick asserted that the 'weeping Latin' was excommunicated by his Greek priest: H. Chadwick, *East and west*, 239. Such a conclusion is not supported by the report of the friars, which says only that the priest had condemned the Latin, *dicens papatem suum eum supposuisse sententie*: Golubovich, 'Disputatio,' 430 lines 13–14.

21 19 January 1234.

22 Nikephoros Blemmydes also testifies to the presence of an imperial palace in Nicaea: Nikephoros Blemmydes, *Autobiographia*, ed. J. Munitiz, Book 2, ch. 7, 49 line 6 – 50 line 2; transl. J. A. Munitiz, *A partial account*, 97–98.

23 The word *thesaurarius* is somewhat misleading. The chartophylax oversaw the notarial duties of the patriarch and served as an intermediary with lower clergy, especially at conciliar gatherings: *ODB* I, sub Chartophylax; J. Darrouzès, *Recherches sur les ΟΦΦΙΚΙΑ de l'eglise byzantine* (Paris: Institut français d'études byzantines, 1970), 508; R. Macrides, 'Nomos and Kanon on paper and in court,' in *Church and people in Byzantium: Society for the Promotion of Byzantine Studies twentieth spring symposium of Byzantine Studies, Manchester, 1986*, ed. R. Morris (Birmingham: Centre for Byzantine, Ottoman and Modern

THE REPORT OF THE FRIARS 139

and at the command of both the Patriarch and the Emperor, he began to speak thus: 'Do you believe that there is one God in three persons?' We answered: 'We believe.' And he continued: 'Do you believe that the Father is unbegotten, that the Son is the only begotten, and that the Holy Spirit proceeds from the Father?' We answered: 'We believe, just as you say.' But [the Chartophylax], appearing remarkably naïve, raised his hands to heaven and began to bless God in a loud voice, and when he had repeated the same words a second and a third time, as we repeated the same reply, he added: 'Here we find no controversy between you and us; God be blessed through all things!' To this we began to reply in the following manner: 'If in this article you do not find disagreement between the Roman and the Greek Church – and through the grace of God we do not believe that disagreement is found in the Sacrament of the altar, and there have been no other reasons for the schism like that one – then the schism is without cause, and the Church of the Greeks removed itself from obedience to the Roman Church unjustly and without cause.' After these words, having received the advice of the wise men, the Emperor said: 'We hear you speak in the same way as us; but what the lord Patriarch asks is if you say anything more, because we have heard that you have added something to the creed composed by the holy Fathers in council:[24] and they forbade under anathema that anyone should dare to add or to alter either a letter or a syllable or phrase.' To which we said: 'Let the lord Patriarch show to us where that is written.' Then the Patriarch answered and said: 'I beseech your charity, that today you spare me for a while, because I am weary and infirm: tomorrow, God willing, I will recover and will show to you that which I have promised.'[25] And thus we mutually retired.

Greek Studies, University of Birmingham, 1990), 69. Girolamo Golubovich identified this individual as Aulenos: Golubovich, 'Disputatio,' 423. This identification is verified by the profession of faith of the Greek synod at Nymphaion in spring 1234, authored and signed *Chartophylax summae Dei ecclesiae Constantinopolitanae Aulinus*: J. Mansi, *Sacrorum conciliorum*, XXIII, col. 319 A.

24 The First Council of Nicaea in 325.

25 One cannot help but wonder if the patriarch is playing for time in the hopes of delaying the proceedings until he can identify the texts he intended to use because they are not at hand. Henry Chadwick maintained that the friars thought the patriarch's claims of illness to be a diplomatic ploy, but the friars never explicitly express such a suspicion in their report: H. Chadwick, *East and west*, 240.

THE DISPUTATIO

6. On Friday,[26] at an early hour, after celebrating mass and solemnly completing those things pertaining to the hours, we came to the *disputatio*. To begin we asked that the Patriarch keep his promise. He instructed one of his learned men to read the letter from Cyril[27] to John, Patriarch of Antioch, which begins: *Let the heavens rejoice and the earth be glad.*[28] And he began to read from around the middle of the letter. The text of the reading was as follows: *'Concerning God and the Virgin Mother, and about the means of incarnation necessary for the Son, we shall say briefly what we know and declare, not by way of addition, but for the sake of clarity, as we have received first from the divine scriptures and from what has been handed down by the tradition of the holy fathers, adding nothing to the creed promulgated by those who were at the Council of Nicaea, because this is sufficient for all religious knowledge, and for the rebuttal of every evil and heretical opinion.*[29] Here it is said that one must not add to the published creed of the holy Fathers of Nicaea. Then why have you added?' To which we responded in this manner: 'This Cyril does not say no one should add, but he says: *We will speak briefly, adding nothing to the creed published at the synod of Nicaea by the fathers.*[30] Neither do we have in this authority [proof] that it is not permitted for us to add, nor has the Patriarch discharged his promise.' When this had been said, they began to examine the proposition more keenly, and went back to that letter. After a short delay, they began to read, and the passage read was as follows: *In no way is the faith – that is, the creed of the faith as defined by our holy Fathers, who were assembled for the occasion in Nicaea – to be changed by anyone; nor indeed do we allow ourselves or others to alter even a phrase of what was ordained there, or to change one syllable, being mindful of him who said: Nor will you transgress the eternal boundaries, which your fathers ordained.*[31] *It was not they who were speaking, it was the Spirit of God the Father, who proceeds from the Father himself. However, he is not*

---

26 20 January 1234.

27 Cyril of Alexandria (ca. 375–444), the 'main architect of patristic Christology': E. Ferguson, *Encyclopedia of early Christianity*, 310–12.

28 The letter in question is Cyril of Alexandria, *Epistle* 39, Migne *PG* 77, cols 173–82; transl. J. McGuckin, *St Cyril of Alexandria: the Christological controversy*, 343–48.

29 Cyril of Alexandria, *Epistle* 39, Migne *PG* 77, col. 176 C–D; transl. J. McGuckin, *St Cyril of Alexandria: the Christological controversy*, 344.

30 Cyril of Alexandria, *Epistle* 39, Migne *PG* 77, col. 176 C–D; transl. J. McGuckin, *St Cyril of Alexandria: the Christological controversy*, 344.

31 Proverbs, 22:28.

THE REPORT OF THE FRIARS 141

alien to the Son by reason of his essence.[32] Notice, he said that neither he nor anyone was allowed to alter or change the phrase or syllable of these things which were laid down in the Nicaean creed. To which we gave the following response: 'Concerning the faith itself we have altered nothing, nor have we changed either syllable or iota. This evidence you have presented supports our position and is against yours, who say that the Spirit does not proceed from the Son, which you will find is maintained nowhere by your saints or by anyone. Again, nor did he prohibit anything to be added to the Nicaean creed.' Therefore, seeing that they were unable to prove their own proposition, they put to us the following question: 'We ask if you have added something to the creed.' We said: 'Let the creed be read and you will understand.' And a certain man began to read the creed of Constantinople, which had been made at the second council.[33] In truth, planning to extract the reason for our addition from their own mouth, we said 'The creed of Nicaea was produced first, and you have said that nothing should be added to that, and blessed Cyril did not dare to add [to it], and he forbade that anyone should alter or change any phrase or syllable, or transgress it. Therefore, we wish to hear that first.' While they put up much resistance to our request, finally [the creed] of Nicaea was read first, which contained the entire creed in full up to this passage: *I believe in the Holy Spirit*, and the following, namely as it is contained in that creed. This having been read in full, [the creed] of Constantinople was then read, in which they had added in addition things which they left out in the first creed.[34] Recognizing that the second synod had added to the Nicaean creed, we posed the following question: 'If the truth is what you say, that your saints forbade anyone to add to the Nicaean creed or to change or alter anything, who added, or had the audacity to add to it, those things which were added to the Nicaean creed in the Council at Constantinople?' Because they were afraid to answer that question, they laboured to divert to another. Therefore, we insisted all the more on that question. Finally, after lengthy consultations and ploys, they were compelled to answer that it had not been an addition,

---

32 Cyril of Alexandria, *Epistle* 39, Migne *PG* 77, col. 180 D – 181 A; transl. J. McGuckin, *St Cyril of Alexandria: the Christological controversy*, 347.

33 First Council of Constantinople, 381.

34 The 'additions' to the creed of the Council of Nicaea made at the Council of Constantinople are illustrated in J. Stevenson and W. Frend, *Creeds, councils and controversies: documents illustrating the history of the Church, AD 337–461*, revised edn (London: SPCK, 1989), 114–15.

142   THE DISPUTATIO

but an expression of truth. Then when we asked whether it was a different creed from the first one on account of that expression, they answered that it was the same creed, not an alteration, because the expression of truth does not make a different creed, nor does it alter, nor does it make an addition to the creed. From the things already said we had our conclusion to our case and what we said was confirmed, because that addition which they say that we made, namely the *filioque*, is not some addition, nor an alteration to the creed, nor does it make a different creed, providing that what was added was true. Therefore, they insisted on asking what we had added to the creed. And although we could have replied well and truly: 'We have added nothing,' according to the explanation which they had given to us, we nevertheless responded carefully in this way: 'We ask whether it was permitted for us to believe, what is [in accord with] the truth of the creed?' They answered: 'It is permitted.' 'And that which is permitted for us to believe, is it permitted for us to write that?' 'It is permitted' they answered. 'Likewise, what is permitted to believe and to write, is it not permitted to sing and to preach?' They answered: 'On the contrary, it is permitted.' 'But that the Holy Spirit proceeds from the Son is in accordance with the truth of the creed. Therefore, for us it is permitted to believe it, to write it, to sing and to preach it. For this reason we believe and we sing in the creed, *who proceeds from the Father and the Son*, and therefore we preach [the same].' To this they answered: 'Prove that it is true.' We answered: 'Let your saints prove it. Let us listen to blessed Cyril in the first sermon on worship, where he said thus: *The Holy Spirit is in no way changeable; for if it is changeable, it is a mark of weakness, [and] that flaw would overflow to the divine nature, seeing as it [the Spirit] is of God the Father and also the Son, who is in its essence poured out from both.*[35] The same is in the letter to Nestorius, which begins thus: *As our saviour says* etc:[36] *Even though the Spirit exists in its own hypostasis, and it is understood in itself in accordance with being the Spirit and not the Son; nonetheless it is not alien to the Son. Indeed it is called the Spirit of truth, and Christ is truth, and it is poured out from him just as it is from God the Father.*[37] To

35 Cyril of Alexandria, *De Adoratione et cultu in spiritu et veritate*, Migne *PG* 68, col. 148 A.

36 Cyril of Alexandria, *Epistle* 17, Migne *PG* 77, cols 105–122; transl. with Greek edition in L. Wickham, *Cyril of Alexandria: select letters*, 12–33.

37 Cyril of Alexandria, *Epistle* 17, Migne *PG* 77, col. 118 C; ed. and transl. L. Wickham, *Cyril of Alexandria: select letters*, 26–27.

THE REPORT OF THE FRIARS
143

these authorities they answered that *to be poured out* is not *to proceed*.[38] But blessed Cyril refuted them, saying that it is also *to be poured out*. For the same Cyril, in his exposition on the creed of Nicaea: *Completing the sermon about Christ the thrice-blessed Fathers make reference to the Holy Spirit. Indeed, they said that they believed in him just as in God the Father and the Son, for he is consubstantial with him, and is poured out, in other words, proceeds*.[39] Also Athanasios[40] in his declaration of faith, which begins *I believe in one unbegotten God*,[41] at the end it says the following: *Likewise the Holy Spirit is an entity destined to proceed from the Father and to proceed from the Son, through whom he filled all things*.[42] Following these authorities it is plain that the Holy Spirit is from the Son just as it is from the Father. And thus the debate on Friday was ended.

7.[43] On the Sabbath[44] they delayed the *disputatio* until after the evening meal[45] because they observed it almost in the same manner as the Jews:[46] whence after they had finished eating and drinking, imperial messengers were sent to us, and they summoned us to the *disputatio*. And considering that on Friday we had against them many authorities of saints and a plentiful multitude of Greek books, which we had carried with us from

---

38 *Profundi* versus *procedere*. Edward Siecienski suggested that it was Nikephoros Blemmydes who pointed out errors in the friars' interpretation of the works of Cyril of Alexandria: A. Siecienski, *The filioque*, 126.

39 Cyril of Alexandria, *Epistle* 55, Migne *PG* 77, col. 316 D; transl. J. McEnerney, *St. Cyril of Alexandria: Letters 51–110*, 34.

40 Athanasios of Alexandria (ca. 300–73). See E. Ferguson, *Encyclopedia of early Christianity*, 137–40.

41 Athanasios, *Expositio Fidei*, Migne *PG* 25, col. 199–220; ed. P. Schaff and H. Wace, *Athanasius: select works and letters*, 364–66.

42 Athanasios, *Expositio Fidei*, Migne *PG* 25, col. 208 A; ed. P. Schaff and H. Wace, *Athanasius: select works and letters*, 366.

43 The exchange reported here corresponds to that found in Nikephoros Blemmydes, *Autobiographia*, ed. J. Munitiz, Book 2, ch. 26, 57 lines 1–9; transl. J. A. Munitiz, *A partial account*, 107.

44 21 January 1234.

45 *post prandium* can be taken to mean after any meal of the day. However, we see below that the friars were referring to events late in the day, as the discussions move well past sundown. Thus, we can deduce that this meal took place in the evening.

46 The friars are referring to the practice of observing Saturday as a day of rest, beginning and ending at dusk: E. Boring, *An introduction to the New Testament: history, literature, theology* (Louisville, KY: Westminster John Knox Press, 2012), 142; E. Ferguson, *Encyclopedia of early Christianity*, 1095–97.

144 THE DISPUTATIO

Constantinople,[47] they devised how they might be able to confuse us with little questions or deceive us with words: indeed they did not care much to rely on a discussion of truth. Therefore, when both parties gathered on either side, there arose a certain great philosopher.[48] He made a grand and lengthy prologue. Finally, coming to the point he had intended to make, he burst forth in these words: 'You, venerable *apocrisiarii*[49] of the most holy Pope of old Rome, we understand that you are men of piety and letters, and

47 Several libraries existed in Constantinople before 1204, especially in churches and monasteries, from which the friars could have gained access to Greek theological texts. In 1239, only five years after the friars' *disputatio* in Nicaea, the Nicaean philosopher Nikephoros Blemmydes embarked on an extended tour looking for different volumes. On this tour he visited Mt. Athos, Thessalonike, Larissa, and even the distant Epirot territories. During this tour, Blemmydes claimed to have found several volumes that were unknown in Nicaea: Nikephoros Blemmydes, *Autobiographia*, ed. J. Munitiz, Book 1, ch. 63, 32 line 1 – ch. 64, 33 line 16; transl. J. A. Munitiz, *A partial account*, 79–80. See also C. Constantinides, *Higher education in Byzantium in the thirteenth and early fourteenth centuries (1204– ca. 1310)* (Nicosia: Cyprus Research Centre, 1982), 16. Moreover, it appears that the Latin monastic orders in Constantinople before 1261 were active in assembling their own libraries: E. Fisher, 'Monks, monasteries and the Latin language in Constantinople,' 394. The use of Greek texts at the meeting with the Byzantines attests to the skill of at least one of the friars in the Greek language.

48 Although the friars indicate a number of distinct Byzantine ecclesiasts and learned men who took part in the *disputatio*, they rarely give enough information to identify any of them by name. Often, identification is possible only with the help of outside sources. Girolamo Golubovich stopped short of definitively identifying the 'great philosopher' specified here: Golubovich, 'Disputatio,' 437 note 2. Joseph Gill and John Langdon expressed confidence that the 'great philosopher' specified here is Demetrios Karykes, who held the title *hypatos ton philosophon*, or 'chief of the philosophers': J. Gill, *Byzantium and the papacy*, 271 note 68; J. Langdon, 'Byzantino-Papal discussions in 1234,' 211. See also C. Foss, *Nicaea: A Byzantine capital and its praises*, 68. C. Constantinides commented that Karykes, after failing to uphold the orthodox position against the Latins in 1234, probably lost his position as *hypatos ton philosophon*: C. Constantinides, *Higher education in Byzantium*, 6–7, 12. For more information on the position of *hypatos ton philosophon*, see *ODB* II, sub Hypatos ton philosophon; R. Macrides, 'Nomos and Kanon on Paper and in Court,' 70.

The best evidence supporting the identification of this philosopher with Demetrios Karykes comes from the account of Nikephoros Blemmydes, who was also present. According to Blemmydes, Karykes was the first individual appointed to advocate the position of the Greek Church, but he was soon 'put to shame' by his poor performance: Nikephoros Blemmydes, *Autobiographia*, ed. J. Munitiz, Book 2, ch. 25, 57 lines 6–10; transl. J. A. Munitiz, *A partial account*, 107. After this episode Karykes absconds from Nicaea and does not return to the *disputatio*: Nikephoros Blemmydes, *Autobiographia*, ed. J. Munitiz, Book 2, ch. 28, 58 lines 1–10; transl. J. A. Munitiz, *A partial account*, 108.

49 The Byzantines are careful to address the friars as *apocrisiarii*, rather than legates.

THE REPORT OF THE FRIARS 145

you value peace and truth, and it is not shameful for a catholic to profess his creed. Tell us: who added, when and where, and for what reason was what you say in the creed added, namely *filioque*?' And we recognized their strategy, since they believed that we could neither understand nor answer these questions, they sought to bewilder us before the multitude, and thus it would be obvious to all that they had won. The question which they had devised we turned back on them in this way: 'You said rightly that a catholic ought not conceal his faith, but publicly confess what he believes. Therefore, if you believe that the Spirit does not proceed from the Son, you are obliged to confess to us who are asking. We ask, therefore, if you believe and say that it is not from the Son?' They answered: 'We do not believe that it is from the Son.' And us: 'We do not ask this, but rather we want to know if you believe what you say, that the Spirit is not from the Son?' And with this they plainly refused to confess, they were convicted by their own words, because what they believed they dare not confess. Therefore, they insisted that we answer their question. Since we saw that it was now night, we believed it would not be good to begin such a question. We suggested a delay, and not to respond at that time. But they insisted, lighting candles and oil lamps throughout the palace as they laboured to turn the night into day. When we saw everyone's determination, we gave the following response: 'So that you may know that the faith of the Roman Church does not seek subterfuge even by way of debate, and neither is it shameful for us to confess our faith, we will answer your questions in this manner. Your first question was: who added it and who said it? We say it was Christ. When and where? In the Gospel when it said: *When the Spirit of truth comes he will show you all truth.*[50] Why? For the instruction of the devout and confusion of heretics, who would deny this article; and whoever does not have this faith is on the road of perdition. And that what we say is true we prove through the Gospels, through the Letters of Paul, through the holy writings of your saints, and through ours, if you are willing to admit them, Augustine,[51] Gregory,[52] Jerome,[53] Ambrose,[54]

---

50 John 16:13.

51 (354–430), bishop of Hippo from 395. See E. Ferguson, *Encyclopedia of early Christianity*, 148–54.

52 Gregory I the Great was bishop of Rome from 590 to 604. See E. Ferguson, *Encyclopedia of early Christianity*, 488–91.

53 Author of the Latin Vulgate (ca. 347–419/20). See E. Ferguson, *Encyclopedia of early Christianity*, 606–09.

54 (ca. 339–397), bishop of Milan from 374. See E. Ferguson, *Encyclopedia of early Christianity*, 41–44.

146   THE DISPUTATIO

Hilary,[55] and many others.' When we had said these things all were astonished. While everyone was quiet, the emperor said in Greek: '*Calo*.'[56] He added, after having a long discussion with his wise men: 'Show us where that is said in the Gospel, that the Holy Spirit proceeds from the Son.' And, scrolling through the Bible, someone began to read that [passage] of John: *When the Spirit of truth comes he will show you all truth.*[57] And he added: 'When it said *Spirit of truth*, it said that the Holy Spirit proceeds from truth, and we wish to prove this.' At this point they introduced a certain philosopher for the purpose of answering, so that he might obstruct our arguments. We began to oppose him in this manner: '*The Spirit*, exactly as it appears in this place, it is taken to mean which spirit?' He answered: 'To mean the Holy Spirit.' 'Likewise *of truth* as it appears here, for which truth is it taken, [the truth of] Christ or not?' He answered: 'There is a variety of truth, some of compounds, others of simplicity etc.' 'And you say that the truth as it appears in this passage, is it said to be compounded, or is it actually compounded?' And then he answered that it is not. But we said: 'Does it refer to Christ or not?' He answered: 'Not.' And we replied: 'But the truth, as it is used here, does it refer to created truth or uncreated?' And he said 'Created.' And we said: 'Therefore it is a creation.' And we added: 'From this follows the heresy of Macedonius,[58] condemned at the second council.' And, terrified, he began to concede the truth, saying: '*The Spirit of truth*, that is the Holy Spirit, which is the Spirit of Christ.' And we: 'The Holy Spirit is and is called the Spirit of Christ the Son of God, as you profess. We ask: for what reason?' Having taken counsel, they answered that the substance of the Spirit is the same as the substance of the Son. To this we said: 'If this is a sufficient and right reason, why is the Holy Spirit called the Spirit of the Son? Because it is consubstantial with him? But the Father is consubstantial with the Son. Therefore, [it would follow that] the Father is and ought to be called the Spirit of the Son. That is false. This is, firstly, what [the idea] leads to, namely that the reason why it is called the Spirit of the Son is because it is consubstantial.' And having said these things we

---

55 (ca. 315–ca. 367), bishop of Poitiers from 353. See E. Ferguson, *Encyclopedia of early Christianity*, 527–28.

56 The friars explain the meaning of the Greek word *kalo* below, ch. 8.

57 John 16:13.

58 Claimant to the see of Constantinople (died ca. 362). See E. Ferguson, *Encyclopedia of early Christianity*, 703; F. Cross and E. Livingstone, *Oxford dictionary of the Christian Church*, 1018; J. Pelikan, *The Christian tradition*, vol. 2, 27.

THE REPORT OF THE FRIARS

mutually departed: we believe it had already come to almost the second watch of the night.[59]

8.[60] On Sunday[61] we kept ourselves free for the divine service. Early on Monday,[62] in the second week, we returned to the *disputatio* at the palace of the Emperor, and when we undertook the *disputatio* against their philosophers, the Emperor rebuked us saying: 'Your task is to show simply, without philosophy, the truth of the question. Nor are you to proceed syllogistically, since from such debates arise controversies and quarrels. It is better that you proceed simply.' To which we responded as follows: 'Since the Apostle[63] says that *the servant of God ought not to quarrel,*[64] it pleases us more to reveal the truth simply, than to hasten to quarrels or stalemates.[65] And we are able to say with the Apostle *we have become fools, but you compelled us,*[66] since in replying you have given not simple, but complex and elaborate answers. But since it is your purpose to learn the truth in simple terms, we will make matters readily and briefly clear to everyone by way of demonstration.' And the Emperor answered in Greek: '*Calo,*' which is translated: it is good. 'Yesterday we asked your philosophers, why the Holy Spirit is called the Spirit of the Son from eternity? To this question there seem to be only three possible reasons: either because he is of the same substance, as your wise man replied; or because the Son sends the Spirit into created things; or because it proceeds from him. That it is not the Spirit of the Son from eternity is apparent because by the same reasoning, the Father would be the Spirit of the Son, because he is consubstantial. Likewise, it is not because the Son sends the Spirit into created things, because the Holy Spirit was of the Son from eternity; but from eternity the Son did not send the Spirit into created things; therefore that was not the reason why it is said that the Spirit of the Son is from eternity,

---

59 i.e. midnight.

60 The exchange reported here corresponds to that found in Nikephoros Blemmydes, *Autobiographia*, ed. J. Munitiz, Book 2, ch. 27, 57 line 1 – ch. 28, 58 line 14; transl. J. A. Munitiz, *A partial account*, 107–08.

61 22 January 1234.

62 23 January 1234.

63 Paul.

64 2 Timothy 2:24.

65 The Latin term *obviationes* brings to mind an almost martial contest, with an army blocking their enemy in a strategic position: Golubovich, 'Disputatio,' 436 line 7.

66 Cf. 2 Corinthians 12:11.

148   THE DISPUTATIO

because from eternity the Son did not send the Spirit into created things. Therefore, the third reason remains, because it proceeds from the Son, therefore it is truly called the Spirit of the Son.' When they had listened to this rationale, they asked that a copy of this reasoning be given to them in writing.[67] It first being given in Latin, they requested that it be translated into Greek for them, and this was done. Afterwards they asked for a truce[68] to ponder over this line of thought, and they had the respite for Monday and Tuesday.[69]

9. On Tuesday,[70] about the evening hour, we were instructed to go to the home of the Patriarch, and we went. When we arrived the clergy were already assembled, and he ordered that a large and copious writing be brought up, in which, he said, was contained the contents of his reasoning in opposition to us. In view of the fact that we had proposed a simple line of reasoning in everyday language, we did not expect that they would write something in response to us, but that they would simply agree to acknowledged truth. But since we recognized that they proceeded wickedly, we desired to hear his own reply in which we heard many reasons and falsehoods and untruths and many childish things, which we were not able to hear without surprise, because they were more ridiculous than true. Therefore, we took counsel among ourselves to determine whether we would accept that very ridiculous writing, or if it was proper that we answer without time to consider his arguments (because even then we were prepared to respond to the things pronounced in our presence). Then, more for confusion than for our consolation, because they had offered their writing to us, we proposed to listen. But when they realized that we attached little value to their writing, they said: 'You may retire with the grace of God, and we will send the writing to you without delay.'[71] After we had retired, they began to

---

67 According to Blemmydes, this was the last action taken by Demetrios Karykes as advocate of the Greek Church before he departed from the *disputatio* in shame: Nikephoros Blemmydes, *Autobiographia*, ed. J. Munitiz, Book 2, ch. 28, 58 lines 1–10; transl. J. A. Munitiz, *A partial account*, 108.

68 *Indutias* – another allusion to combative language: Golubovich, 'Disputatio,' 436 line 27.

69 Blemmydes reports that the patriarch was greatly depressed by this exchange: Nikephoros Blemmydes, *Autobiographia*, ed. J. Munitiz, Book 2, ch. 28, 58 lines 10–14; transl. J. A. Munitiz, *A partial account*, 108.

70 24 January 1234.

71 The implication being that the Byzantine philosophers considered their treatise so

THE REPORT OF THE FRIARS

149

discuss whether they should compose a new writing, and having altered a great part of the first writing, on the advice of their philosophers they wrote new and different things from what had been recited a little before, and they produced such a delay in altering the writing that they sent it to us at a time when we ought to have been going to bed, and because the time of night had passed, we refrained from translation until the next day.[72]

10.[73] On Wednesday,[74] after we had celebrated mass and duly completed our office, we gave attention to the task of translating from Greek into Latin. Meanwhile, the Patriarch sent word to us, that we might excuse him, because he was very unwell, and he was not able to be present for the *disputatio* on that day. Then the Emperor excused himself, sending messengers saying he would not be sending for us, because the Patriarch was not able to be present. But after they had finished eating, the Emperor sent for us to come to the home of the Patriarch to continue the *disputatio*. When we came to the home of the Patriarch, the first question was whether we had considered his latest draft. And in everyone's presence we read aloud the fraud, which they had contrived in that writing, not yet asserting the translated writing, as was the truth. Nevertheless we said: 'Because we do not wish to waste time with that document, let the writing be read to us publicly, and we will give an answer.' One of their philosophers[75] got up and began to read. His first point was such that it contained a falsehood.

---

complex that the friars, whose disdain for the product was clear, could not understand its gravity.

72　Joseph Gill theorized that the first document presented to the friars was the work of Demetrios Karykes, whereas the revised work was composed by Nikephoros Blemmydes: J. Gill, *Byzantium and the papacy*, 66. There is no evidence that Karykes was the author of the earlier treatise. The only thing we know for certain is that Blemmydes wrote the document which the friars eventually received and translated. See below, ch. 11.

73　The exchange reported here corresponds to that found in Nikephoros Blemmydes, *Autobiographia*, ed. J. Munitiz, Book 2, ch. 29, 57 line 1 – ch. 28, 58 lines 1–10; transl. J. A. Munitiz, *A partial account*, 108–09.

74　25 January 1234.

75　It is tempting to identify the 'philosopher' reading this text aloud with the author of that document, Nikephoros Blemmydes. Both Joseph Munitiz and John Langdon maintain that he is the philosopher indicated here: J. A. Munitiz, *A Partial Account*, 108 note 41; J. Langdon, 'Byzantino-Papal discussions in 1234,' 211 note 54. Blemmydes states that he was to champion the Greek cause only after 'the Church's learned men refused': Nikephoros Blemmydes, *Autobiographia*, ed. J. Munitiz, Book 2, ch. 29, 58 lines 2–3; transl. J. A. Munitiz, *A partial account*, 108.

150   THE DISPUTATIO

Then he added another falsehood. He introduced a heresy in the third point that Christ was not from eternity, except in the way he was called the king from eternity. Fourthly, concerning the argument which we had produced to demonstrate that the Spirit was from the Son, they pretended it was a false syllogism, when it was not our intention to reason syllogistically, as the writing which we gave to them demonstrated adequately – even though, if we had wished to, we would have been able to form a good syllogism from that rationale – but we intended to present a simple and common account. The text of the Greek treatise was as follows:

11.[76] You, honourable legates[77] of the most holy Pope, have proposed to us a problem along these lines: 'Why is the Holy Spirit called the Spirit of Christ from eternity? Only three reasons can be given. First, because it is consubstantial with Christ. Second, because it is sent from himself into created things. Third, because it proceeds from him. It is well known that the first reason is not sufficient, because from this follows that the Father is the Spirit of the Son, because he is consubstantial with the Son. That the second cause is not true is clear because the Holy Spirit is the Spirit of Christ from eternity; but he was not sent into created things from eternity; thus this cannot be the reason why it is called the Spirit of Christ. Therefore, the third reason remains the reason why it is called the Spirit of Christ, because it proceeds from him.'

To which we respond as follows:

Every principle, be it of theology, or nature, or mathematics, or of whatever science or art, does not require a demonstration. Indeed it is a common and universal saying, that principles are indemonstrable. For if you seek the principle of a principle you will find no end. However, the

---

76 For a nearly complete Greek version of this treatise, see M. Stavrou, *Œuvres théologiques*, vol. 1, 184–205. An older edition can be found in P. Canart, 'Nicéphore Blemmyde et le mémoire,' 319–25. Nikephoros Blemmydes discusses his own work at length in his autobiography: Nikephoros Blemmydes, *Autobiographia*, ed. J. Munitiz, Book 2, ch. 29, 58 – ch. 40, 63; transl. J. A. Munitiz, *A partial account*, 108–14.

77 The word *legati*, used here to refer to the friars, presents us with numerous problems: Golubovich, 'Disputatio,' 438 line 1. The friars had previously rejected the label (see above, ch. 2), but here have identified themselves as legates. The Greek word Nikephoros Blemmydes uses to identify the friars is ἀποκρισιάριοι: M. Stavrou, *Œuvres théologiques*, I, 184 line 1. Are we to understand that the friars considered an *apocrisarios* as the equivalent of a legate? Or is it possible that the friars did indeed consider themselves as legates, and on this instance they forgot their earlier modesty?

THE REPORT OF THE FRIARS   151

principle of the faith of orthodox Christians, in so far as it pertains to theological truth, are the words of Christ, spoken by God, from which we are taught to believe in the Father, Son and Holy Spirit. Concerning the Son [we are taught to believe] that he has his being from the Father, and the name itself bears witness to his sonship. Concerning the Spirit, since it is not a relative condition,[78] Christ taught us, without syllogism, from whence he has existence, saying: *The Spirit of truth who proceeds from the Father.* Christ spoke of *the Spirit of Truth*; and I[79] accept without syllogism that he is the Spirit, the Spirit of Truth, that is, of Christ. He said that *the Spirit proceeds from the Father*: and I[80] accept without syllogism that he has existence from the Father. We said beforehand that principles are indemonstrable. Both the Apostles and every holy synod observed this doctrine without transgression all the way to the end, and in Baptism we promised to believe thus in Christ, and it will be asked of use before the tribunal of Christ, whether we kept this faith without transgression.

Thus we have met the objection of your wisdom.[81] You have given this reason why the Holy Spirit is called the Spirit of Christ from eternity. Now we say, first: What Scripture called the Holy Spirit the Spirit of Christ from eternity? Indeed, we were aware of holy Scripture calling him the Spirit of Christ, but not with addition, as you say: the Spirit of Christ from eternity. Nor does Christ have co-principality with the Father and the Spirit in so far as He is Christ, but only according to His Godhead;[82] and the Spirit does indeed exist before the ages, but his anointing is recent, just as Christ,

---

78 Here the relative conditions – *ditio habitudinalis* in Latin or λέξις σχετική in Greek – indicate a Byzantine conception of Aristotelian conditions: Golubovich, 'Disputatio,' 438 line 21; M. Stavrou, *Œuvres théologiques*, vol. 1, 184 line 11. For more on these concepts, see C. Constantinides, *Higher education in Byzantium*, 2; A. Bucossi, 'Introduction,' Andronikos Kamateros, *Sacred Arsenal*, xxviii; K. Ierodiakonou and D. O'Meara, 'Philosophies,' in *The Oxford handbook of Byzantine Studies*, ed. E. Jeffreys with J. Haldon and R. Cormack (Oxford: Oxford University Press, 2008), 714.

79 While the Latin uses the singular verb *recipio*, the Greek uses the plural δεχόμεθα: Golubovich, 'Disputatio,' 438 line 24; M. Stavrou, *Œuvres théologiques*, vol. 1, 186 line 14.

80 Again, where the Latin says 'I,' *recipio*, the Greek uses 'we,' δεχόμεθα: Golubovich, 'Disputatio,' 438 line 25; M. Stavrou, *Œuvres théologiques*, vol. 1, 186 line 17.

81 The Latin and Greek verb tenses diverge at this point. The Latin uses the perfect *obviavimus*, indicating that the objection had been addressed, whereas the Greek uses the present ἀπαντῶμεν, indicating that what comes next is intended to answer the question: Golubovich, 'Disputatio,' 438 line 31; M. Stavrou, *Œuvres théologiques*, vol. 1, 186 line 24.

82 i.e., Christ only receives the appellation 'from eternity' when he is considered in the godhead.

152 THE DISPUTATIO

receiving it in himself, uttered the words of Isaiah: *The Spirit of the Lord is upon me because he has anointed me.*[83] However, let us grant out of courtesy to you, that he may be called the Spirit of Christ from eternity. Nevertheless, if this is indeed said, it can be said in the same way that it is understood [that he is] King before the ages,[84] when the things over which he was to reign had not been introduced, and Creator before the ages, when those things which were created were not yet made, and Benefactor, when the things to which he was to act as benefactor did not exist. And thus the Spirit may also be called the *Spirit of Christ before the ages*[85] because of the ancient plan, formed before the ages, and his dispensation in the flesh, according to which Emmanuel was anointed by the Spirit.

You said that there can be only three reasons. The first is because he is consubstantial with Christ: and casting it down, as it seemed, you rejected this, saying that this reason is not sufficient: because from this it follows that the Father is the Spirit of the Son, because he is consubstantial with the Son; and that reason or rationale – that he is called the Spirit of the Son on account of the fact that he is consubstantial with him – is not our word, but that of the saints and the God-bearing Fathers. For Basil the Great,[86] in his eighteenth chapter to Amphilochius,[87] gives this line of reasoning when he says the following: 'He is the Spirit of Christ, inasmuch as he is appropriated or familiar according to his nature.'[88] Blessed Cyril, in his commentary on the Gospel of John,[89] says the following: 'How then [can it be that he] who proceeds from the Father is the Spirit of truth? On account of the likeness and identity of substance, so that he both is and is called truth – how will he have a beginning?'[90] And the same saint, in the

83 Isaiah 61:1.

84 Psalm 74:12.

85 My emphasis.

86 Basil of Caesarea (330–379). See E. Ferguson, *Encyclopedia of early Christianity*, 169–72.

87 Amphilochios of Ikonion (ca. 340–after 394). See *ODB* I, sub Amphilochios of Ikonion; E. Ferguson, *Encyclopedia of early Christianity*, 46. For the text referred to here: Basil of Caesarea, *Liber de Spiritu Sancto*, caput XVIII, Migne *PG* 32, cols 147–54; ed. P. Schaff, *Basil: letters and selected works*, 199–204.

88 Basil of Caesarea, *Liber de Spiritu Sancto*, Migne *PG* 32, col. 152 B; ed. P. Schaff, *Basil: letters and selected works*, 201.

89 Cyril of Alexandria, *In Ioannis Evangelium*, Book X, Migne *PG* 74, cols 283–446; transl. N. Russell, *Cyril of Alexandria*, 96–129.

90 Cyril of Alexandria, *In Ioannis Evangelium*, Book X, Migne *PG* 74, col. 444 A–B; transl. N. Russell, *Cyril of Alexandria*, 123. There are some slight discrepancies between

THE REPORT OF THE FRIARS
153

commentary on the aforementioned Gospel: *When the Spirit of truth comes it will show all truth to you*: 'Indeed he calls the Spirit of truth the Paraclete, that is to say, of himself, for he himself is truth, so that we may recognize that the Holy Spirit is not foreign from the substance of the Only-Begotten, nor is he other from him, by reason of their consubstantiality.'[91] Saint Basil, from the letter to his brother Gregory,[92] says: 'He who said the Spirit alone, included in that phrase also that of which he is the Spirit: namely of Christ; and [he included] the one from whom: namely from God, according to what the Apostle says.'[93] See how in [the case of] the Son it is not said.[94]

Since we have an abundance of different and incontrovertible witnesses on this point, for the sake of brevity we pass over them. Indeed, we have given our answer theologically, using the great testimonies of the holy fathers more than syllogistic demonstration, thus there is no need excessive inquiry, for these are the words of the most Holy Spirit.

Let us, however, discuss that method of empty wisdom, in the proclamation of which some have ruined their faith, as Paul says.[95] You said that when it is said that the Holy Spirit is called the Spirit of Christ because it is consubstantial, it follows that the Father is the Spirit of the Son because he is consubstantial with the Son. Thus, reasoning syllogistically: the Spirit is the Spirit of the Son because it is consubstantial; the Father is consubstantial with the Son; therefore the Father is the Spirit of the Son because

the Greek and the Latin phrasing here, between how Blemmydes and the friars have formed the question: M. Stavrou, *Œuvres théologiques*, vol. 1, 190 lines 12–15; Golubovich, 'Disputatio,' 439 lines 18–21.

91 Cyril of Alexandria, *In Ioannis Evangelium*, Book X, Migne *PG* 74, col. 444 A–B; transl. N. Russell, *Cyril of Alexandria*, 123.

92 Gregory of Nyssa (331/40–ca. 395). See E. Ferguson, *Encyclopedia of early Christianity*, 495–98. For the text referred to here: Basil of Caesarea, *Epistle* 38, Migne *PG* 32, cols 325–40; ed. P. Schaff, *Basil: letters and selected works*, 426–33.

93 Basil of Caesarea, *Epistle* 38, Migne *PG* 32, col. 332 C; ed. P. Schaff, *Basil: letters and selected works*, 429; 1 Corinthians 2:10–12; John 4:2.

94 The Latin here is very problematic. The Greek gives a clearer meaning: 'See how the Son "from whom" is passed over in silence': M. Stavrou, *Œuvres théologiques*, vol. 1, 192 lines 26–27.

95 Both the Latin and the Greek text here are fairly convoluted. Joseph Munitiz offered an insightful solution for this problem. He suggested that Nikephoros Blemmydes was 'behaving badly' in this instance, altering the biblical phrase 'by rejecting conscience, certain persons have made shipwreck of their faith' (I Timothy 1:19) into 'by advertising sophistry, certain persons have made shipwreck of their faith.' Munitiz added that Girolamo Golubovich, editing the Latin text without the Greek for references, was 'quite lost': J. Munitiz, 'A reappraisal of Blemmydes' first discussion with the Latins,' 22 note 19.

154   THE DISPUTATIO

he is consubstantial [with him]. These indeed have the appearance of a syllogism. Hear then of what kind of nature this syllogism is, if it can be called a syllogism at all. Firstly, you have shaped this syllogism of yours in the second figure, from premises of similar quality, and in no way should premises in this figure have similar quality; but by necessity in the second figure one premise must always be affirmative, while the other is negative. Therefore, you mangled the predicate in the major premise by saying in the minor premise: *the Spirit is the Spirit of the Son as it is consubstantial*. Leaving out the first term of the predicate in the major premise, that is the Spirit, you accepted the rest. These are the errors in the premises. But in the conclusion, which is necessarily deduced from the established premises – setting aside the absurdity that the Spirit is the Father – you have made the predicate [of the minor premise] your full conclusion. Therefore, the thing which appears to be a syllogism is not only not a syllogism in truth, but it is not at all like a syllogism. Also, if we do not grant that this is a syllogism, but only a conversion, we say that it is a false conversion, and incompatible with logical methods. For it is not true that if the Spirit is consubstantial with the Son, what is consubstantial with the Son must be his spirit. This conversion can only occur in things that are of equal value and also individual, but by no means in cases where one thing is of a more general nature and the other of a more particular. And the Spirit does not signify the same thing as consubstantiality according to number, nor is consubstantiality particular to the Spirit, so that it can undergo conversion. The former signifies a thing, that is, the identity of essence, while the latter [signifies] the person and hypostasis. One of these [essence] is shared by the three [Persons], while the other [hypostasis] is particular to one of the three. For the Father is called consubstantial with the Son and Spirit, and the Son with the Father and the Spirit, and again the Spirit consubstantial with the Father and the Son. One of these indicates relationship,[96] the consubstantiality, while the other is mentioned without any qualification. One has the status of an antecedent, the other of a consequent: for if the Spirit of Christ is indeed consubstantial with him [Christ], it does not follow that what is consubstantial with him [Christ]

---

96 The term 'relationship,' translated from the Latin *habitudinem* and the Greek σχέσιν, carries certain ontological implications: Golubovich, 'Disputatio,' 440 line 34; M. Stavrou, *Œuvres théologiques*, vol. 1, 196 line 15. For more see I. Vigorelli, 'ΣΧΕΣΙΣ and ΟΜΟΟΥΣΙΟΣ in Gregory of Nyssa's *Contra Eunomium*: metaphysical contest and gains in Trinitarian thought,' *Vox Patrum* 37 (2017), 165–77.

THE REPORT OF THE FRIARS

155

is also the Spirit.[97] However, we have learned from what has been said that given the antecedent then certainly the consequent must follow, but not that the antecedent follows from the consequent. For if a man is also a creature, it does not follow that if something is a creature it is also a man. Thus, if that statement of yours is rejected, it becomes clear that whoever says that the Spirit is the Spirit of Christ because it is consubstantial with him is correct.

But[98] let us also examine the reason why your wisdom says that the Holy Spirit is called the Spirit of Christ, which is this: that the Spirit clearly proceeds from the Son. Listen then. If it is for this reason that the Holy Spirit is called the Spirit of Christ, because he proceeds from him, and that everything which is called the spirit of something, proceeds from it; surely, according to this rationale, the spirits of the prophets have their existence from the prophets themselves. Likewise, we say this, that it is not only on account of consubstantiality that the Spirit is called the Spirit of the Son – just as the holy fathers taught – but also because of the bestowal[99] of spiritual gifts.[100] The Only-Begotten, having been made man, poured out this bestowal [of spiritual gifts] abundantly upon all the faithful, just as the first of the apostles, Peter, related concerning Christ, saying: *Having been raised up by the right hand of God, and having received the promise of the Holy Spirit from the Father, he has now poured out this [Holy Spirit] that you now see and hear.*[101] And Paul, the chief of the apostles, agreed with this, writing to his disciple Titus: *God saved us through the font of rebirth and renewal of the Holy Spirit, which he abundantly poured into us through Jesus Christ our Saviour.*[102] And it is said, again: *The Spirit of Christ is anointing.*[103] *The Father anoints him with the Holy Spirit according to the flesh.*[104]

---

97 In the Latin: *si enim Spiritus Christi et consubstantialis ei, non quidem si consubstantialis et Spiritus*: Golubovich, 'Disputatio,' 440 line 36 – 441 line 1. The Greek here reads: εἰ γάρ, Πνεῦμα Χριστοῦ, καὶ ὁμοούσιον αὐτῷ, οὐ μὴν εἰ ὁμοούσιον, καὶ Πνεῦμα: M. Stavrou, *Œuvres théologiques*, vol. 1, 196 lines 17–18.

98 The opening of this paragraph is preserved only in the Latin.

99 *Administrationem* in Latin, οἰκονομία in Greek: Golubovich, 'Disputatio,' 441 line 13; M. Stavrou, *Œuvres théologiques*, vol. 1, 198 line 11.

100 At this point, the text is preserved in both Latin and Greek.

101 Acts 2:33.

102 Titus 3:5–6.

103 Isaiah 61:1.

104 Once more, the previous phrase, 'And it is said again: the Spirit of Christ is anointing. The Father anoints him with the Holy Spirit according to the flesh,' is not found in the Greek text.

156   THE DISPUTATIO

And again the Spirit is called the Spirit of Christ because he was always with Christ, not as *energon*[105] – that is the one working in – but as giving testimony to one equal-in-honour, according to the theological term. In all the ancient divinely inspired scriptures the Holy Spirit is never found referred to as the Spirit of Christ. But when the Only-Begotten was made man, anointed by the Holy Spirit, and when he poured this out to the faithful, then the Spirit is called of Christ.

In addition we say: If the Holy Spirit is called the Spirit of Christ because it is understood to be said that he proceeds from him, then it is clear that many inconsistencies arise. It is advisable to lay down certain things first for sake of explanation. It is commonly held[106] and professed among theologians that, with respect to the holy and superessential[107] Trinity, certain properties pertain to nature, while others are hypostatic and personal. The natural properties are equally present in the three hypostases, and with regard to these there is no other difference or division between them. The hypostatic properties, however, are personal and unique to each, and it is according to these that the hypostases are differentiated the one from the other both in number and division. And because procession is a mode of existence, from this it is evident that procession is a hypostatic property. If it were a natural property, it would be common to the three hypostases, and all would be subject to procession: but this is absurd and repugnant to theological conceptions of the mind. Procession is, therefore, not a natural property, but is instead hypostatic, and belongs to one of the three. Therefore, it is agreed that it belongs to the Spirit. And indeed, theological learning separates procession in this way. Therefore, procession is a mutual relationship between the one proceeding and that from which it proceeds, considered just as generation is between the one being begotten and the one begetting. If procession belongs to one, it is clear that emission also will belong to one. But procession is of the Spirit alone, thus it is clear that emission will belong to one alone, and this will

105 The Latin term here, *energon*, is a transliteration from the Greek, ἐνεργοῦν, from ἐνεργέω, literally meaning 'the one acting/operating/influencing': Golubovich, 'Disputatio,' 441 line 24; M. Stavrou, *Œuvres théologiques*, vol. 1, 200 lines 23–24.

106 The Latin here employs a noun, *Dignitas*, while the Greek uses a verb, Ἠξίωται, 'to deem worthy': Golubovich, 'Disputatio,' 441 line 33; M. Stavrou, *Œuvres théologiques*, vol. 1, 200 line 4.

107 *Superessentia* in Latin, ὑπερούσιος in Greek: Golubovich, 'Disputatio,' 441 line 35; M. Stavrou, *Œuvres théologiques*, vol. 1, 200 lines 5–6, meaning 'supersubstantial.' For more on this term, see J. Erickson, 'Leavened and unleavened,' 162.

THE REPORT OF THE FRIARS

157

be either the Father or the Son, and not both. But we are taught by the holy Gospels that [the Spirit] proceeds from the Father. From [the Father] alone then does the Spirit have procession. But if [the Spirit] is also from the Son, the property will be made common, and can no longer be hypostatic, but is transferred to the natural and shared properties, and it is clear that it will be common to all three. This had been shown to be impossible. And moreover, if the Spirit is from the Father and the Son, then the Father and Son will be reduced to one person, or the Spirit itself will be not be one in number, but will be divided into a duality of persons. If [the Spirit] is one and simple, it will come from one. But if it does not come from one, it is not one and simple. But the Holy Spirit certainly is one and simple. Therefore, it is from one in number. Likewise, if the things that emit are different from one another in number and the differences are in accord with their hypostatic properties, then certainly they will emit things that are different in number and there will be two Spirits: one from the Father, and the other coming forth from the Son. Also, it is commonly held among those who study theology that the Holy Trinity is at one and the same time a Unity and a Trinity; and not first a unity, and then a duality, and after this a Trinity. Therefore, when your honour says there are two principles, the Father and the Son, of the Holy Spirit who is consubstantial with them, they will need some other principle before themselves which gathers the two into one. For unity must proceed all and every duality, and it follows in your theology that there will be four things that are deities. For as we Greeks say: The first principle is the Father, who exists as the principle of two who are consubstantial, and also exists as unity, and to him belongs from that unity a duality which unites, and he does not require any other in so far as there is no need for something that initiates the unity. But, following on what you say, positing that the principle is a duality, it is necessary that something other, a single, come before it. Again, unity is before duality in nature. But for duality to precede a unity, and one which is simple, is against nature and impossible. And if that which is according to nature is good, then certainly and in every way that which is against nature is likewise evil.

12. The emperor, however, since he heard that they could not defend their own writing, wishing to cover up their disgrace, said: 'Let that writing be disregarded, because it produces only controversy. Let us proceed to your case; demonstrate through the writings of the saints that these things which you say are true.' And straightaway one of our brothers, upon whom the

158 THE DISPUTATIO

Lord had bestowed favour in the literature of the Greeks,[108] opened the book of blessed Cyril on the ninth anathema and began to read in Greek. What he read was as follows:

'Blessed Cyril says: *if anyone says that the one Lord Jesus Christ is glorified by the Spirit as if by some foreign power, which by using him and being received by him is able to work against the unclean spirits, and to fulfill in men divine signs, and does not say rather that it is through his own Spirit that he worked the divine signs, let him be anathema.*[109] Likewise, later on, he says these words explaining the matter more openly: *being made man, he remained the Only-Begotten Word of God, and thus God, being everything that the Father was, except alone being the Father, and having as his own the Holy Spirit, which was from him and essential in nature with him, he performed the divine miracles.*[110] In this authoritative [text] of Cyril, the Holy Spirit is said to be the Spirit proper to the Son, who is from the Son with respect to substance; but he is not able to be the Spirit from the Son with respect to substance, unless it is by birth or procession, because there are not many modes of being in the Trinity, one person from another. But he is not able to be from him through generation, because then there would be two Fathers and two Sons in the Trinity. Therefore, what remains is that he is from him through procession. And Cyril says that those who do not believe this are anathematised.'

Then, being confused by this authoritative [text], not having here anything to criticise, they said: 'Read on, you will hear what the saint opposes: *And they brought a certain heretic, Theodoticus by name,*[111] *who had been condemned in the fifth council,*[112] *who spoke against the saint as a heretic saying: 'Cyril, who said the Holy Spirit was the proper Spirit of the Son, blasphemed not only men, but the Seraphim and God himself. To*

---

108 The text specifically refers to the literature, or *litteratura*, of the Greeks, as opposed to merely Greek letters: Golubovich, 'Disputatio,' 443 line 4.

109 Cyril of Alexandria, *Explicatio duodecimo capitum*, Anathema IX, Migne *PG* 76, col. 308 C–D; transl. N. Russell, *Cyril of Alexandria*, 186.

110 Cyril of Alexandria, *Explicatio duodecimo capitum*, Anathema IX, Migne *PG* 76, cols 308 D – 309 A; transl. N. Russell, *Cyril of Alexandria*, 186.

111 Theodoret of Cyrrhus (393–460 [or 457/8 or 466]) was an avid supporter of Nestorius. His writings in opposition to Cyril of Alexandria were anathematized as part of the Three Chapters: E. Ferguson, *Encyclopedia of early Christianity*, 1117–18; F. Cross and E. Livingstone, *Oxford dictionary of the Christian Church*, 1600–01; *ODB* III, sub Theodoret of Cyrrhus.

112 Second Council of Constantinople, 553.

THE REPORT OF THE FRIARS

159

which words blessed Cyril answers saying: Behold how he has spoken, he who knows only how to accuse. And again he repeated what he said previously.'[113]

And when they saw that they did not have anything they could rightly contradict, the Emperor began to excuse them, saying: 'There Cyril spoke against the heretic, and for that reason he spoke more than was proper.'[114] To which we responded: 'Is it possible that blessed Cyril lied on account of the heretic?' He answered: 'No.' 'Therefore the Holy Spirit proceeds from the Son, as he himself says, and he who does not believe this is anathema.' And when these things were said we mutually retired.

13. On Thursday,[115] as they laboured to disguise their own confusion and contrived excuses for their sin, we responded that we no longer wished to debate over this article with them, because we had revealed clear reasons and authoritative opinions of the saints, in which the truth of this question is sufficiently revealed. And: 'If you flagrantly do not wish to assent to the truth, what more will we be able to show to you, which you might be willing to believe? And the lord Emperor is about to retire from this city[116] tomorrow; we wish in his presence to debate the second cause you gave, namely disobedience.'[117]

At last, although unwilling, in a certain way they agreed that we should move on to the *Sacrament of the altar*. And they said: 'You speak.' To which we responded thus: 'Since this pleases you, we will say what we maintain, beginning as follows: we have heard from you that it seems very tedious to you to debate syllogistically or philosophically. This is not surprising, because often it begets quarrels and unduly tender consciences. Therefore,

---

113 Cf. J. Mansi, *Sacrorum conciliorum*, V, cols 82 D – 83 D, and VI, cols 414–18. See also R. Price, *The acts of the Council of Constantinople of 553 with related texts on the Three Chapters controversy*, vol. 1, *General introduction, letters and edicts, Sessions I–V* (Liverpool: Liverpool University Press, 2009), 281–82.

114 For the first time, Emperor John III Vatatzes personally contributes to the arguments.

115 26 January 1234.

116 Nicaea.

117 It is unclear what the friars mean by 'disobedience,' *inobedientie*: Golubovich, 'Disputatio,' 444 line 7. This may be a reference to the issue of papal primacy, a recurrent issue in ecclesiastical negotiations between East and West, especially after 1204, but neither the friars nor the patriarch and his clergy have identified this as a 'reason' for schism. Indeed, the 'second reason you gave' suggests that the friars want to move on to the problem of azymes.

160   THE DISPUTATIO

we have determined, concerning a Sacrament of such nature, to discuss the truth simply, but nevertheless truthfully and faithfully. Therefore, we will start by putting to you a simple question, in which the truth will appear immediately, if you answer correctly.' And they answered: 'That approach greatly pleases us; you may speak.' But wishing to divert to other questions on the azymes and fermenting and trifles and nonsense, they spun out the time all the way to the hour for the midday meal.[118] Finally the Patriarch said: 'Show us in what manner and with what material you work, and we will answer you.' Therefore, when we had shown our method and material, he begged a truce until after lunch.[119] When we agreed to delay the *disputatio* until after lunch, he answered saying: 'These are difficult questions. And we have our brothers, the Patriarch[s] of Jerusalem, Alexandria, Antioch, without whose counsel it is not for us to answer those things. We will assemble a council for around the middle of March. We ask that you be present at that council, and you will hear what will be answered to you regarding the questions you have posed to us.' To this we answered in this way: 'We have sufficiently explained to you that the lord Pope, of whose holiness we are servants, sent us to no council, nor to another Patriarch, but to you. For this reason we do not dare, nor do we wish, to extend beyond his mandate to something else, which might be prejudicial to his holiness or to the Roman Church. Nevertheless, we advise you to gather your brothers so that you may have good and effective and timely counsel about the peace and reformation of the Church, and then write to us in Constantinople. We will remain in that place until your petition in the middle of March, and we will await your answer, so that we may know what we can report with certainty on this matter to him who sent us. And may God grant to us to hear such things to report, that it may be to the glory of his name and to the shared joy of each Church; and may God be blessed in all and through all.' And thus we mutually retired.

14. On Friday,[120] after celebrating mass, we were received at court, that we might take leave from the Emperor, since he was about to depart early

---

118 *prandendi*, from *prandeo*, probably refers to a midday meal. See P. Glare, *Oxford Latin dictionary*, 1450.

119 Again, the term to denote a meal, *prandium*, is ambiguous. However, if we are correct about the earlier mention of a midday meal with *prandendi*, we can interpret *prandium* here in the same way: Golubovich, 'Disputatio,' 444 line 21.

120 27 January 1234.

THE REPORT OF THE FRIARS 161

the next morning.[121] And finding the Emperor and Patriarch together, the Emperor began to discuss with us, in what manner the Patriarch and the Church of the Greeks might be able to be reconciled with the Church of the Romans. To which we gave the following answer: 'It could be reconciled in this way, if it were to believe and preach what the Roman Church believes (whether or not it sings [the same] would not make much difference, we believe, to the Roman Church),[122] and if [the Church of the Greeks] were to obey in the same way, and in the same matters concerning which it obeyed before the schism.' And the Emperor added: 'If the lord Patriarch wished to submit to the Church of the Romans, would the lord Pope restore to him his right?'[123] To this we answered in this way: 'If the Patriarch were to pay the obedience and other things which are owed to his mother [church], we believe[124] that he will find greater mercy than he expects, in the presence of the lord Pope and the whole Church of the

121 The friars give no indication of a reason for the emperor's departure from Nicaea. George Akropolites relates that Nymphaion was a favoured residence of Vatatzes, especially during winter. As these events were taking place in January, we might imagine that Vatatzes was preparing to make his way there: Akropolites, *History*, 68 lines 1–2, 85 lines 1–2; transl. R. Macrides, 41.220, 47.245. For more on Nymphaion as an imperial residence, see R. Macrides, *George Akropolites, The History*, 87–88.

122 The friars are careful to make a distinction between what is *required* for reconciliation and what *may be required*: Golubovich, 'Disputatio,' 445 line 5. They are conscious that their response to the inquiry from Vatatzes might well come up in future negotiations between Rome and Nicaea, and they do not want to bind Gregory IX to an offer or agreement to which he did not consent.

123 The Latin word *ius* leaves this question open to interpretation: Golubovich, 'Disputatio,' 445 line 8. Vatatzes may be asking whether the Greeks would be allowed to keep their customs and liturgy in the event of a restored union. The more common interpretation of *ius* in this question is that it refers to the patriarch's rightful See in Constantinople: R. Wolff, 'The Latin Empire of Constantinople and the Franciscans,' 226; M. Angold, *Church and society in Byzantium*, 523; A. Siecienski, *The papacy and the Orthodox*, 294; J. Doran, 'Rites and wrongs in 1234,' 139; J. Hussey, *The Orthodox Church in the Byzantine Empire*, 215; R. Spence, 'Gregory IX's attempted expeditions,' 168. If this interpretation is correct, the true intent of Vatatzes' question to the friars would be 'if the patriarch submitted to the Church of the Romans, would the pope restore Constantinople to us?' The only historian to express reservations about this interpretation was John Langdon, who agreed that *ius* refers to the patriarch's authority over Constantinople but insisted that the term is limited to the issue of ecclesiastical jurisdiction, not political control: J. Langdon, 'Byzantino-Papal discussions in 1234,' 213.

124 Again, the friars are careful to state how they 'believe' (*credimus*) the pope will react: Golubovich, 'Disputatio,' 445 line 10.

162   THE DISPUTATIO

Romans.'[125] And, accepting his leave, we withdrew from Nicaea and left for Constantinople.[126]

15. About the middle of March, the Patriarch sent a messenger with letters inviting us to a certain *Leschara*[127] of Vatatzes, where he promised to unite his own prelates and patriarchs, and to convoke a council. And, as if forgetting the meeting which happened between us in Nicaea, in every way in his letter he assumed that we would go there. Therefore, astonished by such a command, we wrote back in reply that we were very much surprised. At this time we were awaiting the response after he had summoned the prelates to a council, and now he asks us to come to that council, when we should be returning to the Roman Curia. But lest our work be unfruitful, and because we are compelled by the love of God, which *does not seek its own, but that which is of Jesus Christ*,[128] and puts common good before individual advantage, for your sake[129] we decided to wait again until the end of March. Therefore, we continued to petition him to do what he was going to do as quickly as possible.

Part II. *Deeds at Nymphaion in Lydia*

16. At the end of March, [the Patriarch] wrote back to us saying that he had received the letters, but he could scarcely hear[130] them because of the pain

---

125 Robert Wolff saw in this response a tremendous ability by the friars to give straight-forward yet 'evasive answers': R. Wolff, 'The Latin Empire of Constantinople and the Franciscans,' 226.

126 It is difficult to measure the attitude of Vatatzes based on the depiction of the friars here. He appears eager for a possible compromise, but the friars offer no information regarding his reaction to their answers. Robert Wolff maintained that Vatatzes, who had high hopes for the results of the *disputatio*, was greatly discouraged by this particular exchange. He argued that, from this point on, the emperor, who had 'maintained a friendly attitude toward the envoys,' becomes increasingly angry with them: R. Wolff, 'The Latin Empire of Constantinople and the Franciscans,' 226.

127 It is not clear if Leschara refers to a building or a settlement, but the name may be a Latin corruption of Achyraous, a fortress overlooking the Makestos (Simav) River between Lopadion and Nymphaion.

128 1 Corinthians 13:5; Philippians 2:21.

129 i.e. Pope Gregory IX's sake.

130 *audire poterat*, suggesting that the letter was read aloud: Golubovich, 'Disputatio,' 445 line 29.

THE REPORT OF THE FRIARS
163

in his heart, as their content filled his heart with sadness. He added that he was alone in Nicaea, and he could not respond to us because to make and restore peace and discuss our faith pertains to everyone collectively, 'I had come to believe [it would be possible] to discuss these things with them and with you together. But if you depart now, it will seem to us that you have not come for peace, but in order to test us.' He even wrote to our Brothers, namely brother *Benedict*, Minister of Romania,[131] and brother *Jacob of Russano*,[132] who were then present in Constantinople, that they should in every way put to us what he had in mind, promising that if we went to the council, we would return to the curia with great joy.[133] And in addition, we received letters from the Emperor,[134] who urged us in every way to return to him at *Leschara*, because he had prepared a ship for us, and all necessities for our crossing, and that of his own messengers, whom he intended to send to the presence of the lord Pope.[135] In addition, the land of Constantinople was as if abandoned by all protection. The lord emperor *John*[136] was poor. All the mercenary

131 Benedict of Arezzo, identified by Salimbene de Adam as Franciscan provincial minister of the East, Salimbene de Adam, *Cronica*, ed. G. Scalia, 63 lines 16–17; transl. J. Baird, *The Chronicle of Salimbene de Adam*, 18. See also R. Wolff, 'The Latin Empire of Constantinople and the Franciscans,' 226.

132 Jacob of Russano, a Franciscan missionary who was delivering papal letters to the king of Georgia: Potthast, *Reg.*, no. 9141, 783; G. Golubovich, *Biblioteca*, vol. 1, 162–63; vol. 2, 299–300; R. Wolff, 'The Latin Empire of Constantinople and the Franciscans,' 226.

133 It is unclear if Germanos II was only attempting to pressure officials of the Franciscan Order to win over the friars, or if he intended to appeal to the government apparatus of Latin Constantinople to achieve his end. If the latter, then it is notable that he knew enough of the governmental hierarchy of Latin Constantinople to know to whom to direct his appeal.

134 John III Vatatzes.

135 That Vatatzes would prepare a ship to sail to Italy for the sole purpose of union negotiations is significant. It was not uncommon for diplomatic embassies to find travel aboard commercial vessels. Michael McCormick has described the fluid boundaries between merchant and ambassador: M. McCormick, *Origins of the European economy: communications and commerce, AD 300–900* (Cambridge: Cambridge University Press, 2001), 237–43; M. McCormick, 'Byzantium on the move: imagining a communications history,' in *Travel in the Byzantine world: papers from the thirty-fourth spring symposium of Byzantine Studies, Birmingham, April 2000*, ed. R. Macrides (Aldershot: Ashgate, 2002), 6. Therefore, we can deduce from the offer from Vatatzes to take up the expense of outfitting a vessel specifically for the sake of continued union negotiations that he placed a high priority on those proceedings, and that he was optimistic that those discussions would succeed.

136 John of Brienne, died 1237, king of Jerusalem and Latin emperor of Constantinople, father-in-law to both Frederick II Hohenstaufen and Baldwin II. George Akropolites comments on the rise of John of Brienne as Latin emperor: Akropolites, *History*, 44 line 6

164 THE DISPUTATIO

soldiers had departed. The ships of the Venetians, Pisans, Anconitans, and other nations were preparing to withdraw, and indeed some had already departed.[137] Considering, therefore, the desolate land, we feared danger, because that land was situated in the middle of its enemies. *Asan*,[138] king of the Bulgarians, in the North, *Vatatzes* from the East and South, and *Manuel*[139] surrounded it from the West.[140] For this reason we proposed to discuss a truce between the Emperor of Constantinople and Vatatzes to last till the end of the year.[141] Compelled by these reasons, it was the desire of all that we return to the land of Vatatzes. Nevertheless, lest we should be seen to attempt these things for our own intentions alone, we consulted the chapter of Holy Sophia and the prelates of the land, and moreover the Emperor himself,[142] about this matter, who all unanimously gave to us the same advice.

– 45 line 22; transl. R. Macrides 27.184–85. For the agreement making John of Brienne senior emperor in Constantinople, see G. Tafel and G. Thomas, *Urkunden zur alteren Handels- und Staatsgeschichte der Republik Venedig mit besonderen Beziehungen auf Byzanz und die Levante*, vol. 2 (Vienna: Hof- und Staatsdrucker, 1856), no. 273, 265–70. For more on John of Brienne's career see R. Wolff, 'The Latin Empire of Constantinople and the Franciscans,' 214–15; R. Spence, 'Gregory IX's attempted expeditions,' 164; P. Lock, *Franks in the Aegean*, 62–63; G. Perry, *John of Brienne*, 157–88.

137 This remark indicates a truly desperate situation. The friars state that several Italian ships had already abandoned Constantinople by March of 1234. Modern scholarship has shown that sailing before March was a dangerous proposition. John Pryor explains that it was only in the thirteenth century that new technology made the sea voyage from east to west in winter safer to attempt, but it was still a prospect to be avoided: J. Pryor, *Geography, technology, and war: studies in the maritime history of the Mediterranean, 649–1571* (Cambridge: Cambridge University Press, 1988), 88. According to Michael McCormick, the optimal sailing season began in April: M. McCormick, *Origins of the European economy*, 450–53. Thus we must consider that the Italians in question were especially eager to depart from the Latin Empire.

138 John II Asen.

139 Manuel Komnenos Doukas, ruler of Thessalonike: Akropolites, *History*, 43 line 19 – 44 line 5; transl. R. Macrides, 26.182.

140 The friars' description of the enemies of the Latin Empire is strikingly similar to that found in a letter of Henry I over two decades earlier: G. Prinzing, 'Der Brief Kaiser Heinrichs von Konstantinopel,' 411–18.

141 The friars here appear to accept the task of envoys from the Latin Empire – an occupation that was probably not part of their mandate from the pope. This was their only mention of serving as representatives of the Latin Empire. They do not indicate whether they were successful in gaining the aforementioned truce.

142 John of Brienne.

THE REPORT OF THE FRIARS   165

17. Therefore, on the third Sunday in Lent,[143] the final Sunday in March,[144] we began the journey to *Leschera*, and the next day, after crossing the sea, we came to the place of *Chalogerorum*,[145] situated on the sea.[146] From here we sent two pairs of letters by different messengers to the Patriarch of Nicaea, asking that he hasten to the aforementioned place, because at that place he would find us prepared, as he had requested in his letters. Departing from that place, we sent a messenger with our letters to the Emperor, apprising him of our approach. Thus that Sunday, *Laetare Ierusalem*,[147] we were near *Lopadion*,[148] and, departing from there on Monday,[149] we came to *Alescheran*. And because that place was assigned to us as much by the Emperor as by the Patriarch, we paused there.

But when our arrival had been announced to the Emperor, he promptly sent his own messenger to us, who came to us on the evening of that Thursday,[150] delivering to us the letters of the Emperor beseeching us to come to *Nymphaion*,[151] because he awaited us there. Because we had heard

---

143 Literally, the 'third Sunday in 40' – *tertia Dominica in XL*: Golubovich, 'Disputatio,' 446 line 20.

144 26 March 1234.

145 i.e., 'the place of monks,' probably the port of Kios in the Gulf of Myrlea on the Sea of Marmara, due west of Nicaea: Golubovich, 'Disputatio,' 446 note 7; W. Ramsay, *Historical geography of Asia Minor*, 180. The friars almost certainly lodged in a monastery in the area, as the word *locus* in the terminology of medieval monastic orders usually refers to a monastic institution: M. Roncaglia, *Les frères mineurs et l'eglise grecque orthodoxe*, 70 note 1.

146 See the map of this journey on p. xv.

147 i.e., the fourth Sunday of Lent, 2 April 1234.

148 Lopadion, modern Ulubad, is on the banks of the Rhyndakos river. This fortress, not far from Lake Apollonias, was built in 1130 and protected a bridge that comprised an important link between the Marmara, Hellespont, and Aegean regions: F. Hasluck, *Cyzicus*, 78–83; Golubovich, 'Disputatio,' 447 note 2; W. Ramsay, *Historical geography of Asia Minor*, 160; C. Foss, 'The defenses of Asia Minor,' 159–61; C. Foss and D. Winfield, *Byzantine fortifications*, 145.

149 3 April 1234.

150 6 April 1234.

151 George Akropolites tells us that the Nicaean emperors spent a good deal of time at Nymphaion since 1204 and indicates that it was a winter residence: Akropolites, *History*, 175 lines 22–26; transl. R. Macrides, 84.369. See also D. Jacoby, 'The economy of Latin Constantinople, 1204–1261,' in *Urbs Capta, the Fourth Crusade and its consequences*, ed. A. Laiou (Paris: Lethielleux, 2005), 207; D. Angelov, *Imperial ideology and political thought in Byzantium*, 5. Ruth Macrides, however, demonstrated that the presence of the Laskarids at Nymphaion was not merely determined by the seasons, and that it was more of a regular imperial residence: R. Macrides, *George Akropolites, The History*, 87–88. Michael Angold noted the government operation at Nymphaion: M. Angold, 'Administration

166 THE DISPUTATIO

no definite reports of the Patriarch or other prelates, we answered that we were not able to respond to him about this, before we had received a messenger from the patriarch.[152] On the following Sabbath[153] a messenger from the Patriarch arrived with letters from him, in which he indicated his arrival to us and implored us to go before him to *Nymphaion*, saying that he would hurry and follow us immediately.

18. Therefore, departing from *Lescherea* on the Sunday of the Passion,[154] after four days we arrived at *Nymphaion*. Finding the Emperor there, we awaited the arrival of the Patriarch, who reached *Nymphaion* on Thursday[155] at about the evening hour.

On Friday,[156] after a meal,[157] we approached him, asking that he expedite our business, should he be able. To which he answered: 'I am prepared, and behold the prelates who have assembled; they too desire to expedite [this business] so that they might be able to be in their own churches on these holy days.' And, as we considered the word of so great a man to be reliable, we happily returned to our lodging.

On the Monday[158] after Palm Sunday,[159] we waited for him to send for us. But when he did not send for us, we sent two of our Brothers to the Patriarch, wishing to learn why he did not send for us. He answered them that his own prelates had not yet assembled. The Brothers, thinking that he intended to prolong the business, sharply urged that he should summon

of the Empire of Nicaea,' *Byzantinische Forschungen* 19 (1993), 13. Girolamo Golubovich described Nymphaion as 'the particular seat of the Greek emperors' of Nicaea: Golubovich, 'Disputatio,' 447 note 6. Clive Foss referred to Nymphaion as the 'regular base of operations' for Vatatzes: C. Foss, *Nicaea: A Byzantine capital and its praises*, 65. Suna Çağaptay pointed out that two emperors, Theodore II Laskaris and Michael VIII Palaiologos, were first proclaimed from Nymphaion: S. Çağaptay, 'How western is it? The palace at Nymphaion and its architectural setting,' in *Change in the Byzantine world in the twelfth and thirteenth centuries* (Istanbul: Koç Üniversitesi Anadolu Medeniyetleri Araştırma Merkezi, 2010), 357.

152 The friars' insistence on waiting for word from the patriarch again emphasizes the ecclesiastical nature of their mission and their mandate from the pope.

153 8 April 1234.

154 Departing on 9 April 1234, which was the fifth Sunday of Lent, and arriving on 12 April 1234.

155 13 April 1234.

156 14 April 1234.

157 *prandium* here probably signifies an early meal – i.e. breakfast – indicated by the urgency the friars place on their business in the following text.

158 17 April 1234.

159 i.e. the sixth Sunday of Lent.

THE REPORT OF THE FRIARS 167

us. For that reason, being provoked against the Brothers, he said: 'We are amazed by the Brothers, when we have 30 headings against you, and you wish to be dealt with in a moment.' And he added: 'Let the Brothers come tomorrow if they wish, and they will have the *disputatio*.' When we heard that, we went to the Emperor, telling him everything in order, believing that he would compel them to keep their promise. At first he began to excuse the prelates for not having assembled, because some of them came from considerable distance, and the Patriarch of Antioch[160] had only just arrived: 'In addition, this is a time of prayer and great affliction. You should not be surprised if they are reluctant at this time to take part in the *disputatio*.' And at length he said: 'I ask that you wait until after Easter; in the meantime, the prelates and the Patriarch will be assembled, and then on the Monday they will answer you.' And thus he obtained a truce from us.

19. When those days had passed, on the Monday[161] after Easter the prelates were assembled after a meal[162] in the home of the Patriarch,[163] and his own messengers were sent to summon us. When we had gathered among them,

---

160 Symeon II, patriarch from 1206–1235, was probably of Syrian origin, and was elevated to the patriarchate as the result of a conflict between the prince of Antioch, Bohemond IV, and the Latin patriarch, Peter I of Angouleme. When the prince and patriarch reconciled Symeon II was exiled from Antioch, and eventually sought refuge in the Byzantine court at Nicaea. See V. Grumel, *Traité d'études Byzantines: I: La Chronologie (Bibliotheque Byzantine publiee sous la direction de P. Lemerle)* (Paris: Presses universitaires de France, 1958), 448; C. Cahen, *La Syrie du Nord à l'epoque des Croisades et la principauté franque d'Antioch* (Paris: Presses de l'Ifpo, 1940), 612–19; B. Hamilton, *The Latin Church in the Crusader states: the secular church* (London: Variorum, 1980), 221, 313–21; J. Prawer, *Crusader institutions* (Oxford: Clarendon Press, 1980), 71–73; N. Jamil and J. Johns, 'An original Arabic document from crusader Antioch (1213 AD),' in *Texts, documents and artefacts: Islamic studies in honour of D. S. Richards*, ed. D. Richards (Leiden: Brill, 2003), 167–68. Symeon II was eventually made to do penance for his submission to the Latin patriarch, Peter II of Ivrea, before being restored to communion with the Greek Orthodox Church: Laurent, *Reg.*, no. 1220, 28.

161 24 April 1234.

162 *prandium* may again refer to breakfast, as the report of the friars continues to express their eagerness to proceed with the discussions.

163 *hospitio Patriarche*: Golubovich, 'Disputatio,' 448 line 20. This comment indicates that the patriarch had a permanent residence in Nymphaion, where the Nicaean emperors, especially John III Vatatzes, often held court. However, it is also possible that the residence was a monastery or a private home made available to the patriarch on this and other occasions. The comments by the Latin friars do not attest definitively to the status of this 'home of the patriarch.'

the Patriarch said: 'It is known to you that we had a *disputatio* in Nicaea about the Holy Spirit, but at that time I was alone. Our prelates who are now present would gladly hear about the progress on that question.' From these words we deduced that he was dissembling in answering our question, wishing to bring us back to the issue of the Holy Spirit. We then began to tell the reason for our journey, and how it was discussed in Nicaea, and how the Patriarch himself promised to send to us around the middle of March a response to the question put to him about our Sacrament, and how often he had altered our agreement. And then, wishing in their presence not to appear compelled by promises or by the orders of our superior, but only by goodwill and love of peace and harmony, and the promises of the Patriarch, which he had intimated to us in his own letters, that if we came, he would make us return happy to the one who had sent us to him. 'Therefore, convinced by the hope of such good things and by brotherly love, we did not plead as an excuse the weariness caused by distant journeys, the perils of the sea, the physical labour, nor the loss of time, but we preferred rather to obey your will through many physical discomforts, rather than to satisfy our own advantage. We have come to listen to your answer.' And they said: 'On what?' 'On the question about which the Patriarch promised to consult you.' And they said: 'We were not present for the question. We did not hear [it].' And we answered: 'This was the question, and we ask the same of you: whether we are able to accomplish the body of Christ in azymes, or not?' To which they answered: 'The issue between us and you is twofold, namely about the procession of the Holy Spirit, and about the body of Christ. Let us first, therefore, discuss the procession of the Holy Spirit in the presence of the whole council, because that question precedes the other, and then we will answer you on the other question.' To which we answered: 'You answered the question on the procession of the Holy Spirit, and we know perfectly well what and how progress was made on that question. The question [now asked] was on the body of Christ, and this has not yet been answered. For that reason we now seek a response from the whole council.' Complaining by way of subterfuge, that they might [avoid] answering the aforementioned question, they said: 'The order of theology is confused, if that which is of higher importance is not to be discussed first.' And we answered: 'The order which you seek was maintained in what was done in Nicaea, when it was right and proper to debate both matters, but we have come to hear only your response on the second matter. Therefore, your rationale concerning the order in which the arguments should be presented is of no concern

THE REPORT OF THE FRIARS 169

to us.' When they had repeatedly gone over the same rationale, a certain Calogerus, in the dress of their philosophers,[164] came forward and said: 'God was without beginning and from eternity, one in essence, three in persons. The flesh of Christ began in time, and had a beginning. But that which is without beginning has precedence over that which is from time. Therefore, one ought to come to the question on the Holy Spirit, which is eternal, before discussion of the body of Christ, which has its origin in time. That order is indeed natural, and if we do not protect this order, we will sin against the order.' To which we answered: 'That which is in the body of Christ about which we speak is the deity itself, for there is true deity and true humanity. Therefore, in dealing with the body of Christ, as we ask, we are dealing with both.[165] Likewise, such is the order in the Gospel, for Matthew began from the incarnation of Christ, and at the end of his Gospel spoke of the Trinity saying: *Go, teach all nations, baptizing them in the name of the Father and of the Son and of the Holy Spirit.*[166] And that is the order which we seek.' When these things had been said, that philosopher became silent, and later was not present.

Then the Patriarch spoke, saying: 'Since you compel us, we will write our response to both questions, and give it to you.' Therefore, realizing that they did not want to answer the question, but to pass over it by dissembling, and to disguise it with their writing, we answered: 'We are not concerned about your writing, since we are present. Please speak your answer to us. Writing is done namely for those who are absent and not for those present. Therefore, seeing as we are present, answer us as though

---

164 At first glance, this phrase appears inherently redundant. The Greek word καλόγηρος, transliterated here to 'Calogerus,' often signified a monk or other ascetic: I. Ševčenko, 'The definition of philosophy in the Life of Saint Constantine,' in *For Roman Jakobson: essays on the occasion of his sixtieth birthday, 11 October 1956,* ed. M. Hale (The Hague: Mouton, 1956), 449–57. In addition, an individual 'in the dress of their philosophers' can also be understood to indicate a monk. Thus, it is possible to interpret this phrase as saying 'a certain monk, in the dress of one of their monks.' In order to resolve this redundancy, we must reconsider what the friars mean by 'Calogerus.' Their report introduces other Byzantine speakers, but never as 'Calogerus' or 'a calogerus': see above, ch. 6 and ch. 7. In addition, the individual is described as 'in the dress of one of their philosophers.' It is possible, therefore, that the friars overheard this individual referred to as a 'calogerus' and mistook that appellation for his name. Thus, we can understand the phrase as saying 'a certain individual, with the name of Calogerus, who was in the dress of their philosophers ... .'

165 A possible corruption in the text makes it difficult to interpret this sentence.

166 Matthew 28:19.

170 THE DISPUTATIO

we were present.'[167] To which the Patriarch said: 'If you wish to recite, in the presence of the whole council, the order and proceedings of the entire *disputatio* which was conducted in Nicaea, in a like manner we will answer your question.' To which we answered with the following: 'Provide us with an answer to this question, whether or not we are able to accomplish the body of Christ in azymes. And when we have been satisfied on this question, we will recite to you the progress and proceedings of the question on the Holy Spirit, and we will answer all doubts which have been raised by the question.' And the patriarch rose and retired together with the other prelates to take counsel. And returning thence they answered: 'We beg a truce until Wednesday, and then we will answer you just as we have promised.' And because we have often found them false, lest they deceive us, we said: 'So that we might not prolong these words and assemblies, behold we repeat our demand.' After we once again repeated our position, they approved it, and thus we mutually retired.

20. On Wednesday,[168] about the first hour, we came to the home of the Patriarch where the council had assembled. And when we were in the middle of the council, the archbishop of Amastris[169] in Paphlagonia began

167 In the 1136 *disputatio* in Constantinople, the western advocate, Anselm of Havelberg, states that everything in the *disputatio* was taken down in writing by appointed notaries, but he himself asked that his speech not be translated literally in a word for word manner, as he might be misunderstood: Anselm of Havelberg, *Antikeimenon*, Migne *PL* 188, col. 1164 A–B; transl. A. Criste and C. Neel, *Anticimenon*, 85–87. The friars never make a statement about concerns over being misunderstood, indicating their confidence with the Greek language as well their eagerness to complete their business and depart.

168 26 April 1234.

169 It is possible to identify this individual as Nicholas Kaloeidas, metropolitan of Amastris. Members of the Kaloeidas family had reached high stations before 1204, such as Constantine Kaloeidas, who was *oikoumenikos didaskalos* in Constantinople before the Fourth Crusade: R. Browning, 'The patriarchal school at Constantinople in the twelfth century,' *Byzantion* 32 (1962), 197. They remained well established in the Empire of Nicaea, especially in and around Smyrna, not far from Nymphaion: M. Angold, *A Byzantine government in exile*, 265–66, 269. One Nicholas Kaloeidas, *nomikos* of Ephesos, is listed on a document from 1216 and may have been the same individual identified here in Nymphaion in 1234: F. Miklosich and J. Müller, *Acta et Diplomata Graeca Medii aevi*, vol. 6, no. 61, 176. Ruth Macrides, however, has presented the possibility that more than one individual was named Nicholas Kaloeidas: R. Macrides, *George Akropolites, The History*, 21 note 128. The archbishop of Amastris identified by the friars is almost certainly the same individual who had served as a favourite champion and representative of Germanos II. He advocated for the rights of the patriarch in Nicaea with the Greek clergy of Epiros and condemned

THE REPORT OF THE FRIARS   171

to speak thus: 'It is known to you, venerable *apocrisarii* of the lord Pope, that the aforementioned most holy Pope sent through you a letter to the lord Patriarch,[170] upon hearing the contents of which, we were amazed to no small extent by a certain argument[171] that he had placed at the end of the letter. From this argument it seems to us that he wants to suggest that our Sacrament in leavened bread and your Sacrament in azymes are two Sacraments. He says that our Sacrament and yours are indicated through the two disciples running together to the tomb, saying:[172] *The Greek – running ahead to the faith with the younger disciple, and not ungrateful for such grace, choosing to be reminded daily of the honour by which God, out of compassion for human misery, chose to become a human capable of suffering, has determined that the host be offered as leavened.*[173] *But the Latin, following scripture, with the elder Peter, had earlier entered the tomb, from which proceeds spiritual meaning, and saw laying there the linens, which had covered the most holy body, designating the Church, and he observed the separate napkin which had been over the head. Thus he chose to celebrate the more marvellous sacrament of the glorified body in the azymes of purity.*[174] From these words it seems

---

the assumption of the imperial title by Theodore Doukas: Laurent, *Reg.*, no. 1248, 55. His service to the patriarch is mentioned in a letter of Germanos II: J. B. Pitra, *Analecta sacra et classica. Spicilegio solesmensi parata*, vol. 6 (Paris: apud Roger et Chernowitz bibliopolas; Rome: ex officina libraria Philippi Cuggiani, 1891), 483–86. Such an individual would have certainly had the trust and faith of the patriarch in addressing the papal representatives in 1234.

170 Tautu, *Acta*, no. 193, 266–68.

171 *verbo*, literally 'word,' but the friars here seem to be translating from the Greek word λόγος, with its more varied meaning: Golubovich, 'Disputatio,' 450 line 20.

172 The following analogy is taken from the letter from Gregory IX to Germanos II: Tautu, *Acta*, no. 193, 267 lines 25–36 (Source IV).

173 This reading of the letter from Gregory IX omits some of the pope's words. 'So, following what the apostle says, that is that the [whole] lump is corrupted by the leaven, the corruption, to which the body of the lord, before the resurrection, was subject, is made manifest in the leaven [of the host].' – *ut, Apostolo dicente, quod ex ferment massa corrumpitur, in ferment corruption, cui ante resurrectionem corpus dominicum subiacere potuit, ostendatur*: Tautu, *Acta*, no. 193, 267 lines 29–31.

174 John 20.4–7; 1 Corinthians 5.8. John Erickson described this as a 'typical position' held by the Latin Church. It acknowledges the symbolism behind the Greek usage while maintaining the preference for unleavened bread: J. Erickson, 'Leavened and unleavened,' 170–71. Pope Innocent III uses this analogy in a letter dated 13 November 1204: Hageneder, *Die Register Innocenz' III*, vol. 7, no. 154, 264–70; transl. A. Andrea, *Contemporary sources for the Fourth Crusade* (Leiden: Brill, 2000), 119–21.

172   THE DISPUTATIO

to us that the lord Pope wishes to suggest two traditions. Therefore, we ask you if it is your belief that these [two] disciples signify two traditions in the Sacrament, [the tradition] of the Greeks and [the tradition] of the Latins.' We considered carefully the cunning way in which they had devised to avoid giving a response in whatever way possible, [using] the opportunity presented by the letter to divert us to other questions.[175] We briefly answered: 'It is true that we bore a letter from the lord Pope, and if you take the time to carefully examine the writing in this letter, you will find that it elegantly answers the uncertainty of your question. But as it is written concerning the law – [the authority] to interpret belongs to the one who composed it[176] – the letter of the lord Pope is not for us to interpret. But if there is something unclear to you, write it in a letter to the lord Pope and he will explain it to you.' And they answered: 'On the contrary, you are the messengers, you ought to explain.' Therefore, they began to press harder, and repeatedly to go over the same question, and we repeated the same response. After wasting time on that nonsense and trifle up to the evening hour, we were afflicted by boredom and anguish of the heart, and not wishing to endure their malice any longer, we answered them: 'We see you are wasting time and that you labour to avoid our question and you do not dare to profess your faith. Henceforth we will open our heart to you in open speech, and we will let you know what we think of you. Now we have determined that you think badly of our Sacrament in azymes. We know this first through your writings, which are full of this heresy. Second, because you do not dare to answer the question put forward on the Sacrament, lest your heresy be laid bare. Third, because your deeds prove it. You wash your altars after a Latin has celebrated on them.[177] Fourth, because you compel Latins who come to your Sacrament

175 The other question: i.e. the procession of the Holy Spirit. The Byzantines may well have been trying to dissemble in their comments, or they may have been expressing genuine concerns over the unity of the Church as demonstrated by the Eucharist. For more on the importance of this matter, see J. Erickson, 'Leavened and unleavened,' 171.

176 For *eius est interpretari*, see A. Fellmeth and M. Horwitz, *Guide to Latin in international law* (Oxford: Oxford University Press, 2011), 89.

177 A very common complaint among Latins, both clergy and laity, was that the Greeks washed altars after Latins had performed their ceremonies upon them. Odo of Deuil famously complains of this in his chronicle of the Second Crusade: Odo of Deuil, *De profectione Ludovici VII in orientem*, ed. and transl. V. Berry, 54–55. The practice was condemned by the Fourth Lateran Council in 1215: ed. and transl. N. Tanner, *Decrees of the Ecumenical Councils*, vol. 1, 235–36. Deno John Geanakoplos argued that continued complaints of this

THE REPORT OF THE FRIARS 173

to apostatise and repudiate the Sacraments of the Roman Church.[178] Fifth, that you have removed the lord Pope from your diptychs, but we know that you only remove excommunicates and heretics; therefore you consider him to be excommunicated and a heretic. Sixth, because once each year you excommunicate him, as some have reported to us what they have heard.' Then the Chartophylax[179] rose in the middle of the council and said: 'As for your accusation that we excommunicate the lord Pope, we say that is false. Whoever says it, let him depart or he will suffer evil things. You should not be surprised by the other things we do, because when your Latins seized Constantinople, they shattered churches, demolished altars, stealing gold and silver, they threw relics of the saints into the sea, they trampled holy icons, and they made churches into stables for mules, so that the prophecy appeared fulfilled: *God, the nations came into your inheritance, they defiled your holy temple, they laid low Jerusalem* etc.'[180] And after these things had been spoken the Patriarch said: 'If you are surprised that we have removed the Pope from our diptychs, I ask why he has removed me from his own diptychs?' And we began by responding to the last objection, we said: 'The lord Pope never removed you from his diptychs, because you were never there. But if you are asking about your predecessors, please read whether the Pope removed you before you removed him.'[181] They did not reply to this at all. 'As for the other things which you lay upon the Roman Church, you lay nothing [upon the Church, because] these deeds were not done with the agreement or at the command of the Roman Church. But if these things were done, the people who did

nature indicate a deepening resentment of Latin occupation from 1204 to 1261 by Greek clergy: D. J. Geanakoplos, *Byzantine east and Latin west,* 104.

178 See above, ch. 4, for the earlier incident involving the 'certain Latin' chastised by his priest in Nicaea.

179 The aforementioned Aulenos. He is the only spokesman for the Greek Church identified by the friars to appear as speaking in the *disputatio* at both Nicaea and Nymphaion.

180 Psalm 79:1. This account of Latin atrocities committed during the conquest of Constantinople in 1204 mirrors those of earlier Byzantine authors: Choniates, *Historia,* 585–95; transl. H. Magoulias, 322–27; Mesarites I, 45–47; transl. M. Angold, 169–71. This was not the first time Latin atrocities committed in Constantinople during the Fourth Crusade were discussed during a *disputatio.* Nicholas Mesarites referenced such actions in the *disputatio* with Cardinal Benedict on 2 October 1206: Mesarites I, 62 lines 12–21.

181 When Pope Urban II asked in 1089 why the Byzantines had omitted his name from the diptychs no one could present a definitive reason: T. Kolbaba, 'The legacy of Humbert and Cerularius,' 51, 59–60; M. Kaplan, 'La place du schism de 1054,' 36; A. Louth, *Greek east and Latin west,* 316–17.

174 THE DISPUTATIO

them were laity, sinners, and excommunicates, presuming to commit such actions on their own authority. The whole Church should not be charged, for these things were done presumptuously by certain wicked persons. But what we say about you is true, and you testify to these things by your words and deeds. And your patriarchs and archbishops do it first, followed by the bishops, and the other prelates of your Church. You commit these acts, and you teach that they should be done. Hence you do not have an excuse for your sins. And because we find such hateful things among you, with no desire for the errors done to this point to be corrected, behold we return to him who sent us.' And thus we withdrew from the council.

21. That same day, after lunch,[182] we came to the Emperor, relating to him in order everything that had happened, with truth leading the way. After we had reported these things, we asked that he grant us safe conduct beyond his own land. Then the Emperor, speaking as an eloquent man, clever and prudent in action, modest in words, amazingly began to make excuses for his own people, and to promise improvement, adding that if the *disputatio* had taken place in his presence it would not have descended to insulting words. 'I do not wish you to depart in such discord. I wish to hear you and them concerning your question, and then you will depart having completed the business with peace and love. And behold my galleys are prepared to convey you to Apulia with my messengers, whom I will send with you to the most holy Pope. Indeed, I intend, as is proper, to show as much respect as is possible to the lord Pope with messengers, gifts and obedience, because I wish him to consider me a friend and intimate and son of his holiness.' To these words we responded: 'Lord, henceforth we wish not to hide the truth from you. It is written: *the Lord had regard for Abel and his gifts*.[183] At first it says 'for Abel,' then 'for his gifts,' as the Lord does not receive men for the sake of their gifts, but he receives their gifts for the sake of the men. Thus we know that the lord Pope will not receive you for the sake of your gifts, but when you are welcomed by him through the unity of faith, then your gifts will be acceptable to him. Please do not believe that the lord Pope wishes to accept you as a friend and son, if there is not first agreement in faith, and unity. Indeed, if you were to give all your gold and silver, he would not accept you as a son or friend, as long as

---

182 Because this meal took place after part of the day had been devoted to substantial meetings with the patriarch and his clergy, *prandium* probably indicates a midday meal.
183 Genesis 4:4.

THE REPORT OF THE FRIARS   175

you are contrary to the faith of the Roman Church. Therefore, how can we escort your messengers to the curia, when we do not dare present them to the lord Pope? Indeed, if by chance they were to come, we would be right to stand against them in the presence of our Lord.' Then the Emperor, his expression changing to grief, spoke thus: 'I saw that the Emperor *Manuel*,[184] *Theodore*[185] and many other Emperors had friendship with the Pope during the schism. Nevertheless, if you insist that I hold back my messengers, I will not send them.' To this we responded: 'We neither insist, nor warn, but know this, that we will not escort your messengers, except under hope of a peace.' And again the Emperor said: 'If you do not wish to escort them, I am unwilling to send them, because I do not wish my men, nor ships, nor property to be exposed to harm.' And he added: 'The schism has lasted for nearly 300 years,[186] and what has lasted for so long cannot be dissolved in

---

184 Manuel I Komnenos, 1143–1180. For his relationship with the papacy see P. Magdalino, 'The phenomenon of Manuel I Komnenos,' 178–85; M. Magdalino, *The empire of Manuel I Komnenos, 1143–1180* (Cambridge: Cambridge University Press, 1993), 87–95; M. Angold, *The Byzantine Empire, 1025–1204: a political history*, 2nd edn (London: Longman, 1997), 211–15, J. Rowe, 'The papacy and the Greeks (1122–1153),' *Church History: Studies in Christianity and Culture* 28:2 (1959), 124.

185 Theodore I Laskaris, 1205–1221, founded the so-called Empire of Nicaea after the Fourth Crusade. His relationship with the papacy was not always positive. In a letter from Innocent III to Theodore I, dated 17 March 1208, the pope addresses the Nicaean emperor as 'noble man' and called on Theodore I to recognize the imperial title of Henry I: Hageneder, *Die Register Innocenz' III*, vol. 11, no. 44(47), 61–64. For more on the correspondence between Innocent III and Theodore I see A. Papayianni, 'The papacy and the Fourth Crusade,' 158–62. One indication of a more amiable relationship between Theodore I and the papacy comes from Nicholas Mesarites, who claims that the emperor spoke so eloquently about peace between the two churches at the talks in Herakleia Pontike in 1214/15 that he moved the Latin representatives to tears: Mesarites III, 33 line 30 – 34 line 10; transl. M. Angold, 276–77. Despite any supposed 'friendship' between Theodore I and Rome, the eastern policies of both Innocent III and Honorius III continued to champion the Latin rite and to use the Latin Empire of Constantinople to support crusader ventures in the Holy Land: R. Spence, 'Gregory IX's attempted expeditions,' 165–66.

186 *CCC*: Golubovich, 'Disputatio,' 453 line 9. Vatatzes' understanding of the duration of the schism between the eastern and western churches puts the beginning of the divide somewhere in the tenth century. His reckoning gives us some possible insight into the Byzantine understanding of the beginning of the schism. The emperor's statement contradicts the traditional view of 1054 as the origin of the schism: S. Runciman, *The Eastern schism*, 22–77; J. Erickson, 'Leavened and unleavened,' 155–56. If we look to an earlier period, the crisis most often cited as the origin of the schism by historians comes with the Patriarch Photios: M. Jugie, *Le schisme Byzantin: aperçu historique et doctrinal* (Paris: Lethielleux, 1941), 102–55; W. Norden, *Das Papsttum und Byzanz*, 6–12; S. Runciman, *The*

176   THE DISPUTATIO

such a short time. Wait. Tomorrow I will speak to the prelates, and I will
ask them to answer your question.' And we withdrew from him.

On Thursday,[187] after the evening hour, the Emperor sent his messenger
to us asking that tomorrow, Friday, we come before him. And we agreed.
When the messenger of the Emperor withdrew, a messenger from the
Patriarch came asking that tomorrow we appear before him in the palace
of the Emperor.[188] And we answered: 'Tomorrow we will be before the
Emperor; if he is present, he will find us there.'

22. On Friday[189] morning we approached the palace of the Emperor, where
the council had assembled. And first the Emperor began to speak, saying:
'Even if the prelates had promised to answer you, it is still not surprising
if they wished first that the confusions they had over the letters of the lord
Pope should be explained to them.' To that we answered: 'We said then and
we still say now that after they have satisfied us on our question, we will
then be prepared to reply not just to that ambiguity but to all other doubts
which arise in the question.' Then, after taking counsel with the Emperor
and other prelates, the Patriarch answered first: 'And we also will answer
you.' Next, the archbishop of Amastris[190] began to speak in this way: 'You
ask if the body of Christ can be accomplished in azymes; and we answer that
it is impossible.' Therefore, wishing to understand his meaning perfectly, we
asked if they had determined it was not possible because it cannot be done
by law, or because it cannot be done at all. And they answered: 'Indeed,
because it cannot be done at all, because we know that the Lord himself used

---

Eastern schism, 22–27; T. Ware, *The Orthodox Church*, 52–56; T. Kolbaba, 'Byzantine
perceptions of Latin errors,' 19–21; F. Dvornik, *Byzantium and the Roman Primacy*, 106–17.
Unfortunately, the Photian Schism would place the beginning of the schism in the ninth
century, which again does not coincide with the comment by Vatatzes. We should not allow
this statement by Vatatzes to cause us serious pause. Dates in medieval texts are notoriously
untrustworthy. Even if we take it for granted that this is a faithful report of words spoken by
Vatatzes, it remains entirely possible that a scribe added a *C* or took one away. In any event,
attempting to identify a starting point for the schism can be inherently misleading: M. Smith,
And taking bread, 156.

187 27 April 1234.

188 The redundancy of a messenger from the emperor, and later one from the patriarch,
both requesting the same action from the friars, is striking. It is possible that the adminis-
trations of the emperor and patriarch simply lacked communication on who was to send the
message, or the episode could indicate a power play going on behind the scenes.

189 28 April 1234.

190 Again, it is possible to identify this individual as Nicholas Kaloeidas.

THE REPORT OF THE FRIARS

177

leavened bread, and so gave it to the Apostles. Whence the Apostle says in 1 Corinthians, chapter 11: *I received from the Lord, that which I passed on to you, that the Lord Jesus, on the night he was betrayed, took arton*[191] etc. Peter and the other Apostles, just as they received [the tradition in this form] from the Lord, in the same form they also passed [the tradition] to the four patriarchal churches. So Peter passed [the tradition] to Antioch, John the Evangelist [passed it] to the churches which were in Asia, Andrew [passed it] to the churches in Achaia, James [passed it] to Jerusalem, and again, blessed Peter [passed it] to blessed Clement, and thus it was first celebrated in the Roman Church, as we believe.[192] This is why we say this, that it cannot be done [using] another bread – that is in the bread of a different quality – from that which Jesus passed down, that is in the leaven.'[193] Listening to this heresy, we asked each one separately, first the Patriarch of Nicaea,[194] next [the Patriarch] of Antioch, then each prelate individually, if this was their faith, and if they believed it. And they answered separately: 'This is our faith, and we believe this.' Then we added: 'We ask that you write this and sign your name to your faith, and give the writing to us.'[195] The Patriarch of

---

191 1 Corinthians 11:23. According to the friars, the disputants make a clear differentiation between *artos*, the Greek word for bread, and the Latin word *panis*. Chris Schabel commented that the two words came to denote two distinct concepts. Greeks insisted that *artos* specifically denoted leavened bread, whereas the Latins argued that *panis* was a generic word used for all bread: C. Schabel, 'The quarrel over unleavened bread in western theology,' 91. The two groups continue to argue this point below in ch. 25. In order to convey the implications of the argument I have chosen to leave the word *arton* as it appears in the text edited by G. Golubovich.

192 What is presented here is a typical Byzantine concept of apostolic tradition. For more on this, see J. Pelikan, *The Christian tradition*, vol. 2, 164; W. de Vries, 'The college of patriarchs,' *Concilium* 8 (1965), 65–80; T. Ware, *The Orthodox Church*, 47–48; A. Papadakis, 'The Byzantines and the rise of the papacy,' 22; A. Siecienski, *The papacy and the Orthodox*, 231–32.

193 John Erickson explained that this response by the archbishop of Amastris emphasizes the gravity of the issue for the Byzantines. At stake was the whole of 'liturgical custom and humanly established ecclesiastical discipline' – an issue that no human practice should be allowed to threaten: J. Erickson, 'Leavened and unleavened,' 158 note 18.

194 Rather than referring to Germanos II as 'Patriarch of Constantinople' or 'Patriarch of the Greeks,' the friars here refer to him as the 'Patriarch of Nicaea,' *Patriarcha Nicee*: Golubovich, 'Disputatio,' 454 line 5. Germanos II referred to himself as archbishop and patriarch of Constantinople in his 1232 letter to Gregory IX, and in his letter to the Roman Cardinals that same year: Tautu, *Acta*, no. 179a, 240 lines 2–3; no. 179b, 249 lines 1–2.

195 It is notable that, whereas previously the friars had refused to allow the *disputatio* to proceed in writing, they now ask to see the Greek position in written form.

178 THE DISPUTATIO

Nicaea responded: 'And may you write for us that the Holy Spirit proceeds from the Son, and whoever disbelieves this is on the road of perdition.' And we agreed. Therefore a truce was given until the next day, so that on that day the document from each side could be written. And thus we retired.

23. On the Sabbath,[196] after a meal,[197] we were summoned to the council, and both sides offered their documents. They presented their own document to us first, the contents of which were as follows:[198] *The most honourable apocrisarii[199] of the most holy Pope of older Rome asked us if it is possible to complete the anemakton, that is, the sacrifice of the body of Christ,[200] in azymes. And we answered that this is impossible for men who wish to follow the new grace, as it [was handed down] from the beginning in the tradition of the Saviour. Indeed he passed it on to his own holy disciples and apostles through [the use of] leavened bread, according to the words of the Gospels. And they likewise passed on the mystery in this form, just as they themselves received [it], as it is written in the words of the magister Paul to the Corinthians: Brothers, I received from the Lord that which I gave to you also, that on the night the Lord Jesus was betrayed he took the arton, and giving thanks he broke it and said: Take it and eat: This is my body, which is broken for you, do this in remembrance of me. And likewise after he had dined he took the cup saying: This cup is the new covenant in my blood: Do this every time you drink in remembrance of me. Indeed as often as you eat this bread and drink this cup, you will proclaim the death of the Lord.[201] Therefore, we*

---

196 29 April 1234.

197 *prandium.* As this is the first mention of activity on this day, the meal indicated is probably breakfast. This is supported by the fact that the length of the description of talks on this day by the friars is quite extensive, from ch. 23 through ch. 25.

198 As we shall see, chs 29–30, the Greek document translated here was kept by the friars as they departed for Constantinople. According to their recollection of events, however, the document was taken from them by force shortly after beginning their return journey. Thus, the Latin translation of this treatise is the only version to survive.

199 Earlier, ch. 11, when Nikephoros Blemmydes referred to the friars as *apocrisarii*, the friars changed the text to refer to themselves as legates: M. Stavrou, *Œuvres théologiques*, vol. 1, 184 line 1; Golubovich, 'Disputatio,' 438 line 1. Unfortunately, the Greek text of this document has not come down to us, so we cannot know what the Byzantines intended to say, but it seems that the friars were content to be addressed as *apocrisarii*.

200 *anemakton*, a transliteration from the Greek word ἀναίμακτος (bloodless), is a reference to the bread of the Eucharist.

201 1 Corinthians 11:23–26.

THE REPORT OF THE FRIARS 179

have received from the well-regarded Apostles, just as they received from Christ, and thus the four ecclesiastical dioceses[202] of the world maintain right up to the present day; indeed, we judge that the diocese of elder Rome also received [it] and will continue to hold [it] in this way. For this reason we say that one cannot consume the sacrifice through azymes, as azymes arise from his part, which was free of legal servitude.[203] And indeed we have written these things as a summary, in accordance with the desire of the apocrisarii, who could not endure to hear more. If, however, the authorities and evidence for our argument are required of us, then we will extend our argument from both the old and new Testament.

In the month of April, the seventh indication,[204] signed by me, the Chartophylax[205] of the most holy great church of God of Constantinople, on the order of the universal[206] [Patriarch] of the most holy patriarchs,

---

202 Constantinople, Antioch, Jerusalem, and Alexandria.

203 The end of this sentence is particularly complex. The text reads *ut azimo parte existente eius, que cessavit legalis servitutis*: Golubovich, 'Disputatio,' 455 lines 2–3. *Parte* may be translated as a 'part' or 'share,' but may also refer to a 'representation' or 'symbol.' If the latter is true, then it must be a symbol of the *legalis servitutis*, literally meaning 'of legal servitude,' probably the genitive of accusation. Issues of legality and slavery often pertain to Jews, just as the use of unleavened bread at the first Passover before their departure from Egypt. If this is the case, then *ut azimo parte existente eius, que cessavit legalis servitutis* can be interpreted as an accusation, on the part of the Greeks, that the Roman Church indulged in Judiasing practices. Indeed, more can be read into this; the Greeks may be accusing the Latins of being slaves to Jewish law. A precedent for such an accusation exists in the polemic of Niketas Stethatos, who states that 'those who still partake of the azymes are under the shadow of the Law and eat of the table of the Jews' – Εἰ οὖν ἔτι τῶν ἀζύμων μετέχετε, πρόδηλον ὑπὸ τὴν σκιὰν τοῦ παλαιοῦ νόμου ἐστὲ καὶ τράπεζαν Ἰουδαίων ἐσθίετε: Niketas Stethatos, *Against the Armenians and Latins*, ed. J. Hergenroether, *Monumenta Graeca ad Photium ejusque historiam pertinentia* (Ratisbon: G. J. Manz, 1869), 140 lines 11–12; translated in J. Erickson, 'Leavened and unleavened,' 161.

This is a somewhat complex reading of the sentence. It is entirely possible that the meaning was not intended to be so subtle. The phrase 'free from legal servitude' may simply be an accusation that the Roman Church has strayed from the traditional use of leavened bread. The lack of clarity may come from the fact that this was initially translated from a Greek text, which the friars may not have understood or they purposely wished to misrepresent.

204 The text here confusingly reads *mense aprilis, indict. VII, I.* What the *I.* refers to is unclear, and indeed Golubovich notes that the mark is omitted in one of the manuscripts (manuscript E, ms. 250), Golubovich, 'Disputatio,' 455.

205 Presumably, the same Aulenos, see above, chs 5 and 20.

206 i.e. ecumenical.

180   THE DISPUTATIO

*of the [Patriarch] of the great Teupolitan[207] city of Antioch, and of the
bishops who were present with them.*

24. And once in the full council, they delivered to us the document they
had read aloud in testimony to their creed. Then we brought forward our
document and read it aloud in the full council. It read as follows:[208]
In the name of the Lord. Amen.

*The Father is fully God in himself. The Son is fully God begotten from
the Father. The Holy Spirit is fully God proceeding from the Father and the
Son, and indeed the Spirit proceeds directly from the Son, from the Father
but by means of the Son.[209] As for the fact that the Holy Spirit proceeds
from the Son, the Son has this from the Father. For that reason he who
believes that the Holy Spirit does not proceed from the Son is on the road
of perdition. Whence St Athanasios, when he was in exile in the west, in his
statement of faith, which he expressed in Latin, said thus: 'The Father is
from nothing, neither made, nor created, nor begotten. The Son is from the
Father alone, not made, nor created, but begotten. The Holy Spirit is from
the Father and Son, not made, nor created, nor begotten, but proceeding.'[210]
And the same St Athanasios in his statement of faith, which he expressed in
Greek, said: 'the Holy Spirit is a being, proceeding from the Father and the
Son who transmits him, through whom he completed all things.'[211] Whence
also blessed Gregory, who is rightly called Thaumaturgus,[212] bishop of
Neocaesarea, in his statement of faith, which he had through revelation
from blessed John the Evangelist, through the mediation of the Mother of
God, clearly proclaimed saying: 'One God, the Father of the living Word,
and existing wisdom, and the eternal virtue and impression, the perfect*

---

207 The name 'Theoupolis' is associated with Antioch going back to the sixth century, see
ODB I, sub Antioch: Antioch on the Orontes.

208 Both the original Latin and a Greek translation of this text can be found in J. Mansi,
Sacrorum conciliorum, XXIII, cols 61–66.

209 *Spiritus Sanctus plenus Deus a Patre Filioque procedens, et Spiritus quidem a Filio
procedit immediate, a Patre vero mediante Filio*: Golubovich, 'Disputatio' 455 lines 16–17.

210 Athanasios, *Symbolum de fide catholica*, Migne *PG* 28, cols 1582 B – 1583 A.

211 Athanasios, *Expositio fidei*, Migne *PG* 25, col. 207A. Note that the friars translate
Athanasios' Greeks words into Latin in this document. This fact may be the cause of some
difficulties in the Latin formation of the statement. For more on problems associated with
translation of treatises dealing with procession of the Holy Spirit, see A. Siecienski, *The
filioque*, 7–8.

212 Gregory Thaumaturgus, 'the Miracle-Worker,' (ca. 210–260). See E. Ferguson,
Encyclopedia of early Christianity, 499–500.

THE REPORT OF THE FRIARS 181

creator of the perfect, Father of the only-begotten Son.[213] *Then about the Son he says thus: 'One Lord, one from one, God from God, impression and likeness of the God-head, efficacious word' etc.*[214] *Speaking here about the Son he says: 'One from one'; therefore the Holy Spirit is not from one; but he is from the Father and another, when he is from something. Although he is said to be from the Father and another, he is not said to be from another according to essence, but according to hypostasis. Gregory, bishop of the city of Nyssa, testifies that the Holy Spirit is directly from the Son, while from the Father by means of the Son, saying: 'In confessing the immutability of nature, we do not deny the difference between causative and cause, by which alone we are able to understand the distinction of one thing from the other. One we believe to be the causative [being]. The other is from the causative [being], and that which is his is from the cause. Again we understand another distinction. One exists proximate from the first, while the other is through him who is proximate from the first.'*[215] *Therefore,*[216] *with regards to that, by which things differ, it is impossible for that to apply to both. It is necessary that the being who is proximate to the first must correspond to either the Son or the Holy Spirit. The saints say that between Father and Son there is no intermediary. Therefore, the Son alone exists proximately from the Father. Therefore, the Holy Spirit does not exist proximately from the Father. It is also widely agreed that whatever is from one, it is especially proximate to that one. Therefore, when the Holy Spirit is from one, it is proximate to that one. But it is not proximate to the Father, as was already explained. Therefore, it is proximate to the Son. Blessed Cyril, following those holy Fathers of yours, and also blessed Ambrose, archbishop of Milan, and blessed Augustine, bishop of the city of Hippo, likewise Saint Jerome, the most resolute opponent of heretical depravity,*

---

213 Gregory Thaumaturgus, *Expositio Fidei*, Migne *PG* 10, col. 983; ed. P. Schaff, *Fathers of the Third Century: Gregory Thaumaturgus, Dionysius the Great, Julius Africanus, Anatolius, and Minor Writers, Methodius, Arnobius. Anti-Nicene Fathers*, vol. 6 (Grand Rapids, MI: Christian Classics Ethereal Library), 12.

214 Gregory Thaumaturgus, *Expositio Fidei*, Migne *PG* 10, cols 983–86; ed. P. Schaff, *Fathers of the Third Century*, 12.

215 Gregory of Nyssa, *Quod non sint tres dii*, Migne *PG* 45, col. 133 B–C; ed. P. Schaff, *Gregory of Nyssa: Dogmatic Treatises. Nicene and Post-Nicene Fathers*, vol. 5, Second Series (Grand Rapids, MI: Christian Classics Ethereal Library), 625.

216 Girolamo Golubovich explained that, in the Latin text, a segment of words not found in the Greek text is repeated. Thus, I have omitted them in this translation: Golubovich, 'Disputatio' 456 note 2.

182 THE DISPUTATIO

and with him the whole holy and universal third synod,[217] *left us a written account, clearly stating that the Spirit exists from the Son. Therefore, he who resists its words is not a catholic, but a deviant from the faith. Indeed, [Cyril], in his address on the proper faith to Emperor Theodosius,*[218] *clearly says that the Spirit is from the Son through these words: 'Indeed, referring to a man not yet present and not yet seen, he says that he baptizes in fire and the Holy Spirit, not sending into the baptized a Spirit other than his own, in the way of a slave or servant, but as God according to [his] nature, in the fullness of power, which exists from him, and is his own.'*[219] *What is more evident than this testimony? Here he plainly says about the Son that he sends the Holy Spirit into the baptized, [the Spirit that is] from himself, and is his own. And Cyril writes the same thing through the words on Jeremiah, in his sermon on the same Jeremiah, which is entitled, 'On the incarnation of the Only-Begotten,'*[220] *and that Christ is one, and Lord, in accordance with the Scriptures. And the same Cyril, in the statement on the ninth anathema,*[221] *says the same. In the ninth anathema, speaking about the Spirit belonging to the Son, when he sets forth the same anathema, he explains in what sense he had said the Spirit was his own, saying: 'The only-begotten Word of God, having become man, remained God, being everything the Father was, except being the Father, and having what was proper from him [i.e. the Father], [thus] the Holy Spirit is essentially innate to him [the Son]' etc.*[222] *Here again the holy father says that the Holy Spirit exists from the Son. There should be no doubt concerning what meaning the saint intended when he published the anathema. The aforementioned third holy and universal synod accepted that anathema with all other anathemas, in the sense in which the saint pronounced it. It is agreed that*

217 The Council of Ephesos, 431.

218 Cyril of Alexandria, *Liber de recta in Dominum nostrum Iesum Christum fide*, Migne *PG* 76, cols 1133–200.

219 Cyril of Alexandria, *Liber de recta in Dominum nostrum Iesum Christum fide*, Migne *PG* 76, ch. XXXVI, col. 1188 A–B.

220 Cyril of Alexandria, *Scholia de Incarnatione Unigeniti*, Migne *PG* 75, cols 1369–412; transl. J. McGuckin, *St Cyril of Alexandria: the Christological controversy*, 294–335. See ch. VI, Migne *PG* 75, col. 1374–75; transl. J. McGuckin, *St Cyril of Alexandria: the Christological controversy*, 298–99; and ch. XIII, Migne *PG* 75, col. 1384–88; transl. J. McGuckin, *St Cyril of Alexandria: the Christological controversy*, 306–08.

221 Cyril of Alexandria, *Explicatio duodecimo capitum*, Anathema IX, Migne *PG* 76, cols 308 C – 309 A; transl. N. Russell, *Cyril of Alexandria*, 186.

222 Cyril of Alexandria, *Explicatio duodecimo capitum*, Anathema IX, Migne *PG* 76, cols 309 C – 309 A; transl. N. Russell, *Cyril of Alexandria*, 186.

THE REPORT OF THE FRIARS 183

the holy Fathers, assembled in the aforementioned holy synod, without any hint of hesitation, received[223] *the entire third letter of the aforementioned Father to the wicked Nestorius, bishop of the city of Constantinople.*[224] *There was no doubt that the final part of the aforementioned letter contains the aforementioned 12 anathemas. If anyone attempts to adduce the most wicked words of bishop Theodoret of Cyrus, which poured out babbling in utter impudence against the 12 articles of the aforementioned blessed Father,*[225] *let him know that the fifth holy and universal synod*[226] *anathematized the aforementioned babbling Theodoret, in accordance with the words of blessed Cyril, to which the aforementioned Theodoret answered by saying: 'He only knows how to accuse.' In the eighth act the fifth holy and universal synod says thus: 'We condemn and anathematize, with every other heretic condemned and anathematized by the aforementioned four councils, and by the holy catholic church, Theodore who was bishop of Mopsuestia*[227] *and his wicked writings, and the wicked things which were impiously written by Theodoret against the correct faith and against the 12 chapters of Saint Cyril at the first holy synod in Ephesos,*[228] *and whatever was written for the defense of Theodore and Nestorius by him.'*[229] *And it is clear from these that those things Theodoret wrote against the 12 articles of Cyril are abominable and full of impiety, and he who alleges them to be true is an enemy of the faith. For Cyril writes to Achacius, bishop of Malta, after the union of the churches, saying thus: 'Indeed what we rightly wrote against the blasphemies of Nestorius, no argument will convince us that it*

---

223 The use of the Latin word *recepisse* indicates that the friars were aware of the Greeks' conciliar tradition and consciously appealed to it. Thus, they speak in a language their hosts can appreciate: Golubovich, 'Disputatio,' 457 line 19.

224 Nestorius (ca. 381–451) became bishop of Constantinople in 428, but was opposed by Cyril of Alexandria and then condemned and deposed by the Council of Ephesos in 431. See E. Ferguson, *Encyclopedia of early Christianity*, 809–810; J. Meyendorff, *Byzantine theology*, 91–93.

225 Theodoret of Cyrrhus charged that Cyril's anathemas against Nestorius smacked of Apollinarianism: F. Cross and E. Livingstone, *Oxford dictionary of the Christian Church*, 1600–01; E. Ferguson, *Encyclopedia of early Christianity*, 1117.

226 The Second Council of Constantinople, 553.

227 Theodore of Mopsuestia (ca. 350–428) was yet another opponent of Cyril of Alexandria. Cyril spoke of Theodore as 'a Nestorian before Nestorius': F. Cross and E. Livingstone, *Oxford dictionary of the Christian Church*, 1598–99; E. Ferguson, *Encyclopedia of early Christianity*, 1116–17.

228 Apparently meaning the first council held in Ephesos, but still the council of 431.

229 J. Mansi, *Sacrorum conciliorum*, IX, cols 375 D – 376 A.

184 THE DISPUTATIO

was not proper to say.[230] *And to his servant Donatus he wrote saying thus: 'We rightly wrote what we wrote, rightly and immaculately advocating the faith, and we deny nothing at all of what we said. None of what was said, as they say, was said without knowledge, but everything was correct, and agreed with the power of truth.*[231]

From these things it is most evident that blessed Cyril denied nothing he had said, but that he believed them in the same sense in which he had said them without a mark of rebuke. Nor would he have been able to correct them by himself, even if he had wanted to do so; far be it for a saint [to alter] what the holy synod had accepted with complete confidence and without any notion of doubt. For it accepted his words[232] *in the same sense that he himself had uttered them. Therefore, he who refuses to accept the ninth article of the holy Father, which he put forth with the holy synod, in the sense he uttered it, justly falls into anathema. All the holy Fathers who attended the subsequent synods venerated this holy synod, and they believed the same things which it too believed. But even the holy Fathers who preceded it were of the same opinion as it was itself.*[233]

25. And after reading the document, we gave it to the Patriarch of Nicaea and to everyone listening we said: 'You have given us your writing which contains heresy. And know this, that whoever believes what is written in your document, the Roman Church considers such a person as a heretic. Nevertheless, because a defence of heresy makes a heretic, we wish to know why you say such things. There can be two reasons why you say

230 Cyril of Alexandria, *Epistle* 40, Migne *PG* 77, col. 184 D; transl. L. Wickham, *Cyril of Alexandria: select letters*, 39.

231 Cyril of Alexandria, *Epistle* 48, Migne *PG* 77, col. 249 C–D.

232 Again, *receipt* can be interpreted as an acknowledgment of Greek traditions: Golubovich, 'Disputatio,' 458 line 12.

233 At the end of this passage, in manuscript A (Cod. Vaticano, now in the Riccardiana library in Florence, n. 228), there follow the signatures of each of the four friars attesting to their belief in the contents of the document: Golubovich, 'Disputatio,' 458 note 6. Find these preserved in both Greek and Latin in J. Mansi, *Sacrorum conciliorum*, XXIII, col. 66 D–E. *Thus we hold, we believe, we understand, and we declare this faith.*

I, Rodulphus from the order of Franciscans, apocrisarius of the lord pope Gregory, bishop of elder Rome, support this faith, write thus, and believe thus.

I, Haymo of the order of Franciscans, apocrisarius of the lord pope Gregory, bishop of elder Rome, hold this faith, believe thus and feel thus.

We, Hugh and Peter of the order of Dominicans, and apocrisarii of the lord pope Gregory, bishop of elder Rome, embrace this same faith, believe thus and feel thus.

THE REPORT OF THE FRIARS   185

this: ignorance or malice. Therefore, we are prepared to show the truth
to you, exposing you to be creators of lies, so that when you have seen
the truth, the heresy that you say may cease and be revoked. Or, if it
does not cease, we may know that what was said all this time was out
of malice, and that you are heretics. But because we do not have judges,
let the books, namely the old and new Testament, and the writings of the
saints, be brought forward, and let them decide between us and you.' And
it is astonishing to tell, when everyone there looked among themselves
for the books, they were unable to find a single Old or New Testament.[234]
Therefore, wishing to show that they were deceitful in all things, we asked
why they said that the Lord had made his body in leavened bread. And
they answered: 'We have that in the Gospel, that *the Lord took the arton,
broke it* etc.' And we added: 'What does *arton* mean?' They answered:
'It means completed bread, risen bread, leavened bread.' And we asked
if *arton* everywhere stands for leavened bread. And they responded: 'No,
because from time to time *arton* is used on its own, and from time to
time it is used with the adjective. When it is used on its own, it indicates
leavened bread. When [it is used] with the adjective, as in Leviticus VII,
unleavened *arton*,[235] there is, so to speak, a contradiction in the adjective,
as when one says: a dead man.'[236] And again we asked: 'If *arton* is used
on its own, does it always indicate leavened bread?' They answered that it
did not. For whenever it is used on its own, it is kept in its proper [sense],
and then it is always kept [in a sense of being] leavened. And whenever
it is used improperly, then it indicates azymes. 'Therefore, *arton* used on
its own retains both senses, it does not always mean leavened, nor does
it always mean unleavened, but sometimes it means the one, sometimes
it means the other. Therefore, the *arton* used on its own stands for bread,
and does not specify [what kind]. Therefore, what you say concerning

---

234 John Doran referred to this embarrassing incident as the effective end of serious
negotiations: J. Doran, 'Rites and wrongs in 1234,' 142.

235 Leviticus 7:13.

236 This is a common argument employed by the Byzantines in disputations with the Latins
over which bread is proper to use in the Eucharist. The twelfth-century monk Euthymios
Zigabenos, quoting John Chrysostom in his *Panoplia Dogmatica*, explains that whenever
Scripture refers to man (ἄνθρωπος) it means 'living man.' In the same way, whenever
Scripture mentions bread (ἄρτος) it means 'leavened bread': Euthymios Zigabenos, *Panoplia
Dogmatica*, Migne *PG* 130, col. 1180 C–D. John Erickson noted that, although this argument
appeared conclusive to the Byzantines, it seems to have made little impact on the Latins:
J. Erickson, 'Leavened and unleavened,' 159.

186   THE DISPUTATIO

the Gospel supports our case as much as it supports yours. And this is what our Gospels call bread [*panem*], where you have *arton*. Likewise, we find in Leviticus 7, where it is dealing with the law of peace offerings, leavened *arton* and unleavened *arton*, according to the letter of the Greek text. When they are specifically different they are referred to as azymes or leavened *arton*, but *arton* on its own can be used for either of them in common, equally for one or the other. Neither genus is used more or less properly as the predicate than the other. Therefore, your distinction, which you made about proper and improper [usage], was meaningless. Therefore, where it is said in the Gospel: *Jesus took the arton*, it stands for bread, not specifying a particular bread. Likewise, having disproved your reasoning, which you thought to have concerning this word *arton*, we prove through the Gospel that the Lord made his body in azymes, and not in leavened bread. It is read in the Gospel of Matthew: *On the first day of azymes they came to Jesus saying: Where do you wish us to prepare for you to eat the passover?*[237] Then we asked them: 'What was the first day of azymes, of which he is speaking?' And they gave the explanation of John Chrysostom:[238] '*The first day of azymes, that is the first day before azymes.*' And on this point, John Chrysostom says: *On the first day before azymes the disciples came to Jesus, on the evening on which the passover was sacrificed.*[239] Therefore, the passover of the Jews was on that evening, and it was mandated that the Jews should not have either yeast or anything leavened in their homes or within their borders. Thus it is read in Exodus 12: *For seven days you will eat azymes. From the first day there will be no yeast in your homes. And whoever eats leavened bread, his soul shall perish from Israel from the first day to the seventh.*[240] Therefore, Christ made his own passover in azymes, because he observed the law up to the end of his life, as Chrysostom and Epiphianus[241] say. Therefore, he made his body from that bread which he had. And because he only had azymes, he made his body from azymes. If, therefore, your rationale is that which you wrote – that it is not possible

---

237 Matthew 26:17.

238 John Chrysostom (ca. 347–407), bishop of Constantinople from 398. See E. Ferguson, *Encyclopedia of early Christianity*, 622–24; *ODB* II, sub John Chrysostom.

239 John Chrysostom, *In Matthaeum. Homilia* LXXXI (al. LXXXII), Migne *PG* 58, col. 729; ed. P. Schaff, *St. Chrysostom: Homilies on the Gospel of Saint Matthew*, 842.

240 Exodus 12:15.

241 Epiphanios of Cyprus (ca. 315–403). See E. Ferguson, *Encyclopedia of early Christianity*, 380–81.

THE REPORT OF THE FRIARS

187

to accomplish the body of Christ if not [if not using the same kind of] bread, in which the Lord made [it], and the Lord made it in azymes, in accordance with what has been demonstrated – then you are not able to make it from leavened bread. And nevertheless we do not say this.[242] And so that you will learn the truth, which so far you have pretended not to learn, we shall demonstrate what we say clearly from the writings of your saints. But because we did not have the books at hand,[243] they refused to hear the obvious authorities. However, the authorities proving what we say were as follows:[244]

John Chrysostom, in homily 81 *On Matthew*, discusses these words: *On the first day of azymes the disciples came to Jesus* etc. At the beginning of the homily he says the following: *He calls the first day of azymes that [day] which is before azymes. They were always accustomed to count the day from the evening, and he mentions it [this day], on the evening on which passover was to be sacrificed. They came on the fifth day of the week [i.e. Thursday]. And this day, which was before azymes, he himself [i.e. the author of the Gospel of Matthew] calls 'the day in which they came.' Indeed he said the following: The day of azymes has come, on which it is proper for passover to be sacrificed. 'Has come,' i.e. was at the door, referring to that evening, for clearly they were to begin [the Passover] that evening, for which reason each adds: when passover is sacrificed.*[245]

Also, the same Chrysostom proves that Jesus observed the law and ritual of the Jews at dinner, saying later in the same homily: *For this reason he fulfilled the passover in every way, showing to the last day that he was not contrary to the law.*[246]

---

242 Chris Schabel observed that this statement by the friars is evidence that the Latins were not interested in forcing the use of unleavened bread upon the Greeks; rather, their goal was to convince the Greeks to simply agree that the Body of Christ could be achieved with either leavened or unleavened bread: C. Schabel, 'The quarrel over unleavened bread in western theology,' 94–95.

243 The friars made a point of bringing Greek books with them to Nicaea, but this statement suggests that they left that material behind in Constantinople before they came to Nymphaion. See above, ch. 7.

244 There is no indication that these examples were put before the Greeks in the council at Nymphaion.

245 John Chrysostom, *In Matthaeum. Homilia* LXXXI (al. LXXXII), Migne *PG* 58, cols 729–30; ed. P. Schaff, *St. Chrysostom: Homilies on the Gospel of Saint Matthew*, 842.

246 John Chrysostom, *In Matthaeum. Homilia* LXXXI (al. LXXXII), Migne *PG* 58, col. 730; ed. P. Schaff, *St. Chrysostom: Homilies on the Gospel of Saint Matthew*, 842.

188 THE DISPUTATIO

In addition, the same Chrysostom, in homily 82 *On Matthew*, says the following: *That at the time of passover he fulfilled that mystery, so that you may learn that he himself is the lawgiver of the new and old Testament, and those things which are prefigured in the one [Old Testament] are for the sake of the other [New Testament]. For this reason, where there is a figure, he establishes the truth. The evening indicated the completion of the ages, and that matters are coming to the end.*[247]

Likewise, blessed Epiphanius of Cyprus, in the book which is called *Panaria*,[248] where he speaks against the Ebionites,[249] just past the middle of the work, says the following: *How is it that their stupidity about the eating of meat is not refuted? Firstly, because the Lord ate the passover of the Jews. The passover of the Jews was sheep and azymes. Roasted sheep is meat. Therefore eat, just as his own disciples say to him: Where do you wish us to prepare for you to eat the passover?*[250]

Also, in the same work, here against the Marcionites,[251] in refutation 61 on the letter of the Gospel – the refutation which begins thus: *Against you a cloud of arrows* etc.[252] – he says the following: *O Marcion, you have introduced refutation against yourself in many ways, or rather, you have been compelled by truth itself. For the old passover was nothing other than the sacrifice of sheep and eating of meats, and partaking of living [meat] with azymes.*[253] And a little later: *Indeed [concerning] the eating of*

247 John Chrysostom, *In Matthaeum. Homilia* LXXXI (al. LXXXII), Migne *PG* 58, col. 738; ed. P. Schaff, *St. Chrysostom: Homilies on the Gospel of Saint Matthew*, 852.

248 The *Panarion* by Epiphanios of Cyprus is a refutation of all known heresies. This work indicates the necessity of leavened bread in the Eucharist for Orthodox Christology: J. Erickson, 'Leavened and unleavened,' 161.

249 Ebionites were an early Christian sect that insisted on closely observing the Old (Jewish) Law. See E. Ferguson, *Encyclopedia of early Christianity*, 357–58; F. Cross and E. Livingstone, *Oxford dictionary of the Christian Church*, 523; C. Schabel, 'The quarrel over unleavened bread in western theology,' 115; M. Goulder, 'A poor man's Christology,' *New Testament Studies* 45 (1999), 332–48; J. Erickson, 'Leavened and unleavened,' 161. For the work of Epiphanios against the Ebionites see Epiphanios of Cyprus, *Adversus Haereses*, Migne *PG* 41, Lib. I, tom. 2, cols 406–74; transl. F. Williams, *The Panarion*, 30.131–65.

250 Ephiphanios of Cyprus, *Adversus Haereses*, Lib. I, tom. 2, Migne *PG* 41, col. 441 B–C; transl. F. Williams, *The Panarion*, 149.

251 An early anti-Jewish Christian sect. See E. Ferguson, *Encyclopedia of early Christianity*, 717–18.

252 Ephiphanios of Cyprus, *Adversus Haereses*, Lib. I, tom. 3, Migne *PG* 41, col. 761 B – 764 B; transl. F. Williams, *The Panarion*, 334.

253 Ephiphanios of Cyprus, *Adversus Haereses*, Lib. I, tom. 3, Migne *PG* 41, col. 764 A–B; transl. F. Williams, *The Panarion*, 334.

THE REPORT OF THE FRIARS 189

meats which you detest, the Lord Jesus ate with his disciples, keeping the passover, in accordance with the law.[254] And *he did not say that he was going to perfom the aforementioned mystery when he said: I wish to eat the passover with you. So that truth might confound you in a general way, he did not perform the mystery at the beginning, so that you cannot deny [it], but after they had eaten he spoke [it], taking this and that, and he left no room for malice. It is clear that after the passover of the Jews, that is, after he had eaten, he came to the mystery.*[255]

Refusing to hear the authoritative [voices] of the saints, they began to oppose us from the Gospel of John: *The Jews did not enter the praetorium lest they be made impure, but they ate the passover.*[256] To which we answered that it is not to be believed that John said anything contrary to the other Evangelists. To their question we responded thus: 'So that they may eat passover, that is the passover food. For thus we read that passover was spoken of [in this way] in the old Testament,[257] and this was the said 15th moon.' And because a great part of the night had already passed, with the permission of the Emperor we mutually retired.

26. Then we rested from the *disputatio* on Sunday, Monday, Tuesday, and Wednesday.[258] Wondering what they were waiting for, we sent a message to the Emperor asking for his leave to depart.[259] He, however, began to test us through his own messenger, seeking if by means of some agreement peace might still be made between the Roman and Greek Church. To the messenger sent to us we answered as follows: 'When we are in the presence of the Emperor, and he speaks to us concerning this matter, then we will know what will be our answer to him.'

Summoning us the next day[260] to his palace, the Emperor said: 'It is the custom of kings and princes, when there was disagreement between

---

254 Ephiphanios of Cyprus, *Adversus Haereses*, Lib. I, tom. 3, Migne *PG* 41, col. 764 B; cf. transl. F. Williams, *The Panarion*, 334.

255 Ephiphanios of Cyprus, *Adversus Haereses*, Lib. I, tom. 3, Migne *PG* 41, col. 764 B; cf. transl. F. Williams, *The Panarion*, 334.

256 John 18:28.

257 Leviticus 23:6.

258 30 April to 3 May 1234.

259 Although no indication is given about why the *disputatio* was delayed, John Langdon speculated that the emperor intentionally delayed the proceedings in order to increase tension: J. Langdon, 'Byzantino-Papal discussions in 1234,' 226.

260 3 May 1234.

190 THE DISPUTATIO

them over the castles or provinces, for example, that each one should give up something which he considered his right, so that they may reach peace through compromise. Thus it seems to me that it ought to be done between your church and ours. There are namely two issues between us and you: first concerning the procession of the Holy Spirit; the other concerning the body of Christ. If, therefore, you desire peace, you ought to give up one of these two. We will venerate and hold your sacrament [to be] acceptable, while you, on the other hand, give up for us your creed, and say with us just as we say, just as we have it established by the holy fathers and their councils. And the part you have added you will say no longer, because it is an offence to us.' To this we answered: 'Understand this, the Lord pope and the Roman Church will not give up one iota of its faith, nor anything that is said in our creed.' And the Emperor said: 'How, then, will we be able to make peace?' And we answered: 'If you wish to know the way, we will briefly describe it to you. Concerning the body of Christ we say this, that you will be required to faithfully believe, and preach to others that the body of Christ can be accomplished in azymes just as in leavened bread. And let all books which your [people] have written against our faith be condemned and burnt. Concerning the Holy Spirit we say thus, it will require that you believe that the Holy Spirit proceeds from the Son just as from the Father. And it is necessary to preach that to the people. As for the issue of you singing this in your creed, unless you wish, the lord Pope will not compel you,[261] once you condemn and burn all books which are contrary to this article.' After hearing [our offer], the Emperor became upset and said: 'I do not now hear the term[s] of peace. And therefore, I will tell the assembled prelates what you have told me.' When they had heard [the report of our exchange with the Emperor, the Greek prelates] became indignant and

---

261 At first glance this does not appear much of an offer, but, when taken in the context of the increasingly divisive and aggressive nature of the negotiations in the council, this exchange shows that both the friars and Vatatzes continued to be open to the possibility of a compromise. The friars required the Byzantines to change neither their practice nor their creed. They did, however, require that the Greeks refrain from condemning the Latin use of azymes and the Latin use of the *filioque*, and that they destroy a large number of books. Martin Hinterberger argued that a similar request was made of the Cypriot monks who were executed in 1231, not because they believed in using leavened bread but because they refused to stop condemning the Latins for their use of unleavened bread: Hinterberger, 'A neglected tool of Orthodox propaganda?' 146. Likewise, Vatatzes' offer to exchange the Byzantine position on the Eucharist for the Latin position on the procession was truly extraordinary, if perhaps a bit too pragmatic for the friars to accept.

THE REPORT OF THE FRIARS
191

were transformed into sedition against us. We believe[262] they contemplated how they might confound us with treachery.

27. And sending for us on Wednesday,[263] at the evening hour, they carefully[264] invited us, so that on Thursday[265] morning we would attend the council. Thus, having said farewell for the day and the council going into recess, we mutually departed in peace and affection. Early the next morning we joined the council again, and we found all of them gathered there, and with them an abundant multitude of lay people, and with the front doors open the council sat in the atrium of the Patriarch's home.[266] When we sat down among the others, the Patriarch said: 'As long as there was hope for peace, we spoke peaceably, but since we have discovered that we are disappointed in our hope, we ask that you listen to us peaceably, and this session finally will complete the matter.'[267] Then he added: 'You gave to us, in writing, the faith of the Roman Church.[268] We examined it, and we want to proclaim it throughout our provinces and to the peoples and the nations.[269] And because it is unknown to us, we wish that all will hear and

---

262 By this statement the friars are confessing that they were not privy to the initial reaction of the Greek prelates to Vatatzes' report of their exchange, and thus they only 'suspect' that the patriarch and those with him sought to act treacherously.

263 3 May 1234.

264 The adverb, *diligenter*, translated here as 'carefully,' may not be enough to convey what the friars were implying as far as the intent of the Greeks on that day: Golubovich, 'Disputatio,' 462 line 28. One suspects that the friars, with hindsight, are accusing the Greeks of plotting and scheming, as we will see shortly hereafter. One should consider the use of the word in the Gospel of Matthew to describe Herod seeking among the wise men where he might find the newborn Jesus: Matthew 2:8.

265 4 May 1234.

266 John Doran interpreted the presence of the popular crowd as a conscious show of strength engineered by the patriarch in the hopes of intimidating the friars: J. Doran, 'Rites and wrongs in 1234,' 144.

267 The patriarch's statement is heavy with meaning. Not only is it clear that he had gained a report of what had been said between the friars and the emperor, but he and the other Greeks at the council apparently interpreted the position of the friars as a list of impossible demands, not a counteroffer in negotiations. Furthermore, the statement, 'As long as there was hope for peace, we spoke peaceably' – *Dum spes fuerat pacis, pacifice locuti sumus*: Golubovich, 'Disputatio,' 462 line 33, suggests that the Greeks were on their best behaviour until this point. Such a claim is difficult for the outside observer to accept.

268 See above, ch. 24.

269 The precise translation of *gentes et nationes* is clearly problematic: Golubovich, 'Disputatio,' 462 lines 37–38. The reader should not view it as a comment on medieval issues

192   THE DISPUTATIO

understand the faith of the Roman Church. Does this please you?' And we answered: 'It pleases us. Indeed this is our wish, that you and everyone in the eastern Church may know and learn and faithfully keep the faith of the Roman Church, which we have given to you in writing.' And after we said this he became silent.

Then one in the middle of the council rose holding a large document, and he began to read it, the beginning of which was as follows: *The venerable apocrisarii of the most holy pope of old Rome gave to us in writing that the Father is fully God in himself. The Son is fully God begotten from the Father. The Holy Spirit is fully God proceeding from the Father and the Son* etc. as is maintained in the aforementioned writing.[270] *And he who does not believe this is on the road of perdition.* To this we answered that it was false. And, reading our document, we found what we had written: *He who believes that the Holy Spirit does not proceed from the Son is on the road of perdition.* There was among them no one who could understand the distinction of those words.[271] Then they introduced authorities to prove their faith, of which one was the opinion that the Holy Spirit proceeds from the Father. Among the many authorities they introduced were those of Pope Damasus,[272] who said: *whoever does not believe the Holy Spirit to be properly from the Father, he is anathema.*[273] To which we answered: 'We believe the Holy Spirit to be properly from the Father, and he who does not believe this, let him

---

of race or nationality. It seems probable, however, that the words do constitute a developing concept of 'us' versus 'them': e.g. T. Kolbaba, 'Byzantine perceptions of Latin errors,' 119.

270 See above, ch. 24.

271 Given the subtlety of the clarification, one can understand how the patriarch and his clergy might miss the point the friars are trying to make. The issue is one of negative versus positive belief. The Greeks quote the friars as saying 'he who does not believe,' whereas the friars say 'he who believes that the Holy Spirit does not.' The only difference in the two statements is the placement of the negative. The friars' original statement – *He who believes that the Holy Spirit does not proceed from the Son, he is on the road of perdition* – condemns those who positively believe that procession from the Son cannot happen. In other words, those who actively profess that the Roman Church is in the wrong are 'on the road of perdition.' This interpretation is in keeping with what the friars had offered to Vatatzes in their meeting on 3 May: Golubovich, 'Disputatio,' ch. 26, 462 lines 18–22.

272 Bishop of Rome (366–384). See E. Ferguson, *Encyclopedia of early Christianity*, 316–17.

273 Damasus, *Epistle* 4, *Confessio Fidei catholicae*, Migne *PL* 13, col. 362, no. xvi; ed. P. Schaff, *Theodoret, Jerome, Gennadius, and Rufinus. Nicene and Post-Nicene Fathers*, vol. 3, Second Series (Grand Rapids, MI: Christian Classics Ethereal Library), 320.

THE REPORT OF THE FRIARS

be anathematized. Still, we say that the Holy Spirit is properly from the Son, just as blessed Cyril says: and he who does not believe that, let him also be anathematized.'[274] They also introduced another authority, which, if I recall correctly,[275] was blessed Basil, whose opinion was such, that the Holy Spirit was from the Father and not from another.[276] To that we answered: 'That the Holy Spirit is from the Father and not from another is true. That is, he is not from any other substance, other than from the substance of the Father.' And they introduced many others, but that one[277] seemed to be the most against us.

28. Considering, therefore, that they had accomplished nothing, the Patriarch called for silence with hand and word, because there was a great uproar among the people. He contemplated, as we believe, when silence had fallen, how to stir up the people against us. Therefore, we had a care for ourselves, by the grace of God, and we cast their deceits back upon their own heads.[278] For when it became silent, and the whole populace was waiting attentively, we said: 'Do you believe that the Holy Spirit proceeds from the Son or not?' The Patriarch answered: 'We believe he does not proceed from the Son.' And we added: 'But blessed Cyril, who presided over the third council, anathematizes all those who do not believe this. Therefore, you are anathematized. Likewise, you believe and say that the body of Christ cannot be made in azymes. But this is heretical, therefore, you are heretics. Thus we found you heretics and excommunicates, and as heretics and excommunicates we leave you.' And after we had said this we left the council, as they shouted after us: 'You, rather, are the heretics.' We agreed among ourselves, therefore, that we would not eat on that day until we had leave from the Emperor to depart. We obtained

---

274 Cyril of Alexandria, *Explicatio duodecimo capitum*, Anathema IX, Migne *PG* 76, col. 308 C–D; transl. N. Russell, *Cyril of Alexandria*, 186.

275 It should be noted that this is the first instance in which the friars acknowledge any possibility that their recollection may not have been the exact truth. This is also the only instance in the text when the author of the report refers to himself in the first person, *recolo*: Golubovich, 'Disputatio,' ch. 27, 463 line 21.

276 A possible reference to Basil of Caesarea, *Liber de Spiritu Sancto*, Migne *PG* 32, cols 67–218; ed. P. Schaff, *Basil: letters and selected works*, 138–250.

277 i.e. Basil.

278 John Doran suggested that the friars interrupted the patriarch at this point 'in spite of, or perhaps because of, their fears' over what he was about to say: J. Doran, 'Rites and wrongs in 1234,' 143.

194 THE DISPUTATIO

it, but the Emperor showed us a countenance perturbed and distressed, as though he were saddened that we had departed in conflict with each other.

29. So it came to pass that, given permission from the Emperor himself, we left from *Nymphaion* on Saturday[279] morning, and continuing our journey we came on Sunday[280] to a town called *Calamus*.[281] And when it was the time for compline, there came to us a messenger from the Emperor Vatatzes, and another messenger on behalf of the council.[282] Upon greeting us the messenger from the Emperor said: 'My lord greets you and benevolently reproaches you for the fact that you left so suddenly, without bidding farewell to the Patriarch and council, and because you did not return to the lord Patriarch and the other prelates, that after gaining their leave and blessing, you might depart with the favour and goodwill of all.' And to this we answered: 'May the lord save the lord Emperor and preserve him for the good of his Church. He should not be surprised, nor should he reproach us, for we have given him satisfaction, and left with his leave and favour. As for the leave and blessing of the Patriarch and council we care not. He himself knows the reasons why. Therefore, we do not believe we have done anything wrong in this against God or man.' Then the messenger from the council spoke, and after repeating the same words that had been said by the [messenger from the Emperor], he added: 'Behold, the writing that you gave to the council.[283] My lord Patriarch, with the whole council, sends it to you, asking you and begging that you send back to him the writing on azymes that he gave to you.[284] In addition, he sends his letter to you, which he asks you to deliver to the most holy Pope.[285] He also sends to you the [statement of] faith of the whole council which he maintains and believes and preaches on the procession of the Holy Spirit, and asks that

---

279 6 May 1234.

280 7 May 1234.

281 The village of Kalamos, modern Gelembe, lies on the way between Nymphaion and Constantinople: W. Ramsay, *Historical geography of Asia Minor*, 129–30. George Akropolites describes it as the place where the theme of Neokastra begins: Akropolites, *History*, 28 lines 3–6; transl. R. Macrides, 15.149.

282 Once again, the emperor and patriarch act independently of each other, almost as if they were unaware of the measures the other party was taking during the negotiations.

283 See above, ch. 24.

284 See above, ch. 23.

285 This letter has not come down to us, and there is no indication that it was ever delivered.

THE REPORT OF THE FRIARS

195

you carry this creed to the presence of the most holy Pope.'[286] To this we answered: 'The document, which we presented to the council, we gave for the very reason that everyone might have a mirror of the faith of the Roman Church, so that, having looked carefully at the things written there, they may believe [it] in their hearts and confess with their mouths and preach [it] to others, and we will all say the same, and there will be no schism between us. Therefore, we refuse to take back that writing, but we leave it to them by way of the mirror. Likewise, the writing that they gave to us is ours, and that mirror is rather a scandal to their faith. Therefore, we refuse to answer you, but we will offer it to the Pope and Church as a testimony of faith, and in that way they will better see the faithlessness of the Church of the Greeks, unless, as was said before, they were to revoke it with the agreement of the whole council.' Then setting aside the dispute they left us that night.

In the morning[287] they approached once more, and again repeating the same words, they threatened that unless we gave it freely, they would not allow us to depart from their land. And in such matters they detained us up to the third hour of the day. Finally, after long struggles and many controversies, we answered as follows: 'We are in your land. You can take from us that which you desire, but you cannot have it freely.' And when these things were said they departed because it was time to eat.[288]

30. As we and they ate, we discussed what we should do. And, summoning that soldier who came on behalf of the Emperor,[289] we asked him whether the Emperor had ordered him to hinder us on the road? And he answered: 'Far be it for me and for my lord. On the contrary, I have come to speed you on your way.' When we heard this we assembled the messengers[290]

---

286 Find this document, in both Latin and Greek, in Golubovich, 'Disputatio,' 466–70.

287 8 May 1234.

288 *Et hiis dictis recesserunt, tempus enim erat prandendi*, Golubovich, 'Disputatio,' 465 lines 6–7. As strange as it may sound to us, it appears that matters of the stomach superseded a developing international incident.

289 This is the first mention by the friars of a military escort given to them by Vatatzes. Whether they enjoyed such an escort on their earlier journey from Nicaea to Constantinople and why only a single 'soldier' (*milite*) was assigned to them are questions that encourage further research.

290 *nuntiis*: Golubovich, 'Disputatio,' 465 line 13. The reference to 'messengers from Vatatzes' indicates that Vatatzes did indeed send a delegation along with the friars destined for Constantinople, and perhaps for Rome, despite their earlier discussion in which both

196 THE DISPUTATIO

whom Vatatzes had entrusted to us, and we instructed them to prepare the horses and tackle, as we were about to depart. They did so, but the Chartophylax,[291] who had come on behalf of the council, heard[292] [what was happening]. He approached, and setting out with a warning what he had said handing over the document, he pronounced a sentence of excommunication on our messengers if they helped us further in any way. When the messengers heard this, they dropped our cargo of books and refused to serve us. Therefore, we took the books that we could carry, and entrusted our other books to the charge of the aforementioned soldier of the Emperor, and we departed alone on foot. We were in an deserted and impassible land, and we were six days removed from the sea of Constantinople. However, trusting in the grace of God, we advanced fearlessly on our journey. But they sent messengers after us, explaining to us the difficulty and impossibility of the journey, and the dangers to our bodies, asserting upon oath that in the mountains and the forests were peasants lying in wait for us. They would kill us if we continued to advance further without a guide.[293] Although terrified, we would not allow this to hinder us in the journey we had begun. Therefore, we crossed six or seven miles, but soon the aforementioned soldier of the Emperor followed us. And when he had come to us, dismounting from his horse, he abased himself before our feet, begging and pleading that we return to the lodging house from where we had come, and he would have the sentence pronounced revoked, and whatever they said or did against us would be corrected.[294] In accordance, therefore, with our unanimous will, we stopped by a certain lodging house nearby, and sent brothers back for the books. When they came to the lodging house, where we had abandoned the books, the Chartophylax approached, and he

---

sides agreed not to take such an action: Golubovich, 'Disputatio,' ch. 21, 452 line 21 – 453 line 7. It is possible that the friars are instead referring to guides assigned to accompany them back to Latin territory.

291 Once more, the aforementioned Aulenos, find previous references to him in chs 5, 20, and 23. There is no mention of the chartophylax serving as an envoy to the friars before this instance. He is apparently the leader of the embassy from the council.

292 The verb in this case (*audissent*) is plural: Golubovich, 'Disputatio,' 465 line 15. However, this may be an example of a scribe incorrectly placing an 'n' before a consonant. Thus the correct spelling should have been the singular *audisset*, making the chartophylax the subject.

293 Nicholas Mesarites, who travelled this route not long before, attests to the dangers: Mesarites II, 35–46: transl. M. Angold, 223–34.

294 It is unclear if the friars thought the soldier to be pleading so urgently out of concern for their safety, or if he had been charged with coaxing the friars back by the chartophylax.

THE REPORT OF THE FRIARS 197

searched every book, and all our baggage – he seized those brothers, and led them separately into a room, and having undone the ropes[295] he finally found the document, and taking it he said: 'I have what I sought.'[296]

Nevertheless, the [Latin text] of that document, which was translated earlier,[297] we kept for ourselves.

---

295 *cordis laxatis*, Golubovich, 'Disputatio,' ch. 30, 465 line 28. There is some room for interpretation of the word *cordis* in this phrase. Joseph Gill held that the term refers to the ropes on the packages of books the friars had left behind: J. Gill, *Byzantium and the papacy*, 71. However, we might interpret *cordis* to refer to the friars' clothing – i.e. belts – meaning that the friars were forcibly disrobed: M. Roncaglia, *Les frères mineurs et l'église grecque orthodoxe*, 84. The idea that the chartophylax subjected the friars to a strip-search is also supported by the friars' comment that he had already searched through their books and baggage, and then took the friars into a separate room one at a time.

296 The chartophylax was clearly unaware that the friars had already translated the document, and that Latin edition survived and appears in their report: Golubovich, 'Disputatio,' ch. 23, 454 line 17 – 455 line 10.

297 See above, ch. 23.

BIBLIOGRAPHY

Primary Sources

Akropolites, George, *The History*, ed. A. Heisenberg and P. Wirth, *Opera*, vol. 1 (Stuttgart: Teubner, 1978); transl. R. Macrides, *George Akropolites, The History. Introduction, translation and commentary* (Oxford: Oxford University Press, 2007).

Akropolites, George, *Opera*, ed. A. Heisenberg and P. Wirth, vol. 2 (Stuttgart: Teubner, 1978).

Allatius, Leo, *De Ecclesiae Occidentalis atque Orientalis perpetua consensione libri tres* (Coloniae Agrippinae, 1648).

Andrea, A., *Contemporary sources for the Fourth Crusade* (Leiden: Brill, 2000).

Annali Genovesi di Caffaro e de' suoi continuatori dal MXCIX al MCCXCIII, ed. L. Belgrano and C. Imperiale di Sant'Angelo, vol. 3 (Rome: Tipografia del Senato, 1923).

Anselm of Canterbury, *Opera omnia*, ed. F. Schmitt, vol. 2 (Rome, 1940).

Anselm of Havelberg, *Antikeimenon*, Migne *PL* 188, cols 1117–40; transl. A. Criste and C. Neel, *Anselm of Havelberg, Anticimenon: on the unity of the faith and the controversies with the Greeks* (Collegeville, MN: Liturgical Press, 2010).

Athanasios, *Expositio Fidei*, Migne *PG* 25, cols 199–220; ed. P. Schaff and H. Wace, *Athanasius: select works and letters. Nicene and Post-Nicene Fathers*, vol. 4, Second Series (Peabody, MA: Hendrickson Publishers, 1995), 364–66.

Athanasios, *Symbolum de fide catholica*, Migne *PG* 28, cols 1581–604.

Attaleiates, Michael, *Historia*, ed. I. Pérez Martín, *Miguel Attaliates: introduccion, edicion, traduccion y comentario* (Madrid: Consejo Superior de Investigaciones Científicas, 2002); transl. A. Kaldellis and D. Krallis, *The History, Michael Attaleiates* (Cambridge, MA: Harvard University Press, 2012).

Aubry of Three Fountains, *Alberici monachi Triumfontium Chronica*, ed. P. Scheffer-Boichorst, Monumenta Germaniae Historica, Scriptores 23 (Hanover, 1874), 631–950.

Auvray, L., *Les Registres de Grégoire IX*, 4 vols (Paris: A. Fontemoing, 1896–1955).

Bacon, Roger, *Opera quaedam hactenus inedita*, ed. J. Brewer (London: Longman, 1859).

200 THE DISPUTATIO

Basil of Caesarea, *Epistle* 38, Migne *PG* 32, cols 325–42; ed. P. Schaff, *Basil: letters and selected works. Nicene and Post-Nicene Fathers*, vol. 8, Second Series (Grand Rapids, MI: Christian Classics Ethereal Library), 426–33.

Basil of Caesarea, *Liber de Spiritu Sancto*, Migne *PG* 32, cols 67–218; ed. P. Schaff, *Basil: letters and selected works. Nicene and Post-Nicene Fathers*, vol. 8, Second Series (Grand Rapids, MI: Christian Classics Ethereal Library), 138–250.

Beihammer, A., *Griechische Briefe und Urkunden aus dem Zypern der Kreuzfahrerzeit. Die Formularsammlung eines königlichen Sekretars im Vaticanus Palatinus Graecus 367* (Nicosia: Zyprisches Forschungszentrum, 2007).

Benvenuto di San Giorgio, *Historia Montis-Ferrati ab origine marchionum illius tractus usque ad annum MCCCCXC*, ed. L. Muratori, *Rerum Italicarum Scriptores*, vol. 23 (Milan, 1733), 305–762.

Blemmydes, Nikephoros, *Imperial statue*, ed. and transl. H. Hunger and I. Ševčenko, *Des Nikephoros Blemmydes Βασιλικος Ἀνδριάς und dessen Metaphrase von Georgios Galesiotes und Georgios Oinaiotes. Ein weiterer Beitrag zum Verständnis der byzantinischen Schrift-Koine* (Vienna: Verlag der Österreichischen Akademie der Wissenschaften, 1986).

Blemmydes, Nikephoros, *Nicephori Blemmydae Autobiographia sive curriculum vitae*, ed. J. A. Munitiz (Turnhout: Brepols, 1984); transl. J. A. Munitiz, *Nikephoros Blemmydes: a partial account* (Louvain: Spicilegium Sacrum Lovaniense, 1988).

Blemmydes, Nikephoros, *Nicéphore Blemmydès: Œuvres théologiques: introduction, texte critique, traduction et notes*, ed. M. Stavrou, vol. 1 (Paris: Les Éditions du Cerf, 2007).

Chrysostom, John, *In Matthaeum. Homilia*, Migne *PG* 58, cols 729–38; ed. P. Schaff, *St. Chrysostom: Homilies on the Gospel of Saint Matthew: Nicene and Post-Nicene Fathers*, vol. 10 (Grand Rapids, MI: Christian Classics Ethereal Library), 842–51.

Coureas, N., and C., Schabel, eds, *The Cartulary of the Cathedral of Holy Wisdom of Nicosia* (Nicosia: Cyprus Research Centre, 1997).

Cyril of Alexandria, *De Adoratione et cultu in spiritu et veritate*, Migne *PG* 68, cols 133–1126.

Cyril of Alexandria, *Epistle* 17, Migne *PG* 77, cols 105–22; ed. and transl. L. Wickham, *Cyril of Alexandria, select letters* (Oxford: Clarendon Press, 1983), 12–33.

Cyril of Alexandria, *Epistle* 39, Migne *PG* 77, cols 173–82; transl. J. McGuckin, *St Cyril of Alexandria: the Christological controversy. Its history, theology and texts* (Leiden: Brill, 1994), 343–48.

Cyril of Alexandria, *Epistle* 40, Migne *PG* 77, cols 181–202; ed. and transl. L. Wickham, *Cyril of Alexandria: select letters* (Oxford: Clarendon Press, 1983), 34–61.

BIBLIOGRAPHY 201

Cyril of Alexandria, *Epistle* 48, Migne *PG* 77, cols 247–50.

Cyril of Alexandria, *Epistle* 55, Migne *PG* 77, cols 287–320; transl. J. McEnerney, *St. Cyril of Alexandria: Letters 51–110* (Washington, D.C.: Catholic University of America Press, 1987), 15–36.

Cyril of Alexandria, *Explicatio duodecimo capitum*, Migne *PG* 76, cols 293–312; transl. N. Russell, *Cyril of Alexandria* (New York: Routledge, 2000), 176–89.

Cyril of Alexandria, *In Ioannis Evangelium*, Migne *PG* 73 and 74, cols 9–756.

Cyril of Alexandria, *Liber de recta in Dominum nostrum Iesum Christum fide*, Migne *PG* 76, cols 1133–200.

Cyril of Alexandria, *Scholia de Incarnatione Unigeniti*, Migne *PG* 75, cols 1369–412; transl. J. McGuckin, *St Cyril of Alexandria: the Christological controversy. Its history, theology and texts* (Leiden: Brill, 1994), 294–335.

Damasus, *Epistle 4, Confessio Fidei catholicae*, Migne *PL* 13, cols 357–65; ed. P. Schaff, *Theodoret, Jerome, Gennadius, and Rufinus. Nicene and Post-Nicene Fathers*, vol. 3, Second Series (Grand Rapids, MI: Christian Classics Ethereal Library), 319–21.

Dandolo, Andrea, *Chronica per extensum descripta*, ed. E. Pastorello, *Rerum Italicarum Scriptores*, vol. 12, part 1 (Bologna, 1938), 1–327.

Davies, B., and Evans, G., *Anselm of Canterbury: the major works* (Oxford: Oxford University Press, 1998).

Dölger, F., and Wirth, P., *Regesten der Kaiserurkunden des oströmischen Reiches, von 565–1453*, vol. III: *Regesten von 1204–1282* (revised edition) (Munich/Berlin: C.H. Beck, 1977).

Dondaine, A., '"Contra Graecos." Premiers ecrits polemiques des dominicains d'Orient,' *Archivum Fratrum Praedicatorum* 21 (1951), 320–446.

Ephraem, *Historia Chronica*, ed. O. Lampsidis (Athens: Academia Atheniensis, 1990).

Epiphanios of Cyprus, *Adversus Haereses*, Migne *PG* 41, col. 173, *PG* 43, col. 832: transl. F. Williams, *The Panarion of Epiphanius of Salamis, Book I (Sects 1–46)*, 2nd edn (Leiden: Brill, 2009).

Eusebios of Caesarea, *Vie de Constantin: texte critique*, ed. F. Winkelmann (Paris: Les Éditions du Cerf, 2013); trans. A. Cameron and S. Hall, *Eusebius: Life of Constantine* (Oxford: Clarendon Press, 1999).

Festa, N., 'Le lettere greche di Federigo II,' *Archivo storico Italiano* 13 (1894), 1–34.

Festa, N., ed., *Theodori Ducae Lascaris Epistulae CCXVII* (Florence: Tipografia G. Carnesecchi e Figli, 1898).

Geoffrey of Villehardouin, *Histoire de la conquête de Constantinople par Geoffroi de Ville-Hardouin avec la continuation de Henri de Valenciennes*, ed. N. de Wailly (Paris: Hachette, 1909).

George of Pelagonia, *Life of Vatatzes*, ed. A. Heisenberg, 'Kaiser Johannes Batatzes der Barmherzige. Ein mittelgriechische Legened,' *Byzantinische Zeitschrift* 14 (1905), 193–233.

202 THE DISPUTATIO

Gerard de Frachet, *Vitae Fratrum Ordinis Praedicatorum necnon Cronica Ordinis*, ed. B. Reichert (Leuven: Charpentier and Schoonjans, 1896); transl. P. Conway, *Lives of the Brethren of the Order of Preachers* (London: Aquin Press, 1955).

Germanos II, *Ἀπάντησις*, ed. F. Alter, *Chronikon Georgiou Phrantze tou protovestiariou eis tessara vivlia diairethen* (Vienna, 1796), 140–49.

Gesta Innocentii III, Migne *PL* 214, cols xvii–ccxxviii; transl. J. Powell, *The Deeds of Pope Innocent III by an anonymous author* (Washington D.C.: Catholic University of America Press, 2004).

Golubovich, G., *Biblioteca Bio-bibliografica della Terra Sancta e dell' Oriente Francescana*, 5 vols (Florence: Collegio di s. Bonaventura, 1906–23).

Golubovich, G., 'Disputatio Latinorum et Graecorum seu Relatio apocrisiarorum Gregorii IX de gestis Nicaeae in Bithynia et Nymphaeae in Lydia (1234),' *Archivum Franciscanum Historicum* 12 (1919), 418–70.

Gregoras, Nikephoros, *Byzantina Historia*, ed. L. Schopen, vol. 1 (Bonn: Weber, 1829).

Gregorii VII Registrum, ed. E. Caspar, Monumenta Germaniae Historica, Epistolae selectae, 2 vols (Berlin, 1920 and 1923); transl. H. Cowdrey, *The register of Pope Gregory VII, 1073–1085* (Oxford: Oxford University Press, 2002).

Gregory of Nyssa, *Quod non sint tres dii*, Migne *PG* 45, cols 115–36; ed. P. Schaff, *Gregory of Nyssa: Dogmatic Treatises. Nicene and Post-Nicene Fathers*, vol. 5, Second Series (Grand Rapids, MI: Christian Classics Ethereal Library), 616–25.

Gregory Thaumaturgus, *Expositio Fidei*, Migne *PG* 10, cols 983–88; ed. P. Schaff, *Fathers of the Third Century: Gregory Thaumaturgus, Dionysius the Great, Julius Africanus, Anatolius, and Minor Writers, Methodius, Arnobius. Anti-Nicene Fathers*, vol. 6 (Grand Rapids, MI: Christian Classics Ethereal Library), 11–12.

Grumel, V., *Les Regestes des actes du Patriarcat de Constantinople*, I, fasc. 2 and 3: *les regestes de 715 à 1206*, revised edition (Paris: Institut français des études byzantines, 1989).

Hageneder, O. et al., *Die Register Innocenz' III*, 13 vols (Graz/Cologne, Rome, Vienna: Verlag der Österreichischen Akademie der Wissenschaften, 1964–2015).

Hendrickx, B., *Regestes des empereurs latins de Constantinople (1204–1261/1272)* (Thessalonike: Aristoteleian University of Thessaloniki, 1988).

Huillard-Bréholles, J., *Historia diplomatica Friderici secundi*, 6 vols (Paris: Excudebant Plon Fratres, 1852–1861).

Kamateros, Andronikos, *Sacred arsenal*, ed. A. Bucossi, *Sacrum armamentarium. Pars prima* (Turnhout: Brepols, 2014).

Kokkinos, Philotheos, *Antirretike VI*, *PG* 151, cols 881–992.

Laurent, V., *Les regestes des actes du patriarcat de Constantinople*, I, fasc. 4: *Les regestes de 1208 à 1309* (Paris: Institut français des études byzantines, 1971).

BIBLIOGRAPHY 203

Liber Pontificalis: texte, introduction et commentaire, ed. L. Duchesne, vol. 1 (Paris: Thorin, 1886); transl. R. Davis, *The Book of Pontiffs (Liber Pontificalis): the ancient biographies of the first ninety Roman bishops to AD 715* (Liverpool: Liverpool University Press, 1989).

Liudprand of Cremona, *Relatio de legatione Constantinopolitana*, ed. P. Chiesa, *Liudprandi Cremonensis opera omnia* (Turnhout: Brepols, 1998), 185–218; transl. P. Squatriti, *The complete works of Liudprand of Cremona* (Washington, D.C.: Catholic University of America Press, 2007), 238–82.

Lorenzo de Monacis, *Historiae Venetae*, ed. F. Cornelius, *Rerum Italicarum Scriptores*, vol. 8 (Venice, 1758), 137–50.

Mansi, J., ed. *Sacrorum conciliorum nova et amplissima collectio*, 53 vols (Florence and Venice, 1759–1798).

Martin de Canale, *La chronique des Veniciens de maistre Martin da Canal*, ed. F. Galvani, *Archivio storico italiano*, series 1, VIII (Florence, 1845), 229–798.

Merendino, E., 'Quattro lettere greche di Federico II,' in *Atti della Accademia di Scienze Lettere e Arti di Palermo*, vol. 34, series 4, part 2 (Palermo, 1974–1975), 293–343.

Mesarites, Nicholas: A. Heisenberg, 'Neue Quellen zur Geschichte des lateinischen Kaisertums und der Kirchenunion: I. Der Epitaphios des Nikolaos Mesarites auf seinen Bruder Johannes,' *Sitzungsberichte der Bayerischen Akademie der Wissenschaften*, philos.-philol. und hist. Klasse, 1922, Abh. 5 (Munich, 1922), 3–75 [= A. Heisenberg, *Quellen und Studien zur spätbyzantinischen Geschichte* (London: Variorum Reprints, 1973), II, i]; transl. M. Angold, *Nicholas Mesarites: his life and works (in translation)* (Liverpool: Liverpool University Press, 2017), 141–92.

Mesarites, Nicholas: A. Heisenberg, 'Neue Quellen zur Geschichte des lateinischen Kaisertums und der Kirchenunion: II. Die Unionsverhandlungen vom 30. August 1206; Patriarchenwahl und Kaiserkrönung in Nikaia 1208: i. Die Disputation vom 30. August 1206; ii. Die Bitteschriften des griechische Klerus in Konstantinopel an den Kaiserhof von Nikaia und die kaiserliche Botschaft; iii. Reisebericht des Nikolaos Mesarites an die Mönche des Euergetisklosters in Konstantinopel,' *Sitzungsberichte der Bayerischen Akademie der Wissenschaften*, philos.-philol. und hist. Klasse, 1923, Abh. 2 (Munich, 1923), 3–46 [= A. Heisenberg, *Quellen und Studien zur spätbyzantinischen Geschichte* (London: Variorum Reprints, 1973), II, ii]; transl. M. Angold, *Nicholas Mesarites: his life and works (in translation)* (Liverpool: Liverpool University Press, 2017), 197–234.

Mesarites, Nicholas: A. Heisenberg, 'Neue Quellen zur Geschichte des lateinischen Kaisertums und der Kirchenunion: II. III – 'Der Bericht des Nikolaos Mesarites über die politischen und kirchlichen Ereignisse des Jahres 1214,' *Sitzungsberichte der Bayerischen Akademie der Wissenschaften*, philos.-philol. und hist. Klasse, 1923, Abh. 3 (Munich, 1923), 3–96 [= A. Heisenberg, *Quellen und Studien zur spätbyzantinischen Geschichte* (London: Variorum

204 THE DISPUTATIO

Reprints, 1973), II, iii]; transl. M. Angold, *Nicholas Mesarites: his life and works (in translation)* (Liverpool: Liverpool University Press, 2017), 251–96.

Mesarites, Nicholas, *Description of the Church of the Holy Apostles, Constantinople*, ed. A. Heisenberg, *Grabeskirche und Apostelkirche. Zwei Basiliken Konstantins: Untersuchungen zur Kunst und Literatur des ausgehenden Altertums* (Leipzig: Hinrichs, 1908), II, 10–96; ed. G. Downey, 'Nikolaos Mesarites: description of the Church of the Holy Apostles at Constantinople,' *Transactions of the American Philosophical Society* 47 (1957), 855–924; transl. M. Angold, *Nicholas Mesarites: his life and works (in translation)* (Liverpool: Liverpool University Press, 2017), 75–133.

Migne, J. P., *Patrologiae cursus completus: series Graeco-Latina*, 166 vols (Paris: Garnier Fratres, 1857–1866).

Miklosich, F., and Müller, J., ed., *Acta et diplomata graeca medii aevi sacra et profana*, 6 vols (Vienna: Carolus Gerold, 1860–1890).

Mouskes, Philippe, *Chronique rimée de Philippe Mouskes*, ed. Le Baron de Reiffenberg, 2 vols (Brussels, 1836, 1838).

Nicetae Choniatae Historia, ed. J.-L. van Dieten, 2 vols (Berlin/New York: De Gruyter, 1975); transl. H. Magoulias, *O City of Byzantium: Annals of Niketas Choniates* (Detroit, MI: Wayne State University Press, 1984).

Nicholas of Otranto, *Nikolaia Hidruntskago tri ealici*, ed. Archimandrite Arsenij (Novgorod, 1896).

Odo of Deuil, *De profetione Ludovici VII in orientem*, ed. and transl. V. Berry (New York: Columbia University Press, 1948).

Pachymeres, George, *Georges Pachymérès. Relations historiques*, ed. A. Failler, transl. V. Laurent vol. 2, III, IV (Paris: Peeters, 1999).

Paris, Matthew, *Chronica majora*, ed. H. Luard, 7 vols (London: Longman, 1872–1883); transl. J. Giles, *Matthew Paris's English History from the year 1235 to 1273*, 3 vols (London: Henry Bohn, 1852–1854).

Pieralli, L., *La corrispondenza diplomatica dell'imperatore byzantino con le potenze estere nel tredicesimo secolo (1204–1282). Studio storicodiplomatistico ed edizione critica* (Vatican: Archivio segreto vaticano, 2006).

Pitra, J. B., *Analecta sacra et classica. Spicilegio solesmensi parata*, vol. 6 (Paris: apud Roger et Chernowitz bibliopolas; Rome: ex officina libraria Philippi Cuggiani, 1891).

Potthast, A., *Regesta Pontificum Romanorum inde ab anno post Christum natum MCXCVIII ad annum MCCCIV*, vol. 1 (Graz: Akademische Druck-U. Verlagsanstalt, 1957).

Price, R., *The acts of the Council of Constantinople of 553 with related texts on the Three Chapters controversy*, vol. 1, *General introduction, letters and edicts, Sessions I–V* (Liverpool: Liverpool University Press, 2009).

Prokopios, *De aedificiis*, ed. G. Dindorf, vol. 3 (Bonn: Weber, 1838); transl. A. Stewart, *Of the buildings of Justinian by Procopius (circ. 560 AD)* (London: Palestine Pilgrims Text Society, 1888).

BIBLIOGRAPHY 205

Quetif, J., and Echard, J., *Scriptores ordinis praedicatorum recensiti, notisque historicis et criticis illustrati*, 2 vols (Paris, 1719).

Richard of San Germano, *Ryccardi de Sancto Germano notarii chronica*, ed. C. Garufi, *Rerum Italicarum Scriptores*, vol. 7, part 2 (Bologna, 1937).

Robert of Clari, *La conquête de Constantinople*, ed. and transl. P. Noble (Edinburgh: British Rencesvals Publications, 2005).

Rodenburg, C., ed., *Epistolae Saeculi XIII e regestis pontificum Romanorum*, vol. 1 (Berlin, 1883).

Salimbene de Adam, *Cronica*, ed. G. Scalia, vol. 1 (Turnhout: Brepols, 1998); transl. J. Baird, *The Chronicle of Salimbene de Adam* (Binghamton, NY: Center for Medieval and Early Renaissance Studies, 1986).

Sanudo, Marino the Younger, *Vite de' duchi di Venezia*, ed. L. Muratori, *Rerum Italicarum Scriptores*, vol. 22 (Milan, 1733), 399–1252.

Sathas, K. N., ed., *Μεσαιωνικὴ Βιβλιοθήκη*, 7 vols (Venice and Paris, 1872–1894).

Schabel, C., *The Synodicum Nicosiense and other documents of the Latin Church of Cyprus, 1196–1373* (Nicosia: Cyprus Research Centre, 2001).

Skoutariotes, Theodore. ed. K. N. Sathas, *Μεσαιωνικὴ Βιβλιοθήκη*, vol. 7 (Paris, 1894).

Stethatos, Niketas, *Against the Armenians and Latins*, ed. J. Hergenroether, *Monumenta Graeca ad Photium ejusque historiam pertinentia* (Ratisbon: G. J. Manz, 1869), 139–54.

Stevenson, J., and Frend, W., eds, *Creeds, councils and controversies: documents illustrating the history of the Church, AD 337–461*, revised edn (London: SPCK, 1989).

Tafel, G., and Thomas, G., *Urkunden zur alteren Handels- und Staatsgeschichte der Republik Venedig mit besonderen Beziehungen auf Byzanz und die Levante*, vol. 2 (Vienna: Hof- und Staatsdrucker, 1856).

Tanner, N., ed. and trans., *Decrees of the ecumenical councils*, vol. 1, *Nicaea I to Lateran V* (London: Georgetown University Press, 1990).

Tartaglia, A., *Theodorus II Ducas Lascaris opuscula rhetorica* (Munich: Saur, 2000).

Tautu, A., *Acta Honorii III (1216–1227) et Gregorii IX (1227–1241)* (Vatican: Typis Polyglottis Vaticanis, 1950).

Theiner, A., ed., *Vetera monumenta historica Hungariam sacram illustrantia*, vol. 1 (Rome: Typis Vaticanis, 1863).

Theophanes, *Chronographia*, ed. C. de Boor (Leipzig: Teubner, 1883); transl. C. Mango and R. Scott, *The chronicle of Theophanes Confessor* (Oxford: Clarendon Press, 1997).

Thomas of Eccleston, *Tractatus De Adventu Fratrum Minorum in Angliam*, ed. A. Little (Manchester: Manchester University Press, 1951); transl. A. Little, *The coming of the Friars Minor to England and Germany* (London: J. M. Dent and Sons, 1926).

Vasiljevski, V., 'Epirotica saeculi XIII,' *Vizantiiskii Vremennik* 3 (1896), 233–99.

206 THE DISPUTATIO

'Vita Gregorii Papae IX,' ed. L. Muratori, *Rerum Italicarum Scriptores*, vol. 3 (Milan, 1723), 570–87; *Le Liber Censuum de l'Eglise Romaine*, ed. P. Fabre, vol. 2, fascimile 5 (Paris, 1905), 18–36.

Vita of St Theodora of Arta, Migne *PG* 127, cols 903–08; transl. A. M. Talbot, *Holy women of Byzantium: ten saints' lives in English translation* (Washington, D.C.: Dumbarton Oaks, 1996), 326–33.

Xanthopoulos, Nikephoros Kallistos, *Nicephori Callisti Xanthopuli enarratio de episcopis Byzantinii et de patriarchis omnibus Constantinopolitanis*, Migne *PG* 147, cols 464–68.

Zigabenos, Euthymios, *Panoplia Dogmatica*, Migne *PG* 130.

Secondary Sources

Abulafia, D., *Frederick II: a medieval emperor* (New York: Oxford University Press, 1988).

Ahrweiler, H., 'L'histoire et la géographie de la région de Smyrne entre les deux occupations turque (1081–1317), particulièrement au XIIIe siècle,' *Travaux et Mémoires* 1 (1965), 1–204.

Anastos, M., 'Constantinople and Rome: a survey of the relations between the Byzantine and the Roman Churches,' in *Aspects of the mind of Byzantium: political theory, theology, and ecclesiastical relations with the See of Rome*, ed. S. Vryonis and N. Goodhue (Aldershot: Ashgate, 2001), 1–119.

Andrea, A., 'Innocent III and the Byzantine Rite,' in *Urbs Capta: the Fourth Crusade and its consequences*, ed. A. Laiou (Paris: Lethielleux, 2005), 111–22.

Andrea, A., 'Latin evidence for the accession date of John X Camateros, Patriarch of Constantinople,' *Byzantinische Zeitschrift* 66 (1973), 354–58.

Angelov, D., *Imperial ideology and political thought in Byzantium, 1204–1330* (Cambridge: Cambridge University Press, 2007).

Angelov, D., 'Prosopography of the Byzantine world (1204–1261) in the light of Bulgarian sources,' in *Identities and allegiances in the Eastern Mediterranean after 1204*, ed. J. Herrin and G. Saint-Guillain (Aldershot: Ashgate, 2011), 101–19.

Angold, M., 'Administration of the Empire of Nicaea,' *Byzantinische Forschungen* 19 (1993), 127–38.

Angold, M., 'After the Fourth Crusade: the Greek rump states and the recovery of Byzantium,' in *The Cambridge history of the Byzantine Empire, c. 500–1492*, ed. J. Shepard (Cambridge: Cambridge University Press, 2008), 731–58.

Angold, M., *The Byzantine Empire, 1025–1204: a political history*, 2nd edn (London: Longman, 1997).

Angold, M., *A Byzantine government in exile* (London: Oxford University Press, 1975).

BIBLIOGRAPHY 207

Angold, M., 'Byzantine "nationalism" and the Nicaean Empire,' *Byzantine and Modern Greek Studies* 1 (1975).

Angold, M., 'Byzantium in exile,' in *The new Cambridge medieval history* V, ed. D. Abulafia (Cambridge: Cambridge University Press, 1999), 543–68.

Angold, M., *Church and society in Byzantium under the Comneni, 1081–1261* (Cambridge: Cambridge University Press, 1995).

Angold, M., 'The Latin Empire of Constantinople: marriage strategies,' in *Identities and allegiances in the Eastern Mediterranean after 1204*, ed. J. Herrin and G. Saint-Guillain (Aldershot: Ashgate, 2011), 47–65.

Angold, M., 'Michael VIII Palaiologos and the Aegean,' in *Liquid and multiple: individuals and identities in the thirteenth-century Aegean*, ed. G. Saint-Guillain and D. Stathakopoulos (Paris: Association des Amis du Centre d'Histoire et Civilisation de Byzance, 2012), 27–44.

Armpatzis, C., Ἀνέκδοτη επιστολή του πατριάρχη Κωνσταντινουπόλεως Γερμανού Β΄ προς τους καρδιναλίους της Ρώμης (1232),' *Αθήνα: Εταιρία Βυζαντινών Σπουδών* (2006), 363–78.

Arnold, B., 'Emperor Frederick II (1194–1250) and the political particularism of the German princes,' *Journal of Medieval History*, 26:3 (2012), 239–52.

Balard, M., 'The Genoese in the Aegean (1204–1566),' in *Latins and Greeks in the Eastern Mediterranean after 1204*, ed. B. Arbel, B. Hamilton and D. Jacoby (London: Frank Cass, 1989), 158–74.

Barber, M., 'Western attitudes to Frankish Greece in the thirteenth century,' *Mediterranean Historical Review* 4 (1989), 111–28.

Beck, H., *Kirche und theologische Literatur im byzantinischen Reich* (Munich: Beck, 1959).

Beihammer, A., and Schabel, C., 'Two small texts on the wider context of the martyrdom of the thirteen monks of Kantara in Cyprus, 1231,' in *ΠΟΛΥΠΤΥΧΟΝ: Αφιέρωμα στον Ιωάννη Χασιώτη*, ed. E. Motos Guirao and M. Morfakidis (Granada: Centro de Estudios Bizantinos, 2008), 69–81.

Boring, E., *An introduction to the New Testament: history, literature, theology* (Louisville, KY: Westminster John Knox Press, 2012).

Borsari, S., 'Federico II e l'Oriente bizantino,' *Rivista Storica Italiana* 63 (1951), 278–91.

Bréhier, L., 'Attempts at reunion of the Greek and Latin Churches,' in *Cambridge medieval history* 4, ed. J. Bury (Cambridge: Cambridge University Press, 1923), 594–626.

Browning, R., 'The patriarchal school at Constantinople in the twelfth century,' *Byzantion* 32 (1962), 167–202.

Brubaker, J., '*Nuncii* or *Legati*: what makes a papal representative in 1234,' in *Cross-cultural exchange in the Byzantine world, 300–1500 AD: selected papers from the XVII International Graduate Conference of the Oxford University Byzantine Society*, ed. K. Stewart and J. Wakeley (Oxford: Peter Lang International Academic Publishers, 2016), 115–28.

208 THE DISPUTATIO

Brubaker, J., "'You are the heretics!" Dialogue and disputation between the Greek east and the Latin west after 1204,' in *Interfaith dialogue and disputation in the medieval Mediterranean*, ed. B. Catlos and A. Novikoff, *Medieval encounters* 24, no. 5/6 (Leiden: Brill, 2018), 613–30.

Bryer, A., 'The late Byzantine identity,' in *Byzantium, identity, image, influence: XIX International Congress of Byzantine Studies, University of Copenhagen, 18–24 August, 1996*, ed. K. Fledelius and P. Schreiner (Copenhagen: Eventus, 1996), 49–50.

Cağaptay, S., 'How western is it? The palace at Nymphaion and its architectural setting,' in *Change in the Byzantine world in the twelfth and thirteenth centuries* (Istanbul: Koç Üniversitesi Anadolu Medeniyetleri Araştırma Merkezi, 2010), 357–62.

Cahen, C., *La Syrie du Nord à l'epoque des Croisades et la principauté franque d'Antioch* (Paris: Presses de l'Ifpo, 1940).

Cameron, A., *Arguing it out: discussion in twelfth-century Byzantium* (Budapest: Central European University Press, 2016).

Canart, P., 'Nicéphore Blemmyde et le mémoire adressé aux envoyés de Grégoire IX (Nicée, 1234),' *Orientalia Christiana Periodica* 25 (1959), 310–25.

Chadwick, H., *East and west: the making of a rift in the Church, from apostolic times until the Council of Florence* (Oxford: Oxford University Press, 2005).

Chrissis, N., 'The city and the cross: the image of Constantinople and the Latin Empire,' *Byzantine and Modern Greek Studies* 36 (2012), 20–37.

Chrissis, N., *Crusading in Frankish Greece: a study of Byzantine–Western relations and attitudes, 1204–1282* (Turnhout: Brepols, 2012).

Chrysos, E., '1054: Schism?' *Cristianità d'Occidente e cristianità d'Oriente* 1 (Spoleto, 2004), 547–67.

Ciggaar, K., 'Flemish counts and emperors: friends and foreigners in Byzantium,' in *The Latin Empire: some contributions*, ed. V. van Aalst and K. N. Ciggaar (Hernen: A. A. Bredius Foundation, 1990), 33–62.

Congourdeau, M., 'Frère Simon le Constantinopolitan, OP (1235?–1325?),' *Revue des études byzantines* 45 (1987), 165–74.

Congourdeau, M., 'Note sur les Dominicains de Constantinople au debut du 14e siècle,' *Revue des études byzantines* 45 (1987), 175–81.

Constantinides, C., *Higher education in Byzantium in the thirteenth and early fourteenth centuries (1204–ca. 1310)* (Nicosia: Cyprus Research Centre, 1982).

Cowdrey, H., 'The Gregorian papacy, Byzantium, and the First Crusade,' in *Byzantium and the west, c. 850–c. 1200: proceedings of the XVIII spring symposium of Byzantine Studies, Oxford 30th March–1st April 1984*, ed. J. Howard-Johnston (Amsterdam: Verlag Adolf M. Hakkert, 1988), 145–69.

Cross, F., and Livingstone, E., eds, *Oxford dictionary of the Christian Church*, 3rd edn (Oxford: Oxford University Press, 2005).

Crown, A., ed., *The Samaritans* (Tübingen: Mohr, 1989)

BIBLIOGRAPHY 209

Dagron, G., *Emperor and priest: the imperial office in Byzantium*, transl. J. Birrell (Cambridge: Cambridge University Press, 2003).

Darrouzès, J., 'Les documents byzantins du XIIe siècle sur la primauté romaine,' *Revue des études byzantines* 23 (1965), 51–59.

Darrouzès, J., *Recherches sur les ΟΦΦΙΚΙΑ de l'église byzantine* (Paris: Institut français d'études byzantines, 1970).

de Vries, W., 'The college of patriarchs,' *Concilium* 8 (1965), 65–80.

Doran, J., 'Rites and wrongs: the Latin mission to Nicaea, 1234,' *Studies in Church History* 32 (1996), 131–44.

Downey, G., 'Nikolaos Mesarites: description of the Church of the Holy Apostles at Constantinople,' *Transactions of the American Philosophical Society* 47 (1957), 855–924.

Duba, W., 'The status of the patriarch of Constantinople after the Fourth Crusade,' in *Diplomatics in the eastern Mediterranean 1000–1500*, ed. M. Parani and C. Schabel (Leiden: Brill, 2008), 63–91.

Dvornik, F., *Byzantium and the Roman Primacy* (New York: Fordham University Press, 1966).

Dvornik, F., *The Photian schism: history and legend* (Cambridge: Cambridge University Press, 1948; reprinted 1970).

Edwards, M., 'The First Council of Nicaea,' in *The Cambridge history of Christianity*, vol. 1, *Origins to Constantine*, ed. M. Mitchell and F. Young (Cambridge: Cambridge University Press, 2006), 552–67.

Erickson, J., 'Leavened and unleavened: some theological implications of the schism of 1054,' *St Vladimir's Theological Quarterly* 14 (1970), 155–76.

Fedalto, G., 'Venice's responsibility in the break down of ecclesiastical unity between Rome and Constantinople,' in *The Fourth Crusade Revisited. Atti della Conferenza Internazionale nell'ottavo centenario della IV Crociata 1204–2004. Andros (Grecia) 27–30 maggio 2004* (Vatican: Libreria Editrice Vaticana, 2008), 185–201.

Fellmeth, A., and Horwitz, M., *Guide to Latin in international law* (Oxford: Oxford University Press, 2011).

Ferguson, E., ed., *Encyclopedia of early Christianity*, 2nd edn (London: Garland Publishing, 1998).

Fisher, E., 'Monks, monasteries and the Latin language in Constantinople,' in *Change in the Byzantine world in the twelfth and thirteenth centuries* (Istanbul: Koç Üniversitesi Anadolu Medeniyetleri Araştırma Merkezi, 2010), 390–95.

Fisher, J., 'Hugh of St. Cher and the development of mediaeval theology,' *Speculum* 31 (1956), 57–69.

Foss, C., 'The defenses of Asia Minor against the Turks,' *Greek Orthodox Theological Review* 27:2 (1982), 145–205.

Foss, C., *Nicaea: A Byzantine capital and its praises* (Brookline, MA: Hellenic College Press, 1996).

210 THE DISPUTATIO

Foss, C., and Winfield, D., *Byzantine fortifications: an introduction* (Pretoria: University of South Africa, 1986).

Franchi, A., *La svolta politico-ecclesiastica tra Roma e Bizanzio (1249–1254) La legazione di Giovanni da Parma* (Rome: Pontificium Athenaeum Antonianum, 1981).

Gardner, A., *The Lascarids of Nicaea* (London: Messrs, Methuen and Co., 1912).

Geanakoplos, D. J., *Byzantine east and Latin west: two worlds of Christendom in the Middle Ages and Renaissance; studies in ecclesiastical and cultural history* (Oxford: Basil Blackwell, 1966).

Geanakoplos, D. J., 'Church and state in the Byzantine Empire: a reconsideration of the problem of caesaropapism,' *Church History* 34 (1965), 381–403.

Geanakoplos, D. J., *Interaction of the 'sibling' Byzantine and western cultures in the Middle Ages and Italian Renaissance 330–1600* (New Haven, CT: Yale University Press, 1976).

Gill, J., *Byzantium and the papacy, 1198–1400* (New Brunswick: Rutgers University Press, 1979).

Gill, J., 'An unpublished letter of Germanus, patriarch of Constantinople (1222–1240),' *Byzantion* 44 (1974), 138–51.

Gilmore, A., 'The date and significance of the Last Supper,' *Scottish Journal of Theology*, 14:3 (1961), 256–69.

Glare, P., ed., *Oxford Latin dictionary*, 2nd edn (Oxford: Oxford University Press, 2012).

Goulder, M., 'A poor man's Christology,' *New Testament Studies* 45 (1999), 332–48.

Grumel, V., 'Autour du voyage de Pierre Grossolanus archevêque de Milan, à Constantinple, en 1112. Notes d'histoire et de littérature,' *Échos d'Orient* 32 (1933), 22–33.

Grumel, V., 'L'Authenticité de la lettre de Jean Vatatzès, empereur de Nicée, au Pape Grégoire IX,' *Échos d'Orient* 29 (1930), 450–58.

Grumel, V., *Traité d'études Byzantines: I: La Chronologie (Bibliotheque Byzantine publiee sous la direction de P. Lemerle)* (Paris: Presses universitaires de France, 1958).

Guran, P., 'From empire to church, and back: in the aftermath of 1204,' *Revue des Études Sud-Est Européennes* 44 (2006), 59–69.

Hamilton, B., *The Latin Church in the Crusader states: the secular church* (London: Variorum, 1980).

Hasluck, F., *Cyzicus: being some account of the history and antiquities of that city, and of the district adjacent to it, with the town of Apollonia ad Rhyndacum, Miletupolis, Hadrianutherae, Priapus, Zeleia, etc.* (Cambridge: Cambridge University Press, 1910).

Hinterberger, M., 'A neglected tool of Orthodox propaganda? The image of the Latins in Byzantine hagiography,' in *Greeks, Latins, and intellectual history, 1204–1500*, ed. M. Hinterberger and C. Schabel (Leuven: Peeters, 2011), 129–49.

BIBLIOGRAPHY
211

Hoeck, J., and Loenertz, R., *Nikolaos-Nektarios von Otranto, Abt von Casole: Beiträge zur Geschichte der ost-westlichen Beziehungen unter Innozenz III. und Friedrich II.* (Ettal: Buch-Kunstverlag, 1965).

Holtzmann, W., 'Unionsverhandlungen zwischen Kaiser Alexios I. und Papst Urban II. im Jahre 1089,' *Byzantinische Zeitschrift* 28 (1928), 38–76. Reprinted in W. Holtzmann, *Beiträge zur Reichs- und Papstgeschichte des hohen Mittelalters* (Bonn: Röhrscheid, 1957), 79–105.

Humphreys, C., *The mystery of the Last Supper: reconstructing the final days of Jesus* (Cambridge: Cambridge University Press, 2011).

Hussey, J., *The Orthodox Church in the Byzantine Empire* (Oxford: Clarendon Press, 1986).

Ierodiakonou, K., and O'Meara, D., 'Philosophies,' in *The Oxford handbook of Byzantine Studies*, ed. E. Jeffreys with J. Haldon and R. Cormack (Oxford: Oxford University Press, 2008), 711–20.

Jacoby, D., 'The economy of Latin Constantinople, 1204–1261,' in *Urbs Capta: the Fourth Crusade and its consequences*, ed. A. Laiou (Paris: Lethielleux, 2005), 195–214.

Jacoby, D., 'From Byzantium to Latin Romania: continuity and change,' in *Latins and Greeks in the Eastern Mediterranean after 1204*, ed. B. Arbel, B. Hamilton and D. Jacoby (London: Frank Cass, 1989), 1–44.

Jacoby, D., 'The Latin Empire of Constantinople and the Frankish states in Greece,' in *The new Cambridge medieval history* V, ed. D. Abulafia (Cambridge: Cambridge University Press, 1999), 527–42.

Jamil, N., and Johns, J., 'An original Arabic document from crusader Antioch (1213 AD),' in *Texts, documents and artefacts: Islamic studies in honour of D. S. Richards*, ed. D. Richards (Leiden: Brill, 2003), 157–90.

Jerman, C., 'Hugh of St. Cher,' *Dominicana* 44 (1959), 338–47.

Jugie, M., *Le schisme Byzantin: aperçu historique et doctrinal* (Paris: Lethielleux, 1941).

Kaldellis, A., *Hellenism in Byzantium: the transformation of Greek identity and the reception of the classical tradition* (Cambridge: Cambridge University Press, 2007).

Kaldellis, A., *Streams of gold, rivers of blood: the rise and fall of Byzantium 955 A.D. to the First Crusade* (Oxford: Oxford University Press, 2017).

Kaplan, M., 'La place du schism de 1054 dans les relations entre Byzance, Rome et l'Italie,' *Byzantinoslavica* 54:1 (1993), 29–37.

Karpozilos, A., *The ecclesiastical controversy between the Kingdom of Nicaea and the Principality of Epiros (1217–1233)* (Thessalonike: Kentron Vyzantinōn Ereunōn, 1973).

Kazhdan, A., 'The notion of Byzantine diplomacy,' in *Byzantine diplomacy: papers from the twenty-fourth spring symposium of Byzantine Studies, Cambridge, March 1990*, ed. J. Shepard and S. Franklin (Aldershot: Ashgate, 1992), 3–21.

212 THE DISPUTATIO

Kazhdan, A., and Talbot, A., eds, *Oxford dictionary of Byzantium*, 3 vols (Oxford: Oxford University Press, 1991).

Kiesewetter, A., 'Die Heirat zwischen Konstanze-Anna von Hohenstaufen und Kaiser Johannes III. Batatzes von Nikaia (Ende 1240 oder Anfang 1241) und der Angriff des Johannes Batatzes auf Konstantinopel im Mai oder Juni 1241,' *Römische Historische Mitteilungen* 41 (1999), 239–50.

Kolbaba, T., *The Byzantine lists: errors of the Latins* (Urbana: University of Illinois Press, 2000).

Kolbaba, T., 'Byzantine perceptions of Latin religious "errors": themes and changes from 850 to 1350,' in *The crusades from the perspective of Byzantium and the Muslim world*, ed. A. Laiou and R. Mottahedeh (Washington, D.C.: Dumbarton Oaks, 2001), 117–43.

Kolbaba, T., *Inventing Latin heretics: Byzantines and the filioque in the ninth century* (Kalamazoo, MI: Medieval Institute Publications, Western Michigan University, 2008).

Kolbaba, T., 'The legacy of Humbert and Cerularius: traditions of the schism of 1054 in Byzantine texts and manuscripts of the twelfth and thirteenth centuries,' in *Porphyrogenita: Essays on the history and literature of Byzantium and the Latin East in honour of Julian Chrysostomides*, eds C. Dendrinos et al. (Aldershot: Ashgate, 2003), 47–62.

Kolbaba, T., 'On the closing of the churches and the rebaptism of Latins: Greek perfidy or Latin slander?' *Byzantine and Modern Greek Studies* 29 (2005), 39–51.

Kolbaba, T., 'Repercussions of the Second Council of Lyon (1274): theological polemic and the boundaries of orthodoxy,' in *Greeks, Latins, and intellectual history, 1204–1500*, ed. M. Hinterberger and C. Schabel (Leuven: Peeters, 2011), 43–68.

Kolbaba, T., 'Theological debates with the west, 1054–1300,' in *The Cambridge intellectual history of Byzantium*, ed. A. Kaldellis and N. Siniossoglou (Cambridge: Cambridge University Press, 2017), 479–93.

Kordoses, M., *Southern Greece under the Franks (1204–1261): a study of the Greek population and the Orthodox Church under the Frankish dominion* (Ioannina: University of Ioannina Press, 1987).

Korobeinikov, D., *Byzantium and the Turks in the thirteenth century* (Oxford: Oxford University Press, 2014).

Kurtz, E., 'Christophoros von Ankyra als Exarch des Patriarchen Germanos II,' *Byzantinische Zeitschrift* 16 (1907), 120–42.

Lagopates, S., Γερμανὸς ὁ β΄, πατριάρχης Κωνσταντινουπόλεως-Νικαίας, 1222–1240: βίος, συγγράμματα καὶ διδασκαλία αὐτοῦ, ἀνέκδοτοι, ὁμιλίαι καὶ ἐπιστολαί (Athens: Μορέας, 1913).

Laiou, A., 'Byzantine trade with Christians and Muslims and the crusades,' in *The crusades from the perspective of Byzantium and the Muslim world*, ed. A. Laiou and R. Mottahedeh (Washington, D.C.: Dumbarton Oaks, 2001), 157–96.

BIBLIOGRAPHY

213

Lampe, G., *A Patristic Greek Lexicon* (Oxford: Clarendon Press, 1961).

Langdon, J., 'Byzantium in Anatolian exile: imperial vicegerency reaffirmed during Byzantino-Papal discussions at Nicaea and Nymphaion, 1234,' *Byzantinische Forschungen* 20 (1994), 197–233.

Langdon, J., *Byzantium's last imperial offensive in Asia Minor* (New Rochelle, NY: Caratzas, 1992).

Langdon, J., 'The forgotten Byzantino-Bulgarian assault and siege of Constantinople, 1235–1236, and the breakup of the *entente cordiale* between John III Ducas Vatatzes and John Asen II in 1236 as background to the genesis of the Hohenstaufen-Vatatzes alliance of 1242,' in *Byzantina kai metabyzantinia*, vol. 4, *Byzantine studies in honor of Milton V. Anastos*, ed. S. Vryonis (Malibu: Undena Publications, 1985), 105–35.

Langdon, J., 'John III Ducas Vatatzes and the Venetians: the episode of his anti-Venetian Cretan campaigns, 1230 and 1234,' in *Novum millennium: studies in Byzantine history and culture dedicated to Paul Speck*, ed. C. Sode and S. Takács (Aldershot: Ashgate, 2001), 231–50.

Lankila, T., 'The saracen raid of Rome in 846: an example of maritime *Ghazw*,' in *Travelling through time: essays in honour of Kaj Öhrnberg*, ed. S. Akar, J. Hämeen-Anttila and I. Nokso-Koivisto, *Studia Orientalia* 114 (Helsinki: Finnish Oriental Society, 2013), 93–120.

Lees, J., *Anselm of Havelberg: deeds into words in the twelfth century* (Leiden and New York: Brill, 1998).

Lewis, S., *The art of Matthew Paris in the Chronica Majora* (Berkeley: University of California Press, 1987).

Liddell, H. G., and Scott, R., *Greek–English lexicon* (New York: Harper and Brothers, 1883).

Little, A., *Franciscan papers, lists, and documents* (Manchester: Manchester University Press, 1943).

Little, A., *Studies in English Franciscan history, being the Ford Lectures, delivered in the University of Oxford in 1916* (Manchester: Manchester University Press, 1917).

Lock, P., *The Franks in the Aegean 1204–1500* (London: Longman, 1995).

Lock, P., 'The Latin emperors as heirs to Byzantium,' in *New Constantines: the rhythm of imperial renewal in Byzantium, 4th–13th centuries*, ed. P. Magdalino (Aldershot: Ashgate, 1994), 295–304.

Loenertz, R., 'Les établissements dominicains de Péra-Constantinople,' *Échos d'Orient* 34 (1935), 332–49.

Longnon, J., *L'Empire latin de Constantinople et la principauté de Morée* (Paris: Payot, 1949).

Loud, G., 'The Papal 'crusade' against Frederick II in 1228–1230,' in *The papacy and the crusades: proceedings of the VIIth conference of the Society for the Study of the Crusades and the Latin East*, ed. M. Balard (Aldershot: Ashgate, 2011), 91–103.

Louth, A., *Greek east and Latin west: the Church AD 681–1071* (Crestwood, NY: St Vladimir's Seminary Press, 2007).

McCormick, M., 'Byzantium on the move: imagining a communications history,' in *Travel in the Byzantine world, papers from the thirty-fourth spring symposium of Byzantine Studies, Birmingham, April 2000*, ed. R. Macrides (Aldershot: Ashgate, 2002), 3–29.

McCormick, M., *Origins of the European economy: communications and commerce, AD 300–900* (Cambridge: Cambridge University Press, 2001).

MacEvitt, C., *The crusades and the Christian world of the east: rough tolerance* (Philadelphia: University of Pennsylvania Press, 2008).

Macrides, R., 'Emperor and church in the last centuries of Byzantium,' *Studies in Church History* 54 (2018), 123–43.

Macrides, R., 'From the Komnenoi to Palaiologoi: imperial models in decline and exile,' in *New Constantines: the rhythm of imperial renewal in Byzantium, 4th–13th centuries*, ed. P. Magdalino (Aldershot: Ashgate, 1994), 269–82.

Macrides, R., 'Nomos and Kanon on paper and in court,' in *Church and people in Byzantium: Society for the Promotion of Byzantine Studies twentieth spring symposium of Byzantine Studies, Manchester, 1986*, ed. R. Morris (Birmingham: Centre for Byzantine, Ottoman and Modern Greek Studies, University of Birmingham, 1990), 61–86. Reprinted in R. Macrides, *Kinship and justice in Byzantium, 11th–15th centuries* (Aldershot: Ashgate, 1999).

Macrides, R., 'The thirteenth century in Byzantine historical writing,' in *Porphyrogenita: essays on the history and literature of Byzantium and the Latin East in honour of Julian Chrysostomides*, eds C. Dendrinos et al. (Aldershot: Ashgate, 2003), 63–76.

Madden, T., 'Vows and contracts in the Fourth Crusade: the Treaty of Zara and the attack on Constantinople in 1204,' *International History Review* 15 (1993), 441–68.

Magdalino, P., 'Byzantine snobbery,' *The Byzantine aristocracy, IX to XIII centuries*, ed. M. Angold (Oxford: British Archaeological Reports, International Series 221, 1984), 58–78.

Magdalino, P., *The empire of Manuel I Komnenos, 1143–1180* (Cambridge: Cambridge University Press, 1993).

Magdalino, P., 'Enlightenment and repression in twelfth-century Byzantium: the evidence of the canonists,' in *Byzantium in the 12th century: canon law, state and society*, ed. N. Oikonomides (Athens: Etareia Byzantinon kai Metabyzantinon Meleton, 1991), 357–73.

Magdalino, P., 'Hellenism and nationalism in Byzantium,' in P. Magdalino, *Tradition and transformation in medieval Byzantium* (Aldershot: Variorum, 1991), 1–29.

Magdalino, P., 'The phenomenon of Manuel I Komnenos,' in *Byzantium and the west, c. 850–c. 1200: proceedings of the XVIII spring symposium of Byzantine Studies, Oxford 30th March–1st April 1984*, ed. J. Howard-Johnston (Amsterdam: Verlag Adolf M. Hakkert, 1988), 171–99.

BIBLIOGRAPHY 215

Maiorov, A., 'Church-union negotiations between Rome, Nicaea and Rus, 1231–1237,' *Orientalia Christiana Periodica* 84 (2018), 385–405.

Mango, C., 'The meeting-place of the first ecumenical council and the church of the Holy Fathers at Nicaea,' *Deltion tes Christianikes Archeologikes Etaireias* 26 (2005), 27–34.

Martin, C., 'Disputing about disputing: The medieval procedure of *positio* and its role in a dispute over the nature of logic and the foundations of metaphysics,' in *Traditions of controversy*, ed. M. Dascal and H. Chang (Amsterdam and Philadelphia: John Benjamins Publishing Company, 2007), 151–64.

Martin, J., 'O felix Asia! Frédéric II, l'Empire de Nicée et le "césaropapisme",' *Travaux et Mémoires* 14, *Melanges Gilbert Dagron* (2002), 473–83.

Mayne, R., 'East and west in 1054,' *The Cambridge Historical Journal* 11:2 (1954), 133–48.

Meyendorff, J., *Byzantine theology: historical trends and doctrinal themes* (New York: Fordham University Press, 1979).

Mitsiou, E., 'Ideology and economy in the politics of John III Vatatzes (1221–1254),' in *Change in the Byzantine world in the twelfth and thirteenth centuries*, ed. A. Ödekan (Istanbul: Koç Üniversitesi Anadolu Medeniyetleri Araştırma Merkezi, 2010), 195–205.

Mitsiou, E., 'Networks of Nicaea: 13th-century socio-economic ties, structures and prosopography,' in *Liquid and multiple: individuals and identities in the thirteenth-century Aegean*, ed. G. Saint-Guillain and D. Stathakopoulos (Paris: Association des Amis du Centre d'Histoire et Civilisation de Byzance, 2012), 91–104.

Moorman, J., *A history of the Franciscan Order: from its origins to the year 1517* (Oxford: Clarendon Press, 1968).

Morris, C., *The papal monarchy: the western Church from 1050 to 1250* (Oxford: Clarendon Press, 1989).

Morrison, C., 'Thirteenth-century Byzantine "metallic" identities,' in *Liquid and multiple: individuals and identities in the thirteenth-century Aegean*, ed. G. Saint-Guillain and D. Stathakopoulos (Paris: Association des Amis du Centre d'Histoire et Civilisation de Byzance, 2012), 133–64.

Munitiz, J., 'A reappraisal of Blemmydes' first discussion with the Latins,' *Byzantinoslavica* 51 (1990), 20–26.

Munitiz, J., 'A "wicked woman" in the 13th century,' *Jahrbuch der österreichischen Byzantinistik* 32:2 (1982), 529–37.

Nicol, D., 'The crusades and the unity of Christendom,' Lecture to the friends of Dr. Williams's Library (London: Dr. Williams's Trust, 1986).

Nicol, D., *The Despotate of Epiros* (Oxford: Basil Blackwell, 1957).

Nicol, D., 'The fate of Peter of Courtenay, Latin Emperor of Constantinople, and a treaty that never was,' in *Καθηγήτρια: Essays presented to Joan Hussey* (Camberley: Porphyrogenitus, 1988), 377–83.

216 THE DISPUTATIO

Nicol, D., 'The Fourth Crusade and the Greek and Latin empires,' in *Cambridge medieval history* IV/1, ed. J. Hussey (Cambridge: Cambridge University Press, 1966), 275–330.

Nicol, D., 'Mixed marriages in Byzantium in the thirteenth century,' *Studies in Church History* 1 (1964), 160–72. Reprinted in D. Nicol, *Byzantium: its ecclesiastical history and relations with the western world* (London: Variorum, 1972).

Nikolov, A., 'The medieval Slavonic "dossier" of the Great Schism: historical narrations and lists of Latin errors among the Balkan Slavs,' in *Contra Latinos and Adversus Graecos: the separation between Rome and Constantinople from the ninth to the fifteenth century*, ed. A. Bucossi and A. Calia (Leuven: Peeters, 2020), 297–310.

Nilsson, I., '"The same story, but another": a reappraisal of literary imitation in Byzantium,' in *Imitatio – Aemulatio – Variatio*, ed. E. Shiffer and A. Rhoby (Vienna: Österreichischen Akademie der Wissenschaften, 2010), 195–208.

Norden, W., *Das Papsttum und Byzanz. Die Trennung der beiden Mächte und das Problem ihrer Wiedervereinigung bis zum Untergange des byzantinischen Reichs (1453)* (Berlin: Behr, 1903).

Novikoff, A., 'Anselm, dialogue, and the rise of disputation,' *Speculum* 86 (2011), 387–418.

Novikoff, A., *The medieval culture of disputation: pedagogy, practice, and performance* (Philadelphia: University of Pennsylvania Press, 2013).

Novikoff, A., 'Towards a cultural history of scholastic disputation,' *American Historical Review* 117:2 (2012), 331–64.

Oikonomides, N., 'Byzantine diplomacy, A.D. 1204–1453: means and ends,' in *Byzantine diplomacy, papers from the twenty-fourth spring symposium of Byzantine Studies, Cambridge, March 1990*, ed. J. Shepard and S. Franklin (Aldershot: Ashgate, 1992), 73–88.

Page, G., *Being Byzantine: Greek identity before the Ottomans* (Cambridge: Cambridge University Press, 2008).

Palau, C., 'L'*Arsenale Sacro* di Andronico Camatero. Il proemio ed il dialogo dell'imperatore con i cardinali latini: originale, imitazioni, arrangiamenti,' *Revue Revue des études byzantines* 51 (1993), 5–62.

Palau, C., 'Nicholas Mésaritès: deux lettres inédites (Milan, *Ambrosianus* F 96 Sup., ff. 15v–16r),' in *Manuscripta Graeca et Orientalia, Mélanges monastiques et patristiques en l'honneur de Paul Géhin*, ed. A. Binggeli, A. Boud'hors and M. Cassin (Leuven: Peeters, 2016), 187–232.

Papadakis, A., 'Byzantine perceptions of the Latin west,' *Greek Orthodox Theological Review* 36 (1991), 231–42.

Papadakis, A., 'The Byzantines and the rise of the papacy: points for reflection, 1204–1453,' in *Greeks, Latins, and intellectual history, 1204–1500*, ed. M. Hinterberger and C. Schabel (Leuven: Peeters, 2011), 19–42.

BIBLIOGRAPHY 217

Papadakis, A., *Crisis in Byzantium: the filioque controversy in the patriarchate of Gregory II of Cyprus (1283–1289)*, 2nd edn (Crestwood, NY: St Vladimir's Seminary Press, 1997).

Papadakis, A., and Meyendorff, J., *The Christian east and the rise of the papacy: the church 1071–1453 A.D.* (Crestwood, NY: St Vladimir's Seminary Press, 1994).

Papadakis, A., and Talbot, A. M., 'John X Camaterus confronts Innocent III: an unpublished correspondence,' *Byzantinoslavica* 33 (1972), 26–41.

Papadopoulou, T., 'The terms *Ρωμαῖος, Ἕλλην, Γραικὸς* the Byzantine texts of the first half of the 13th century,' *Byzantina Symmeikta* 24 (Athens, 2014), 157–76.

Papayianni, A., 'The papacy and the Fourth Crusade in the correspondence of the Nicaean Emperors with the Popes,' in *The papacy and the crusades: proceedings of the VIIth conference of the Society for the Study of the Crusades and the Latin East*, ed. M. Balard (Aldershot: Ashgate, 2011), 157–63.

Pelikan, J., *The Christian tradition: a history of the development of doctrine*, vol. 2, *The spirit of eastern Christendom* (Chicago, IL: University of Chicago Press, 1988).

Perry, G., *John of Brienne: King of Jerusalem, Emperor of Constantinople, c. 1175–1237* (Cambridge: Cambridge University Press, 2013).

Prawer, J., *Crusader institutions* (Oxford: Clarendon Press, 1980).

Price, R., 'Precedence and papal primacy,' in *Sylvester Syropoulos on politics and culture in the fifteenth-century Mediterranean: themes and problems in the memoirs*, ed. F. Kondyli et al. (Aldershot: Ashgate, 2014), 33–47.

Principe, W., *The theology of the hypostatic union in the early thirteenth century*, vol. 2, *Hugh of Saint-Cher's theology of the hypostatic union* (Toronto: Pontifical Institute of Medieval Studies, 1970).

Prinzing, G., 'Der Brief Kaiser Heinrichs von Konstantinopel vom 13. Januar 1212,' *Byzantion* 43 (1973), 395–431.

Prinzing, G., 'Epiros, 1204–1261: historical outline – sources – prosopography,' in *Identities and allegiances in the Eastern Mediterranean after 1204*, ed. J. Herrin and G. Saint-Guillain (Aldershot: Ashgate, 2011), 81–99.

Pryor, J., *Geography, technology, and war: studies in the maritime history of the Mediterranean, 649–1571* (Cambridge: Cambridge University Press, 1988).

Queller, D., *The office of ambassador in the Middle Ages* (Princeton, NJ: Princeton University Press, 1967).

Queller, D., 'Thirteenth-century diplomatic envoys: "*Nuncii*" and "*Procuratores*",' *Speculum* 35 (1960), 196–213.

Queller, D., and Madden, T., *The Fourth Crusade: the conquest of Constantinople*, 2nd edn (Philadelphia: University of Pennsylvania Press, 1997).

Ramsay, W., *Historical geography of Asia Minor* (London: John Murray, 1890).

218 THE DISPUTATIO

Reinert, S., 'Fragmentation (1204–1453),' in *The expansion of Orthodox Europe: Byzantium, the Balkans and Russia*, ed. J. Shepard (Aldershot: Ashgate, 2007), 307–26.

Richard, J., 'The establishment of the Latin church in the Empire of Constantinople (1204–1227),' in *Latins and Greeks in the Eastern Mediterranean after 1204*, ed. B. Arbel, B. Hamilton and D. Jacoby (London: Frank Cass, 1989), 45–62.

Roncaglia, M., *Les frères mineurs et l'église grecque orthodoxe au XIIIe siècle (1231–1274)* (Cairo: Le Caire Centre d'études orientales de la Custodie franciscaine de Terre-Sainte, 1954).

Rouéché, C., 'Defining identities and allegiances in the Eastern Mediterranean after 1204,' in *Identities and allegiances in the Eastern Mediterranean after 1204*, ed. J. Herrin and G. Saint-Guillain (Aldershot: Ashgate, 2011), 1–5.

Rowe, J., 'The papacy and the Greeks (1122–1153),' *Church History: Studies in Christianity and Culture* 28:2 (1959), 115–30.

Runciman, S., *The Eastern schism: a study of the papacy and the Eastern Churches during the XIth and XIIth centuries* (Oxford: Oxford University Press, 1955).

Ryder, J., 'Changing perspectives on 1054,' *Byzantine and Modern Greek Studies* 35 (2011), 20–37.

Salaville, S., 'Fragment inédit de traduction grecque de la Règle de saint François,' *Échos d'Orient*, 28 (1929), 167–72.

Santifaller, L., *Beiträge zur Geschichte des lateinischen Patriarchats von Konstantinopel (1204–1261)* (Weimar, 1938).

Schabel, C., 'Antelm the Nasty, first Latin archbishop of Patras (1205–ca. 1241),' in *Diplomatics in the eastern Mediterranean 1000–1500*, ed. M. Parani and C. Schabel (Leiden: Brill, 2008), 93–137.

Schabel, C., 'Martyrs and heretics, intolerance of intolerance: the Greek–Latin azymo dispute and the execution of thirteen monks in Cyprus in 1231,' in *Greeks, Latins, and the Church in Early Frankish Cyprus*, ed. C. Schabel (Aldershot: Ashgate, 2010), 1–33.

Schabel, C., 'The quarrel over unleavened bread in western theology, 1234–1439,' in *Greeks, Latins, and intellectual history, 1204–1500*, ed. M. Hinterberger and C. Schabel (Leuven: Peeters, 2011), 85–127.

Schmidt, H., 'The papal and imperial concept of *plenitudo potestatis*: the influence of Pope Innocent III on Emperor Frederick II,' in *Pope Innocent III and his world*, ed. J. Moore (Aldershot: Ashgate, 1999), 305–14.

Schmutz, R., 'Medieval papal representatives, legates, nuncios, and judges-delegate,' *Studia Gratiana* 15 (1972), 443–63.

Setton, K., *The papacy and the Levant 1204–1571*, vol. 1, *The thirteenth and fourteenth centuries* (Philadelphia, PA: The American Philosophical Society, 1976).

BIBLIOGRAPHY 219

Ševčenko, I., 'The definition of philosophy in the Life of Saint Constantine,' in *For Roman Jakobson: essays on the occasion of his sixtieth birthday, 11 October 1956*, ed. M. Hale (The Hague: Mouton, 1956), 449–57.

Shawcross, T., 'The lost generation (*c.* 1204–*c.* 1222): political allegiance and local interests under the impact of the Fourth Crusade,' in *Identities and allegiances in the Eastern Mediterranean after 1204*, ed. J. Herrin and G. Saint-Guillain (Aldershot: Ashgate, 2011), 9–37.

Siecienski, A., *The filioque: history of a doctrinal controversy* (Oxford: Oxford University Press, 2010).

Siecienski, A., *The papacy and the Orthodox: sources and history of a debate* (Oxford: Oxford University Press, 2017).

Sinogowitz, B., 'Über das Byzantinische Kaisertum nach dem vierten Kreuzzuge (1204–1205),' *Byzantinische Zeitschrift* 45 (1952), 345–56.

Skedros, J., '"You cannot have a church without an empire": political orthodoxy in Byzantium,' in *Christianity, democracy, and the shadow of Constantine*, ed. G. Demacopoulos and A. Papanikolaou (New York: Fordham University Press, 2016), 219–31.

Smith, A., 'Hugh of Saint-Cher,' in *New Catholic encyclopedia*, 2nd edn, vol. 7 (Washington, D.C.: Catholic University of America Press, 2002), 193–94.

Smith, M., *And taking bread...: Cerularius and the azyme controversy of 1054* (Paris: Beauchesne, 1978).

Smythe, D., 'Byzantine identity and labeling theory,' in *Byzantium, identity, image, influence: XIX International Congress of Byzantine Studies, University of Copenhagen, 18–24 August, 1996*, ed. K. Fledelius and P. Schreiner (Copenhagen: Eventus, 1996), 26–36.

Spence, R., 'Gregory IX's attempted expeditions to the Latin Empire of Constantinople: the crusade for the union of the Latin and Greek churches,' *Journal of Medieval History* 5 (1979), 163–76.

Spiteris, G., 'I dialoghi di Nicolas Mesarites coi Latini: opera storica o finzione letteraria,' *Orientala Christiana Analecta* 204 (1977), 181–86.

Stavrou, M., 'Heurs et malheurs du dialogue théologique gréco-latin au XIIIe siècle,' in *Réduire le schisme? Ecclésiologies et politiques de l'Union entre Orient et Occident (XIIIe–XVIIIe siècles)*, ed. M. Blanchet and F. Gabriel (Paris: Peeters, 2013), 41–56.

Stavrou, M., 'Rassembler et rénover une église en crise: la politique ecclésiale du patriarche Germain II (1223–1240),' in *Le patriarcat oecuménique de Constantinople et Byzance hors frontières (1204–1586)*, ed. M. Blanchet, M. Congourdeau and D. Muresan (Paris: Centre d'études byzantines, 2014), 23–36.

Stiernon, L., 'Les origines du Despotat d'Épire: A propos d'un livre recent,' *Revue des études byzantines* 17 (1959), 90–126.

Striker, C., and Kuban, D., *Kalenderhane in Istanbul: the buildings, their history, architecture, and decoration* (Mainz: Zabern, 1997).

220 THE DISPUTATIO

Trigg, J., 'The angel of great counsel: Christ and the angelic hierarchy in Origen's theology,' *Journal of Theological Studies* 42 (1991), 35–51.

Tsougarakis, N., *The Latin religious orders of medieval Greece, 1204–1500* (Turnhout: Brepols, 2012).

Ullmann, W., *The growth of papal government in the Middle Ages: a study in the ideological relation of clerical to lay power*, 2nd edn (London: Messrs, Methuen and Co., 1962).

Van Cleve, T., *The Emperor Frederick II of Hohenstaufen, Immutator Mundi* (Oxford: Oxford University Press, 1972).

Van Tricht, F., *The Latin* Renovatio *of Byzantium: the Empire of Constantinople (1204–1228)*, English translation by P. Longbottom (Leiden: Brill, 2011).

Vasiliev, A., 'Mesarites as a source,' *Speculum* 13 (1938), 180–82.

Vaughan, R., *Matthew Paris* (Cambridge: Cambridge University Press, 1958).

Venning, T., *A chronology of the Byzantine Empire* (New York: Palgrave, 2006).

Vigorelli, I., 'ΣΧΕΣΙΣ and ΟΜΟΟΥΣΙΟΣ in Gregory of Nyssa's *Contra Eunomium*: metaphysical contest and gains in Trinitarian thought,' *Vox Patrum* 37 (2017), 165–77.

Ware, T. *The Orthodox Church* (London: Penguin, 1997).

Watt, J., 'The papacy,' in *The new Cambridge medieval history*, vol. 5, *c. 1198–c. 1300*, ed. D. Abulafia (Cambridge: Cambridge University Press, 1999), 105–63.

Weijers, O., *In search of the truth: a history of disputation techniques from antiquity to early modern times* (Turnhout: Brepols, 2013).

Weijers, O., *La 'disputatio' dans les Facultés des arts au moyen âge* (Turnhout: Brepols, 2002).

Weijers, O., 'The medieval *disputatio*,' in *Traditions of controversy*, ed. M. Dascal and H. Chang (Amsterdam and Philadelphia, PA: John Benjamins Publishing Company, 2007), 141–49.

Weiler, B., 'Matthew Paris on the writing of history,' *Journal of Medieval History* 35 (2009), 254–78.

Whittow, M., *The making of Orthodox Byzantium, 600–1025* (Basingstoke: Macmillan, 1996).

Wolff, R., 'The Latin Empire of Constantinople, 1204–1261,' in *A history of the crusades*, ed. K. Setton, vol. 2 (Madison: University of Wisconsin Press, 1969), 187–233.

Wolff, R., 'The Latin Empire of Constantinople and the Franciscans,' *Traditio* 2 (1944), 213–37. Reprinted in R. Wolff, *Studies in the Latin Empire of Constantinople* (London, 1976).

INDEX

Abasgs (see Georgians)
Achacius 183
Achaia 177
Achyraous xv, 72–73, 162n127
Adam 130, 131n10
Adam of Oxford 27n107
Adrianople 24n98
Aegean Sea 73n360, 135n8, 165n148
Agapetus, Pope 118
Akropolites, George 3, 14n53, 20,
    23n97, 24n98, 25n99, 25n101,
    97, 98n474, 98n476, 100n483,
    112n39, 161n121, 163n136,
    165n151, 194n281
Alans 38, 120
Albert of Pisa 54
Alescheran 72, 165
Alexandria 65n315, 66, 79–80, 89n435,
    140n27–28, 143n38, 158n111,
    160, 179n202, 183n223, 183n227
Alexios I Komnenos 10n31, 42,
    43n193, 77n377
Alexios III Angelos 18
Amastris 170, 176, 177n193
Ambrose of Milan 67n322, 80n396,
    145, 181
Amphilochius of Ikonion 152
Anaplous 32
Anatolia 18, 23, 27–28, 72, 83n411
Anconitans 164
Andrew, Apostle 177
Angelina, Anna 18
Anselm of Cahieu 24n98

Anselm of Canterbury 12
Anselm of Havelberg 10n32, 55,
    170n167
Antioch 66, 119, 140, 160, 167, 177,
    179n202, 180
apokrisarios/apocrisarius 13, 14, 58,
    150n77, 171, 178–79, 184n233,
    192
Apollinarianism 183
Apollo 117
Apostle, the (see Paul, Apostle)
Aquila 123
Aquinas, Thomas 51n240
Arab/Arabic 118n17, 134n4, 167n160
Ark of the Covenant 131
Aristotle 54n260
artos/arton 78–79, 177–78, 185–86
Asen, Helen 97, 98n475
Asia 97n474, 177
Athanasios of Alexandria 65n315, 66,
    79–80, 143, 180
Attaleiates, Michael 134n4
Aubry of Three Fountains 99n478
Augustine of Hippo 67n322, 80n396,
    145, 181
Aulenos 85, 139n23, 173n179, 179n205,
    196n291
autokrator 92, 109
Aymo (see Haymo of Faversham)
Azymes 44–46, 49, 60, 65, 70, 76–79,
    81–82, 85, 132, 137n17, 159n117,
    160, 168, 170–72, 176, 178–79,
    185–88, 190, 193–94

222 THE DISPUTATIO

Bacon, Roger 49, 57
Baldwin I, Latin Emperor 20, 22
Baldwin II, Latin Emperor 50,
    163n136
Basil of Caesarea 65n315, 66, 79–80,
    129, 152–53, 193
Bela IV 93
Benedict of Arezzo 163
Benedict of St Susanna, Cardinal
    21n89, 22n90, 55, 173n180
Benvenuto di San Giorgio 100
Bithynia 133
Blemmydes, Nikephoros 11, 14n53,
    16n69, 32, 58, 59n280–81,
    63n304, 65n315, 66–69,
    88–89n435, 99n480, 138n22,
    143n38, 143n43, 144n47–48,
    147n60, 148n67, 148n69,
    149n72–73, 149n75, 150n76–77,
    153n90, 153n95, 178n199
Bogomils 92
Bohemond IV 167n160
Bologna 54
Boniface of Montferrat 19n78
Bosporos 25, 32
Bulgaria/Bulgarians 14n53, 25, 38,
    96–99, 120, 164
Byzantine(s), Byzantium 1, 2, 4,
    5, 7–9, 10–14, 16–18, 20, 23,
    31, 36, 41, 48, 50–51, 60–61,
    75–78, 80–83, 86, 88, 90, 92,
    96, 98–99, 102, 118n17, 118n19,
    133n3, 134n4–5, 137n15,
    137n18, 144n47–49, 148n71,
    151n78, 167n160, 169n164,
    172n175, 173n180–81, 175n186,
    177n192–93, 178n199, 185n236,
    190n261
    Emperor/Empire 1, 5n14, 7–8, 10,
        15, 19–20, 23, 25–27, 32–34,
        41–44, 46, 50, 59, 62, 64, 69–75,
        83–91, 93, 95–97, 99n480,

        101–103, 109, 118, 133, 135–36,
        139, 146–47, 149, 157, 159–61,
        162n126, 163, 165–67, 174–76,
        182, 189–90, 191n267, 193–96

Cain and Abel 35, 111
Calamus (see Kalamos)
Calogerus 169
Cephas (see Peter, Apostle)
Chalogerorum (see Kios)
Chartophylax 79n392, 85–87, 89,
    138–39, 173, 179, 196, 197n295
Cherubim 131
Chios 73n360
Choniates, Niketas 1, 2n5, 19n80
Christ, Jesus 34, 44, 78–79, 113–14,
    130–31, 155, 158, 162, 177–78,
    186–87, 189, 191n264
Christopher of Ankyra 96–97
Chrysostom, John 79, 185n236, 186–87
Cilicia 123
Cistercian Order 48n216
Clement I, Pope 177
compline 194
Constantine IX Monomachos, 42
Constantinople 1, 3–5, 10n31–32, 15,
    17–22, 31–32, 34n149, 35, 43,
    48n217, 48n220, 50–52, 55–57,
    70–73, 75, 77, 78, 83–89, 92n454,
    93n455, 96–99, 102, 107, 112n39,
    118, 125n34, 134n5, 141, 144,
    146n58, 160, 161n123, 162–64,
    170n167, 170n169, 173, 186n238,
    187n243, 194n281, 195n289–90,
    196
    Church of Hagia Sophia 164
    Church of the Holy Apostles 125n34
    First Council of (381) 141, 146
    Second Council of (553) 65n315,
        158, 183
    Latin Emperor of 20, 22, 50, 71, 83,
        98, 163n136

INDEX

223

Latin Empire of 5, 17, 23, 24n98, 25n99, 28, 31, 38, 48, 50, 53n247, 56, 71, 86, 91–93, 95–99, 100n482, 102, 136n13, 163, 164n137, 164n140–41, 175n185, 196n290

Latin Patriarch of 20–21, 22

Constanza-Anna 101

consubstantiality 108n8, 116n3, 143, 146–47, 150, 152–55, 157

Contra graecos 49

Corinth 117, 178

Cumans 47

Cyprus vii, 25–28, 31, 33, 35–36, 46, 112, 113n40

Cyril of Alexandria 65n315, 66, 67, 69, 79–80, 82, 89n435, 129, 140–43, 152, 158–59, 181–84, 193

Damasus I, Pope 79n392, 80, 192

Damietta 50n236

Dandolo, Andrea 21n85, 97n471

Daniel 40n180, 122

David 110, 132

Derbe 123

Disputatio 6–7, 9–17, 33–35, 42n191, 44, 46–47, 49n222, 52, 54–56, 58–59, 63–68, 70–72, 74–77, 79–85, 87–91, 93–95, 97, 102–103, 133, 140, 143, 144n47–48, 147, 148n67, 149, 160, 162n126, 167–68, 170, 173n179–80, 174, 177n195, 189

Dominic the Venetian 15

Dominican Order 34n146, 47–52, 53n247, 57, 65n313, 94, 130n7, 133, 184n233

Donatus 183

Ebionites 188

Egypt 179n203

Elias 125

Elias (Franciscan Friar) 54n258

Elijah 130

Elisha 125, 130

Emmanuel 152

energon 156

England/English 39–40, 49, 53–54, 57, 60, 61n287, 137

Ephesos 22, 69n335, 79n392, 170n169, 182n217, 183

Council of 79n39, 182, 183

Epiphanios of Cyrus 79–80, 186, 188

Epiros 18, 19n79, 23n95, 24n98, 25, 32n136, 38, 170n169

Esau and Jacob 111

Esseron (see Achyraous)

Ethiopian 38, 120

Eucharist 2, 44–46, 65, 78–79, 82–83, 131, 137n17, 172n175, 178n200, 185n236, 188n247, 190n261

Europe 24n98, 25, 32, 34, 49, 57, 99

Eusebios of Caesarea 134n4

Eustorge 26n104, 31

Eve 131n10

Ezekiel 122, 130

Ferrara-Florence, Council of 42n191, 64n307

filioque 2, 63, 65, 67, 76n371, 81–82, 85, 90, 92, 137n16, 142, 145, 180n209, 190n261

Fourth Crusade 1, 3–4, 7, 18–19, 22, 29, 32, 43, 46, 71, 77, 80–81, 170n169, 173n180, 175n185

France/French 2, 51, 53, 57, 60, 61n287, 93, 137

Francis I, Pope vii

Francis of Assisi 48, 50n236

Franciscan Order 27–29, 34n146, 35, 47–51, 53–54, 58, 94, 109n21, 116n5, 130n8, 133, 163n131–33, 184n233

Franks/Frankish 3n5, 92, 98, 99n478, 116
Frederick II Hohenstaufen 24n98, 30, 34, 43, 50n232, 54n258, 93–94, 99–102, 163n136

Gelembe 194n281
Gemlik 73
Genoa 24n98, 99
Geoffrey of Villehardouin 18n78
Geoffrey II Villehardouin 99n478
George of Pelagonia 98n476
Georgia/Georgian 38, 120n28–29, 163n132
Germanos II, Patriarch 1, 9–11, 15, 27–29, 32–41, 43–48, 58–65, 67n325, 70, 72, 73n358, 74–76, 78, 81–85, 87–92, 96, 103–104, 107, 109n21, 112n36, 113n40, 115, 116n3, 116n5, 116n7, 118n19, 121, 129, 133n3, 134n4, 135n7–8, 136n10, 136n14, 163n133, 170n169, 171n169, 171n172, 177n194
Germany/German 43, 50n232, 52n242
Goths 38, 118n19, 120
  Ostrogoth 118n20
Great Schism 1, 3–4, 29, 35, 92n451
Greece 48n216, 48n220, 98, 99n478
Greek(s) 1–4, 8–9, 17–18, 19n79, 21–22, 23n95, 24n97, 25–28, 31, 33, 35–37, 42, 44–46, 48–50, 52, 54–57, 60–70, 74–81, 89, 91, 93–94, 109, 111–13, 117, 120–21, 124, 129, 131, 133, 137, 138n20, 139n23, 149n75, 157, 161n123, 170n169, 171, 172n177, 173n177, 177n191, 177n194, 179n203, 187n242, 187n244, 190, 191n262, 191n264, 191n267, 192n271
  anti-Greek sentiments 49n221

Church vii, 1, 4–5, 6n15, 7, 9, 17–18, 21–23, 31, 35–38, 40–41, 42n191, 43–47, 49, 56n266, 60, 64, 70–71, 85, 87, 90, 91n447, 92n451, 94, 114, 116n7, 125–27, 135n8, 137, 139, 144n48, 148n67, 161, 167n160, 173n179, 189, 195
  doctrine/practice 2–3, 12n43, 26n104, 45–46, 49, 77, 85, 131, 172, 177n195, 183n223, 184n232–33
  Emperor (see Byzantine Emperor)
  Empire of the (see Byzantine Empire)
  language/text/translation 11, 14, 28, 29n116, 35, 39, 48n217, 49, 51, 54–57, 58n276, 67, 68n328, 72, 78, 81, 107n1, 109n20, 110n26–27, 111n30, 112n37, 117n9, 118n18, 142n36, 143, 144n47, 146–50, 151n78–79, 151n81, 153n90, 153n94–95, 154n96, 155n97, 155n99–100, 155n104, 156n105–107, 158, 169n164, 170n167, 171n171, 171n174, 177n191, 178n198–200, 179n203, 180, 181n216, 186, 187n243, 195n286
Gregoras, Nikephoros 14n53, 67n325, 97n471, 98n476
Gregory I, Pope 67, 145n52
Gregory VII, Pope 38
Gregory IX, Pope 1, 8–10, 13, 15–16, 26n104, 28–32, 34–47, 50–52, 58, 60, 64–65, 70, 78n383, 79, 82–83, 90, 92–95, 97n473, 98, 100, 103, 107, 117n9, 121, 122n9, 123n19–21, 129, 131n10, 135n7–8, 136n13, 161n122–23, 162n129, 171n172–73, 177n194, 184n233
Gregory of Nazianzus 129

INDEX

225

Gregory of Nyssa 79n392, 80, 153, 154n96, 181

Gregory Thaumaturgus 79n392, 80, 180

Grossolano, Peter 10n32, 43

Gulf of Myrlea 165n145

Haymo of Faversham 47, 53–54, 57, 130, 133, 184n233

Hellene 17

Hellespont 97n474, 165n148

Henry I, Latin Emperor 22–23, 73, 136n13, 164n140, 175n185

Henry VI 100

Herakleia Pontike 43, 55, 175n185

Hilary of Poitiers 67n322, 146

Holy Land 27, 31, 93, 175n185

Holy Spirit/Ghost 6, 12n43, 13, 35n153, 43n193, 56, 58, 65, 66n316, 67–69, 76, 80n396, 81–82, 85n419, 88n435, 92, 112n37, 114, 116, 132, 137–39, 141–43, 145–48, 150–59, 168–70, 172n175, 178, 180–82, 190, 192–94

  Spirit of Christ 146, 150–56

  Spirit of God the Father 140

  Spirit of the Lord 152

  Spirit of the Son 146–48, 150,152–55, 158

  Spirit of Truth 67, 88n435, 142, 145–46, 151–53

Honorius III, Pope 29, 47n214, 102n491, 175n185

Hugh (see Hugo of St Cher)

Hugo of St Cher 47, 51–52, 54n256, 57, 130, 133, 184n233

Hungary 93–94, 97n473, 98n475

hypatos ton philosophon 144n48

hypostasis/hypostatic 68, 142, 154, 156–57, 181

  enhypostatic 108, 116

Iberian 120

Innocent III, Pope 4, 21, 29, 31, 38, 45n205, 47n214, 48, 78, 92n454, 96n467, 136n13, 171n174, 175n185

Innocent IV, Pope 14n53, 52, 94

Ionia 72

Isaiah 108, 115, 152

Israel/Israelites 35, 44, 110, 123n18, 126, 129, 186

Istanbul 48

Italy/Italian 24n98, 30–31, 43, 50, 57, 89, 98, 100n483, 112, 117, 118n19, 163n135, 164n137

Jacob of Russano 27n107, 163

Jacobites 47

James, Apostle 177

Jeremiah 182

Jerobo'am 44, 129

Jerome 67n322, 80n396, 145, 181

Jerusalem 4, 28, 31, 35, 40, 77, 93, 99, 110, 122, 124, 160, 163n136, 173, 177, 179n202

Job 40n180, 122

John (author of the Book of Revelation) 108, 126

John of Brienne 50, 71, 83, 98, 163, 164n136, 164

John the Evangelist 177, 180

John of Parma 11

John, Patriarch of Antioch 66, 140

John II Asen/Asan 96, 97n470, 97n473, 98n475, 102, 164

John X Kamateros, Patriarch 19–20, 38

John II Komnenos 72

John III Vatatzes 23, 24n98, 25, 27–8, 29n116–17, 32, 46, 50, 59, 61, 69n335, 71–75, 82–97, 98n474–77, 99–102, 103n494, 109n15, 133n3, 136n10, 136n12–13, 159n114,

226 THE DISPUTATIO

161n121–23, 162, 163n134–35, 164, 166n151, 167n163, 175n186, 176n186, 190n261, 191n262, 192n271, 194, 195n289–90, 196

John, 'younger disciple' 45, 125

Joseph 108, 109n14, 124, 126, 131

Judaea/Judah 35, 110

Justinian I 134n4

Kalamos xv, 85–86, 194

Kalenderhane Camii 48

Kallipolis 97

Kaloeidas, Nicholas 170, 176n190

Kamateros, Andronikos 22

Kantara 26

Karykes, Demetrios 144n48, 148n67, 149n72

Kenchreai 123

Kephas (see Peter, Apostle)

Khazars 38, 120

Kios xv, 73, 165n145

Klokotnitza 25, 38, 96, 100

Komnenoi 7, 10

Lake Apollonias 165n148

Lamech 131

Laquera (see Achyraous)

Larissa 144n47

Laskarids 8, 165 n151

Laskarina, Eirene 97n474

Laskarina, Eudokia 24n98

Last Supper 78–79

Lateran 127, 132
　Council of (1215) 172n177

Latin(s) 1–5, 7–12, 14n51, 17–18, 19n80, 21, 23–28, 31, 33–37, 45–46, 48n216, 49–50, 51n237, 55–56, 60–61, 63, 65n310, 65n312, 68n331, 69n332, 69n335, 70–71, 73, 77, 80–81, 84, 86, 92–93, 96, 98–99, 100n482–83, 109, 111–12, 113n40, 114, 116n7,

124, 131–33, 137–38, 144n47–48, 167n163, 171–73, 175, 177n191, 179n203, 185n236, 187n242, 190n261

anti-Latin sentiments 33–34, 58, 59n280, 61, 92

atrocities/persecutions 36, 77, 79n392, 89, 173

Church 17, 116n7, 127, 171n174

crusaders 2

doctrine/practice 3, 45, 64, 78n383, 79n392, 81, 85n419, 92, 98n476, 175n185, 190n261

language/text/translation 35, 39, 50n234, 51, 56–57, 61, 68n328, 108n5, 108n8, 109n14–15, 109n21, 110n26–27, 111n29–30, 112n35, 112n37, 116n2–3, 116n7–8, 117n14–16, 118n20, 120n29, 147n65, 148–49, 151n78–81, 153n90, 153n94–95, 154n96, 155n97–100, 156n105–107, 161n123, 162n127, 177n191, 178n198, 180, 181n216, 183n223, 184n233, 195n286, 197

Latin West 9, 12–13, 24, 49n222, 56n266, 78n383

missionaries 34

scholasticism 49n222

Lazi 38, 120

Leavened (bread) 2, 44–46, 49, 65, 70, 76n374, 78–79, 131–32, 137n17, 171, 177–78, 179n203, 185–87, 188n247, 190

Lebanon 122

Legate 14, 16, 135, 136n14, 144n49, 150, 178n199

Legatus 13–14, 16, 150n77

Lembos 101n485

Lescaram 72

Leschara xv, 72–74, 84, 162–63

Leschera 72, 165

INDEX

Lescherea 72, 166
Liudprand of Cremona 15, 135n5
Lombards 118n19
Lopadion xv, 72–73, 162n127, 165
Louis VII, King of France 2
Louis IX, King of France 51
Lydia 72, 162
Lyons
    Council of (1245) 94, 95n462
    Council of (1274) 8, 51, 103
Lystra 123

Macedonius 146
Makestos River 72, 162n127
Manuel Doukas, ruler of Thessalonike
    164
Manuel I Komnenos 175
Marcion/Marcionites 188
Mercy Seat 131
Mesarites, Nicholas viii, 3, 7n21, 11,
    14, 21–23, 43n194, 81, 125n34,
    173n180, 175n185, 196n293
Michael IV Autoreianos, Patriarch 20
Michael Doukas, ruler of Epiros 18,
    19n78
Michael Kerularios, Patriarch 42,
    43n192
Michael VIII Palaiologos 8, 24n98, 51,
    99, 166n151
Milan 10n32, 43, 145n54, 181
Minor, Order of Friars (see Franciscan
    Order)
Moses 123, 131
Moses of Bergamo 55
Mouskes, Philippe 99n478
Mouth Athos 144n47
Mysia 72

Nazarites 123
Negroponte 51
Neophytos 26, 33
Nestorian 47, 183n227

Nestorius 66n320, 142, 158n111, 183
New Testament 37, 44, 65n315,
    78n386, 79n392, 123n19, 179,
    185, 188
Nicaea 1, 5n15, 6, 8, 14, 18–20, 22,
    24, 26–29, 32–33, 35, 44, 46–47,
    50, 52–56, 58–64, 66n315, 67,
    69n335, 70–72, 75–76, 77n376,
    79–80, 84, 87–88, 89n436, 90,
    92–99, 102–103, 133, 134n4,
    136n13, 137n18, 138n22,
    140–41, 144n47–48, 159n116,
    161n121–22, 162–63, 165,
    167n160, 168, 170, 173n178–79,
    177–78, 184, 187n243, 195n289
    Church of Hyakinthos of 134n4
    Church of St Sophia of 134n4
    Creed of 66n320, 88n435, 139–43,
        145
    Emperor/Empire of 18, 20n83,
        22–26, 28, 32–33, 38n171, 55,
        59–61, 71, 84–85, 91, 93n456,
        95–96, 97n473, 99, 102,
        165–66n151, 167n163, 170n169,
        175n185
    First Council of (325) 65n315, 133,
        134n4, 139n24, 140, 141n34
    Second Council of (787) 134n4
Nicholas III, Patriarch 10n31
Nicolas of Otranto 11n34, 55
Nicosia 26, 31
Nikephoros II Phokas 15, 135n5
Niketas of Nicomedia 10n32, 55
Noah 40n180, 122, 131
nuncio/nuntio 13–16, 24n98, 60, 133n3,
    135n10, 136n14, 195n290
Nymphaion xv, 6n32, 46–47, 56,
    58, 69n335, 70, 72–76, 78–82,
    84–86, 88–93, 103, 139n23,
    161n121, 162, 165–66, 167n163,
    170n169, 173n179, 187n243–44,
    194

228 THE DISPUTATIO

Odo of Deuil 2, 65n310, 77n376, 172n177
oikoumene 108, 112
Old Testament 35, 44, 77n386, 79n392, 107n1, 131n10, 179, 185, 188, 189
Orsini, Matthew 24n98
Otto I 15, 135n5
Oxford 27n107, 49, 54, 57

Pachymeres, George 51n238, 103n494
Padua 54
Paphlagonia 170
Parastron, John 51
Paris 49, 51, 54
Paris, Matthew 39–40, 50, 95n462, 112n37, 117n16, 119n20, 119n23, 120n31, 122n9, 132n21, 132n24–25
Patras 36n155
Paul, Apostle 37, 41, 78, 108, 111, 113, 117, 119, 123–26, 135, 145, 147, 153, 155, 171n173, 177–78
Pelagius, Cardinal 4, 43, 112n39
Pentarchy 38
Pera 48
Peter, Apostle 16, 29, 37–38, 40–42, 45, 110, 113, 117, 119–25, 126n36, 130, 132, 135, 155, 171, 177
Peter I of Angouleme, Latin Patriarch of Antioch 167n160
Peter II of Ivrea, Latin Patriarch of Antioch 167n160
Peter of Sézanne 47, 51–53, 57, 130, 133, 184n233
Photian Schism 1, 176n186
Photios 175n186
Pisa/Pisan 99n378, 164
Poimanenon 23, 24n98
Preachers, Order of the (see Dominican Order)
Priscilla 123

Procession (of the Holy Spirit/Ghost) 6, 12n43, 13, 35n153, 43n193, 56, 58, 59n280, 65–70, 80n396, 81, 85n419, 88n435, 137–38, 156–58, 168, 172n175, 180n211, 190, 192n271, 194
Prokopios of Caesarea 134n4
Propontis 72

Rhyndakos River 165n148
Richard of San Germano 24n98
Robert of Clari 20n84
Rodulphus of Remis 47, 53, 57–58, 130, 133, 184n233
Roman(s) 17, 100n483, 115, 118n16
 Church vii, 1, 5, 6n15, 7, 9, 11, 13–14, 16–18, 21–23, 26, 31, 33n144, 34–42, 43n194, 45n205, 46–47, 54, 60, 63–64, 77, 81, 87, 90, 91n447, 118n16, 121, 126–27, 129–30, 135n8, 136–37, 139, 145, 160–62, 173, 175, 177, 179n203, 184, 189–92, 195
 Curia 36n156, 70, 162–63, 175
 Pontiff 127, 130
 see 42, 64n308, 125
Romania (see Latin Empire of Constantinople)
Rome 4, 13, 16, 35–36, 38, 41–42, 44, 46, 59, 64, 71, 72n352, 83, 89–90, 101, 103, 107, 113–14, 115–16, 118–20, 123n21, 135n8, 135n10, 137, 144, 145n52, 161n122, 175n185, 178–79, 184n233, 192, 195n290
Rus 103
Russia/Russian 38, 120
Ruthenians 47

Sacrament of the Altar 137–39, 159
St John the Baptist at Petra, monastery of 34

INDEX

229

Salimbene de Adam 50–51, 54n258, 57, 163n131
Salisbury 53
Samaria 35, 110, 125, 129
Samson 121n3
Satan 114, 126
Sea of Marmara 165n145
Second Crusade 2, 77n376, 172n177
Seljuk Turks 25, 27
Septuagint 107n1
Sicily 43, 99
Simon of Constantinople 51
Simon of Faversham 54n260
Solomon 111, 115, 120, 126n42, 127n44
Stethatos, Niketas 179n203
successor states 5, 18, 84n413
superessential Trinity 156
Sycheron (see Achyraous)
Symeon II, Patriarch of Antioch 167
Syria/Syrian 38, 120, 123, 167n160

Teupolitan 180
Theodahad 118n20
Theodore II Eirenikos, Patriarch 43
Theodore I Laskaris 14, 18–20, 22n91, 23, 43, 73, 78n381, 95, 99, 136n13, 175
Theodore II Laskaris 14n53, 97, 98n474, 166n151
Theodore Doukas, ruler of Epiros 18–19, 24n98, 32, 38, 100, 171n169
Theodore of Mopsuestia 183
Theodoret of Cyrrhus/Theodoticus 158, 183

Theodosios II 182
Theophanes the Confessor 134n4
Thessalonike 18, 19n78, 32, 100, 144n47, 164n139
Thomas of Eccleston 49, 53
Thomas Morosini, Latin Patriarch 21
Thrace 19, 24n98, 98
Three Chapters 118n20, 158n111
Tiepolo, Jacopo, Doge 101n485
Timothy 123
Titus 155
Tobias 126
Tours 54
transubstantiation 45, 78n383, 132
trilemma 67, 68n331
Trinity 68n331, 156–58, 169

Ulubad 73, 165n148
unleavened (bread) 2, 44–46, 65, 70, 76n374, 78–79, 90, 132, 137n17, 171n174, 179n203, 185–86, 187n242, 190n261
Urban II, Pope 10n31, 77n377, 173n181

Venice/Venetians 15, 21, 25n99, 51n238, 97, 98n478, 99n478, 101n485, 164
Vigilius, Pope 118, 119n20
Vulgate 122n9, 145n53

William VI, marquis of Montferrat 100

Zigabenos, Euthymios 185n236
Zion 110

Printed and bound by CPI Group (UK) Ltd, Croydon, CR0 4YY
10/03/2024
14467795-0004